SPLIT IMAGE

Edited by

Jannette L. Dates

and William Barlow

SPLIT IMAGE

AFRICAN AMERICANS IN THE MASS MEDIA

HOWARD UNIVERSITY PRESS   WASHINGTON, D.C.   1990

Printed in the United States of America
This book is printed on acid-free paper.

Library of Congress Cataloging-in-Publication-Data

Split image : African Americans in the mass media / edited by Jannette L. Dates
and William Barlow.
    p. cm.
   ISBN 0-88258-035-3: $29.95.—ISBN 0-88258-063-9 (pbk.): $14.95
   1. Afro-Americans and mass media—United States. I. Dates,
Jannette Lakes, 1939–   . II. Barlow, William, 1943–   .
P94.5.A372U574 1990
302.23'089'96073—dc20

90-4410
CIP

This book is dedicated to

Victor, Karen, Chip, Matt, and Craig Dates;
Iantha Lake, Mabel and Teddy Murray, Iantha Tucker,
Moses Lake, Cecial and Richard Mosley, Marva and
Stephen Belt, Loretta Moody, Cheryl Wethersford,
and the rest of the Lake/Dates family
for their support

and Dorothy Goodman Barlow

CONTENTS

ACKNOWLEDGMENTS

We would like to acknowledge and thank colleagues and friends who contributed encouragement, criticism, and support. They include: O. Rudolph Aggrey and Ruby M. Essien of Howard University Press, Orlando L. Taylor, Carolyn Stroman, Bishetta Merritt, Clint C. Wilson II, Oscar H. Gandy, Jr., and Paula Matabane. The following persons deserve thanks for their assistance with research efforts: Elinor D. Sinnette, Maricia Battle, Janet Sims-Wood, Doris Hull, Avril Madison, Malik Azeez of the Moorland-Spingarn Research Center at Howard University; Frances Ziegler, Ruth E. Westin, Julius Whitaker, Carrie Hackney, and Eric White of Founder's Library and the Undergraduate Library at Howard University; Marva Belt and Faye L. Houston of Enoch Pratt Library in Baltimore; Ed Jones of WHMM-TV; Mildred Morse of the Corporation for Public Broadcasting, and Cary Beth Cryor of the Afro-American Newspaper Archives. This book could not have been completed without the typing assistance of Brenda Alexander and Kimberly Ellison.

INTRODUCTION: A WAR OF IMAGES

JANNETTE L. DATES AND WILLIAM BARLOW

Writing at the dawn of the twentieth century, W. E. B. Du Bois in *The Souls of Black Folk* prophesied more than once that "the problem of the color line" would dominate the planet's historical landscape for at least the next one hundred years. Having thus established race as the primary theoretical framework for his perceiving and being perceived by the world, Du Bois proceeded to delineate the cultural legacy of the "color line" with respect to African Americans, revealing that a deeply rooted "double consciousness" lay at the heart of his people's common racial memory. In his own words:

> After the Egyptian and the Indian, the Greek and Roman, the Teuton and Mongolian, the Negro is a sort of seventh son, born with a veil, and gifted with second sight in this American world, a world which yields him no true self-consciousness, but only lets him see himself through the revelation of the other world. It is a peculiar sensation this double consciousness, this sense of always looking at one's self through the eyes of others, of measuring one's soul by the tape of a world that looks on in amused contempt and pity. One ever feels his twoness, an American, a Negro; two souls, two thoughts, two unreconciled strivings, two warring ideals in one dark body, whose dogged strength alone keeps it from being torn asunder.
>
> The history of the American Negro is the history of this strife, this longing to attain self-conscious manhood, to merge his double self into a better and truer self. In this merging he wishes neither of the old selves to be lost. He would not Africanize America, for America has

NOTE: The terms Colored, Negro, black, Black American, Afro-American, and African American are all used to designate Americans of African ancestry more or less in correspondence with the trend of the period under discussion.

I

too much to teach the world and Africa. He would not bleach his Negro soul in a flood of white Americanism, for he knows that Negro blood has a message for the world. He simply wishes to make it possible for a man to be both a Negro and an American, without being cursed and spit upon by his fellows, without having the doors of opportunity closed roughly in his face.[1]

In many respects, the "double self" that Du Bois describes in the above passage is the inverse of the "split image" which, we shall argue, has characterized African American representations in the mass media throughout the twentieth century. When juxtaposed, the exterior "image" and the interior "self" constitute the complex and interdependent relationships between the media and society, as well as between the individual and the mass, which this book seeks to scrutinize through the cultural prism of race.

Sterling A. Brown was one of the first African American scholars to identify and comment extensively on the bifurcation of black images in American culture along racial lines. In his pioneering study, *The Negro in American Fiction*, he discussed the striking differences between fictional representations of African Americans by white authors and those by black authors. In the process, Brown identified recurring caricatures, particularly the "contented slave," the "wretched freedman," the "tragic mulatto," the "brute Negro," and the "comic Negro," as the most persistent African American stereotypes to emerge from the nineteenth century and carry over into his era.[2] Likewise, his *Negro Poetry and Drama* drew distinctions between "Negro poetry" and "white poetry of Negro life" as well as between "Negro folk drama" and blackface minstrelsy: "The minstrel show had a great deal to do with setting up the American stereotype of the comic Negro, addicted to the use of big words, to gaudy finery, to brawling with a razor, and to raiding chicken roosts." It was "produced by whites for whites, and soon lost even its most rudimentary realism; the dialect became gibberish and the caricature a cartoon."[3]

It is interesting to note that Brown was also one of the first scholars of American culture to use Walter Lippmann's media-centered concept of the stereotype in his writings on literature, the arts, and the African American oral folk tradition. According to Lippmann's classic formulation, the stereotype "precedes reason" and "as a form of perception imposes a certain character on the data of our senses."[4] Hence, to be effective a stereotype must be anticipated by the conditioned perceptions of the beholder as well as existent in the imagination of the image maker. Ten years after Lippmann introduced the concept, Brown used it to characterize distinctive clusters of black representations in novels, poetry, and on the stage. Like the revelation implicit in Du Bois's "double consciousness" trope, Brown's unmasking of black stereotypes worked to deconstruct them, both metaphorically and mythically. His purpose was to expose the racial bias inherent in the most persistent caricatures of African Americans in the popular culture and then to replace them with less contrived and more authentic characterizations created, for the most part, by black image makers.

This collection of historical essays seeks to follow the intellectual lead of Du Bois and Brown by using the cultural prism of race to examine critically the images of African Americans that exist in the mass media. As our title suggests, the study focuses on the schizoid nature of these black representations. The dominant trend in African American portraiture has been created and nurtured by succeeding generations of white image makers, beginning as far back as the colonial era. Its opposite has been created and maintained by black image makers in response to the omissions and distortions of the former. This war of images casts light on the historical trajectory of the race issue in American society from both sides of the controversy. Thus, the definition and control of black images in the mass media have been contested from the outset along racial lines, with white cultural domination provoking African American cultural resistance. This theoretical framework is drawn from the Gramscian concept of ideological hegemony, of which it is an integral part. In brief, Antonio Gramsci argues that ruling-class alliances in modern societies maintain their power by cultivating a consensus among subordinate classes; coercion is used only as a last resort. Cultural domination is the best means of achieving ideological hegemony because it ensures the triumph of a single consensus, or "common sense," among all sectors of the social order. But hegemony is always in the making—or unmaking— for Gramsci also argues that cultural domination provokes its opposite, cultural resistance, in subordinate classes. Hence, even at its best, ideological hegemony is still an "unstable equilibrium." The dominant culture must constantly strive to expand its hegemony while fending off challenges and interventions from the very classes and groups it seeks to subjugate.   Consequently, culture itself becomes an arena for historical contest.[5]

In the wake of Gramsci's formulations on class, culture, and ideological hegemony, Stuart Hall and his associates have more recently focused attention on popular culture and the mass media as sites of ideological struggle between the dominant culture and those subordinate classes and/or groups threatened by its cultural imperialism.   In his studies of representation and ideology, Hall and others have noted the importance of the rituals of social behavior in which ideologies imprint or inscribe themselves.   "These rituals . . . occur in social sites and are linked with social apparatuses. This is why we need to deconstruct language and behavior in order to decipher the patterns of ideological thinking which are inscribed in them."[6] The mass media function as the producers and transmitters of ideologies because the rituals and myths they reproduce for public consumption "explain, instruct and justify practices and institutions . . . linking symbols, formulas, plot and characters in a pattern that is conventional, appealing and gratifying . . . in tales of redemption that show how order is restored."[7]   This is done routinely to encourage dutiful submission to authority.

In American society, by reproducing the ideological hegemony of the dominant white culture, the mass media help to legitimate the inequalities in class and race relations.   In *Beyond Agenda-Setting*, Oscar Gandy argues that there is strong evidence that the media tilt toward the upper classes, that information systems "tend to distribute information, including the mass media, in a form most familiar to users with more education,"[8] thus widening the knowledge gap between the poor and poorly educated and the rich and well-educated as well as the disparity between the races.

In addition, racial images in the mass media are infused with color-coded positive and negative moralistic features.   Once these symbols become familiar and accepted, they fuel misperceptions and perpetuate misunderstandings among the races.   Hall, Jefferson, and other researchers point out that groups and classes are ranked in relation to each other in terms of productivity, wealth, and power, and that cultures may be similarly ranked in terms of "domination and subordination, along the scale of 'cultural power.' " Further, they support the position that the ruling class rules as thinkers and producers of ideas, as well as regulating their distribution.   Its ideas, therefore, are the dominant ideas of any period.[9]

When this framework is applied to race relations in American society, a similar pattern of unequal cultural power emerges. Racial representations help to mold public opinion, then hold it in place and set the agenda for public discourse on the race issue in the media and in the society at large. Black media stereotypes are not the natural, much less harmless, products of an idealized popular culture; rather, they are more commonly socially constructed images that are selective, partial, one-dimensional, and distorted in their portrayal of African Americans. Moreover, stereotyped black images most often are frozen, incapable of growth, change, innovation, or transformation. As T. W. Adorno has observed: "The more stereotypes become reified and rigid in the present setup of the culture industries, the less people are likely to change their preconceived ideas with the progress of experience. The more opaque and complicated modern life becomes, the more people are tempted to cling desperately to clichés which seem to bring some order into the otherwise un-understandable."[10]

Stereotypes are especially effective in conveying ideological messages because they are so laden with ritual and myth, particularly in the case of African Americans; but, invariably, these black representations are totally at odds with the reality of African Americans as individual people. The end result, a series of sharply conflicting black images in the mass media, has grave implications for American society as a whole. The conflict is indicative of a deep cultural schism, which precipitated the ideological struggle between white and black image makers in the first place. Hence the situation offers scholars a unique opportunity to explore the dynamics of cultural conflict as manifested in mass-media imagery. By tracking African American images, their audience, and their producers over time and across the various media strategically involved in the production and distribution of those images, we can pinpoint their common characteristics and sources, the ways in which they evolved, and the context in which they competed for the attention of both black and white Americans. Ultimately, this unmasking of black stereotypes deeply embedded in the popular culture brings the question of racial identity to the forefront, both at the individual and the national level. It was James Baldwin who expressed the quintessential paradox of America's race relations when he stated prophetically to a white television audience: "If I'm not who you say I am, then you're not who you think you are."[11]

Antebellum Popular Culture

The roots of the schism go back to slavery. Both the popular theater and the literature of the antebellum period created standardized images of slaves and their masters. These initial representations were used to rationalize the enslavement of African people and to justify the institution of slavery in the South. As early as 1781, in a play called *The Divorce*, and then again in 1795, in a romantic farce entitled *The Triumphs of Love*, a black character named Sambo appeared on the American stage. In both cases, he was cast in a familiar mold: always singing nonsense songs and dancing around the stage. His dress was gaudy, his manners pretentious, his speech riddled with malapropisms, and he was played by white actors in blackface. The subsequent popularity of the "comic Negro" stereotype had profound social implications. As historian Joseph Boskin noted:

> Sambo was an extraordinary type of social control, at once extremely subtle, devious, and encompassing. To exercise a high degree of control meant also to be able to manipulate the full range of humor; to create, ultimately, an insidious type of buffoon. To make the black male into an object of laughter, and conversely, to force him to devise laughter, was to strip him of masculinity, dignity, and self-respect. Sambo was, then, an illustration of humor as a device of oppression, and one of the most potent in American popular culture. The ultimate objective for whites was to effect mastery, to render the black male powerless as a potential warrior, as a sexual competitor, as an economic adversary.[12]

The first slave to appear in a major American novel was Caesar Thompson Wharton, a house servant in James Fenimore Cooper's *The Spy*. Caesar was the epitome of the early contented slave stereotype. He was loyal, devoted to his master's welfare, and seemingly comfortable with his own servitude. He also provided the story with comic relief due to his fear of ghosts and other superstitions. The novel was adapted to the stage soon after it was written and became one of the most popular plays of the era. Theater and literature were the major conduits for cultural images in America throughout the nineteenth century. Popular songs were integral to both, being performed on stage and published as sheet music or broadsides. Late in the 1820s, white actors began doing imitations of African American song and dance in urban theaters in the North and South. Their performances presented clownlike images of black Americans, portraying them as comic buffoons. The actors continued the practice of blackening their faces with burnt cork to accent the caricatures. The most renowned of the early blackface performers was Thomas D. Rice, who popularized the song and dance, "Jump Jim Crow," a theatrical sensation in the 1830s. Rice modeled his famous character on an elderly, crippled African American stable hand and reputedly even borrowed his suit of ragged clothing for the first stage performance. His new stage act was an instant success, catapulting him into a much heralded tour of the major entertainment halls in the United States and England. In the process, the "Jim Crow" stereotype was born. He was a comically deformed song-and-dance man, wearing ragged, ill-fitting clothes—a burlesque of African American fashion, speech, and physiognomy.[13] As historian William Van Deburg observed: "The early slave image offered white audiences a comforting psychological reassurance. In the real world of . . . Santo Domingo, or Stono, South Carolina, rebellious African slaves might conspire and revolt, but on stage blackface bondsmen were loyally imitative and greatly dependent on their masters. Such intellectually inferior clowns posed little threat to white hegemony."[14]

By the 1840s, blackface minstrelsy had evolved into a formalized entertainment genre, complete with a standardized stage extravaganza that required an entire troupe of actors. But from its inception, antebellum minstrelsy's characterization of black Americans was a damaging one. African Americans living in the cities were invariably portrayed as urban dandies and dummies who futilely aped white manners. Plantation slaves were depicted as childlike, comical, and contented with their lot. With the slavery issue increasingly preoccupying the nation, such representations tended to reinforce the ideology of racism, especially in the minds of white working-class males, the major audience of the minstrel shows. As a result, they were not inclined to want the slaves emancipated, and most of them were openly hostile to the abolitionist movement.

Many of the popular white performers in antebellum minstrel shows had some knowledge of black folklore prior to putting on the burnt cork. The most prominent of these performers were Thomas Rice, George Dixon, Dan Emmett, E. P. Christy, and Stephen Foster. But their assumption of the slave population's inherent inferiority and their perceptions of African American "peculiarities" were in league with the condescending and inhumane views advanced by southern slave owners. Historian Robert Toll ably summarized the social dynamics of antebellum ministrelsy:

> Blackface performers were like puppets operated by a white puppet master. Their physical appearance proclaimed their non-humanity; yet they could be manipulated not only to mock themselves but also to act like human beings. They expressed human emotions such as joy and grief, love, fear, longing. The white audience then identified with the emotions, admired the skills of the puppeteer, even sympathized laughingly with the hopeless aspiration of the puppets to become human, and at the same time feasted on the assurance that they could not do so. Blackface minstrelsy's dominance of popular entertainment amounted to a half a century of inurement to the uses of white supremacy.[15]

By the 1850s, the slavery controversy had engulfed the nation in a war of political rhetoric and racial imagery. For the first time, key stereotypes in the arsenal of the proslavery forces, like the contented slave and the benevolent master, were being seriously challenged by antislavery activists at public forums and in the media. In particular, white abolitionists rallied around the publication of Harriet Beecher Stowe's *Uncle Tom's Cabin*, which they found to be an ideal vehicle for projecting their image of African American slaves and their antislavery sentiments. The book received a great deal of fanfare, inspiring a rash of imitative fiction and stage melodramas, and ultimately becoming the media event of the decade. Although Stowe stood the stereotype of the benevolent slave master on its head, portraying him as the novel's lecherous and malevolent villain, it was her reworking of the slave stereotype through the character of Uncle Tom that attracted the most attention. Uncle Tom was hardly a contented or comic slave, but neither was he an angry or rebellious one; instead, he was a gentle and long-suffering bondsman, imbued with childlike innocence and a "natural" Christian piety. Lurking behind these idealized character traits was an unusual collusion of middle-class white abolitionist and feminist beliefs, referred to by historian George Fredrickson as "romantic racialism."[16] Through the Uncle Tom stereotype, the major Christian virtues associated with the domestic realm of women were elevated and favored over secular patriarchial virtues. As one enthusiastic male supporter proclaimed: "It is sometimes said . . . that the Negro race is the feminine race of the world. This is not only because of [the Negro's] social and affectionate nature, but because he possesses that strange, moral, instinctive insight that belongs more to women than men."[17]

While Uncle Tom proved to be a prized new addition to the pantheon of popular American racial stereotypes, the other major black figures in Stowe's book were pretty much old hat, even back then. Like her white proslavery adversaries, Stowe resorted to long-standing popular cultural stereotypes in order to round out her cast of characters. The tragic mulattoes are represented by Cassy and George Harris, whose white blood gives them a genetic edge in intellect and temperament over their full-blooded African compatriots, but whose mixed blood dooms them to a life in limbo, stranded indefinitely between two cultures. The comic minstrel stereotypes are present in the slave duo of Sam and Andy, who could easily be considered the original Amos 'n' Andy prototypes. There is a black pickaninny child, Topsy, who is juxtaposed to her angelic blond opposite, Little Eva. Although there are no misguided rebel slaves in *Uncle Tom's Cabin*, Stowe made amends by devoting her next novel, appropriately named *Dred*, to just such a figure. Based in part on Nat Turner, the slave insurrectionist is depicted as a religious fanatic tormented by evil spirits and visions, while the idealized virtues of Uncle Tom are transferred to Dred's patient and docile wife, Milly.[18]

The nationwide publicity surrounding the publication of *Uncle Tom's Cabin* provoked a deluge of schemes to cash in on its popularity. These included everything from a cornucopia of Uncle Tom memorabilia to a plethora of amateurish "Uncle Tom Shows" that crisscrossed the country, staging the melodrama wherever they could solicit an audience. As one amused observer noted, " 'Uncle Tom' became, in his various forms, the most frequently sold slave in American history."[19] The longevity of Uncle Tom's lifespan as a well-known national stereotype, rivaled only by the ubiquitous Sambo, is testimony to his staying power—especially with white audiences. As recently as 1946, *The Negro Digest* reported that a large majority of the whites they polled thought that *Uncle Tom's Cabin* was not an "Anti-Negro" fable, while a clear majority of the African Americans polled viewed the same story and its hero as "Anti-Negro."[20]

The contested image of the slave in the antebellum era was at the eye of an ideological storm that shattered the hegemony of the dominant white culture, eventually dividing the country into two camps. For the white proslavery apologists, the black bondsmen were invariably a happy lot who had much to be thankful for while living on plantations. In contrast, white antislavery advocates depicted the black bondsmen as victims of an inhumane plantation system, waiting patiently to be set free by righteous white eman-cipators. It was left to ex-bondsmen such as Frederick Douglass, Soloman Northrup, William Wells Brown, and Henry Bibb to publicize accounts of defiant slaves who took their lives into their own hands. Each of them wrote a slave narrative detailing the inhumane conditions of their captivity and their eventual escape to freedom.

It is interesting to note that the mastery of reading, and especially writing, was also seen as an act of liberation for these former bondsmen. The slave narratives were the first instances of African American voices reaching the outside world, moving beyond the black oral tradition and the slave community. In essence, these written narratives are the beginnings of an African American literary tradition, one that responded to the pervasive white images of slavery by becoming "double voiced." Former slaves were recognized as speaking subjects in the dominant culture only to the extent that they could inscribe their voices in the written word. It was only by writing their thoughts down on paper that slaves could obtain a hearing in the outside world. Ironically, learning to read and write was strictly prohibited to slaves. Moreover, as Henry Louis Gates, Jr., has observed: "In slave narratives . . . making the white written text speak with a black voice is the initial mode of inscription of the double voiced."[21]

In addition to the slave narratives, the fiction written by former bondsmen during the antebellum era also championed bold and rebellious slave heroes who actively opposed their bondage. Fred-erick Douglass's The Heroic Slave is a classic example of this genre. It is based on a real mutiny carried out by bondsmen aboard the slaveship Creole in 1841. The novel's black hero is Madison Washington, who, after leading the successful slave revolt, returns to the South to rescue his kin, even though this action places his newly won freedom in great jeopardy. Another example of this genre is J. T. Trowbridge's Cudjo's Cave, the story of two escaped slaves in eastern Tennessee who live in a secret cave and wage guerrilla warfare against the Confederacy in the region. In both novels, the slave protagonists' active resistance to the bondage of their people stands in sharp contrast to Uncle Tom's passive resistance to slavery.[22]

Postbellum Popular Culture

After the Civil War, popular literature and the stage continued to be the chief media channels for cultural images of African Americans. Likewise, the debate over slavery continued, but now from a historical vantage point. Most white southern writers in the postbellum era routinely romanticized the Confederacy. Genteel slave masters and chivalrous military leaders were venerated as the cultural heroes of a mythical golden age of southern gallantry and glory—gone but not forgotten. Slaves continued to be characterized as contented and comical. But as a postbellum literature evolved, new black stereotypes emerged, updating those from the antebellum period. The place of the contented slave was taken over by the faithful servant: the female side of this stereotype became the domestic mammy caricature, while the male side matured into elderly Uncle Toms. Thomas Nelson Page invented Uncle Billy to sing the author's praises of slavery days in the slaves' own vernacular. Joel Chandler Harris created Uncle Remus as a sort of folksy apologist for the plantation social system and antebellum southern culture. His stories were expropriated from the African American oral tradition and related in black dialect. Next, the wretched freedman stereotype devolved into the bestial, brutish Negro, also a doomed figure—but in this case because of his ignorance, insolence, and lust for white women. Likewise, the mulatto became more degenerate as well as more tragic. Thomas Nelson Page helped to popularize the brute Negro stereotype in his novel *Red Rock* by inventing the character Moses, a mulatto villain who lusts after political power and white females. He is described by the author as a "reptile" and a "wild beast." Perhaps the most notorious of the depraved mulatto creatures, Silas Lynch, first appeared in Thomas Dixon's novel *The Clansmen* and then later in D. W. Griffith's film "Birth of a Nation." Dixon was an infamous southern Negrophobe who was also responsible for inventing the renegade Gus, a classic brute Negro stereotype equally prominent in Griffith's controversial film.[23]

In contrast and reaction to this new onslaught of black stereotypes from the southern white literary mainstream, African American writers created cultural heroes who were masters of their own destiny, and they also sought to repossess the black vernacular tradition for their own literature. The first order of business was the veneration of African American heroes. In William Still's *The Underground Railroad*, a fugitive slave who works as an underground railroad conductor is the novel's major character and role model.[24] Another favorite fictional African American hero during this period was the black soldier who fought for the Union during the Civil War. His courage and skill as a combatant was lauded in novels, histories, and personal reminiscences.

It was Charles Chesnutt, however, who first used black dialect and parody, cultural resources drawn from the wellspring of the black oral tradition, as a means of undermining the dominant white literary discourse on African Americans and their vernacular. In addition to the masking function of the dialect, what Gates refers to as "the self-conscious switch of linguistic codes from white to black, or more properly, from standard English to black vernacular," Chesnutt also made use of its subversive qualities.[25] His dialect-speaking folk hero in *The Conjure Woman*, Uncle Julius, is the antithesis of Uncle Remus; this wily raconteur is more interested in preserving his integrity and surviving in the postbellum era than in glorifying antebellum slavery and remaining loyal to his former masters. Moreover, Uncle Julius also uses witchcraft in his adversarial relationships with white people.[26] Chesnutt's use of black folklore and dialect in his writing set the stage for other African American authors—from Jean Toomer to Langston Hughes, Zora Neal Hurston, and Sterling A. Brown—to mine the black oral tradition for materials to incorporate into their novels, short stories, and poetry. As Gates points out: "The poet has in this mutation—this dialect—an accessible linguistic system that turns the literate language upon itself, exploiting the metaphor against the master."[27] In the ongoing war of racial images during this period, "one didn't believe one's eyes, if one were black," according to Sterling Brown, "one believed one's ears."[28]

Within the context of the black vernacular, two key strategies were readily adopted by black writers: parody and signifying. Literary scholar Mikhail Bakhtin defines the former as follows. In parody, "the author employs the speech of another . . . he introduces into that other speech an intention which is directly opposed to the original one. The second voice, having lodged in the other speech, clashes antagonistically with the original, host voice and forces it to serve directly opposite aims. Speech becomes a battlefield for opposing intentions."[29] In light of this definition, parody has a very special significance for an African American literary tradition because of its tendency to invert social hierarchies: "By appropriating an existing discourse for its own ends, parody is especially well-suited to the needs of the powerless, precisely because it assumes the force of the dominant discourse only to deploy that force, through a kind of artistic jujitsu, against domination."[30] Signifying, on the other hand, is a rhetorical strategy calculated to reverse dialogue by turning a statement back on itself in order to gain the upper hand in a verbal contest; it is yet another "double-voiced" or intertextual practice that seeks to subvert existing power relations. The act of signifying is, of course, associated with the "Signifying Monkey," a well-known fixture in African American folklore; but its roots go all the way back to trickster figures from traditional West African cultures like the Yoruban Esu-Elegbara and the Fon's Legba. One of the most famous examples of literary signifying was created by Sterling A. Brown: in response to Robert Penn Warren's line from his poem, "Piney Woods," "Nigger, your breed ain't metaphysical," Brown retorts, "Cracker, your breed ain't exegetical."[31]

Popular theater was also an important cultural arena in which racial images were contested during the postbellum period. In the aftermath of the Civil War, African American minstrel troupes began appearing before both white and black audiences. These entertainers adopted the blackface minstrelsy format, the plantation subject matter, and, to a certain extent, the blackface stereotypes of slave life; but they did so while infusing their minstrel routines with authentic folk materials drawn from the African American oral tradition. This contradiction set the stage for what would follow: a protracted tug-of-war within minstrelsy between the forces of the still dominant antebellum blackface tradition and those of a slowly emerging postbellum African American minstrelsy.

Although black entertainers eventually came to dominate postbellum minstrelsy, white businessmen owned and controlled it. In addition to reaping the profits, these white entrepreneurs insisted that the material and structure of the shows remain faithful to the content and the format of the early blackface tradition. They demanded that the black performers they hired reproduce the outdated routines and caricatures of the antebellum minstrel show. In essence, they functioned as guardians of the old cultural order, and their collective influence resulted in the perpetuation of demeaning racial stereotypes in American show business, a trend that persisted well into the twentieth century. Talented black entertainers who worked for white-owned minstrel troupes often found themselves between the hammer and the anvil with respect to their artistic and racial integrity. The white owners decided who could work in the most prestigious troupes and offered a certain amount of fame and fortune in exchange for African American compliance with the blackface legacy. Although there was some latitude in negotiating these arrangements, even the most popular, and therefore potentially the most powerful, of the black performers in these shows sacrificed a good deal of their artistic independence in return for stardom and financial gain. The careers of James Bland, Billy Kersands, and Bert Williams offer clear, if somewhat disheartening, illustrations of the pitfalls inherent in postbellum minstrelsy. Each of them accommodated minstrel stereotypes on the road to success. Bland's song "Carry Me Back to Old Virginny" told the story of a former slave longing for his master and his life on the old plantation. It became the state anthem of Virginia. Bert Williams was the last significant African American entertainer to perform in blackface on the American stage.[32]

Toward the end of the nineteenth century, the infamous "coon song" became fashionable. The term "coon" was a shortened version of raccoon used by southern whites as a derisive reference to black males. Gradually it came to represent the image of a dandified urban black male. In 1896, the African American songwriter Ernest Hogan published "All Coons Look Alike to Me." The song became an overnight sensation, inspiring a flood of commercial coon songs over the next two decades. Hogan would later regret that he had helped to popularize the derogatory connotations of the term and its image. At their worst, the coon songs were degrading burlesques of African American physical and cultural traits. However, the songs written by black composers for their new vaudeville musical revues were also commonly referred to as coon songs during this period. They were usually optimistic, ragtime numbers tinged with a whimsical sort of irony. "Darktown Is Out Tonite" by Will Marion Cook is an example of this sort of coon song. It celebrated the good times and musical vitality found in black urban enclaves, while also playfully chiding whites for their inability to break through their own rigid formalities and move past racial stereotypes to have some fun themselves. African American tunesmiths were thus able to reclaim a portion of a song genre that was rightfully theirs, but only after it had been thoroughly exploited by Tin Pan Alley and Broadway. As late as 1925, black entertainment columnist S. T. Whitney, after complaining bitterly about the white business interests in control of black show business, acknowledged that "the real musical show and drama of race life will have to be promoted by our own men before the desired result is obtained."[33]

Enter the Mass Media

Like popular theater and literature, popular song was another battlefield in the war of images between black and white image makers. With the advent of phonograph recordings, motion pictures, and radio broadcasting, the end of an era in American culture was close at hand. Popular theater and literature were no longer the dominant image making media in the country. Minstrelsy and its offspring, vaudeville, were fast becoming relics of the past. Unfortunately, the legacy of derogatory racial caricatures and restricted employment opportunities reemerged in the new mass-media industries that dominated the production and distribution of African American images in the twentieth century. White-owned record, film, radio, advertising, news, and later television industries based most of the black images they produced on the prevailing nineteenth-century stereotypes. They also continued the discriminatory practice of limiting the roles African Americans could play in these media.

This study is first and foremost a historical and comparative analysis of African American portrayal and participation in the mass media in the United States. It develops the theme of "the war of images" to foster some understanding of how and why the mass media have evolved as they have with respect to African American imagery and participation. Every chapter addresses the racial duality of the individual media industries under scrutiny. Each one explores the ways in which, on the one hand, African American images have been distorted and talent exploited, while, on the other hand, African Americans have been systematically denied by those in power the opportunity to act as full participants in the industries. What evolved were mass media that favored black stereotypes created by whites over the more authentic and positive black characters created by black image makers. It is therefore understandable that, for the most part, African Americans have been disappointed in many of the mass-media products featuring their group as seen in mainstream America's popular culture, because so little of their own culture and values that differ from the mainstream has been given any exposure. Thus, whenever and wherever they could, African Americans tried to develop their own media products and their own means of distributing them. White domination of mainstream culture inevitably gave rise to African American cultural resistance, splitting the black image.

As could be expected, very few scholarly books or critical articles have focused substantively on the participation and portrayal of African Americans in media industries, contributing to the perception that black Americans have played no part in the creation and evolution of the various mass media. Almost all the scholarly material written on African Americans in the mass media has been published since 1970 (see Bibliography).

While disparate amounts of scholarship on African American participation and portrayal in each of the media industries discussed here do exist, there is no book that attempts to survey all of them in historical and comparative terms. This study conscientiously attempts to use the cultural prism of race in order to assess the development of the American mass media in the twentieth century and, within this historical context, specifically to trace the negative portrayals and restricted participation of African Americans in the mass media, on the one hand, and their responses to such stereotyping and discrimination, on the other. These responses have been varied, ranging from cautious accommodation, through angry protest, to endeavors to create alternatives both inside and outside the dominant white media.

In the first chapter, "Cashing In: 1900–1939," William Barlow analyzes the commercial music industry's relationship to African American music from the turn of the century to World War II. He shows in detail how the industry served as an important catalyst in the development of certain styles of popular black music, while in the process financially and artistically exploiting African American musicians. The financial exploitation usually involved the theft of royalty monies and/or song copyrights. The artistic exploitation involved the expropriation of new styles of African American music by the white-dominated music industry, which, in turn, diluted its rhythms and trivialized its content in order to make it more palatable to white music consumers.

In chapter 2, "Crossing Over: 1939–1989," Reebee Garofalo extends the line of analysis to the postwar development of rhythm and blues and its offspring, rock 'n' roll. He points out that most white artists who "covered" songs originally conceived by black artists were able to reap huge profits and achieve tremendous popularity while exerting little or no original creativity of their own. At the same time, many of the black artists who were responsible for the popular music of the era went unrecognized and unrewarded. Garofalo demonstrates how this pattern of expropriation repeated itself in the rock music of the 1960s and the disco music of the 1970s. But he also describes how black popular music continued to rejuvenate its traditions and styles as a means of resisting such expropriation—rap music being the latest innovation that demonstrates this effort. As a result of this continuous creative output on a collective level, black music makers are able to control their own images and musical products better vis-à-vis the music industry.

In chapter 3, "Film," Thomas Cripps analyzes the portrayal and the participation of African Americans in motion pictures, revealing how black cinema evolved from African American history. Noting how African Americans by their very presence altered the substance of American politics, Cripps explores the participation of blacks in films made by whites and by themselves. By the time the film industry developed sound and settled into Hollywood, motion picture roles for African Americans had already become narrowly proscribed. During the 1920s and 1930s the two roles open to them were either as entertainers or servants. After World War II, some progress was made toward broadening that image, as African American characters became more realistic and a token black hero, Sidney Poitier, made his film debut. Most African American actors and directors, however, still could not gain entrance into the Hollywood film industry, and the old stereotypes never faded away. The political and cultural ferment of the 1960s brought stronger black role models into Hollywood motion pictures, but then came the "Blaxploitation" films of the 1970s, which glamorized African American decadence, hedonism, and violence. Cripps concludes his chapter by arguing that even now, although some African Americans have moved into directing and producing Hollywood movies, the film industry continues to limit black participation in its work force and still controls, in the majority of cases, the black screen image. Thus, in spite of some important gains made by stars like Richard Pryor, Eddie Murphy, and Spike Lee, Hollywood's hegemony over African Americans in the film industry is still formidable.

In chapter 4, "Commercial and Noncommercial Radio," William Barlow critically assesses the radio industry's portrayal of African Americans since the 1920s, the limited nature of black participation in the industry, and the role African Americans have managed to play in fashioning radio's black audio images. Prior to the 1950s, when radio was the country's most popular form of mass media, African Americans were systematically excluded from working in the industry; most black characters were created and played by white writers and performers. With the advent of television, the radio networks lost their national audience. The radio market became more localized and thus demographically segmented, resulting in the rise of black formatted radio stations in the 1950s and 1960s. The tendency has continued up to the present; yet, even though these stations are programmed for black listeners, they remain for the most part white-owned. On the other hand, Barlow points out that this pattern of white control in African American radio operations is not found presently in the fifty-odd noncommercial black university and community radio stations established since the 1960s.

In chapter 5, "Commercial Television," Jannette L. Dates argues that commercial television failed to reflect African American culture adequately, and distorted the few aspects of the culture it did include. It systematically deterred whites from learning about blacks while it prevented blacks from fully participating in the industry. Despite these constraints, African Americans gained entrance into the medium in whatever ways they could. Their presence developed over the years, and by the mid-1980s African Americans were a potent force in network commercial television, particularly on camera.

In chapter 6, "Public Television," Dates argues that the nonprofit public sector sought access to noncommercial television in order to offer a viable alternative to commercial enterprises. It sought an avenue for meeting the needs of minorities not served by commercial broadcasting, including cultural, regional, and, eventually, racial minorities. She concludes that, for the most part, public television failed to address the needs or desires of African American audiences, despite the fact that the system was subsidized by the public purse. She goes on to demonstrate how, like its commercial counterpart, public television gradually began to include racial minority groups in program offerings, personnel, and ownership/licensing, but these changes occurred well after the time of the civil rights movement.

In chapter 7, "Print News," Dates describes the portraiture of African Americans found in the black press in comparison with the white print media. She argues that the black press has historically seen the black community from a vastly different perspective from that of the white press, thus providing the raison d'être for the existence and continuation of the black press. She argues that, despite black press enfeeblement resulting from the very integration for which it had so conscientiously fought, the black press, particularly magazines, continues to offer viable alternatives for expressing African American views and perspectives.

Lee Thornton, in chapter 8, "Broadcast News," focuses on the strides African Americans made between 1955 and 1990 in radio and television newsrooms. In 1955, for example, there was not a single black person in radio or television newsrooms above the caretaker level, whereas in the 1980s Americans saw Ed Bradley, Carole Simpson, George Strait, Bernard Shaw, and other black people reporting regularly. Thornton documents and analyzes how and why these dramatic changes came about. She concludes that broadcast journalists in general, and African Americans in particular, have a responsibility to African Americans and other minorities to bring the media at all levels into greater congruence with the institutional, cultural, and intellectual diversity of American society.

In chapter 9, "Advertising," Dates develops the argument that African American consumers were seldom courted as an actively targeted advertising market until years after the civil rights movement had ground to a halt. She demonstrates how the African American consumer, practitioner, and activist all figured in the development of the advertising industry's increased interest in the black community as a market. She also discusses how advertising opportunities became more available to African Americans as the new electronic environment emerged.

The Conclusion identifies the major contradictions still evident in the portrayals and participation of African Americans in the media industries. Within the framework of the tension between the potential of African Americans in the mass media and the constraints encountered by black people in those same media, the writers suggest a strategy for the future. This would involve both working within the media industries to broaden black participation and upgrade black images and working outside the industries to develop alternatives that would make users and suppliers aware of the power that resides in the hands of those who shape the image of the African American. The strategy also involves a new and more accurate understanding of the role played by economics and distribution in media operations, from the perspective of the African American entrepreneur. Only through the implementation of this dual strategy, the authors argue, can the schism between black and white images of the African American be significantly narrowed. Only by struggling on at least two fronts, we believe, can the split in the black image be minimized.

1. W. E. B. Du Bois, *The Souls of Black Folk* (New York: Fawcett, 1961), 16–17.

2. Sterling A. Brown, *The Negro in American Fiction*, 2d ed. (New York: Atheneum, 1972).

3. Sterling A. Brown, *Negro Poetry and Drama*, 2d ed. (New York: Atheneum, 1972), 106.

4. Walter Lippmann, *Public Opinion* (New York: Macmillan, 1922), 88–89.

5. Antonio Gramsci, *Selections from the Prison Notebooks* (New York: International Publishers, 1971); Stuart Hall, "Gramsci's Relevance for the Study of Race and Ethnicity," *Journal of Communication Inquiry* 10 (Summer 1986): 5–27.

6. Stuart Hall, "Signification, Representation, Ideology: Althusser and the Poststructuralist Debates," *Critical Studies in Mass Communication* (June 1985):98–100.

7. Douglas Kellner, "Television, Ideology and Emancipatory Popular Culture," in *Television: The Critical View*, 4th ed., ed. Horace Newcomb (New York: Oxford University Press, 1987), 471–506.

8. Oscar H. Gandy, Jr., *Beyond Agenda Setting: Information Subsidies and Public Policy* (New Jersey: Ablex, 1982), 178–81; D. Roberts and C. Bachen "Mass Communication Effects," *Annual Review of Psychology* 32 (1981): 307–56; and Oscar H. Gandy, Jr. and M. ElWaylly, "The Knowledge Gap and Foreign Affairs: The Palestinian-Israeli Conflict," *Journalism Quarterly* 62 (1985): 777–83.

9. John Clarke, Stuart Hall, Tony Jefferson, and Brian Roberts, "Subcultures, Cultures and Class," in *Resistance Through Rituals: Youth Subcultures in Post-War*

Britain, ed. Stuart Hall and Tony Jefferson (London: Hutchinson & Company, 1980), 11.

10. T. W. Adorno, "Television and Patterns of Mass Culture," in *Mass Culture: The Popular Arts in America*, ed. Bernard Rosenburg and David Manning White (New York: Free Press, 1957), 484.

11. James Baldwin, interviewed on CBS News, October 1967.

12. Joseph Boskin, *Sambo: The Rise and Demise of an American Jester* (New York: Oxford University Press, 1986), 13–14.

13. Brown, *Negro Poetry and Drama*, 105.

14. William L. Van Deburg, *Slavery and Race in American Popular Culture* (Madison: University of Wisconsin Press, 1984), 24.

15. Richard C. Toll, *Blacking Up: The Minstrel Show in Nineteenth-Century America* (New York: Oxford University Press, 1974), 274.

16. George M. Fredrickson, *The Black Image in the White Mind* (Middletown, Conn.: Wesleyan University Press, 1971), 101–2, 125–27.

17. Ibid., 114–15.

18. Harriet Beecher Stowe, *Dred: A Tale of the Great Dismal Swamp* (Boston: Phillips Sampson & Company, 1856).

19. Richard Yarborough, "Strategies of Black Characterization in 'Uncle Tom's Cabin' and the Early Afro-American Novel," in *New Essays on Uncle Tom's Cabin*, ed. Eric J. Sundquist (Cambridge: Cambridge University Press, 1986), 63.

20. Wallace Lee, "Is 'Uncle Tom's Cabin' Anti-Negro?", *Negro Digest*, January 1946, 68.

21. Henry Louis Gates, Jr., *The Signifying Monkey: A Theory of Afro-American Literary Criticism* (New York: Oxford University Press, 1988), 131.

22. See Frederick Douglass, *The Heroic Slave* 1853; J.T. Trowbridge, *Cudjo's Cave* (1863).

23. See Thomas Nelson Page, *Red Rock* (1900); Joel Chandler Harris, *Tales of Uncle Remus*; and Thomas Dixon, *The Clansmen* (1905).

24. William Still, *The Underground Railroad: A Record of Facts, Authentic Narratives, Letters, & C., Narrating the Hardships, Hair-breadth Escapes and Death Struggles of the Slaves in Their Efforts for Freedom* (Philadelphia, Pa.: Porter & Coates, 1872).

25. Henry Louis Gates, Jr., *Figures in Black: Words, Signs and the Racial Self* (New York: Oxford University Press, 1987), 171.

26. Charles Chesnutt, *The Conjure Woman* (Boston and New York: Houghton Mifflin, 1899).

27. Gates, *Figures in Black*, 172.

28. Ibid., 186.

29. Mikhail Bakhtin, "Discourse Typology in Prose," in *Readings in Russian Poetics: Formalist and Structuralist Views*, ed. Ladislav Matejka and Kaystyna Pomorska (Cambridge, Mass.: MIT University Press, 1971), 185–86.

30. Robert Stam, "Mikhail Bakhtin and Left Cultural Critique," in *Post-modernism and Its Discontent: Theories, Practices*, ed. E. Ann Caplan (London: Verso, 1988), 139.

31. Interview with Sterling Brown by William Barlow, 4 May 1984.

32. Lewis Bland, "James Allen Bland, Negro Composer: A Study of His Life and Work," MA. thesis, Howard University, 1958; Ann Charters, *Nobody: The Story of Bert Williams* (New York: Macmillan, 1970); and Toll, *Blacking Up*.

33. Daphne Duval Harrison, *Black Pearls: Blues Queens of the 1920s* (New Brunswick, N.J.: Rutgers University Press, 1988), 30.

Part One

CULTURE FOR SALE:
THE MUSIC INDUSTRY

1 CASHING IN: 1900–1939

WILLIAM BARLOW

The growth of the commercial record industry in the United States in this century has had a paradoxical influence on African American folk music; it has both encouraged and impeded its development as a black working-class art form. On the positive side of the ledger, the mechanical reproduction of millions of blues, jazz, and gospel discs made the music far more accessible to the public in general and to black people in particular. With the invention and subsequent mass production of the phonograph player, the potential to reach large audiences with a musical product was considerably enhanced. The eventual ramifications for the local and regional African American folk traditions that spawned blues, jazz, and gospel music were that they, in turn, were infused with new songs, rhythms, and styles to an extent that was never before possible. Black American music entered an era of unprecedented growth and vitality; it mushroomed as a multifaceted cultural movement at an exhilarating pace. The formation of the African American race record industry enabled blues and jazz to surface as a national phenomena by the 1920s. The music not only reached a mass audience but also enabled a new generation of African American musicians to use selectively the best of the commercial recordings as educational tools in expanding their mastery of the various idioms while enhancing their instrumental and vocal techniques. Within these parameters, the race record business served as an important catalyst in the development of blues and jazz, helping them become a part of the mainstream of popular American music.

On the other hand, the transformation of living musical traditions into commodities to be sold in a capitalist marketplace was bound to have drawbacks. For one thing, the profits garnered from the sale of race records invariably went into the coffers of the white businessmen who owned or managed the record companies; the black musicians and vocalists who created the music in the recording studios received a mere pittance for their labors. Furthermore, the major record companies went to great lengths to get African American music to conform to their clichéd, formula-prone, Tin Pan Alley standards, and they often expected black recording artists to conform to racist stereotypes inherited from blackface minstrelsy. Another predilection of the industry was to push white performers' "cover" versions of popular blues or jazz numbers. "Covering" was a frequently used technique designed to introduce a smaller sub-culture into the audience sphere of a larger cultural group. In this instance its purpose was both to entice a curious white public to buy the records and to "upgrade" the music. Upgrading was synonymous with commercializing; it attempted to bring African American music more in line with European musical conventions while superimposing upon it a veneer of middle-class Anglo-Amer-ican respectability. The net result was that a significant percentage of the blues and jazz recorded prior to World War II was drained of its African characteristics and working-class content. This diluting process and the technical constraints, like time and fidelity, inherent in the early recording process, converged to stifle, to a certain degree, both musical authenticity and innovation in the race record releases.

The invention of the mechanical phonograph in 1887 was credited to Thomas Edison, the erratic genius of applied technology in the gilded age of American show business. By the 1890s, a commercial market was developing for the phonograph machines and the crude cylinder recordings that the machine played. They would prove to be the first in a long line of home entertainment luxury items mass-produced for public consumption. The most popular cylinder recordings of the era were marches, sentimental ballads, after-dinner speeches, novelty tunes, opera selections, ragtime numbers, and the infamous "coon" songs. Only a few black entertainers were re-corded on cylinder, the most prominent being George W. Johnson, who performed his "Whistling Coon" minstrel number for Edison's company. At the turn of the century, the cylinder recording was being supplanted by the disc recording, which somewhat improved the quality of the recorded sound and was easier to handle.[1]

During the initial upsurge in the recording and marketing of the disc product, the leading record companies continued virtually to ignore African American talent. The Columbia Record Company, founded in 1899, excluded black performers from their stable of exclusive recording artists until the aftermath of World War I. Bert Williams auditioned for them and was initially turned down. However, the famous black comedian quickly demonstrated his ability to appeal to a white audience when he was given an opportunity to record for Columbia's chief rival. The Victor Talking Machine Company, founded in 1901, adopted a more liberal racial policy. In their second year of operation, sensing that the comic would be popular with white record buyers, they were shrewd enough to record Bert Williams. Williams recorded a total of fifteen titles for Victor between 1902 and 1903, most of them show tunes or comedy routines from his stage repertoire. His recording of his popular "Elder Eatmore's Sermon" eventually sold over half a million copies.[2] Victor also released six sides made by a group called the Dinwiddle Colored Quartet; their material included parodic verses in minstrel style, as well as renditions of authentic African American spirituals like "Steal Away" and "My Way Is Cloudy." The next breakthrough for black musicians was not until 1914, when James Reese Europe's Society Orchestra recorded some dance music for the Victor company as part of a series endorsed by the popular white dance team, Mr. and Mrs. Vernon Castle. In fact, it was Europe who provided the music for both the fox-trot and the turkey trot during this period.[3] Jim Europe's orchestra was made up of members of the Clef Club, an all-black musician's union he had helped to organize in New York in 1910. The club was active in fielding bands from its ranks to play at hotel ballrooms and for society events around town. The size of these orchestras ranged from the eleven musicians used by Europe for his Victor recording sessions to the hundred and thirty musicians who participated in a Clef Club extravaganza staged at Carnegie Hall in 1914. At the center of the club's activities was a core group of talented composers and orchestra leaders that included Europe, Will Marion Cook, James P. Johnson, Tim Bryn, Will Vodery, and Ford Dabney.

Collectively, the Clef Club pioneered the use of ragtime syncopation and unorthodox instrumentation in the various dance and concert ensembles they organized. Jim Europe, like the others, was a school-trained musician of the highest caliber. He played piano and violin, while he also wrote and arranged his own compositions.

His greatest triumph as a bandleader came during World War I when he was commissioned to organize and lead the now legendary 309th Infantry Regiment's military band, nicknamed the "Hellfighters." This group was an elite aggregation of African American musicians. The drum major was the popular showman, Bill "Bojangles" Robinson. Their tour of France at the conclusion of the war caused a major sensation. The French lavished praise on the group, proclaiming them the world's best military band. When they returned to America, they were greeted with great fanfare. Like the Clef Club orchestras, Jim Europe's 309th Regimental Band used syncopation and an unusual instrumental lineup that favored banjos and mandolins over violins.

Although none of Europe's ensembles could properly be called jazz bands, they were precursors to the coming of jazz, helping to prepare the groundwork for its immediate popularity with white audiences in the United States and Europe. Unfortunately, Jim Europe died before big band jazz made its breakthrough in the music industry. He was killed during an altercation with a member of his band in 1919.[4] His tragic death came at the height of his popularity as a bandleader and musical innovator. It marked the end of an era in African American dance and concert music. A second African American musical unit that was lauded by white audiences and critics on two continents and given the opportunity to record for a major record label prior to the 1920s was the Fisk Jubilee Singers from Fisk College in Nashville, Tennessee. The group was established by a white instructor at the college, named George L. White, in the aftermath of the Civil War. White trained his student vocal ensemble to sing the European classics, but he also encouraged them to sing "their own music"—meaning the spirituals. In 1871, White took the Fisk troupe on its first national tour to raise funds for the college. Their concert repertoire included patriotic anthems ("Battle Hymn of the Republic") and sentimental ballads of the era ("Old Folks at Home" and "Home Sweet Home"), as well as a selection of spirituals. The Fisk Jubilee Singers were not professional minstrel performers but rather church singers with some musical training. Their uniqueness stemmed from their being the first black vocal ensemble to introduce the African American spiritual to white audiences at home and abroad. In seven years they were able to raise $150,000 for their college—no small amount in the 1870s. Their success initiated a vocal ensemble tradition at black colleges throughout the United States, starting with the Hampton Jubilee Singers, formed at Hampton, Virginia, in 1872. These African American jubilee singing troupes were still popular enough after the turn of the century to attract the attention of the fledgling record industry. The Fisk Jubilee Singers remained an active and ongoing vocal unit. They even made a series of recordings for the Columbia label that were quite popular in the 1910s.[5] This not only helped pave the way for similar vocal groups, like the Pace Jubilee Singers and the Mitchell Christian Singers, to be recorded, it also set the stage for the recording of various genres of sacred music associated with the African American religious tradition. These included the sermons of famous black preachers, the "holy blues" of the sanctified street singers, and the new songs of the gospel quartets.

While only the exceptional black entertainer, orchestra, or singing group was recorded prior to 1920, the major record companies released a variety of African American-inspired music interpreted by white performers during this same period. It was a trend that would continue throughout the next two decades. Columbia Record's catalog listed a "Negro novelty" section, while Victor boasted of "Up-to-date comic songs in negro dialect." This material was also referred to as "plantation airs," "Ethiopian airs," or, most often, "coon" songs; they were a legacy of blackface minstrelsy and were indicative of the entrenched racism in the entertainment industry. The early career of vaudeville star Sophie Tucker provides a good example of this social malaise. She was a Russian-born immigrant who broke into show business in New York in the early 1900s. Because she was a robust, heavyset woman, she was considered unattractive by the kingpins of the local vaudeville theaters. They forced her to wear blackface and perform "coon" songs, likening her to the antebellum "Mammy" stereotype, until she was able to prove that she could be successful on the stage without them. Yet, although she did away with blackface and "coon" songs, she continued to be a popularizer of African American songs and scored her greatest triumphs with ragtime and blues compositions written by black composers. These included Sheldon Brooks's "Some of These Days" (1909) and "Darktown Strutter's Ball" (1912), as well W. C. Handy's famous "Saint Louis Blues" (1914) and "A Good Man Is Hard to Find" (1918). The Victor label issued its first jazz and blues recordings by white performers in 1917; they included two discs that were destined to be among the biggest commercial hits of the decade. The one million seller in the blues category was Sophie Tucker's rendition of "Saint Louis Blues." In the jazz category, it was the Original Dixieland Jass Band's "Livery Stable Blues" and "Dixieland Jass Band One Step" which also sold over one million copies.[6]

The Original Dixieland Jass Band was a group of five white musicians from New Orleans, the birthplace of jazz. They grew up in the Crescent City and were inspired by the burgeoning "hot" ensemble style that was in vogue among the city's black working class. The group's first national booking was in Chicago in 1916. Several months later, the band moved on to an engagement in New York City, and within a matter of weeks their popularity skyrocketed. The new hot jazz they played became the rage of the town, and they were immediately signed to record for the Victor label. Their first release was a jazz novelty tune featuring cornet and trombone barnyard imitations of horses and cows. It suggested a minstrel mentality, which may have accounted for their stylized, self-conscious approach to the new African American musical genre.[7] The spectacular success of the Original Dixieland Jass Band was the catalyst that launched the post–World War I "jazz age" for a younger and so-called "lost generation" of white artists, musicians, writers, and radical intellectuals. The music came to symbolize the rebellious spirit of the "roaring twenties."

The most publicized and financially successful jazz musician of the decade was Paul Whiteman, the self-proclaimed white "King of Jazz." Whiteman was a classically trained violinist who formed his own "symphonic jazz" dance band in order to capitalize on the music's sudden popularity. His large orchestra owed more to modern European musical conventions than to the "hot" improvisational New Orleans jazz style founded by black musicians, but he was able to define the music on his own terms and to convince a naive white public that it was the real thing. To his credit, however, Whiteman did employ a number of talented white jazz musicians, like trumpeter Bix Beiderbecke, and he helped to create a more favorable climate for the acceptance of jazz by the American public, paving the way for the recording and eventual recognition of pivotal black jazz giants of the 1920s, such as King Oliver, Louis Armstrong, Jelly Roll Morton, Sidney Bechet, Coleman Hawkins, Earl Hines, Fletcher Henderson, and Duke Ellington.[8]

The blues took a similarly circuitous route to reach the American public. The blues were discovered by Tin Pan Alley tunesmiths in 1912; they were a well-known entity when composer W. C. Handy moved to New York from Memphis in 1915. The sheet music publishing business was based on 28th Street between Fifth Avenue and Broadway; most of the major music firms were located there. These firms had received a big boost in 1909 when the first copyright law was passed by the U.S. Congress. Under the law, record companies had to pay royalty fees to the composers of the music they used or to the publishing firm that owned the composition's copyright. The fixed fee was two cents per record sold, or a penny for each of the two songs on the disc. One half of this fee went to the composer of the song, and the other to the publishing company that filed for the copyright.

Many of the more successful black composers who migrated to New York during this period, like many white composers, established their own music publishing firms. Handy and his partner, Harry Pace, went into business there in 1918. Others who formed their own companies included Sheldon Brooks from Mobile, Alabama, Clarence Williams from New Orleans, and Perry Bradford from Atlanta. Even entertainer Bert Williams formed his own company. The advantages were obvious: the songwriter could get his company to copyright his own songs and thus collect all royalty fees from the record companies rather than splitting them with a middle party.[9]

W. C. Handy published his most renowned blues compositions in the 1910s: "Memphis Blues" (1914), "Joe Turner Blues" (1916), and "Beale Street Blues" (1917). All of them were based almost exclusively on folk blues that Handy had heard in his early travels in the South.[10] However, their subsequent popular acclaim in the bastion of America's entertainment industry soon put the blues in a new cultural context. Handy's sudden success demonstrated their commercial potential, which in turn made the genre attractive to the Tin Pan Alley song hacks, who wasted little time in turning out a deluge of imitations. By the end of the decade, a blues craze was in full swing throughout the entertainment industry; not only were they the hottest items coming off the Tin Pan Alley assembly lines, but they were also in great demand in vaudeville theaters, dance halls, and cabarets all across the country. In short, they had entered into the mainstream of American popular music. As a

1917 Tin Pan Alley title proclaimed, "Everybody's Crazy about the Doggone Blues."[11]

The leap from a handful of folk blues interpreters with direct links to the African American oral tradition to a host of imitators with little feeling for or understanding of their subject matter led to a reformulation of the style and the themes of the music. This commercially motivated revisionism gave birth to a new popular song hybrid, referred to as "vaudeville blues" by a number of scholars in the field.[12] The vaudeville blues were based on long-standing black musical traditions, but they were reproduced in a commercial setting as opposed to a folk community. As a result, the intentions of the songwriters and the makeup of their audience changed dramatically. At their worst, the vaudeville blues were degrading burlesques of the music they attempted to duplicate; their style was diffused and the content trivialized. Legions of Tin Pan Alley song manufacturers simply applied their clichéd song formulas to a standardized twelve bar, aab stanza format. The result was a flood of third-rate imitations that glutted the market, polluted the authenticity of the folk originals, and distorted the meaning of the blues in the public's mind.

At their best, however, the vaudeville blues were updated versions of real folk blues translated into popular standards by a relatively small group of African American performers and composers. The best-known performers were female vocalists Ma Rainey, Ida Cox, Sara Martin, Alberta Hunter, Sippie Wallace, and Bessie Smith. These women also wrote some of their own lyrics. The most prominent male composers of vaudeville blues were W. C. Handy, Perry Bradford, James and Rosmond Johnson, Spencer Williams, Porter Grainger, Clarence Williams, and Thomas Dorsey. These men were also usually their own music publishers, and, like their female counterparts, they were well acquainted with the South where they were schooled in the performance and application of black folk music. In an interview with E. Simms Campbell, a blues scholar, Clarence Williams stated: "Why, I'd never have written blues if I had been white. You don't study to write blues, you feel them. It's the mood you're in—lay for hours in the swamp in Louisiana. Spanish moss dripping everywhere. . . . White men were looking for me with guns. I wasn't scared, just sorry I didn't have a gun. I began to hum a tune, a little sighing kinda tune."[13]

Williams had a reputation as a shady operator in the race record business, and he may well have been telling a tall tale to a white interrogator. Nevertheless, the final product was a blues composition fired in the crucible of experience, most likely taken from a folk source, and difficult to duplicate on Tin Pan Alley.

W. C. Handy's approach to blues composition relied heavily on his firsthand exposure to African American folk songs. In his autobiography, he describes how he went about writing his earliest blues effort, "Mr. Crump," later retitled "Memphis Blues":

> The melody of "Mr. Crump" was mine throughout. On the other hand, the twelve bar, three line form of the first and third strains, with its three chord basic harmonic structure (tonic, subdominant, dominant seventh) was already used by Negro roustabouts, honky tonk piano players, wanderers, and others of their underprivileged but undaunted class from Missouri to the Gulf, and had become a common medium through which any such individual might express his personal feelings in a sort of musical soliloquy. My part in their history was to introduce this, the "blues" form to the general public, as the medium for my own feelings and my own musical ideas. And the transitional flat thirds and sevenths in my melody, by which I was attempting to suggest the typical slurs of the Negro voice, were what have since become known as blue notes.[14]

With other numbers, like "Yellow Dog Blues" and "Joe Turner Blues," Handy reconstructed the melodies and the lyrics of commonly known folk blues from memory and published them under his own name; this was not an uncommon practice in the race record industry during the heyday of the blues and jazz bonanza.

Perry "Mule" Bradford was, along with Handy, the other major black songwriter and publisher who played a crucial role in helping to stimulate the commercial boom in vaudeville blues. He was the first show business entrepreneur to talk a record company executive into recording a blues composition, one of his own, by an African American female vocalist backed up by an African American jazz band. The title was "Crazy Blues," recorded by Mamie Smith and Her Jazz Hounds for Okeh Records in 1920; it was a song that she was singing regularly in a New York musical revue called "Made in Harlem." Bradford was a seasoned vaudeville entertainer with an entrepreneurial flair and a street hustler's instincts. He was born in Montgomery, Alabama, in 1895, but spent much of his youth in Atlanta, where his family moved in 1902. The Bradfords first lived in a house next to the Fulton Street Jail. In the evenings, the jail's black inmates would pass the time singing blues and other folk songs; this was where young Perry first heard the music that would soon become his livelihood and claim to fame. Like Handy, Bradford became a popularizer of the blues. In his autobiography, he cites two blues numbers that he used in his repertoire by writing down their lyrical cores. Both of them were well-known folk blues that he had reconstructed:

> Baby you don't know my mind. No—no—no?
> My gal's quit me—and treated me so unkind
> So when you see me laughing—now
> I'm only laughing just to keep from cryin'
>
> My gal walked the streets till she got soaked and wet
> And this is what she said to every man she met
> Don't want your dollars, just give me a lousy dime
> So I can feed that hungry man of mine.[15]

The second verse was a variation of a blues that Jelly Roll Morton used in his repertoire; he credited it to Mamie Desdoumes, the first New Orleans singer to be identified with the blues.[16] Before the emergence of the race record industry, the folk nature of the traditional blues allowed many individuals to have their own personal versions of a song commonly known in the black oral tradition. This became more difficult when copyrighting and then recording came along.

Perry Bradford broke into black vaudeville in his hometown Atlanta as a singer, dancer, and piano player. In 1907, he went on the road with Allen's New Orleans Minstrels, traveling to New Orleans and then on to Chicago, where he lived for a few years. By 1918, Bradford had moved to New York and was involved in staging a musical revue, "Made in Harlem," which showcased his "Harlem Blues." The song was a revision of a number he had learned in 1912 called "Nervous Blues." One of Bradford's pet schemes was to convince a major record company that there was a profit in issuing blues records made by black artists. He argued that "fourteen million Negroes . . . will buy records if recorded by one of their own."[17] The two dominant record labels in the business, Victor and Columbia, turned Bradford down. A smaller label called Okeh, managed by a white businessman named Fred Hager for the General Phonograph Company, agreed to record a few of Perry Bradford's songs, but only if they were sung by Sophie Tucker. When contract commitments made it impossible for Tucker to do the session, Bradford's original choice for vocals was offered the contract. She was Mamie Smith, the female star of "Made in Harlem," who sang "Harlem Blues" in the show. After an undistinguished first release, Mamie Smith recorded her rendition of "Harlem Blues." The title was changed to "Crazy Blues" to avoid a possible copyright suit by the backers of the musical revue. The phenomenal success of "Crazy Blues," issued in August 1920, proved that Bradford's prediction had been correct; it opened the floodgates for the rush to record vaudeville blues sung by black women. The lyrics to "Crazy Blues" went, in part:

> I can't sleep at night, I can't eat a bite
> 'Cause the man I love, he don't treat me right.
> Now I got the crazy blues, since my baby went away
> I got no time to lose, I must find him today.
> Now the doctor gonna do all he can
> But what you're gonna need is an undertaker man
> I ain't had nothing but bad news
> Now I got the crazy blues.[18]

The backup group for this historic session was five local black musicians, called the Jazz Hounds. They included Johnny Dunn on cornet, Dope Andrews on trombone, Earnest Elliott on clarinet, fiddler Leroy Parker, and pianist Willie "the Lion" Smith. In his autobiography, Smith recalled the following about "Crazy Blues":

> The tune was just an ordinary old blues strain that had been used in other songs. Mamie said she first used it in a show called "Maid of Harlem" at the Lincoln Theatre under the title "Harlem Blues." James P. Johnson once claimed he used the same strain in his "Mama and Papa Blues," which he composed back in 1916. Other pianists remembered that part of the melody came from an old bawdy song played in the sporting houses, "Baby Get That Towel Wet."[19]

Okeh Records sold seventy-five thousand copies of "Crazy Blues" in the first month, and surpassed the hundred thousand mark during its first year in the stores. Perry Bradford received close to twenty thousand dollars in royalties, according to his own records; this was less than he was legally entitled to, given the sales figures and the fact that his copyrighted songs were on both sides of the record. At that time, it was extremely difficult to collect royalties from the record labels because they kept score of how many records were manufactured and sold. In addition, the companies tried to buy the copyrights to the songs they recorded, and, failing to do that, they would offer contracts that paid the copyright holders only a fraction of the royalty monies. Bradford, in turn, also engaged in controversial business practices. He owned his own publishing firm, the Perry Bradford Music Company, and was accused of publishing other people's songs under his own name. He even spent some time in jail for subordination of perjury, the result of a copyright suit brought against him. However, Bradford's wheeling and dealing was no different from that of other entrepreneurs in the race record business; it was common practice to avoid or exploit the copyright laws whenever possible. For example, Bradford was at first pressured by Okeh Records to waive his royalty rights to "Crazy Blues." His written response was a patriotic parody. "Please be advised that the only thing Perry Bradford waives is the American flag."[20]

A number of small, newly formed record companies were in the forefront of the upsurge in blues recording that followed in the wake of Okeh's success with "Crazy Blues." The Arto label released Lucille Hegamin's "The Jazz Me Blues" and "Everybody's Blues" in February 1921; Emerson issued blues titles sung by Lillian Brown later in 1921, and Gennett recorded Daisy Martin that same year. Other independent labels attempted to capitalize on the blues and jazz boom in the early twenties, including Perfect, Pathe, Ajax, Vocalion, and Paramount. However, only a few of these smaller companies managed to survive the decade. Promotion and distribution problems usually caused their early demise. The two dominant companies in the recording industry, Victor and Columbia, also hopped on the blues and jazz bandwagon when it became apparent that a new black market did indeed exist. Both were suffering from serious losses in revenue caused by the advent of commercial radio, so their motive for getting into jazz and blues recordings was most likely monetary. Columbia's sales had declined from 7 million dollars to a loss of 4.5 million, forcing the company to file for bankruptcy in 1923; Victor's sales went down from 51 million to 25 million dollars between 1921 and 1925.[21]

The decade also witnessed the rise and fall of a handful of black-owned record companies. W. C. Handy and his partner, Harry Pace, founded the Black Swan record label in January 1921 and proceeded immediately to record Ethel Waters and Alberta Hunter. The company reported over a hundred thousand dollars in sales during 1921, but three years later it was deeply in debt, and Handy and Pace were forced to sell the company's remaining assets to Paramount. Two black record store owners based in Los Angeles launched the Sunshine label in 1922 by issuing separate blues titles by Roberta Dudley and Ruth Lee, as well as a jazz instrumental by Kid Ory's jazz band. But, after these initial three releases, the label never was heard from again. The other black-owned record enterprises started in the 1920s suffered a similar fate. Winston Holmes's Meritt Records was formed in Kansas City in 1925; it lasted three years but only issued seven discs during that period. Female blues vocalist Lottie Kimbrough was Holmes's major recording artist; she was a native of Kansas City and was well known in the town's notorious red-light district. J. Mayo ("Ink") Williams, Chicago's premiere black talent scout in the 1920s, started his own label, Black Patti, in 1927. It folded in less than a year. Although Williams had access to the best African American singers and musicians in the business, he was unable to distribute his product effectively, especially outside of Chicago.[22] Overall, the smaller record companies were at a disadvantage in comparison with the major labels; they could not afford to advertise their product extensively on a national level, and they had no viable means of distributing their product beyond their home bases. As a result, they were invariably forced out of the record industry, while the larger companies were able slowly to take over the new markets, markets they entered only belatedly. This was particularly true for the black-owned record labels, which never gained a foothold in the race record business even though it was aimed at a black consumer market. The economic structure of the industry, coupled with its biased cultural standards, ultimately proved to be insuperable obstacles.

The three white-owned record companies that emerged as the undisputed leaders in the race record market during the early 1920s were Okeh, Columbia, and Paramount. Okeh, which initiated the trend in 1920, continued to set the pace for the next few years. Much of the credit for its success is given to Ralph Peer, who handled the company's race recording ventures after Fred Hager. Peer grew up in Missouri where he gained some appreciation for African American folk music; he was primarily responsible for putting together the Okeh label's special eight thousand series of race records. By the end of 1922, forty selections had been released in the series; they included six jazz instrumentals, eleven gospel numbers, and twenty-three vaudeville blues. Okeh initially advertised this material as "colored" records, and grouped them together in a "Colored Catalogue." In 1922, however, it placed ads in the Chicago *Defender* for "Race phonograph stars" and "Okeh race records." Within a year, Okeh had dropped the word *colored* from its advertising copy. Peer would later claim that he coined the term "race records" as part of Okeh's classification system. More than likely, he adopted the term from the Chicago *Defender*, which frequently used it as a progressive and positive connotation for African Americans. The word *race* was symbolic of black pride, militancy, and solidarity in the 1920s, and it was generally favored over *colored* or *Negro* by African American city dwellers. Peer certainly did not wish to offend potential black customers, which is probably why he made the switch. In any event, soon thereafter the term was adopted by most of the other record companies that were attempting to market African American musical products.[23]

The Okeh label usually paid a twenty-five-dollar per-title flat fee to its race recording artists. The fee was either the price paid for the copyright to the number or an advance on royalty payments when they were unable to obtain the copyright. Okeh's standard royalty deal was to give the songwriter 40 percent of the penny per side; the other 60 percent was kept by the label. Louisville guitarist Sylvester Weaver was a typical Okeh race record artist in the 1920s. He backed up the label's most consistent vaudeville blues vocalist, Sarah Martin, on many of her records and also recorded a number of his own compositions. Nine of those titles were copywritten for him by the Clarence Williams Music Publishing Company. Williams had initially tried to buy Weaver's royalty shares from him but was turned down. Over a four-year period, Williams paid Weaver a meager $137.84 in royalty fees for the nine compositions. If Williams's figures were correct, and he was giving Weaver the same deal that Okeh offered its race record artists, then the nine titles written by Weaver sold about twenty thousand copies on the commercial market. His most popular record was "Guitar Rag" and "Guitar Blues." He received under $100 for his guitar instrumental milestone—$58 in recording fees and less than $50 in royalties.[24] "Guitar Rag" would eventually become one of the biggest country music hits of the 1930s, when it was recorded by

Bob Wills and his Texas Playboys as "Steel Guitar Rag." As could be expected, Weaver was not listed as the songwriter on the Wills recording and he received no royalty money from it.

Much of Columbia Records' success in the race record market was due to its exclusive recording contract with Bessie Smith, the highly acclaimed "Queen of the Blues" during the culturally turbulent twenties. In 1923, Smith was brought to the attention of Frank Walker, who supervised the Columbia Records race record series, after Fred Hager at Okeh decided against recording her because her vocal style was "too rough."[25] Smith's agent with Columbia, Clarence Williams, negotiated her first contract with the label. Williams had his own music publishing firm and worked as a talent scout for Walker. Williams got Smith $125 per selection, plus the royalties for her own material; however, the royalty checks went to his company and he also pocketed half of her recording fees. When Smith discovered the deal, she angrily fired Williams and renegotiated her contract directly with Walker.

This time around, Smith got all of her $125 fee per title and a $1,500 guarantee for the year; however, Walker dropped Smith's royalty clause, which allowed him to copyright her songs for Columbia Records. His own music publishing firms, Frank Music Company and, later, Empress Music Inc., filed for the copyrights, which allowed him to collect a percentage of the royalties while the balance remained in Columbia's coffers.[26] This was a common business practice among race record executives. Fred Hager helped to found Helf and Hager's Music Firm, and Ralph Peer started the Southern Music Publishing Company and the Peer International Corporation. The firms enabled these men to take full advantage of their strategic positions in the industry for their own benefit and for the benefit of their employers.

Bessie Smith recorded 160 titles for the Columbia label from 1923 to 1933; 38 of these songs were copyrighted in her name. She was paid a total of $28,575 by the company over that period of time. Her record sales averaged about twenty thousand copies per release, but some of the biggest hits sold up to seven hundred and eighty thousand in the first six months; this put her earnings for Columbia easily over one million dollars.[27] Yet she never got a penny in royalties and, in all probability, knew nothing about the copyright law—the case with most of the race record artists. Meanwhile,

Walker made a fortune on his music publishing firms, and Columbia Records legally pilfered thousands of dollars from an employee.

Columbia was prosperous enough by 1925 to purchase the patents necessary to introduce electric recording techniques into the record industry. In 1926, Columbia also bought Okeh label's entire record catalog. That same year the record business reached a highwater mark in sales—$128 million—a figure the industry would not surpass until after World War II. The sales of race records were also on the the rise during this period. Researchers Howard Odem and Guy Johnson estimated that in 1925 African Americans were buying five to six million discs yearly. These figures were based on data from only three of the top race record labels, which indicates that the estimate was low. A record sold for one dollar in 1920, but by 1923 the price had dropped to seventy-five cents per copy. The number of race record releases peaked in 1928, when the yearly total of individual titles reached the five hundred mark. Even latecomers, like the front-running Victor label, were now devoting a hefty portion of their catalogs, 21.7 percent in 1928, to race records.[28] In addition to the vaudeville blues and instrumental jazz being recorded in New York, the leading record companies also had started to record some of the most renowned African American singers and musicians based in the South and grounded in their native folk traditions.

Paramount Records was the first label fully to take advantage of the wealth of talented black performers popular in the South. The label was started by the Wisconsin Chair Company in 1917 as an outgrowth of its phonograph manufacturing business. Paramount launched a race record series in New York in 1922 by issuing a handful of vaudeville blues titles sung by Harlem natives Lucille Hegamin and Alberta Hunter. In 1924, Paramount established a second recording base in Chicago, and hired "Ink" Williams to spearhead the race record operations there.[29] Chicago had a burgeoning black ghetto in its rundown southside neighborhoods and a red-light district controlled by a constellation of underworld vice lords. This translated into jobs for black musicians, who came from all over the country, especially from New Orleans, the hometown of jazz, and from the Mississippi delta, the birthplace of the blues.

"Ink" Williams's nickname stemmed from the fact that he was the first businessman to get the signatures of talented African

American entertainers on a record contract. After joining Paramount, he quickly signed up two of the most popular female blues singers on the black vaudeville circuit, Gertrude "Ma" Rainey and Ida Cox. Ma Rainey, the much loved "Mother of the Blues," was at the height of her career as a performer. She recorded ninety-three selections for Paramount between 1923 and 1928, one-third of which were listed as her own compositions while another nineteen did not list a composer. The publisher for all of the titles she recorded was the Chicago Music Publishing Company (CMPC). This firm was set up by "Ink" Williams, and it filed for copyrights to all the race records he supervised. His secretary, Althea Dickerson, typed the lyrics and music on CMPC stationary, then sent them to the United States copyright office in Washington, D.C.

A gifted young Georgia musician, Thomas A. Dorsey, worked as a studio pianist, arranger, and composer for "Ink" Williams in the 1920s. He recalled the following about the company's copyright operation: "A guy'd come in with a song, and he'd sing it. He had nobody to arrange it or put it down on paper. So I put it down on paper and then the company could copyright it."[30] The CMPC collected all royalty payments generated by the material it held the copyrights on; it was then responsible for passing some of that money on to the appropriate composer or performer under contract. To his credit, Williams did share some of the firm's royalty money with his closer associates, like Dorsey. Dorsey said of the royalty situation back then: "Oh, royalties were kinda late coming. You know, we had to kinda organize on these people to get the royalties, and we had a hard time. 'Course I've gotten mine, some of it with Paramount Records. 'Cause Williams had that sewed up, and he got his. And if he got his, then we got ours. And if he didn't get his, then we didn't get ours. Yeah, it was hard back there."[31]

"Ink" Williams was also responsible for recording two of the race record industry's most popular rural folk blues performers, Blind Blake and Blind Lemon Jefferson. Arthur Blind Blake was the mercurial blues bard who pioneered the ragtime guitar style associated with the rural blues played in the southeastern United States. He was born in Florida and spent his early youth in Georgia before becoming a vagabond bluesman. His travels took him as far north as Chicago, where he was discovered by Williams. He was hired as a studio musician for Paramount and worked there intermittently between 1926 and 1932. During this period, he also recorded over eighty titles on his own for the label. It is unlikely that Blind Blake got any royalties for his unique repertoire, even though his records were a commercial success. Because he was an alcoholic, he was usually given a bottle for a recording session, and was paid a flat fee for his guitar playing and singing. Even though Blind Blake was probably content with this arrangement, he was vulnerable because of his alcoholism and sight handicap. His employers in the music business could easily take advantage of him, and the evidence suggests that they did just that with respect to copyrights and royalties.[32]

The same could be said for Blind Lemon Jefferson, the legendary Texas blues oracle who recorded seventy-five songs for Paramount between 1926 and 1930. He was brought to the attention of the label by a Dallas talent scout, and he proved to be the best-selling rural bluesman of the decade. Jefferson got credit as composer of thirty-one of his recordings, while another twenty-four did not list a composer. He probably received a flat fee for his studio sessions and waived his royalties. Ironically, the most popular of the down-home blues folk artists were also the most exploitable, because of the complicated and confusing copyright procedures. Unfortunately, a few black record producers, like "Ink" WIlliams, Clarence Williams, and Perry Bradford, were involved in pocketing royalty money that rightfully belonged to the recording artists. In his autobiography, Big Bill Broonzy recalled how "Ink" Williams was able to trick him out of the copyrights to the songs he recorded at a 1927 session for Paramount:

> They had my head in a horn of some kind and I had to pull my head out of the horn to read the words and back in it to sing it. And they had Thomas put on a pillar about two feet high and they kept on telling us to relax and giving us moonshine whiskey to drink, and I got drunk. I went to sleep after the recording and when I woke up, on my way home, John Thomas told me that I had signed some paper. I told him I hadn't.
> Look in your jumper pocket, he said.
> And sure enough, there was the paper, signed in ink.
> You've let them make you drunk, Thomas said, and you've signed our rights away.[33]

The unfamiliarity of these rural blues musicians with copyright laws, coupled with the custom of providing free liquor at the recording sessions, made them especially susceptible to the chicanery of race record entrepreneurs.

The successful marketing of discs recorded by traditional African American folk artists encouraged a number of field recording expeditions to southern urban centers by the record companies. The trend had been initiated by Ralph Peer in the early twenties while he was still working for the Okeh label. He took a unit to Atlanta, where he recorded blues singer Lucille Bogan and Fiddlin' John Carson, a traditional Anglo-American folk musician. Peer did so at the urging of Polk Brockman, a white furniture-store owner who doubled as a talent scout for Okeh. Carson's single disc sold so well that it launched the "hillbilly" record bonanza of the 1920s. When he moved over to the Victor label in the middle of the decade to supervise their race and hillbilly catalogs, Peer continued to organize field recording ventures in the South. By this time, the development of portable electric recording equipment made it more feasible and profitable to do on-site recording sessions. Peer was the first to record the two most influential hillbilly acts of the era, Jimmie Rodgers and the Carter Family, as well as a host of southern blues musicians like Tommy Johnson, Blind Willie McTell, Furry Lewis, Gus Cannon and His Jug Stompers, and the Memphis Jug Band. Victor sent field units to Nashville, Bristol, and Memphis, Tennessee; Louisville, Kentucky; Cincinnati, Ohio; Charlotte, North Carolina; Dallas, Texas; Savannah and Atlanta, Georgia; and New Orleans, Louisiana—all under Peer's supervision. Columbia recorded in Atlanta, Memphis, New Orleans, and Dallas. Okeh held sessions in Memphis, Saint Louis, Kansas City, Louisville, Shreveport, Atlanta, Richmond, Virginia, Jackson, Mississippi, and San Antonio, Texas. Vocalion also visited San Antonio, as well as Dallas, Memphis, Atlanta, New Orleans, Birmingham, Alabama, Knoxville, Tennessee, and Columbia, South Carolina; Gennett sent a field unit to Birmingham, Alabama. There also was a network of white talent scouts in the South, usually furniture-store managers or owners, who sold phonograph machines and records. It was in conjunction with their business operations that they got involved in seeking out talent for the race and hillbilly labels. The most successful were Polk Brockman in Atlanta, Sam Price in Dallas, and Henry C. Spier in Jackson. Generally, the rural African American folk musicians who made commercial recordings in the twenties were paid much less than even the vaudeville blues performers. Georgia blues pioneer Peg Leg Howell's record contract with Columbia in 1926 netted him fifteen dollars per side at a time when Bessie Smith was getting two hundred dollars a title from the same label. "Mississippi" John Hurt received twenty dollars per side from Okeh in 1928; Son House was promised fifteen per selection by Paramount in 1930. Royalty fees for these rural bluesmen were habitually excluded from their contracts.[34] In fact, Ralph Peer and others who followed in his wake undertook the field recording ventures in order to find new songs to copyright for their music publishing firms. However, while the profits from better-selling race recordings went to the record companies, there was a trade-off for African Americans. The record company documented a crucial period in the development of African American folk music in the South and made that material available to both black and white record buyers throughout the country.

The onset of the depression quickly reversed the fortunes of the entire record industry. Sales fell from over one hundred million dollars in 1927 to merely six million dollars by 1933.[35] Consequently, race record releases were drastically cut back, field recording forays in the South were discontinued, the labels manufactured fewer and fewer copies of each title, and record prices fell from seventy-five cents to thirty-five cents per disc. Where the average race record on the market sold approximately ten thousand copies in the mid-1920s, it plummeted to two thousand in 1930 and bottomed out at a dismal four hundred in 1932. The smaller labels were gradually forced out of business, while the major record companies with large catalogs that went into debt were purchased by more prosperous media corporations based in radio and film. RCA took over the Victor Record Company; Majestic Radio Corporation acquired the Columbia Record Company for a short period of time; and Warner Brothers Pictures got into the business briefly when it bought Brunswick. Later, Warner sold Brunswick to Consolidated Film Industries, which also acquired Vocalion and a few other smaller labels. The record companies' race catalogs that totally succumbed to the economic downturn were Paramount, Okeh, and Gennett.[36] By 1933, the race record industry appeared to be a fatality of the depression.

The New Deal era brought a new lease on life to the record business from some unlikely sources. The repeal of federal prohibition laws in 1933 revitalized the nightclubs and saloons of urban America. Simultaneously, the demand for popular recordings was stimulated by a new technical innovation, the jukebox, which began to supplant live music in the bars and clubs. This was good news for the record manufacturers. By 1939, there were 255,000 jukeboxes in operation, utilizing thirteen million discs.[37] However, the curtailment of live performances tended to hurt professional jazz and blues musicians by denying them a long-established source of employment. Record sales rebounded to the nine-million-dollar mark in 1935, and the few surviving race record labels began to replenish the marketplace with new products.[38] At this juncture, the major emphasis was on recording jazz bands, gospel quartets, traditional rural blues performers, and the newly coalescing urban blues bands, in that order. The vaudeville blues were a relic of the past. However, the industry's policy of segregated labels and markets remained intact, and the major conduit of advertising for race records remained the Chicago *Defender* and a few other black urban newspapers.

The music that characterized the 1930s as the "Swing Era," in spite of the Great Depression, evolved from the African American big band jazz of the 1920s. In particular, the lively arrangements of the Fletcher Henderson band became the prototype for the popular swing bands of the next decade. Henderson's New York-based orchestra showcased many of the top black jazz soloists of the "Jazz Age," such as trumpeter Louis Armstrong and tenor saxophone pioneer Coleman Hawkins. But, more importantly, along with his brilliant young arranger, Don Redman, Henderson established the primary golden rule of jazz band arranging—the need for interplay between a brass and a reed section. In the 1930s, there were a number of important African American swing bands that took up where Henderson's group left off. They included drummer Chick Webb's band, based at the Savoy Ballroom in Harlem, during the heyday of the Swing Era. Webb showcased jazz luminaries like trombonist Jimmy Harrison and a young vocalist named Ella Fitzgerald, who was the band's biggest attraction from 1935 until Chick Webb's death in 1939. Jimmy Lunceford's band was based at the Cotton Club in New York during the mid-thirties. Led by Willie Smith, it featured one of the most acclaimed saxophone sections in jazz. Lunceford's chief arranger during this period was a young musical genius named Sy Oliver, who was responsible for the band's brilliant orchestral scores. Other black swing bands popular in the 1930s included units led by Cab Calloway, Lionel Hampton, Erskine Hawkins, Earl Hines, Lucky Millander, Don Redman, and Louis

Russell. But, undoubtedly, the two most innovative African American swing bands during this period were those led by Edward "Duke" Ellington and Bill "Count" Basie.

Today, Duke Ellington is honored as one of this nation's greatest twentieth-century composers. His stature is such that he has transcended the jazz category. In the 1920s, he was just starting out as a novice bandleader, arranger, and composer in New York, after moving there from Washington, D.C., his hometown. His major influences during these formative years were former Clef Club bandleader Will Vodery and Will Marion Cook, the highly acclaimed African American composer also associated with the old Clef Club. It was Cook who taught Ellington how to compose melodies during this early period of his development.[39]

In 1925, Duke Ellington and his band were spotted by an enterprising young white music publisher and booking agent named Irving Mills. In exchange for 45 percent of the profits, he agreed to manage Ellington and his band. It was a lot to ask but was not that unusual in the early years of the race record business. And to his credit, Mills opened certain music industry doors that were most often closed to African Americans. He negotiated a record deal with Columbia, and he got the band booked into the Cotton Club for what developed into a five-year run.[40] The Cotton Club showcased African American entertainers for a rich white clientele, hence the pay was higher than what the group had been earning, even taking into account Mill's 45 percent cut. More importantly, their extended engagement gave Ellington the time and space he needed to develop both his talent for composition and his band's unique tonal style of swing.

For his part in the Ellington success story Irving Mills was paid handsomely, and he went on to become a major force in the music business. He later managed Cab Calloway and the Mills Blue Rhythm Band, a unit he stamped with his own name. As an equal partner with Ellington in their joint enterprise, Mills saw fit to add his name to the copyright on Ellington's compositions. He got equal credit and royalties from songs like "The Mooch," "Mood Indigo," and "Rockin' in Rhythm." This also was not an uncommon practice in the race record industry. In 1939, after a decade of artistic and financial success, Duke Ellington severed his fourteen-year relationship with Mills and Columbia Records. Thereafter, he never uttered a word about the subject, in public.[41] After the break,

Ellington signed on with RCA Victor Records and brought new talent into his band, the most prominent being bassist Jimmy Blanton and arranger/composer Billy Strayhorn. For the next three decades, Ellington continued to compose an incredible range of music, thus solidifying his reputation as a jazz giant and a great American composer.

Whereas Ellington's orchestra was in the forefront of swing music on the East Coast in the 1930s, Count Basie's band from Kansas City, Kansas, achieved fame as the Southwest's foremost exponent of their own brand of swinging big band jazz. Basie was from New Jersey, but he spent the formative years of his career as a jazz pianist and then bandleader with bands in the Southwest. In particular, he formed the Blue Devils unit out of Oklahoma City in the late 1920s and then joined Bennie Moten's band in Kansas City, which he eventually took over after Bennie Moten passed away in 1934.[42]

The Blue Devils' stellar aggregation included some of the finest African American jazzmen in the region—musicians like bassist Walter Page, trombonist/guitarist Eddie Durham, trumpeter Oran "Hot Lips" Page, and blues shouter Jimmy Rushing—all of whom moved on to Kansas City along with Basie. The addition of saxophonist Ben Webster and the incomparable Lester Young rounded out this formidable array of master musicians, making Basie's band one of the most talented and innovative in the land. Instead of relying on written arrangements like most of the eastern swing bands, Basie and company favored unwritten head arrangements built around simple blues structures. Tension was created between the brass and the reed sections by means of an ingenious call and response pattern called a "riff." Improvised solos were mandatory. Other jazz bands from the region played a similar style of music—the best being the Texas-based Alfonso Trent band, the Clouds of Joy led by Terrence Holder and then Andy Kirk, and Harlan Leonard's Rockets. But Basie's orchestra was easily the most talented and durable of the lot.

Although Count Basie's band was highly touted by jazz musicians and fans in the Southwest, it took a white New York record producer to bring it to the attention of the eastern musical establishment. That man was John Hammond, who worked as a freelance producer for Columbia Records. Hammond was a scion of the wealthy Vanderbilt family, an active member of the NAACP, and an avid follower of African American music. In addition to arranging for

Basie's recording sessions with Columbia, he was responsible for their last dates with Bessie Smith. Other talent he helped to line up for Columbia in the 1930s included Charlie Christian, Ida Cox, Benny Goodman, Coleman Hawkins, Fletcher Henderson, the Golden Gate Quartet, and Clara Hudmon, the "Georgia Peach."[43] Hammond was not in the music business to make his fortune; he had already inherited a substantial one. Hence his business practices were altruistic and honorable. He treated African American musicians with respect and understanding, securing for them the best record deals possible within the confines of the music industry.

By the 1930s, there were three major record companies involved in race recording ventures, Columbia, RCA Victor, and Decca. Columbia Records had languished through most of the depression under the ownership of the Majestic Radio Corporation and then, in 1935, the American Record Company. In contrast, the fortunes of the Columbia Broadcasting System (CBS) mushroomed because of its prosperous radio network, and the corporation was wealthy enough to buy the ailing Columbia label in 1938. CBS also purchased the Vocalion catalog, but the label was discontinued. With the financial clout of William Paley's millions, Columbia launched a talent raid on RCA Victor and Decca recording artists that was reminiscent of the CBS raid on NBC radio talent earlier in the decade. Hoping to capitalize on the popularity of the swing band craze, Columbia signed up Count Basie and Benny Goodman, the white "King of Swing." Basie came over from the Decca label, while Goodman was lured away from RCA Victor. Columbia's productive race record talent scout John Hammond also brought pianist Teddy Wilson, alto saxophonist Lester Young, and a promising young vocalist named Billie Holiday into the fold. One of the more interesting sessions he set up was a 1941 tribute to Joe Louis, entitled "King Joe." The piece was written by novelist Richard Wright and sung by Paul Robeson, accompanied by the Count Basie Orchestra.[44]

RCA Victor countered Columbia's raid on its swing artists by signing Duke Ellington in 1939. Other important African American jazz masters on its Bluebird label in the 1930s included Earl Hines, Cab Calloway, Erskine Hawkins, Coleman Hawkins, and Thomas "Fats" Waller. Coleman Hawkins recorded his classic jazz version of "Body and Soul" for the Bluebird label in 1939. Fats Waller was the label's most prolific artist. He recorded more than five hundred sides for them between 1934 and 1943.[45] Waller was a talented singer, pianist, and composer who also hosted his own radio show in the 1930s. His overall popularity was second only to Louis Armstrong's during this period.

While the RCA Victor Bluebird label controlled a hefty portion of the jazz record market during the Swing Era, it was even more dominant in the blues category. This was due to the efforts of Lester Melrose, a white native of Illinois who, along with his brother, ran a music store and publishing company in Chicago during the twenties. In 1934, he was hired as the local manager for RCA Victor's Bluebird label. Melrose had published compositions by Jelly Roll Morton and Joseph "King" Oliver; he was familiar with African American musicians in Chicago and had a good ear for their music. For almost two decades, he would dominate the race recordings operations in Chicago through his exclusive agent contract with RCA Victor and Columbia Records. By his own estimate, he was responsible for 90 percent of the blues recorded on these labels from 1934 to 1950. Melrose operated much like "Ink" Williams: he selected a close-knit group of local black musicians and songwriters who made recordings on their own but were used mostly to back up any outside talent he brought into the studio. This group was a "who's who" of Chicago blues during the depression and the war years and included guitarists Lonnie Johnson, Big Bill Broonzy, Tampa Red, Amos Easton, Johnny Temple, and Memphis Minnie; pianists Blind John Davis, Black Bob, Little Brother Montgomery, Roosevelt Sykes, Walter Davis, Josh Altheimer, Memphis Slim, and Big Maceo Merriweather; female blues singers Victoria Spivey and Lil Green; harp blowers Jazz Gillum and Sonny Boy Williamson; bass players Ransome Knowling, Alfred Elkins, Bill Settle, and a youthful Willie Dixon; the studio drummer was usually Fred Williams. The major songwriters in the group were Broonzy; his half brother Robert Brown, better known as Washboard Sam; Amos Easton, who recorded as Bumble Bee Slim; Tampa Red, Memphis Minnie, Sonny Boy Williamson, and Memphis Slim. Melrose also set up a music publishing company. As had been the case with Williams, it allowed him to control the copyrights of the material recorded under his auspices. A final similarity between Williams and Melrose was that both had an ear for folk blues talent, even if it was of an unpolished southern variety. Whereas Williams had found success recording rural bluesmen like

Blind Lemon Jefferson and Blind Blake in the 1920s, Melrose sought to duplicate it in the following decade by recording country blues singers Bukka White, Big Joe Williams, Tommy McClennan, and Arthur "Big Boy" Crudup.[46]

RCA Victor's Bluebird label was soon challenged in the revived race record market by the emergence of a new record company. Late in 1934, Decca was launched in Chicago and New York under the direction of Jack Kapp, a crafty veteran of the recording business. Kapp previously had been Columbia's representative in Chicago and then the head of the Brunswick/Vocalion race record catalog. The Decca label was bankrolled by E. R. Lewis, the owner of the London-based Decca Record Company. But from the outset, Kapp called the shots in the United States. He supervised the recording operations in New York City himself, signing on jazz artists like Louis Armstrong, Jimmy Lunceford, Chick Webb and Ella Fitzgerald, Lionel Hampton, Lucky Millander, and Willie "the Lion" Smith.[47] In Chicago he hired "Ink" Williams as his chief black talent scout, and together they mapped out their recording strategy. It had much in common with the operation of Lester Melrose, and the one that Williams himself developed while working for Paramount a decade earlier. They hired a studio band to back up the local blues artists they contracted, such as Johnny Temple, Rosetta Howard, and Frankie "Half Pint" Jackson. The studio musicians also recorded themselves as the "Harlem Hamfats."

Over the next seven years, Decca released material in all of the race categories: the jazz just mentioned; country blues by Kokomo Arnold, Blind Boy Fuller, and Sleepy John Estes; city blues by Roosevelt Sykes, Pettie Wheatstraw, Louis Jordan, and the Harlem Hamfats; gospel discs by Mahalia Jackson, Sister Rosetta Thorpe, the Norfolk Quartet, and the Dixie Hummingbirds. Decca also produced the Mills Brothers, and the Ink Spots, who were the first black vocal groups to record popular Tin Pan Alley songs for black and white record buyers. The Mills Brothers' and the Ink Spots' success challenged the economic wisdom of the industry's segregationist policies, but the label's most lucrative properties were still the white dance bands, such as the Dorsey Brothers and Guy Lombardo, as well as a new young crooner named Bing Crosby.[48]

On the eve of World War II, the record industry had totally reversed the economic downslide brought on by the depression. With the expansion of a resuscitated record market, a renewed emphasis was placed on manufacturing and selling race records. This time, the music would be labeled "rhythm and blues" by the entertainment industry. It would also be less inhibited by the discriminatory practices and the lingering plantation stereotypes that had characterized both the attitudes and the advertising of the race record labels from 1920 until 1942. During these two decades, the record industry's efforts to stimulate and supply a black record-buying public were constantly inspired by the profit motive; once transcribed onto discs, African American music was perceived as a salable commodity just like the other varieties of ethnic music on the market. However, the record market, like the entire entertainment industry, remained segregated. The record labels gained access to the race market by advertising in the African American press, especially the Chicago *Defender*, discreetly carried into the South by black entertainers and Pullman porters, where it was eagerly read. Radio was dominated by the major commercial networks; their promise to deliver massive nationwide audiences to the sponsors dictated a policy of token participation for African Americans, especially in programming aimed at a national audience. Only with the advent of commercial television would radio be forced to become a more significant factor in the promotion and preservation of black recorded music.

The bottom line in the race record business was, invariably, whether or not the product sold. When the records sold, the industry responded with more records and advertisements. When sales fell off, the records were dropped from the catalogs and the advertisements terminated. In control of this million-dollar business operation was a group of business executives and their agents, predominantly white middle-class males. In most cases, they also managed the day-to-day operations of the race record labels. Where there were black managers and agents involved, they often engaged in the same suspect business practices as their white colleagues. This situation led to the institutionalization of additional economic stratification and cultural bias. Black musicians and performers were paid less for their work in the studio than their white counterparts in the record industry, and the evidence further indicates that African American composers and recording artists were systematically denied their royalty monies. Not only did the race record label owners and operators determine how much they would pay their talent, they also decided whom to record, what to record, and how to do it.

The first commercial jazz and blues hits were recorded by the Original Dixieland Jass Band and Sophie Tucker; both did second-hand imitations of a music that would make them rich and famous, while legions of the real architects of jazz and blues remained entrenched in poverty and unrecognized. Paul Whitman gained fame and fortune as the so-called King of Jazz in the twenties, as did Glenn Miller and Benny Goodman, the "King of Swing" during the next decade's Swing Era. The best big band leader in the jazz tradition during this same period, Fletcher Henderson, was unable to afford to keep his band together and eventually had to resort to selling his arrangements to Goodman's band. Similarly, the pioneer New Orleans jazz cornetist and bandleader Joseph "King" Oliver died in 1938 while working as a janitor in a pool hall in Savannah, Georgia. At the time of his death, he was unable to make a living playing the music that he helped to create.

The cultural biases inherent in the business practices of the managers and producers who controlled the race record operation created a series of obstacles that confronted black musicians even after they signed with a record label. The inability of the industry's hierarchy to appreciate blues, gospel, and jazz as anything other than entertaining modes of music popular among a lower socio-economic class of citizens reinforced their stereotypical understanding of African American music and its creators. Very few were able to recognize that gospel, jazz, and blues were a family of musical art forms with long-standing, cherished folk traditions. This cultural blind spot often worked to compromise the artistic careers of black musicians and performers who managed to secure employment in the industry. They quickly discovered that their employers had preconceived ideas about how they should sound, and even look. Louis Armstrong's career illustrates this dilemma.

Armstrong was the first true melodic genius of the jazz tradition in the twentieth century. He was raised in New Orleans, the birthplace of early jazz, and schooled by the city's premier jazz cornetist, King Oliver. When he emerged on the Chicago jazz scene in the early 1920s, his technical skills and the full-bodied tone he extracted from his horn were already advanced for the time. Armstrong considerably enhanced the role of the instrumental solo in New Orleans jazz ensembles. His improvisational flights of storytelling on a series of selections recorded in the mid-twenties were melodic masterpieces that revolutionized the jazz tradition from that point on. During the depression, Armstrong hired a white nightclub operator from Chicago named Joe Glaser, a distinguished veteran of show business who had befriended him in the 1920s, as his personal manager. Glaser took full control of his career, securing for him new record, radio, and even film contracts. Armstrong quickly achieved celebrity status and made a lot of money, as did Joe Glaser, but not without paying a price. Glaser shaped for him a career as an entertainer, not as a jazz artist, setting up Armstrong's appearances on network radio and in Hollywood movies where there was a certain degree of "shuffling" and "tomming" involved. Armstrong began to cultivate an image more appropriate to a comedian than a jazz artist. In return, he was given high visibility in the national media. Consequently, he worked at being a popular entertainer in show business and was only superficially involved in the ongoing jazz tradition. The choice of careers was ultimately Armstrong's alone, and it reflected a certain mind-set of that time not unusual among black musicians living in the postbellum South. Armstrong articulated this attitude, perhaps unknowingly, in a line he was fond of repeating later in his career to justify its direction: "Always keep a white man behind you that'll put his hand on you and say, 'That's my nigger!' "[49]

Even though Armstrong found it convenient to play the clown on occasion, he still made a major contribution to jazz in the 1920s, a contribution that is well documented on records. Also to his credit, the efforts he made to expand the jazz audience helped to foster a more receptive climate for the music all over the world. Co-optation of the musicians, along with the expropriation of their music, were the twin perils facing African Americans when dealing with the agents of the entertainment industry, whether they were managers or race record executives. Yet if black musicians were taken advantage of by the record industry, they also seized the opportunity to document their music for posterity. And by using the recording technology as a means to extend their musical culture, they also began to make visible inroads into the mainstream of American popular music. During the 1920s and 1930s, there were close to 15,000 race records released by the industry; approximately 10,000 blues titles, 1,750 gospel titles, and 3,250 jazz titles.[50] Thousands of African American musicians—folk singers and professional artists—were involved in amassing this audio evidence of a peoples' feelings, experiences, and struggles over a twenty-year span. In addition, millions of African Americans purchased race records for home entertainment during this period. They were an important source of culture, especially as radio in the pre–World War II era programmed mostly white popular music. The result was that phonograph players and race records were much more prevalent than radio sets in black urban and rural communities. Along with live music, they were at the center of African American social life, and they played a vital role in enriching, broadening, and prolonging the black oral tradition.

1. Ronald G. Foreman, Jr., "Jazz and Race Records, 1920–1932: Their Origins and Their Significance for the Record Industry and Society" (Ph.D. diss., University of Illinois, Chicago, 1972), 15, 18.

2. Roland C. Gelatt, *The Fabulous Phonograph* (New York: Appleton-Century, 1965), 94–95.

3. Robert Dixon and John Godrich, *Recording the Blues* (New York: Stein and Day, 1980).

4. Albert McCarthy, *Big Band Jazz* (New York: Berkley Publishing Corp., 1974), 10.

5. Eileen Southern, *The Music of Black Americans* (New York: W. W. Norton, 1971), 249–50.

6. David Ewen, *All the Years of American Popular Music* (Englewood Cliffs, N.J.: Prentice-Hall, 1977), 180–87; James Lincoln Collier, *The Making of Jazz: A Comprehensive History* (New York: Dell Publishing, 1976), 72.

7. Ibid., 78–79.

8. Richard M. Sadhalter, Phillip R. Evans, with William Dean Myott, *Bix: Man and Legend* (New York: Macmillan, 1974), 191, 225–27.

9. Ewen, *Popular Music*, 219–28; Paula Drunon, *Inside the Music Publishing Industry* (New York: Knowledge Industries Publications, 1980), 12, 13.

10. W. C. Handy, *Father of the Blues* (New York: Colliers, 1941), 127–210.

11. Ewen, *Popular Music*, 221.

12. Derrick Stewart-Baxter, *Ma Rainey and the Classic Blues Singers* (London: Oak Publications, 1957), 10–31; Jeff Titon, *Early Downhome Blues* (Urbana: University of Illinois Press, 1977), 25–29; Bill C. Malone, *Southern Music: American Music* (Lexington: University of Kentucky Press, 1979), 45.

13. Clarence Williams, quoted in E. Simms Campbell, "Blues," in *Jazzmen*, ed. Frederic Ramsey and Charles E. Smith (New York: Harcourt Brace Jovanovich, 1939), 110–11.

14. Handy, *Father of the Blues*, 103.

15. Perry Bradford, *Born with the Blues* (New York: Oak Publications, 1965), 98.

16. Alan Lomax, *"Mister Jelly Roll": The Fortunes of Jelly Roll Morton, New Orleans Creole and "Inventor of Jazz,"* 2d ed. (Berkeley: University of California Press, 1973), 21.

17. Bradford, *Born with the Blues*, 108.

18. "Crazy Blues," by Mamie Smith and Her Jazz Hounds, Okeh Records (4143-A), New York, 6 August 1920.

19. Willie "The Lion" Smith, *Music on My Mind: The Memoirs of an American Pianist* (New York: Doubleday, 1964), 105.

20. Bradford, *Born with the Blues*, 155.

21. Dixon and Godrich, *Recording the Blues*, 10–13, 44; Titon, *Downhome Blues*, 204.

22. Dixon and Godrich, *Recording the Blues*, 13–16; Foreman, "Jazz and Race Records," 60–62.

23. Dixon and Godrich, *Recording the Blues*, 17; Titon, *Downhome Blues*, 205, 206; Foreman, "Jazz and Race Records," 92–94.

24. Jim O'Neal, "Guitar Blues: Sylvester Weaver," *Living Blues* 52 (Spring 1982), 19–20.

25. Chris Albertson, *Bessie* (New York: Stein and Day, 1972), 39.

26. Ibid., 44–46.

27. Ibid., 46, 182.

28. Titon, *Downhome Blues*, 205.

29. Sandra Lieb, *Mother of the Blues: A Study of Ma Rainey* (Boston: University of Massachusetts Press, 1982), 21–22, 50–52.

30. "Georgia" Tom Dorsey interviewed by Jim and Amy O'Neal, *Living Blues* 20 (March–April 1975): 23.

31. Ibid., 26.

32. Titon, *Downhome Blues*, 76–79; Samuel Charters, *Sweet as Showers of Rain* (New York: Oak Publications, 1977), 143–49.

33. Big Bill Broonzy, quoted in *"Big Bill's Blues:" Big Bill Broonzy's Story as told to Yunnick Bruynoghe* (London: Cassell and Company, 1955), 47; David Evans, *Big Road Blues* (Berkeley: University of California Press, 1982), 75–77. Titon, *Downhome Blues*, 212.

34. Malone, *Southern Music*, 65–66. Evans, *Big Band Blues*, 72–74; Titon, *Downhome Blues*, 210–11, 218–21; Albertson, *Bessie*, 165; Dixon and Godrich, *Recording the Blues*, 106–7.

35. Drunon, *Music Publishing Industry*, 101.

36. Dixon and Godrich, *Recording the Blues*, 64, 73, 94.

37. Ibid., 78

38. Ibid., 97.

39. Collier, *The Making of Jazz*, 244–45; James Lincoln Collier, *Duke Ellington* (New York: Oxford University Press, 1987), 108–9, 182–83.

40. Collier, *The Making of Jazz*, 245.

41. Ibid., 246; Collier, *Duke Ellington*, 193–94.

42. Collier, *The Making of Jazz*, 226.

43. John Hammond, *John Hammond on Record* (New York: Summit Books, 1977), 404–9.

44. Ibid., 351.

45. McCarthy, *Big Band Jazz*, 176–78.

46. Mike Rowe, *Chicago Breakdown* (London: Edison Press, 1972), 17–25.

47. Collier, *The Making of Jazz*, 281.

48. C. A. Schike, *Revolution in Sound* (Boston: Little, Brown and Company, 1974), 98. Dixon and Godrich, *Recording the Blues*, 84, 87.

49. James Lincoln Collier, *Louis Armstrong: An American Genius* (New York: Oxford University Press, 1983), 13.

50. Titon, *Downhome Blues*, 204–5.

2 CROSSING OVER: 1939-1989

REEBEE GAROFALO

The history of popular music in this country—at least, in the twentieth century—can be described in terms of a pattern of black innovation and white popularization, which I have referred to elsewhere as "black roots, white fruits."[1] The pattern is built not only on the wellspring of creativity that black artists bring to popular music but also on the systematic exclusion of black personnel from positions of power within the industry and on the artificial separation of black and white audiences. Because of industry and audience racism, black music has been relegated to a separate and unequal marketing structure. As a result, it is only on rare occasions that black music "crosses over" into the mainstream market on its own terms. The specific practices and mechanisms that tend to institutionalize its exclusion and dilution change over time and, for the most part, remain unchallenged even to this day. In the last half-century, the relative success of black artists has been determined by variables that range from individual preference and personal prejudice to organizational memberships, population migrations, material shortages, technological advances, corporate configurations, informal networks, and government investigations. Inevit-

NOTE: Part of the research for this essay was undertaken earlier by Steve Chapple and Reebee Garofalo for *Rock 'n' Roll Is Here to Pay: The History and Politics of the Music Industry* (Chicago: Nelson-Hall, 1977). Portions of that text are reprinted with the permission of the publisher. Other passages have previously appeared in: "From ASCAP to Alan Freed: The Pre-History of Rock 'n' Roll," *Popular Music and Society* VI (1978), and "Hip Hop for High School: An Abbreviated History for Students," *Radical America* (Nov.-Dec. 1984). All previously published passages are reprinted with the permission of the publishers.

ably, black popular music is affected by the prevailing economic and political climate. Still, black music (and the musicians who create it) continues on its creative course and also continues, against all odds, to exert a disproportionate influence on popular music in general. In this chapter, we shall investigate the phenomenon of "crossover" beginning with an analysis of the social forces that gave rise to rhythm and blues in the 1940s.

The Rise of Rhythm and Blues

Prior to World War II, the popular music market was dominated by writers and publishers of the Broadway-Hollywood axis of popular music. They exercised their collective power through the American Society of Authors, Composers, and Publishers (ASCAP), a "performance rights" organization that recovers royalty payments for the performance of copyrighted music. Until 1939, ASCAP was a closed society with a virtual monopoly on all copyrighted music. As proprietor of the compositions of its members, ASCAP could regulate the use of any selection in its catalog. The organization exercised considerable power in the shaping of public taste. Membership in the society was generally skewed toward writers of show tunes and semiserious works such as Richard Rodgers and Lorenz Hart, Cole Porter, George Gershwin, Irving Berlin, and George M. Cohan. Of the society's 170 charter members, six were black: Harry Burleigh, Will Marion Cook, J. Rosamond and James Weldon Johnson, Cecil Mack, and Will Tyers.[2] While other "literate" black writers and composers (W. C. Handy, Duke Ellington) would be able to gain entrance to ASCAP, the vast majority of "untutored" black artists were routinely excluded from the society and thereby systematically denied the full benefits of copyright protection. It was primarily artists in this latter group who would later create rhythm and blues.

Earlier in the century, after a hard-fought battle, ASCAP established in practice the principle, articulated in the 1909 copyright law, that writers are entitled to compensation for the public performance of their work. But it was not until the legal principle was extended to include radio that ASCAP began to realize its full economic potential. "ASCAP income from radio, of which the networks paid about 20 percent, had risen from $757,450 in 1932 to $5.9 million in 1937, and had then dropped to $3.8 million the following year. It increased by 12 percent, to $4.3 million, in 1939."[3]

In 1940, after more than a year of rocky negotiations with radio, ASCAP announced its intention of doubling the fee for a license when the existing agreement expired on 31 December. For broadcasters, who had always considered ASCAP's demands excessive, this was the last straw. The National Association of Broadcasters (NAB), representing some six hundred radio stations, formed their own performing rights organization, Broadcast Music Incorporated (BMI). "Taking advantage of ASCAP's stringent membership requirements, as well as its relative indifference to the popular and folk music being produced outside of New York and Hollywood, BMI sought out and acquired its support from the 'have not' publishers and writers in the grassroots areas."[4] When broadcasters decided to boycott ASCAP in 1941, BMI was ready with a catalog of its own. For the next ten months the United States was treated to an earful of its own root music. Authentic regional styles were broadcast to a mass public intact, not yet boiled down in the national pop melting pot. Though, in its initial stages, BMI came up with few songs of lasting significance, the Broadway-Hollywood monopoly on popular music was challenged publicly for the first time. Without this challenge, we might never have heard from composers like Huddie Ledbetter, Arthur (Big Boy) Crudup, Roy Brown, Ivory Joe Hunter, Johnny Otis, Fats Domino, and Wynonie Harris.

The success of these artists testifies to what critic Nelson George has referred to as "an aesthetic schism between high-brow, more assimilated black styles and working-class, grassroots sounds" that had existed in the black community for a long time.[5] A number of writers, notably Imamu Amiri Baraka (Leroi Jones), have written at length about class differences between jazz and the blues. While jazz was unquestionably an immensely popular and influential crossover music that introduced elements of the African American tradition into the mainstream, it was also in some ways a product of the black middle class. Many of its most notable practitioners such as Duke Ellington, Coleman Hawkins, and Fletcher Henderson were college educated. By the thirties it was a music that had "moved away from the older *lowdown* forms of blues, . . . a music that still relied on [an] older Afro-American musical tradition, but one that had begun to utilize still greater amounts of popular

American music as well as certain formal European traditions."[6] The artists who pioneered rhythm and blues in the forties were much closer to their blues roots. While they often retained some semblance of the big band sound, their initial popularity in the black community represented, in many ways, a resuscitation of the "race" record market of the twenties and thirties. "While the term 'jazz' gave Whiteman equal weight with Ellington, and Bix Beiderbecke comparable standing with Louis Armstrong," writes Nelson George, "the term 'race' was applied to forms of black music—primarily blues—that whites and, again, the black elite disdained."[7] The race records of the twenties and thirties sold well but primarily in regional markets.

The creation of a national audience for this regional music was aided significantly by the population migrations associated with World War II. Eastern and midwestern GIs, who were stationed in southern military bases, were exposed to musical styles that had not yet become popular in the North. At the same time, large numbers of southern African Americans moved north and west to find work in defense plants, and they brought their music with them. In the forties, more than one million black people left the South, three times as many as the decade before. Newly emigrated African Americans had enough money from wartime prosperity to establish themselves as an identifiable consumer group. In areas that received a high concentration of black immigrants, it was in the interest of radio stations to introduce some programming that would cater to this new audience. Gradually, some black-oriented programs, usually slotted late at night, began to appear on a few stations. It was this kind of "specialty" programming that would begin to tear down the walls of the race market at the end of the decade.

Having already alienated the music publishing establishment of the day, the broadcasters—which is to say, radio—managed to arouse the anger of established musicians as well. The period before the end of World War II was the era of big bands, fancy ballrooms, and, most important for the musicians, live music on the radio. Radio was, in essence, their electronic ballroom; it provided very steady work. By and large, live music on radio meant live music performed by white musicians. As a rule, black musicians were barred from radio performances. Of course, there were exceptions such as:

live broadcasts of Duke Ellington at the Cotton Club and Chick Webb at the Savoy in Harlem, Earl (Fatha) Hines from Chicago's Grand Terrace, or maybe a late set from some California band from the West Coast Cotton Club. Significantly, these broadcasts weren't aimed at blacks. Broadcasters and advertisers were simply meeting America's demand for big-band music. These bands just happened to be black and popular.[8]

In the forties, radio began to experiment with programming recorded music. The musicians were not about to surrender their best gig to records without a fight. In 1942 the American Federation of Musicians (AFM) struck the major record labels and ordered a ban on recording. Months later, the musicians returned to the studios to find vocalists in charge. Vocalists belong to a different union—currently called the American Federation of Television and Radio Artists (AFTRA)—and AFTRA did not join the strike. The AFM itself thus aided the rise of solo vocalists, who were now becoming the main attraction of the big bands, by allowing them free rein in the recording studios. With the rise of vocalists, the pop charts were gradually taken over by such figures as Bing Crosby, Perry Como, Dinah Shore, Vaughn Monroe, Frankie Laine, Doris Day, Jo Stafford, and, of course, Frank Sinatra. Throughout the postwar forties the only black vocal acts to make the year-end pop charts were the more pop-sounding artists like Nat "King" Cole ("For Sentimental Reasons"), Ella Fitzgerald ("My Happiness"), the Mills Brothers ("Across the Valley from the Alamo"), and the Ink Spots ("The Gypsy"). There were never more than two black vocalists on the year-end charts in a given year.

If the rise of the solo vocalist was a psychological blow to the big bands, it was the postwar economy that dealt the death blow. After the war, it was no longer feasible to support the elaborate production of twenty-piece orchestras as a regular attraction. Ballrooms disappeared and, unable to find steady work, the big bands gradually broke up. The black big bands, which had provided much of the impetus for the big band sound, limped along for a while on one-nighters on the dying dance-hall circuit. The better known black bands, like Count Basie's band and Duke Ellington's, could also count on an occasional hit record such as Basie's recording of "Open the Door, Richard" for Victor, which made the year-end pop charts in 1947. Still, it was clear by 1947 that a musical era in the United States had come to an end, and it was reflected in record sales. Between 1947 and 1949 sales dropped off more than fifty million dollars, which at the time represented more than 20 percent of the dollar volume of the industry. The situation was worse for black artists. By the end of the decade not a single black performer could be found on the year-end pop charts.

The population migrations previously mentioned opened the possibility of a nationwide market for black music, which did not exist prior to World War II. The major companies never exploited this new market during the war because a shellac shortage caused significant cutbacks in the number of records that could be manufactured. Shellac was the principal ingredient used in making the old 78 rpm records. During the Pacific blockade it became almost impossible to obtain the material from India where it is secreted by a tree-crawling insect. At the height of the shortage, in order to buy a new record it was often necessary to return an old one so that it could be recycled. Since the pop music market alone was capable of absorbing virtually all the records that could be produced, the major labels concentrated their efforts there. The specialty fields, especially blues, jazz, and gospel, bore the brunt of the cutbacks, and were essentially abandoned by the major labels.

Whereas the shellac shortage had seriously limited the supply of specialty music, cross-cultural contact had, if anything, increased the demand. Thus, after the war ended, the major companies tried to regain control of the specialty markets. In the country and western field this proved to be relatively simple. According to pop historian Charlie Gillett:

> [T]he companies responded by heavily promoting various songs performed in versions of country and western styles. One tactic was to promote the strong southern accent of most country and western singers as a "novelty," as Capitol did successfully with Tex Williams' "Smoke That Cigarette" in 1947, and as Columbia did for several years with various Gene Autrey songs, including "Rudolph, the Red-Nosed Reindeer" (1950). Alternatively, the country and western songs that were closest to the melodramatic or sentimental modes of conventional popular songs were promoted as popular songs—or, more frequently, recorded by popular singers in a style that was halfway between country and pop.[9]

Performers such as Frankie Laine and Guy Mitchell fit this latter category. Through these various manipulations, the country music field was soon firmly back in the hands of the major companies.

The black music market proved much more difficult to absorb. Having ignored black music for a number of years, the major companies had lost touch with recent developments in the rich and constantly evolving black culture. While these companies contented themselves with connections to the most prominent black innovators of the big band sound, other black musicians were developing styles that were much closer to the blues. As the swing era declined, the music that was brought to the fore in working-class black communities came to be called rhythm and blues. If there was a transitional figure in this development, it was Louis Jordan. Signed to Decca, a major label, Jordan and his group, the Tympani Five (actually seven members), anticipated the decline of the big bands and helped to define the instrumentation for the black dance bands that followed. With a much smaller horn section, the rhythm became more pronounced. Jordan's material was composed and arranged, but selections like "Saturday Night Fishfry," "Honey Chile," and "Ain't Nobody Here But Us Chickens" evoked blues images not found in most black pop of the day.

While Jordan was said to have "jumped the blues," the rhythm and blues stars who followed in the late forties screeched, honked, and shouted. The raucous sounds of artists such as Wynonie Harris ("Good Rockin' Tonight"), John Lee Hooker ("Boogie Chillen"), saxophonist Big Jay McNeely ("Deacon's Hop"), and pianist Amos Milburn ("Chicken Shack Boogie") were something of a break from the recent musical past and a harbinger of sounds to come:

> Suddenly it was as if a great deal of the Euro-American humanist facade Afro-American music had taken on had been washed away by the war. Rhythm & blues singers literally had to shout to be heard above the clanging and strumming of the various electrified instruments and the churning rhythm sections. And somehow the louder the instrumental accompaniment and the more harshly screamed the singing, the more expressive the music was.[10]

Since this music did not readily lend itself to the production styles of the major labels, they continued to ignore the relatively smaller race market. This situation made it possible for a large number of independent labels to enter the business. It is estimated that by 1949 over four hundred new labels came into existence. Most important among these were Atlantic in New York; Savoy in Newark; King in Cincinnati; Chess in Chicago; Peacock in Houston; and Modern, Imperial, and Specialty in Los Angeles. The independents were generally hampered by a shortage of materials, lack of funds, and inadequate distribution. Yet, with a hit, profits could be substantial. Modern was able to sell its blues singles for $1.05 in the late forties, while the major companies were only getting seventy-eight cents for pop singles. Particularly with the increased affluence provided by the war, black people were willing to spend more for their music. The relatively small number of independents that survived the forties gained a foothold in the industry that would not be dislodged.

A number of technological advances set the stage for the growth and further expansion of rhythm and blues music and its eventual takeover of the pop market as rock 'n' roll. The first of these was the introduction of magnetic tape, an invention stolen from the Nazis during World War II.[11] Prior to this innovation, quality recording was tied to elaborate studios, cumbersome equipment, and a substantial capital investment. Recording facilities were located in relatively few city centers and were firmly under the control of established corporate powers. Magnetic tape and its more versatile hardware changed that. Aside from bringing the obvious technical advantages of editing and better sound reproduction, magnetic tape made it possible for anyone to record anywhere. Operating from a small studio in Memphis, an enterprising young engineer named Sam Phillips could record B. B. King, Howlin' Wolf, Junior Parker, Rufus Thomas, and, later, Elvis Presley. The new technology clearly encouraged independent production and the formation of independent labels.

In 1948 Columbia's Dr. Peter Goldmark invented high fidelity. In what was to become known as the "battle of the speeds"—a contest that pitted Columbia's 33-rpm record against RCA's 45-rpm record—competition between the two giant firms yielded discs of excellent sound quality and maximum durability. These records were lighter and less breakable than the 78-rpm records and were well suited to the rapidly changing pop market because they could be shipped faster and more cheaply. Again, independent production was encouraged.

Most audio and visual media—television, film, and, to a lesser extent, radio—are capital intensive industries. They require huge sums of money for production. Records, on the other hand, do not depend on an elaborate transmission system as does television, and they are not affected by such government regulations as the assignment of frequencies on the electromagnetic spectrum. Particularly in the late forties, records emerged as a relatively inexpensive medium. It was in part for this reason that it was not as easy for a few giant electronics firms to monopolize the business. Records soon became the staple of the music industry, surpassing sheet music as the major source of revenue in 1952. About the same time, radio overtook juke boxes as the number one hit-maker.

Another technological development strengthened local radio as the main vehicle for popularizing rhythm and blues; it involved a major media policy decision that had been made earlier in the century but which came to fruition in the early fifties. As early as 1935, RCA had announced plans to commit its research capabilities to the development of a then unheard of broadcast medium— television. In the late forties television became available as a consumer item. By 1951, RCA had already recovered from the cost of research and development and from the initial period of programming television stations at a loss. By 1957 there were thirty-nine million television sets in use, filling 80 percent of the homes in the United States. Because television quickly attracted most of the national advertising, network radio ad revenues fell off. Local radio grew as an effective medium for local advertisers. Experimenting successfully with new music, new programming, and new personalities, these independent stations eventually pushed aside the more staid network stations and in the process helped to revitalize the then smaller record industry.

Local radio in the early fifties was very loosely structured. The independent deejays, or "personality jocks" as they were called, were in control. These men were not subject to the dictates of music directors, and there was nothing approaching the tightly structured programming and restrictive playlists that we see today. In the search for cheaper forms of programming, records provided the obvious answer. Record programming soon became the rule for radio, and the disc jockey replaced the live entertainment personalities who had dominated radio in the thirties and forties. Until the 1959 congressional payola hearings curtailed their power and "Top Forty" programming rationalized the AM format, the independent deejays were the central figures in the record industry. They could and did make hits. Relying on their own inventiveness for popularity, they often experimented with "specialty" music as an antidote to the trivial popular fare of network radio. Rhythm and blues proved to be quite popular with white as well as black audiences. As early as 1952, Dolphin's Hollywood Record Shop, a black retail outlet, reported that its business suddenly consisted of

40 percent white customers. They attributed it to independent deejays playing rhythm and blues records. Early rhythm and blues hits that were popular among both black and white audiences included Fats Domino's "The Fat Man" for Imperial (1950), Jackie Brenston's "Rocket 88" for Modern (1951), Lloyd Price's "Lawdy Miss Clawdy" for Specialty (1952), and Joe Turner's "Chains of Love" (1951), "Sweet Sixteen" (1952), and "Honey Hush" (1953) for Atlantic. All were recorded for independent labels.

As the market for black popular music expanded, so did the number of stations that played it. At first, the Deep South was the center for rhythm and blues radio. Gradually, white-oriented stations began programming some rhythm and blues shows to accommodate the potential audience for black music in northern cities. As record sales indicated the growing popularity of rhythm and blues among white teenagers, white stations made a growing commitment to the music, and pioneering black deejays like "Jockey" Jack Gibson in Atlanta, "Professor Bop" in Shreveport, and "Sugar Daddy" in Birmingham were soon followed by white rhythm and blues deejays such as Alan Freed, who is remembered as the "Father of Rock 'n' Roll."

Rhythm and Blues Begets Rock 'n' Roll

The rhythm and blues that these stations were playing, the fore-runner of rock 'n' roll, was itself a hybrid form. As a category, it had been adopted by the music business in 1949 as a more palatable catch-all phrase, replacing the designation "race" music. Still a code word for black music, it encompassed styles as diverse as gospel, blues, and jazz. In the nationwide musical market made possible by radio, a number of these traditions converged with some country influence to become rock 'n' roll. Rhythm and blues artist Johnny Otis recalled the phenomenon from a West Coast perspective:

> In the early forties a hybrid form of music developed on the West Coast. What was happening in Chicago was another kind of thing altogether. It was all rhythm & blues later, but the Chicago bands, the people that came up from the Delta, came up with harmonicas and guitars—the Muddy Waters and the rest of them. They had a certain thing, and we loved it, and we were influenced by it to a certain degree. But on the

Coast, the people who were there, like myself and Roy Milton, T-Bone Walker, and Joe Liggins and the Honeydrippers, we all had big band experience. We all thought in terms of big bands, but when it became impossible to maintain a big band and work and make a living we all had to break down, and when we broke down, we didn't break down to just a guitar and a rhythm section. We still tried to maintain some of that sound of the jazz bands. We kept maybe a trumpet, a trombone, and saxes—this was a semblance of brass and reeds, and they continued to play the bop and swing riffs. And this superimposed on the country blues and boogie structure began to become rhythm & blues. And out of rhythm & blues grew rock 'n' roll.[12]

By the time rock 'n' roll established itself as an independent style, the horn section described by Otis had been reduced even further, first to a single saxophone, and then to no horns at all. The rhythmic base of the boogie structure had become even more dominant. And the music was hardly limited to California.

Although its roots were in the Deep South, the music that became rock 'n' roll issued from just about every region in the country. Most of its formative influences, as well as virtually all of its early innovators, were black. T-Bone Walker's pioneering work with the electric guitar on the West Coast had an obvious effect on the Memphis-based B. B. King ("Three O'Clock Blues," "The Thrill is Gone"), whose single string runs influenced dozens of rock guitarists to follow. Delta-born Muddy Waters ("Got My Mojo Working") "electrified" the blues in Chicago; shortly thereafter Bo Didley ("Bo Didley") crossed over into the pop market as a rock 'n' roll star with his distinctive variant of the style. The New Orleans boogie piano of Professor Longhair influenced Fats Domino whose successful rhythm and blues career was transformed into rock 'n' roll legend with hits such as "Ain't That a Shame," "I'm in Love Again," and "Blueberry Hill." The jazz/gospel fusions of Ray Charles ("I Got a Woman," "What'd I Say") and the more pop-oriented gospel stylings of vocalists like Clyde McPhatter ("Treasure of Love," "A Lover's Question") and Sam Cooke ("You Send Me," "For Sentimental Reasons") brought the traditions of the black church into the secular world of rock 'n' roll. The assertiveness of Joe Turner, veteran blues shouter from Kansas City, was taken up by female vocalists such as Ruth Brown ("5-10-15 Hours," "Mama, He Treats Your Daughter Mean") and Laverne Baker ("Tweedle Dee," "Jim Dandy"), and carried to an extreme in the outrageous rock 'n' roll performances of Little Richard ("Tutti-Frutti," "Long Tall Sally,"

"Rip It Up"). The elegant harmonies of urban vocal groups like the Orioles ("Crying in the Chapel"), the Crows ("Gee"), the Chords ("Sh-Boom"), and the Penguins ("Earth Angel") ushered in a whole genre of rock 'n' roll known as doo wop. Even with the new name, however, there was no mistaking where this music came from. As late as 1956, *Billboard* referred to the music as "a popularized form of rhythm & blues." What made the mainstream popularity of this music that much more incredible was the vast array of social forces that stood in its way.

In the fifties one of the factors that kept rhythm and blues from expanding in popularity in its original form was the rapid turnover of artists working in the field. *Billboard* reported the following in a retrospective article on the year 1952: "On the whole, the older more established artists held their own throughout the year, less than a handful of new names established themselves in the pop field, and less than that in the country and western division. The rhythm and blues department where artists turn over like leaves in the fall followed its usual pattern this year."[13]

The "usual pattern" of rhythm and blues turnover continued throughout the 1950s. Groups like the Chords, the Charms, the Spiders, the Spaniels, the Crows, and the Four Tunes, all of whom had pop hits in 1954, could not be found on the year-end pop charts one year later. Often catapulted to success from a neighborhood street corner or, like Little Richard, from a bus terminal kitchen where he was washing dishes, black musicians seldom had access to good advice about record contracts, royalty payments, marketing, promotion, or career development. As a result, they were routinely swindled out of their publishing rights and underpaid for record sales.

Rhythm and blues artist Jimmy Witherspoon recorded "Ain't Nobody's Business" on the Supreme label owned by a dentist named Al Patrick. "But, I didn't get one penny royalty," complained Witherspoon. "Patrick paid me a flat fee for the session. I was supposed to get so much on each record sold, which he never paid me."[14] In some cases black artists were not paid for recording at all. Said Saul Bihari, founder of Modern, an independent label that included on its roster Lightnin' Hopkins, John Lee Hooker, Etta James, and B. B. King:

> We used to bring 'em in, give 'em a bottle of booze and say, "Sing me a song about your girl." Or, "Sing me a song about Christmas." They'd

pluck around a little on their guitars, then say "O.K." and make up a song as they went along. We'd give them a subject and off they'd go. When it came time to quit, we'd give them a wave that they had ten seconds to finish.[15]

The major companies were no more principled in their treatment of black musicians. Ahmet Ertegun, the president of Atlantic, tells an interesting story about a Columbia representative who came to see him in the early years of Atlantic:

He wanted to make a deal whereby Columbia would distribute for Atlantic records because we seemed to be very good at what he called "race" records. So I said, "Well, what would you offer us?" He said, "Three percent." "Three percent!" I said, "We're paying our artists more than that!" And he said, "You're paying those people royalties? You must be out of your mind!" Of course he didn't call them "people." He called them something else.[16]

Another practice that served to limit the crossover potential of black artists was the widespread use of "cover versions" of rhythm and blues hits. Strictly speaking, a cover record is a copy of an original recording performed by another artist in a style thought to be more appropriate for the mainstream market. Table 2.1 lists some of the better-known cover records. In the vast majority of cases, black artists recording for independent labels were covered by white artists signed to one of the majors. In the 1950s, covers were commonly used by the major companies to capitalize on the growing popularity of rhythm and blues among white listeners. Cover records were often released within the expected chart life of the original and, owing to the superior distribution channels and promotional power of the majors, often outsold the originals. But most of them lacked the feeling and sense of excitement that the originals conveyed.

Several dozen songs were successfully covered by the majors in the early years of rock 'n' roll. RCA began by covering Gene and Eunice's "Kokomo" with a version by Perry Como. Columbia covered the same song using Tony Bennett. Columbia and Victor were so reluctant to have anything to do with rock 'n' roll that they were less aggressive with cover versions than other majors. Mercury and Decca had the most luck of the major companies. Mercury's Crew Cuts, aptly named for the fifties teenage audience, recorded a cover version of the Chords' "Sh-Boom" (originally on Atlantic's Cat label) that became the fifth best-selling popular song of 1954.

Following the success of "Sh-Boom," the Crew Cuts systematically pillaged the rhythm and blues charts, covering hits like Nappy Brown's "Don't Be Angry" (Savoy), the Charms' "Gum Drop" (Deluxe), and the Penguins' "Earth Angel" (DooTone). Georgia Gibbs, also signed to Mercury, covered Etta James's "Wallflower" with a cleaned-up version called "Dance with Me, Henry." The original version sold four hundred thousand copies for Modern while the Gibbs cover sold one million records for Mercury. Decca used the McGuire Sisters (on their Coral subsidiary) to cover the Moonglows' "Sincerely" (Chess) and made it the seventh best-selling pop single in 1955.

Table 2.1 Cover Records

Song	Original Artist	Cover Artist
"Crying in the Chapel"	Sonny Till and the Orioles	June Valli
"Sh-Boom"	Chords	Crew Cuts
"Earth Angel"	Penguins	Crew Cuts
"Don't Be Angry"	Nappy Brown	Crew Cuts
"Gum Drop"	Charms	Crew Cuts
"Goodnight, Well It's Time to Go"	Spaniels	McGuire Sisters
"Sincerely"	Moonglows	McGuire Sisters
"Dance with Me, Henry" ("Wallflower")	Etta James	Georgia Gibbs
"Tweedle Dee"	LaVerne Baker	Georgia Gibbs
"Kokomo"	Gene and Eunice	Perry Como
"Shake, Rattle and Roll"	Joe Turner	Bill Haley
"Hound Dog"	Big Mama Thornton	Elvis Presley
"Money Honey"	The Drifters	Elvis Presley
"Lawdy Miss Clawdy"	Lloyd Price	Elvis Presley
"Ain't That a Shame"	Fat's Domino	Pat Boone
"I Almost Lost My Mind"	Ivory Joe Hunter	Pat Boone
"Tutti Frutti"	Little Richard	Pat Boone
"Long Tall Sally"	Little Richard	Pat Boone
"I'll Be Home"	Flamingos	Pat Boone
"Hearts of Stone"	Charms	Fontaine Sisters
"Little Darlin'"	Gladiolas	Diamonds
"I'm Walkin'"	Fats Domino	Ricky Nelson
"Party Doll"	Buddy Knox	Steve Lawrence
"Butterfly"	Charlie Gracie	Andy Williams
"I Hear You Knocking"	Smiley Lewis	Gale Storm

Pat Boone, more than any other artist, built his reputation as a rock 'n' roll singer by covering black rhythm and blues tunes. His label, Dot, was the most successful company at the practice. In 1955 Dot got 15 percent of the popular singles on the charts and shortly after achieved the status of a major company by setting up its own distribution system. Boone recorded "Ain't That a Shame" (Fats Domino), "I Almost Lost My Mind" (Ivory Joe Hunter), and "Tutti Frutti" (Little Richard), among others.

In order to obtain the far larger royalties from performances, record sales, and sheet-music sales available in the white-audience market, small record companies that consigned publishing and copyrights to themselves sometimes took their rhythm and blues songs to the big companies to be covered. Such practices kept the black version of the song out of the popular market and denied the original singer the royalties that would have come if the record company/publisher had pushed the first version as a potential crossover hit. By 1956, however, this initial suppression of black music was less generally successful. Rhythm and blues had merged with and changed into rock 'n' roll, which was becoming a dominant popular style, and the original versions of songs were in demand by a more sophisticated white audience.

The profitable practice of covering records was greatly aided by the copyright laws. The appropriate law under which artists worked in the fifties had been written in 1909 and thus did not include recorded material. Under the 1909 copyright law, it was impossible to copyright a particular recording of a song; one could only copyright the original sheet music. Thus, while a publisher received a royalty payment for the use of his publication and a composer received a royalty payment for the performance of his music, no royalty was derived from the actual recording. The performer was paid only for the sales of his records. In this period of heavy cover activity it was the performer who suffered. Most of the performers whose songs were covered were black.

The wording of the 1909 copyright law often led to other abuses. Even though the royalty payments on any piece of music were supposed to be divided by the writer and the publisher (usually 50 percent each), many performers who wrote their own material never got their royalties. According to Lee Berk, lawyer and founder of the Berklee School of Music in Boston:

> The U.S. Copyright Act speaks of a situation in which, in the case of an "employee for hire," it is the employer and not the composer who will have the right to be considered author or composer of the work. In

such a case, then, the employer would also be the proprietor of the work by the fact of the employment relationship, and would have not only the right to copyright the work and name himself as copyright proprietor, but also the right to name himself composer as well.[17]

The name that appeared on the record might not have been the actual author of the song. More important, even if the real author was credited on the record, his name might not have been registered with the publishing rights organizations (ASCAP and BMI) that collected the royalty payments for artists.

Fred Parris, for example, wrote "In the Still of the Night" and recorded it with his own group, The Five Satins. The record is a rock 'n' roll classic. Rereleased in a number of oldies anthologies, the record has probably sold millions of copies. With proper credits, "In the Still of the Night" should have been worth tens of thousands of dollars for Parris in mechanical royalties alone (one cent for every record sold), not to mention performance royalties of two and one-half cents for every radio play. Had Parris also owned the publishing, the record would have been worth more than twice that figure. As to what really happened with the recording, Parris claimed:

> I don't know about BMI. Okay, I used to see BMI on every label, but I never knew what it meant. I didn't become a BMI writer—and this is very sad—until after the bulk of the plays on "In the Still of the Night." So what was happening was my name was on the label, I'm the writer, I'm getting a fair shake. . . . I'm not going to try and incriminate anyone, but somebody else's name was in at BMI as the writer, and that was where the money came from. When I got out of the service and went to them with my problem, they said "Okay, we feel sorry for you." And again, I still didn't have enough knowledge of the business, and I didn't have enough patience, you know, to say "Well, I'll see my attorney about this. I'll wait." Instead I wanted the money right then. They said, "Okay we'll make it retroactive from such and such a date." But that "such and such a date" was nowhere near where the bulk of the sales were. So I came up with a figure of something like $783.[18]

A final factor that helped to suppress black music and musicians was the technological innovations in the industry that required equipment changeover in the record-buying public. The late 1940s saw the development of unbreakable 45-rpm and 33-rpm records that required different playback equipment than had been used for the 78-rpm records. Because of a simple lack of money, the black record audience was slower to make this switch than the white. Victor and Columbia were marketing three-speed record changers by 1952, but as late as 1956, rhythm and blues records were still sold in the black community as shellac-based 78s. Independent distributers evolved formulas for predicting when a song would cross over into the white market on the basis of the demand for the disk in the 45-rpm configuration. Of course, to go into a separate 45-rpm pressing, a rhythm and blues record would have to show evidence of very strong sales potential. The dual technology had the effect of delaying mainstream exposure for many rhythm and blues artists. While not a conspiracy of the major record companies, the lock-and-key relationship of new and better records and the new record changers tended to isolate black music.

Even with such obstacles to overcome, the mainstream acceptance of rhythm and blues surpassed all expectations. A *Billboard* headline announced: "1955—The Year R&B Took Over Pop Field." The dramatic numerical increase of black artists in the popular market was second only to their influence in shaping public taste. Reviewing the year 1956, *Billboard* offered the following assessment:

> Looking closely at the 25 rhythm and blues platters that made the pop charts, it is interesting to note the great variety of rhythm and blues artists and styles that found pop acceptance. It was not only the slicker, pop-oriented singers like Clyde McPhatter and Otis Williams who hit in the pop market but also those working in the traditional style like Shirley and Lee, Little Richard, and Fats Domino. Their impact, in fact, has virtually changed the conception of what a pop record is.[19]

By the mid-1950s this music, now called rock 'n' roll, had become "perhaps the most profound and enduring reshaping of a dominant musical style to have taken place since the Renaissance."[20]

Rock 'n' Roll: Black or White

Were it not for the dynamics of racism in our society, the man who would most likely have been crowned the "King of Rock 'n' Roll" was the son of a carpenter from St. Louis—Chuck Berry. When Berry walked into the offices of Chess Records on the recommendation of Muddy Waters, his demo of "Ida Red" (backed with a blues number, "Wee Wee Hours") had already been turned down at both Capitol and Mercury because it sounded "too country" for a black man. On the advice of Leonard Chess, Berry gave the tune a "bigger beat" and changed the title to "Maybellene," taking the name from a hair creme bottle. Said Chess a few weeks before he died:

> I liked it, thought it was something new. I was going to New York anyway, and I took a dub to Alan [Freed] and said "Play this." The dub didn't have Chuck's name on it or nothing. By the time I got back to Chicago, Freed had called a dozen times, saying it was his biggest record ever. History, the rest, y' know? Sure, "Wee Wee Hour," that was on the back side of the release, was a good tune too, but the kids wanted the big beat, cars, and young love.[21]

For his part, Freed and another deejay named Russ Fratto were credited as co-writers of the song. The country-tinged "Maybellene" went to number five on the pop charts in 1955.

> But his next four singles, performed in a blues style and presenting in their themes some strong criticisms of aspects of American life, showed his interests much more obviously. Judges and courts in "Thirty Days," credit and car salesmen in "No Money Down," high culture in "Roll Over Beethoven," and all these and more in "Too Much Monkey Business" were cause for complaint. Since these records were performed in a strong "blues" voice, the songs . . . received relatively little attention from disc jockeys.[22]

The songs Berry is best remembered for are the simpler, teen-directed, but still socially relevant recordings he turned out later, such as "School Day" and "Rock and Roll Music" in 1957, and "Sweet Little Sixteen" and "Johnny B. Goode" in 1958, all of which reached the "Top Ten" on the pop charts.

Other rock 'n' roll artists may have had more and bigger hits than Chuck Berry, but none matched his influence in defining the style. "As rock & roll's first guitar hero, Berry, along with various rockabilly musicians, made that instrument the genre's dominant musical element, supplanting the sax of previous black stars."[23] In his writing and performing, he had the uncanny ability to relate rhythm and blues to white teenage culture without disowning his blackness. He was a true storyteller in the folkloric sense of the term, but he was also a man for his time. As he recently told his fans: "I said: 'Why can't I do as Pat Boone does and play good music for the white people and sell as well there as I could in the neighborhood?' And that's what I shot for writing 'School Day.' "[24]

Berry's career was interrupted in 1962 when he was convicted of a violation of the Mann Act and sent to prison. He had done no more than bring a girl back with him from a tour in Mexico, but because she was underage, he was convicted. It took two trials. The first was vacated because of the prejudice shown by the judge, who referred to Berry as "this Negro." The underlying meaning of the conviction was shown in a headline of the time, cited by Michael Lydon. It read "Rock 'n' Roll Singer Lured Me to St. Louis, Says 14 Year Old."[25] Berry's songs continued to be recorded, and he staged a comeback in 1972 with a song as commercially successful as it was puerile: "My Ding-a-Ling."

The second wave of rock 'n' roll performers to hit the charts were white. These were the rockabilly artists Elvis Presley, Carl Perkins, Gene Vincent, Jerry Lee Lewis, and Johnny Cash and their country cousins, the Everly Brothers and Buddy Holly. Their music was widely regarded as an amalgam of rhythm and blues and country and western, the first tradition being upheld by black artists, and the second by predominantly white ones. Both rhythm and blues and country and western exhibited a spontaneity that differentiated them from the Tin Pan Alley pop of their day. But the relative contribution of each to the equally authentic rockabilly strain is more difficult to pinpoint. Johnny Cash's "I Walk the Line," for example, was closer to traditional country material, with country phrasing and the bass line providing a steady country rhythm. The Everly Brothers' close harmonies were also characteristic of the country genre, but their unorthodox, syncopated guitar riffs clearly established them as a rock 'n' roll act. Similarly, Presley, Perkins, and Lewis often sang with a traditional country drawl, but in their up-tempo tunes the lyric phrasing and driving rhythms clearly came from the rhythm and blues tradition.

The phenomenon of country-flavored rock 'n' roll had its origins in the rather unlikely figure of Bill Haley ("Rock Around the Clock"), a middle-aged, slightly balding guitarist who was signed to a major label. His heroes were Bob Wills and his Texas Playboys, who played a culturally mixed brand of music known as western swing, but his sound came closer to Louis Jordan. His producer, Milt Gabler (who had also been Jordan's producer in the forties), told chronicler Arnold Shaw that he consciously modeled Haley's sound on Jordan's jump beat. "We'd begin with Jordan's shuffle rhythm," said Gabler. "You know, dotted eighth notes and six-teenths, and we'd build on it. I'd sing Jordan riffs to the group that would be picked up by the electric guitars and tenor sax. . . . They got a sound that had the drive of The Tympani Five and the color of country and western."[26]

Country music is usually seen as having developed from the Anglo-Celtic folk tradition. Among those immigrants from the British Isles who settled in the valleys of the Appalachian Mountains, this music retained much of its original character. In the slave owning South, however, where most of the rockabilly artists came from, there was a continuing interaction between the European and African cultures, despite the legally enforced separation of the races. While there is no question that cultural crossover was a two-way process, there is considerable controversy over which musical elements can legitimately be considered Africanisms—and, therefore, the contribution of black artists—and to what extent they influenced styles generally performed by whites—in this case, rockabilly. The debate usually includes a discussion of variables such as tonal inflection, instrumentation, "blue notes" and musical scales, the call-and-response style, and rhythmic patterns.

According to African music scholar John Storm Roberts, there is an "intimate connection between speech and melody in African music, which arises partly from the fact that so many African languages are tonal."[27] As Hettie Jones commented, "The song you sing is what you mean to say."[28] This heightened sense of music-as-language extends to African concepts of musical instrumentation as well. In traditional African music, instruments are often used to approximate human speech. They are not simply external devices used to produce notes and "melody," as in European music. African talking drums, for example, did not send messages by using an abstract Morse code-like system of tapping. They replicated the pitch and rhythmic patterns of the language; they really talked. In addition to this " 'talking' function that goes far beyond the well-known use of talking drums, or even talking flutes, xylophones, and so forth," Roberts notes that there is also a "semi-personification of instruments, which are considered to have some form of soul."[29] Centuries later, Ray Charles said that it was this human quality that attracted him to country music instrumentation: "I really thought that it was somethin' about country music, even as a youngster. I couldn't figure out what it was then, but I know what it was now. . . . Although I was bred in and around the blues, I always did have interest in other music, and I felt the closest music, really, to the blues [was country and western]. They'd make them steel guitars cry and whine, and it really attracted me."[30]

At first the blues was a largely improvisational music, with no standard form or rhythmic pattern. Interacting with the European diatonic scale, the blues eventually became standardized into two or three common forms, the best known of which is called the "classic" blues. The notation of the diatonic scale, however, did not accommodate the way the bluesmen really sang. Their deviations from European melodic regularity came to be known as "blue notes." A blue note sounds a little flat, but not flat enough to be the next note down on the scale. There is some controversy over not whether such tones exist but whether they constitute an Africanism. While "an ambiguous third," to use John Storm Roberts's term, appears in the music of more than one continent, the flatted seventh is more of a defining characteristic of the blues. According to noted African scholar Kwabena Nketia, "The flatted seventh is frequent and well-established in Akan vocal music."[31] Such tones are also common in rockabilly songs such as Elvis Presley's recording of "Hound Dog," and Jerry Lee Lewis's "Whole Lotta Shakin'," both of which also follow a classic twelve-bar blues structure.

Another Africanism that found its way into rock 'n' roll was the call-and-response style. In African culture this style is used in religious ceremonies as well as collective work. Most commonly identified with gospel music, the style was probably introduced to America in the work songs of the slaves. In traditional African music the call-and-response style exists primarily as a vocal form where a lead singer is answered by a chorus but in America instrumental variations of this device also developed in blues and jazz. Both forms of call-and-response were evident in blues-based rock 'n' roll. It is also possible, however, to establish a link to the more country-oriented rockabilly strain, which at times employed instrumental fills in a way that suggested an African influence.

"European and Anglo-American folk music sometimes has instrumental bridges between the verses," says Roberts. "It must be said that this is rare, however, and most Anglo-American singing was unaccompanied until so late that a black influence could be postulated," especially in those cases where the "instrumental sections were clearly used not as a bridge to lead to the next vocal line, as a European musician might use them, but as an answer to the previous one."[32] One can hear such instrumental responses in rockabilly songs such as Bill Haley's "See You Later, Alligator," and in "Wake Up Little Susie" by the Everly Brothers. In these instances, to use the words of musicologist Christopher Small, "the instrument is too much like a second voice to allow us to call it merely accompaniment; this second voice seems to work in a way which reminds us more of African call-and-response procedures than of European concepts of melody and accompaniment."[33]

The most significant contribution black music made to rock 'n' roll, of course, was its rhythmic base. Says Small, "Rhythm is to the African musician what harmony is to the European—the central organizing principle of the art."[34] Not surprisingly, African music is polyrhythmic. In America, where slaves were generally denied the use of drums (thought to be politically dangerous, since they could be used to signal an uprising), other percussive practices such as finger popping, hand clapping, and foot stomping were developed. Polyrhythms were not found in European folk forms, or their American country derivatives, which invariably accented the so-called strong beats and reinforced a single unsyncopated sustaining rhythm. The "Big Beat" that was rock 'n' roll, which accents the second and fourth beats of each measure, was African-derived. It is found in virtually every up-tempo rock 'n' roll tune, including the rockabilly style. In 1954 *Billboard* described Elvis Presley as "the youngster with the hillbilly blues beat."[35] Bill Haley stated the issue most clearly when he told his audience, "I felt that if I could take a Dixieland tune and drop the first and third beats and accentuate the second and fourth, and add a beat the listeners could clap to as well as dance, this would be what we were after."[36]

In addition to the musical Africanisms that pervade rock 'n' roll, including the rockabilly strain, the influence of black music and musicians can be seen in the personal lives and styles of the most memorable rockabilly performers. Prior to the emergence of rock-abilly, Sam Phillips, founder of the archetypal rockabilly label, Sun, had been almost exclusively a blues producer, having recorded blues giants like B. B. King, Bobby Bland, Howlin' Wolf, and James Cotton very early in their careers. According to his secretary, Marion Keisker, Phillips used to say: "If only I could find a white man who had the Negro sound and the Negro feel, I could make a billion dollars."[37] With Elvis Presley, his dream of a white man who could sing black came true, and it transformed Sun Records into an overwhelming commercial success.

Each of Phillips's white singers had grown up in an environment that mixed black and white cultures to a degree unknown in the North. This crossover of cultures created the conditions that gave rise to rockabilly, and through it to the dominant strain of rock 'n' roll itself. Presley was reared in Mississippi until his late teens when his family moved to Memphis, Tennessee, in search of work. Later he described growing up:

> I'd play along with the radio or phonograph, and taught myself the chord positions. We were a religious family, going round together to sing at camp meetings and revivals, and I'd take my guitar with us when I could. I also dug the real low-down Mississippi singers, mostly Big Bill Broonzy and Big Boy Crudup, although they would scold me at home for listening to them. "Sinful music," the townsfolk in Memphis said it was. Which never bothered me, I guess.[38]

Margaret McKee and Fred Chisenhall described "Elvis Presley watching Old Charlie Burse, 'Ukulele Ike,' twitching his knee, rocking his pelvis, and rolling his syllables during a show at a Beale Street honky-tonk (the style Elvis copied to launch the blue-suede blues)."[39] Similarly, Jerry Lee Lewis explained how he

> used to hang around Haney's Big House, that was a colored establishment where they had dances and such. . . . We was just kids, we wasn't allowed in. So we'd slip around to the back and sneak in whenever we could. I saw a lot of 'em there, all those blues players. No, it wasn't anything about us being white, we was just too young. See, it wasn't no big thing just because it was a colored place. Of course we was about the only ones down there.[40]

Carl Perkins, the son of a sharecropper, said that he

> was raised on a plantation in the flatlands of Lake Country, Tennessee, and we were about the only white people on it. I played with coloured kids, played football with socks stuffed with sand. Working in the cotton fields in the sun, music was the only escape. The coloured people would sing, and I'd join in, just a little kid, and that was colored rhythm and blues, got named rock 'n' roll, got named that in 1956, but the same music was there years before, and it was my music."[41]

Although it borrowed heavily from black culture, rockabilly was still a legitimate musical movement that integrated black-based blues with country and western styles. It had its own identity and, obviously, in singers like Presley, Perkins, and Lewis, performers of real originality and talent. Unfortunately, it is impossible to separate the popularity of white rock 'n' roll from a racist pattern that exists in American music whereby a style that is pioneered by black artists eventually comes to be popularized, dominated, and even defined by whites as if it were their own. That has been the history of black music in America from ragtime, to jazz, to swing, and rock 'n' roll was no exception. Johnny Otis commented that

> black artists have always been the ones in America to innovate and create and breathe life into new forms. Jazz grew out of black America and there's no question about that. However, Paul Whiteman became the king of jazz. Swing music grew out of black America, created by black artists Count Basie, Duke Ellington. Benny Goodman was crowned king of swing. In the case of rock 'n' roll, Elvis Presley—and in this case not without some justification because he brought a lot of originality with him—became king. Not the true kings of rock 'n' roll—Fats Domino, Little Richard, Chuck Berry. . . . What happens is black people— the artists—continue to develop these things and create them and get ripped off, and the glory and the money goes to white artists. This pressure is constantly on them to find something that whitey can't rip off.[42]

This skewed racial pattern makes the task of unearthing an accurate history of American popular music that much more difficult, and it seriously underestimates the degree of cross-cultural collaboration that has taken place. Styles are described (and defended) in terms that are clearly racial rather than musical. "[R]ockabilly is hillbilly rock-and-roll," insists Nick Tosches. "It was not a usurpation of black music by whites because its soul, its pneuma, was white, full of the redneck ethos."[43] "[I]t was that to a degree," acknowledges Arnold Shaw, "though it would probably be more accurate to describe it as the sound of young, white Southerners imitating black bluesmen."[44]

Were it not for the artificial separation of the races, popular music history might read surprisingly differently. According to Jimmy Witherspoon, "Chuck Berry is a country singer. People put everybody in categories, black, white, this. Now if Chuck Berry was white, with the lyrics he writes, he would be the top country star in the world."[45] Just as an artist need not be limited to a single performance style, so pieces of music do not automatically have a genre; they can be performed in many idioms. There have been any number of country and western covers of Chuck Berry songs including Hoyt Axton's "Maybelline," Freddy Weller's "To Much

Monkey Business" and "Promised Land," Waylon Jennings's "Brown Eyed Handsome Man," Buck Owen's "Johnny B. Goode," Linda Rondstadt's "Back in the U.S.A.," Emmy Lou Harris's "You Never Can Tell," and Johnny Rivers's "Memphis."[46]

Even with these contradictions, however, the vintage rock 'n' roll years were generally good for black musicians. From a low point of 3 percent in 1954, the percentage of black artists on the year-end pop charts rose to an unprecedented 29 percent in 1957. In addition to Chuck Berry, black artists like The Platters ("Only You," "My Prayer," "Great Pretender," "Magic Touch"); Bill Doggett ("Honky Tonk"); Fats Domino ("I'm in Love Again," "Blueberry Hill," "I'm Walkin'," "Blue Monday"); Frankie Lyman and the Teenagers ("Why Do Fools Fall in Love"); Little Richard ("Long Tall Sally"); Sam Cooke ("You Send Me"); The Coasters ("Searchin' "); Johnny Mathis ("Chances Are," "It's Not for Me to Say"); The Bobettes ("Mr. Lee"); and Larry Williams ("Short Fat Fanny"), all made the year-end top fifty during this period. These and other black performers also scored with lesser hits on the weekly pop charts as well.

From the War on Rock to the British Invasion: The Struggle Continues

Significant black encroachment into the coveted pop music terrain would not be taken lightly. It posed a potential economic threat to the established powers of the music industry and, in a larger social sense, it smacked of miscegenation. "It was a time when many a mother ripped pictures of Fats Domino off her daughter's bedroom wall," recalled former BMI vice president Russ Sanjek. "She remembered what she felt toward her Bing Crosby pinup, and she didn't want her daughter creaming for Fats."[47] The reaction came in the form of a loosely coordinated series of government investigations and legislative actions. Acting in concert, ASCAP, the major recording companies, and the United States government waged a protracted public battle for a return to "good music" in what Sanjek has called "the war on rock."[48]

ASCAP, of course, had been at war with BMI since its inception. For them, the attack on rock 'n' roll was simply an escalation of their continuing efforts to put BMI out of business. Most of the rock material was penned by BMI writers. For the major labels, the fight was an attempt to halt the expansion of the independents. Although the independents never represented a substantial economic threat overall, they did make significant inroads into the singles charts as rock 'n' roll took over the popular market. Forty of the seventy records to make the "Top Ten" in 1957, for example, were produced by independent labels.[49] To conservative elected officials, jumping on the bandwagon with the likes of Frank Sinatra, Bing Crosby, Steve Allen, Ira Gershwin, and Oscar Hammerstein to denounce a music that was widely regarded as immoral and subversive, not to mention black, must have seemed like a sure way of grabbing some quick and memorable headlines. In the mid-fifties these roughly convergeant interests erupted in a series of campaigns that culminated in the infamous congressional payola hearings of 1959. Rock 'n' roll became the political football in what was essentially economic warfare with moral, esthetic, and racial overtones.

As had been the case throughout the forties and early fifties, ASCAP led the charge. In 1956, under pressure from the Songwriters of America, an "independent" group of some seven hundred ASCAP writers, the Anti-Trust Subcommittee of the House Judiciary Committee, chaired by Congressman Emmanuel Celler, halted an investigation of television to initiate a probe into BMI. The congressman made clear the racial aspects of the investigation when he said, according to Sanjek: "Well rock and roll has its place. There's no question about it. It's given great impetus to talent, particularly among the colored people. It's a natural expression of their emotions and feelings."[50] Despite testimony from a parade of influential ASCAP writers, the investigation could find no evidence of wrongdoing on the part of BMI, and the matter was referred to the Justice department.

The next battle occurred in 1958 when ASCAP succeeded in having introduced before Congress a bill that would have prevented broadcasters from owning any BMI stock. Again, a parade of ASCAP sympathizers held forth. No less a figure than Sinatra, for example, testified:

> My only sorrow is the unrelenting insistence of recording and motion picture companies upon purveying the most brutal, ugly, degenerate, vicious form of expression it has been my misfortune to hear—naturally, I refer to the bulk of rock 'n' roll. It fosters almost totally negative and

destructive reactions in young people. It smells phony and false. It is sung, played and written for the most part by cretinous goons and by means of its almost imbecilic reiterations and sly—lewd—in plain fact, dirty—lyrics and, as I said before, it manages to be the martial music of every sideburned delinquent on the face of the earth. This rancid aphrodisiac I deplore.[51]

If there was any doubt about the racial implications of Sinatra's statement, they were certainly made clear by Vance Packard who, appearing at a hearing for pay, declared that rock 'n' roll "was inspired by what had been called *race* music modified to stir the animal instinct in modern teenagers."[52] Even supported by twelve hundred pages of such testimony the bill died.

Payola, the practice of paying for record play, certainly did not originate with rock 'n' roll. As early as World War I, it was estimated that about $400 thousand per year was being paid to singers for the express purpose of plugging certain songs. In 1959, however, it was the disc jockeys who were in the limelight, as the Legislative Oversight Subcommittee of the House Commerce Committee, chaired by Arkansas Democrat Oren Harris, launched a new probe into the practice just as their investigation of rigged television quiz shows was coming to an end. While the committee was convened to investigate abuses at all levels of the recording industry, the deejays became the main target of the hearings. They were considered largely responsible for the crossover of black music into the pop market.

The most damning indictment in the payola hearings was that of Alan Freed, the self-appointed "Father of Rock 'n' Roll." While other deejays also fell victim to the self-righteous probe, Freed was the most visible symbol of everything that was threatening about the new music. Freed had played a major role in popularizing rhythm and blues among white audiences, and he continued to push original black recordings during periods of heavy cover activity. He also refused "on principle" to sign a statement saying that he had never received money or gifts to promote records. In 1960, Freed was indicted for accepting $30 thousand in payola, and two years later, after a partial guilty plea, was fined and given a suspended sentence. Unemployed and penniless, he was indicted again in 1964 for income-tax evasion. He died the following year, a broken man.

At the end of their investigation, the Harris Committee had

identified $263,245 in payola to disc jockeys. Not even comparable to World War I levels of abuse, this amount represented a small portion of total industry payola. Still, in all these investigations, the reams of public testimony and extensive media coverage did succeed in helping to create a climate sufficiently unfavorable to rock 'n' roll that more "palatable" forms of popular music were encouraged. Chief among these was what I have called "schlock rock"—a watered-down version of the real thing.[53]

If the rockabilly artists were not frauds, then the next wave of white heroes to make the rock 'n' roll scene certainly were. Aided by the national success of American Bandstand, television drew a final, clear line between rock 'n' roll and its black roots. While black artists like Sam Cooke, Clyde McPhatter, and Jackie Wilson turned out classic "Top Ten" pop hits such as "You Send Me," "Chain Gang," "A Lover's Question," "Lonely Teardrops," and "Night," television was used to promote the new white teen idols: Frankie Avalon, Fabian, Bobby Rydell, Ricky Nelson, Paul Anka, and Neil Sedaka. These were the "schlock rockers," descendants of Pat Boone and winners of Elvis Presley look-alike contests. "The focus in Philadelphia in particular was on image," according to British rock historian Charlie Gillett. "The unsophisticated white southern singers, and the unfashionable black ones, were supplanted by kids who could be the boy-next-door, whose visual appeal was more important than their musical ability."[54] Nevertheless, their vacuous hits would soon glut the pop market and give rock 'n' roll its final facelift of the fifties by softening the music and whitening up the charts.

Central to this process was the role played by the host of American Bandstand, Dick Clark. Bandstand actually started in 1952 as a local Philadelphia TV dance party. Clark took over as host in 1956, and by 1957 the show had been picked up for national broadcast. "Within two years, it was being broadcast by 101 affiliates to an audience of 20 million. . . . Because of program policy, [the performers who appeared on Bandstand] were invariably white in the early years."[55] Under Clark's leadership the show quickly became one of the most important promotional vehicles in the music industry, especially for schlock rock. "Dick Clark, the youthful, debonair host with the Dentyne smile," is remembered by Arnold Shaw, "as the ballast to Alan Freed, representing cool, white rock as Freed was the avatar of hot black rock."[56] Schlock rock was never original or interesting enough to halt the progress of black music completely, but it did contain its growth and limit its crossover appeal, for the next few years.

In addition to the continuing parade of squeaky-clean white vocalists like Freddy Cannon, Brian Hyland, Bobby Vee, and Bobby Vinton, the second generation of "schlock" brought to the fore its first black entertainer, Chubby Checker, whose "The Twist" was the first in a series of dance crazes that swept the country in the early 1960s. Checker's version of "The Twist" covered the Hank Ballard and the Midnighters original of two years earlier. Ballard's funkier single sold extremely well in the rhythm and blues market, but there was little crossover into pop, and it did not even hint at the national fad Checker triggered later. Checker was a real pop phenomenon. Like Bobby Rydell before him, he was created by a corporate decision in the offices of Philadelphia-based Cameo/Parkway Records. Even his name seems to have been manufactured, made to sound vaguely like Fats Domino (Fats-Chubby, Domino-Checker). But his success was unparalleled at the time. To date "The Twist" remains the only record to reach No. 1 on the pop charts twice, once in 1960 and then again in 1962. It was still listed as the best-selling single of all time well into the seventies. Before "The Twist" hit No. 1 for the second time, Checker had already followed it up with a series of short-lived faddish dance records like the "Hucklebuck," the "Pony," and the "Fly."

The twist craze occurred during a period of profound transitions in our history. America's most youthful president was capturing the hearts and minds of the nation. The "ban the bomb" movement foretold the potential horrors of the Cuban missile crisis, and the burgeoning civil rights movement echoed the emergence of independent African nations. No awareness of such historic changes was able to penetrate the popular market. Quite to the contrary, the twist craze was welcomed as a retreat from the worries of bomb shelters and an imagined ever more imminent war with the Soviet Union. Still, its leading exponent was a black man, however unthreatening, and it released middle-class white bodies from their repressed stiffness while anticipating more openly sexual dances like the "Monkey," the "Jerk," and the "Philly Dog." The twist craze was so powerful that major rhythm and blues artists and labels felt compelled to jump on the bandwagon. Sam Cooke recorded "Twist the Night Away" in 1962. The same year Gary

"U. S." Bonds released "Dear Lady Twist" and "Twist, Twist Senora." The Isley Brothers followed their classic "Shout" with "Twist and Shout," also in 1962. Atlantic Records reissued an album of old Ray Charles material as "Do the Twist with Ray Charles," which actually made the "Top Forty" album charts. More in the "schlock" mold, relative unknowns Little Eva and Dee Dee Sharp had hits with two twist spin-offs, "The Locomotion" and "Mashed Potato Time," respectively.

Even with a few refreshing breakthroughs among the dance-craze records like "Twist and Shout," the dominant trend was still "schlock," performed overwhelmingly by bland white singers. Because these performers were marketed as rock 'n' rollers, the connections between rock 'n' roll and rhythm and blues became less clear, which interestingly contributed to a resurgence of the latter as a separate style with crossover potential. Between 1959 and 1962, artists like Ray Charles ("What'd I Say," "Georgia on My Mind," "Hit the Road Jack," "Unchain My Heart"), Wilbert Harrison ("Kansas City"), Barrett Strong ("Money"), Jimmy Jones ("Handy Man," "Good Timin' "), and Gary "U. S." Bonds ("New Orleans," "Quarter to Three," "School Is Out") provided counterpoint to schlock in the pop market.

By the early sixties, rhythm and blues had moved "uptown," to use Gillett's term. In the hands of northern studio producers the rhythm and blues sensibility merged with lavish production to create a calculated effect. The style was established in Lieber and Stoller's pioneering work with the Drifters ("There Goes My Baby," "Dance With Me," "This Magic Moment," "Save the Last Dance for Me") in 1959–60. Developing the style further, independent producers like Luther Dixon, Phil Spector, and Berry Gordy rekindled the spirit of early rock 'n' roll, and the results were overwhelming. In 1962 there were more black acts on the year-end singles charts (but not the album charts) than at any time in history. Chiefly responsible were the recordings of a score of black female vocal groups known collectively as the "girl groups."

In the early sixties women became a recognized trend in rock 'n' roll for the first time, as the "girl groups," almost exclusively black women, began to hit the top of the charts. As talented as these new vocal groups were, their artistic appeal was almost invariably a product of the producers—such rising powers as Spector and Gordy—who molded their sound. In the 1962–63 period, the best-selling lists included groups like the Orlons ("The Wah Watusi," "Don't Hang Up," "South Street"), the Crystals ("He's a Rebel," "Da Doo Ron Ron," "Then He Kissed Me"), the Sensations ("Let Me In"), the Chiffons ("He's So Fine," "One Fine Day"), the Essex ("Easier Said Than Done"), the Ronnettes ("Be My Baby"), the Jaynettes ("Sally Go Round the Roses"), Ruby and the Romantics ("Our Day Will Come"), and the Motown groups like Martha and the Vandellas ("Come and Get These Memories," "Heat Wave," "Quicksand"), and the Marvelettes ("Please Mr. Postman," "Playboy"). By 1964 Motown's Supremes had also come into their own, turning out fifteen hit singles in a row over the next few years.

Prototypical of the "girl groups" were the Shirelles. The group first recorded for Decca, producing the hit "I Met Him on a Sunday." Decca had no faith in the group, however, and their next records were put out on Scepter Records. Scepter had been initially formed by Florence Greenberg, one of the very few women ever to emerge as a record company executive. Greenberg formed her company to handle the Shirelles, who had been classmates of her daughter in Passaic, New Jersey. Combining a plaintive gospel call-and-response style with the urban sensibilities of producer Luther Dixon, the Shirelles produced a string of rock 'n' roll classics between 1960 and 1962: "Will You Still Love Me Tomorrow," "Dedicated to the One I Love," "Mama Said," "Baby, It's You," and "Soldier Boy." By 1962 the commercial appeal of the female vocal groups had been proven and Dixon's production techniques, simultaneously developed by Phil Spector and Berry Gordy, had become a virtual science.

The reasons for the popularity of the girl groups lies largely in what they were *not*: "schlock rock." They were the diametric opposite of the other major trend of the time. Whereas the "schlock" scene was dominated by white male individuals, these acts were black female groups. The Angels and Shangri-Las were the only significant girl groups that were white. With their roots in gospel and rhythm and blues, and with historical ties to the "a cappella" style of the fifties vocal harmony groups, these women demonstrated considerable talent. Still, they were marketed as much for their sexual appeal as for their musical abilities. Remembering the Ronnettes, *Rolling Stone* wrote in 1968:

> They were the tough whorish females of the lower class, female Hell's Angels who had about them the aura of brazen sex. The Ronnettes were Negro Puerto Rican hooker types with long black hair and skin

tight dresses revealing their well-shaped but not quite Tina Turner behinds. . . . Ronnettes records should have been sold under the counter along with girly magazines and condoms.[57]

The other female groups may have been less brazen than the Ronnettes but they were often received in the same way. Charlie Gillett found that "the appeal was obvious as soon as the Shirelles were seen and heard, offering themselves with demure insistence and requiring only the easiest promises before giving themselves up with spine-tingling willingness."[58]

In their role as sex objects for the largely white rock 'n' roll audience, the girl groups were treated not unlike the blues women of the twenties. Although black male singers at the time were often effectively confined to clubs, these black women singers were allowed to record because they posed no threat to white male sexual standards. As Ortiz Walton explained:

> Mamie Smith was the first singer to make a Blues recording. It was so successful that record companies sought out a number of singers [female] hoping to get another Mamie Smith. Some of these "finds" were Eliza Brown, Ida Cox, Lil Green, Lucille Hegamin, Rosa Henderson, Victoria Spivey, Ethel Waters, and Edith Wilson. LeRoi Jones has astutely pointed out that the reason black women, rather than black men, were hired for these appearances is that America could always tolerate orgiastic interplay between white men and black women but could not stand white girls or women being titillated sexually by black men.[59]

The female vocal groups of the early sixties were different from the "schlock" roster in another way. The Philadelphia schlock rock crowd had few roots in anything that could be considered authentic rock 'n' roll. They were image stars, the creations of television. The female groups could be traced directly to the rhythm and blues and vocal group styles of the fifties and, as in fifties rock 'n' roll, the medium of their popularity was exclusively their records, not television. Like the vocal groups of the fifties, the female groups of the early sixties were anonymous. Women had no culture heroes of their own; they did not have role models who existed independent of relationships with men. The music of the "girl groups" did not talk about the women themselves but rather about those who were "Rebels" and "Leader(s) of the Pack." Restrictive gender roles had not yet been challenged. In the popular market, this was still the era of Saturday night dates, going steady, and nice girls who don't. The "girl groups" sang: "He's So Fine," I wish he would "Be My Baby;" when he called me on the phone I pleaded, "Don't Hang Up" until "One Fine Day" he walked me home and "Then He Kissed Me." I hoped that I'd be "Goin' to the Chapel," but of course, that was "Easier Said Than Done," "Da Doo Ron Ron Ron, Da Doo Ron Ron."

Aside from the blockbuster Motown acts, the "girl groups" were a short-lived phenomenon. After 1963 only the Chiffons ever had another "Top-Ten" single, "Sweet Talkin' Guy," in 1966. Despite their sophisticated production, these artists simply faced too many obstacles; they were in many ways a throwback to a fifties style, they were women, and they were black. They were simply unable to stand up to the onslaught of the Beatles and the "British Invasion." All the factors limiting the popularity of the girl groups helped the growth of the Beatles, white males performing in a more contemporary style, as well as being very competent musicians and brilliant songwriters. Like the other English invaders, their early sound was derived from black American music, and their inspirations and many early recordings were taken directly from black American artists.

Shortly after their introduction to America in 1963, the Beatles covered such black rock 'n' roll classics as "Roll Over Beethoven" by Chuck Berry, "Twist and Shout" by the Isley Brothers, Barret Strong's "Money," the Shirelles' "Boys," "You've Really Got a Hold on Me" by Smokey Robinson and the Miracles, and "Long Tall Sally" by Little Richard. Similarly, the Animals brought back Ray Charles's "Hit the Road Jack" and Sam Cooke's "Shake." The Rolling Stones did "Walking the Dog" by Rufus Thomas, "Hitchhike" by Marvin Gaye, a number of Chuck Berry tunes including "Carol," "Talking About You," and "Around and Around," and went deeper into the country blues genre with Slim Harpo's "I'm a King Bee." The Beatles were open about crediting black artists as their early influences, especially Chuck Berry, the Miracles, Chuck Jackson, and Ben E. King. But while openly and repeatedly acknowledging their debt to black music, and touring with black rhythm and blues greats like Little Richard, the Beatles, along with the dozens of other English groups that quickly followed them, were simply much more marketable than the black artists they admired and imitated.

Within two years of the Beatles' arrival, there were no less than twenty English rock groups on the American charts; before them there had been none. In April 1964, just four months after their introduction to America, Beatles' records were issued on five different labels, and they had twelve singles in *Billboard*'s "Hot 100," including the top five positions. Black acts in general showed a sharp decline on the singles charts from an all-time high of 42 percent in 1962 to 22 percent in 1966, the lowest point since the initial surge of rock 'n' roll in the mid-fifties. On the album charts, only three of the top fifty albums for the years 1964 and 1965 were by black artists.

Black Artists and the Civil Rights Era

In its early stages, the civil rights movement, as embodied by Dr. Martin Luther King, Jr., had two predominant themes: nonviolence and integration. As other, more militant tendencies developed in the black community, such a stance would soon appear to be quite moderate by comparison. At the time, however, it seemed to many that the primary task facing black people was to become integrated into the mainstream of American life. It was in this context that Motown developed and defined itself. The company soon "integrated" the popular charts with a success unmatched in the history of the record business.

Until its recent purchase by MCA, Motown was the largest black-owned corporation in the United States. It was founded in the early sixties by Berry Gordy, a middle-class jazz buff from Detroit, who intuitively recognized the commercial potential for highly produced black popular music. First, he evolved a production technique aimed at maximum crossover. Gordy once commented that any successful Motown hit sold at least 70 percent to white audiences. Working closely with Smokey Robinson on the label's early releases, he laid rich gospel harmonies over extravagant studio work with a strong bass line and came up with the perfect popular formula for the early civil rights era: upbeat black pop, that was acceptable to a white audience, and irresistibly danceable. This was the "Motown Sound."

Gordy organized his company as a completely in-house operation under his control. It included not only production but also writing, publishing, tour bookings, and personal management, including lessons on etiquette. Remembering the female director of the

Motown "charm school" in somewhat unflattering terms after she left the label, Martha Reeves recalled that "she taught us how to walk, how to sit proper, and how to get up. She'd have a line of us—the Marvelettes, the Supremes, and the Vandellas all learned together."[60] To his credit, Gordy built all of his acts from the ground up and groomed them for the long commercial haul; he did not simply bleed his talent for one or two hits, a practice all too common with black artists in the fifties. As a result, original Motown acts like the Miracles, the Supremes, the Temptations, and the Four Tops enjoyed a longevity that was unheard of for black artists in the pop market. While other labels may have treated a particularly successful group like the Platters with such care, only Motown approached its whole roster in these terms.

Motown didn't just produce successful records; they made classic "Top-Ten" hits too numerous to mention. The label's Detroit recording studio was aptly named "Hitsville, U.S.A." Key to producing hits was the understanding that on top forty radio, records were literally squeezed in between commercials and deejays who talked like used car salesmen. Typical of Motown's successful writers, Smokey Robinson sought to exercise maximum creativity within the constraints of the AM radio format. In his own words: "My theory of writing is to write a song that has a complete idea and tells a story in the time allotted for a record. . . . I've just geared myself to radio time. The shorter a record is nowadays, the more its gonna be played. This is a key thing in radio time, you dig? If you have a record that's 2:15 long it's definitely gonna get more play than one that's 3:15 *at first*, which is *very* important."[61]

In providing a commercial context for black artists that addressed all aspects of career development, Motown, in its initial stages, was clearly a progressive force in the music business. The original formula, however, became reified. The internal discipline and centralized control once necessary to the survival of the organization eventually became oppressive to writers, producers, and performers who had become successes in their own right. As Motown's artists matured, they came to resent Gordy's total control over their lives and work. *Fortune* magazine reported in 1967 that Gordy himself owned every single share of Motown stock. The company was grossing about $30 million per year at the time. A number of important musicians left the label. As Martha Reeves explained: "The company grew, the tree got weak, and the limbs started falling off.   The first limb that fell off the tree was Brenda Holloway. That's when it started happening—Florence Ballard [of the Supremes].   Then the leaves started falling off, everybody felt it."[62] What had begun as a haven for black singers and songwriters became artistically constraining.   As late as 1971, *Rolling Stone*'s Jon Landau noted that "of all the major record companies, only Motown remains a completely in-house operation.   One has the feeling, whether it's true or not, that Berry Gordy passes personal judgment on every single that comes out on his label."[63]

In addition to controlling artistic freedom, there is some evidence of financial malfeasance on Gordy's part.   In 1968 Holland, Dozier, and Holland, the company's most successful writer-producer team, sued the corporation for $22 million, charging "conspiracy, fraud, deceit, overreaching, and breach of fiduciary relationships."[64]   They stopped producing for Gordy.   David Ruffin of the Temptations was allegedly fired for asking "hard" questions about financial affairs. According to Ruffin, when the Temptations were earning $10 thousand a night, the group members were only being paid $500 a week.   Eddie Kendericks left the Temptations in sympathy with Ruffin, but he could not leave the label.   "They have me," he commented in 1971, "I think they even own my face." As to how much artistic freedom he was allowed, he said simply, "None."[65] Martha Reeves complained that she never handled her own finances. "I always had a road manager who collected my money and took it back to Motown, with a green sheet.   When the money ran out I couldn't pay the Vandellas anymore and I lost the Vandellas."[66] Even during the height of her group's popularity, Reeves claims she was paid only $200 a week.   In 1974 she got a release from Motown after MCA, her new label, paid Motown some $200 thousand in past debts, and she set about rebuilding her career.   The Four Tops and Gladys Knight and the Pips left when their contracts ran out.

Important exceptions to the initial exodus of name talent were Stevie Wonder and the late Marvin Gaye, both long time successful Motown artists.   For both, the struggle to gain artistic freedom was hard-fought.   As soon as he turned twenty-one in 1972, Stevie Wonder reacted against Motown's restrictiveness by demanding his royalty payments, a sum of about $1 million (representing, on sales of some 30 million units, a very low royalty rate of about 3.3 percent) that had been held in trust for him by Gordy.   Independent of Motown, he spent about $250 thousand of this money on the production of his first progressive album, "Music of My Mind" in 1972. Following its overwhelming success, he returned to the label, but under much more favorable conditions. Wonder gained control of his own publishing rights and was the first Motown artist to do so. Marvin Gaye also came a long way from the days when Motown paid him "five dollars a side" for some early sessions. Always seen as a maverick, Gaye resisted Motown's formula mentality right from the beginning: "I didn't like the feeling of being made to do something, simply because a bunch of people said that this is what I should do, as though I'm a robot and couldn't think for myself or didn't know what I liked or disliked, and the biggest insult was that they always claimed they recognized me as a talent, but they never proved it by letting me do my own thing."[67]

Unlike Stevie Wonder, Gaye's sense of loyalty (he was married to Anna Gordy) would not permit him to leave the label at that time. But years of stubbornness succeeded in getting the company to back his first concept album, "What's Goin' On," followed by "Let's Get It On," both million sellers in the seventies. Through such experiences with Gay and Wonder, Motown began to learn that loosening the reins could add millions to their coffers.

Motown enjoyed a second generation of success in the youth market with the Jackson Five. But their early hits, "I Want You Back," "ABC," "The Love You Save," "I'll Be There," "Mamma's Pearl," "Never Can Say Goodbye," and "Sugar Daddy" were a throwback to Motown formula production. Eventually the Jacksons, Marvin Gaye, and even Diana Ross left the label under strained conditions. Ross is recording successfully for RCA. After a series of personal and professional problems, including a self-imposed exile in Belgium, Gaye engineered something of a comeback with the success of his million-selling Epic album, "Midnight Love" and its Grammy award-winning single "Sexual Healing," prior to his death on 1 April 1984. The Jacksons (minus Jermaine, who went to Arista) also left Motown for Epic, where Michael went on to achieve his greatest success as a solo artist with "Thriller," currently the largest-selling album in history.

All the Motown artists were briefly reunited when the company celebrated its twenty-fifth anniversary on 16 May 1984. Broadcast on NBC-TV, the show was not without its tensions. Michael Jackson, for example, agreed to appear only after Motown consented to let him perform his hit single "Billie Jean," the only non-Motown song of the evening. Still, Diana Ross captured the feeling of the event when she announced to her former boss who was sitting in the audience: "It's not about who leaves, it's about who comes back. And tonight, everybody came back." For the most part, the celebration recalled the spirit and enthusiasm of Motown in its prime.

While an enterprise like Motown was encouraged by the climate of the early civil rights movement, Motown never became a "voice" for the cause. At the time, civil rights themes were evident primarily in the folk arena. Of critical importance in linking "folk consciousness" with pop appeal was the often underappreciated Curtis Mayfield. Early in his career, Mayfield left the gospel choir for the secular world of popular music, there to become, in the words of Nelson George, "black music's most unflagging civil rights champion."[68] With his pop/gospel trio, the Impressions, Mayfield achieved major pop successes with a series of "sermon" songs like "Keep on Pushing" and "Amen" in 1964, and "People Get Ready" in 1965, "We're a Winner" in 1968, and "Choice of Colors" in 1969. In 1964, Sam Cooke attempted a similar fusion with "A Change is Gonna Come." By the time the record was released as a single, though, Cooke had already been shot to death. When his friend Malcolm X was assassinated on 21 February 1965, just two months later, "A Change is Gonna Come" was a pop hit. It stands as Cooke's monument to civil rights.

As the moderate civil rights movement gave way to the more militant demand for "black power," Motown's hegemony over black pop was successfully challenged by a resurgence of closer-to-the-roots, hard-driving rhythm and blues recorded in the Memphis-Muscle Shoals region of the Deep South. Chiefly responsible for the popularization of this grittier rhythm and blues music was a temporary but highly successful collaboration between Atlantic Records and a number of southern studios, most notably Stax-Volt in Memphis and Fame in Muscle Shoals. The fruits of this collaboration captured the spirit of the emerging black militancy not so much in content as in tone. From 1965 on, artists like Otis Redding ("I've Been Loving You Too Long"), Wilson Pickett ("In the Midnight Hour"), Sam and Dave ("Soul Man"), Arthur Conley ("Sweet Soul Music"), and Percy Sledge ("When a Man Loves a Woman") were prominent among the new chart toppers. Their recordings were raw, basic, almost angry, and much less "produced" than the cleaner, brighter Motown sound.

Striking differences between Motown and southern soul can be seen in a comparison of Motown and its chief competitor—Stax. Both founded in 1960, Motown was as secretive and tightly controlled as Stax was open and disorganized. Stax was originally a white-owned company; its creative functions were as likely to be handled by whites as by blacks, and the "Memphis sound" they spawned was almost invariably the product of cross-racial teamwork. Initially the credits on all Stax recordings read simply: "produced by the Stax staff." Motown was not only black-owned, but virtually all of its creative personnel—artists, writers, producers, and session musicians—were black as well. It was clearly a haven for black talent. Paradoxically, Motown is remembered by Nelson George as being "totally committed to reaching white audiences," while Stax recordings, by contrast, were "consistently aimed at r&b fans first, the pop market second."[69]

In the context of black pride, Motown's lavish use of multitrack studio production to achieve a more "pop" sound seemed somehow out of sync with the search for African roots. Commenting on the difference in styles between Stax-Volt and Motown, Otis Redding once said:

> Motown does a lot of overdubbing. It's mechanically done. At Stax the rule is: whatever you feel, play it. We cut together, horns, rhythms, and vocal. We'll do it three or four times and listen to the results and pick the best one. If somebody doesn't like a line in the song we'll go back and cut the whole song over. Until last year [1967], we didn't even have a four track tape recorder. You can't overdub on a one track machine.[70]

In many ways, it was the very simplicity and straightforwardness of southern soul production that gave the music its claim on authenticity. When this sound crossed over into the pop market, it wasn't because the music had changed, it was because black pride had briefly created a climate wherein unrefined rhythm and blues could find mainstream acceptance on its own terms.

With southern soul in its ascendency, unencumbered production was soon joined by social consciousness in black popular music. In January of 1967, Aretha Franklin was signed to Atlantic Records and after one legendary session in Muscle Shoals, she found her sound. Later that spring she cut a version of what had been Otis

Redding's signature tune. "Respect" was instantly "transformed from a demand for conjugal rights into a soaring cry of freedom."[71] Shortly thereafter, Aretha was crowned "Lady Soul." The vocal and emotional range of her early Atlantic releases ("Baby, I Love You," "Natural Woman," "Chain of Fools," and "Think," to name a few) uniquely expressed all the passion and forcefulness of the era.

> Aretha did not pray like Mahalia for the endurance to make it on through, nor make you believe her pain as Billie Holiday had. The statement black artists wished to make had changed, the blues had been transfigured by anger and pride. Aretha's music was a celebration, she was "earthmother" exhorting, preacher woman denouncing, militant demanding, forgotten woman wailing. She was black, she was beautiful, and she was the best. Someone called that time in 1967 the summer of "Retha, Rap, and revolt."[72]

The career of James Brown is perhaps the most dramatic parallel to the trajectory of black politics. In the 1950s he was an ambitious and headstrong rhythm and blues artist whose music was intended for, and in many ways confined to, the black audience. At the time of his first "Top-Ten" pop hit, "Papa's Got a Brand New Bag" (1965), he billed himself, with some justification, as "the hardest working man in show business." By 1968, he was "Soul Brother No. 1." When he came to the attention of the white audience, he did so on his own terms. His string of uncompromising "Top-Ten" hits ("I Got You," "It's a Man's Man's Man's World," "Cold Sweat," "I Got the Feelin' ") made fewer concessions to mainstream sensibilities than any other music in the pop market. His connection to black pride was made explicit in his hit single of the same year, "Say it Loud—I'm Black and I'm Proud," which became an anthem in the struggle for black liberation. Critic Robert Palmer described this music as follows:

> With no chord changes and precious little melodic variety to sustain listener interest, rhythm became everything. Brown and his musicians and arrangers began to treat every instrument and voice in the group as if each were a drum. The horns played single-note bursts that were often sprung against the downbeats. The bass lines were broken up into choppy two- or three-note patterns, a procedure common in Latin music but rare in R & B. Brown's rhythm guitarist choked his guitar strings against the instrument's neck so hard that his playing began to sound like a jagged tin can being scraped with a pocketknife. Only

occasionally were the horns, organ or backing vocalists allowed to provide a harmonic continuum by holding a chord.[73]

This was prototypical "funk" and, through it, James Brown has been cited as a formative influence in the music of a formidable array of black talent, including the early Commodores, the Blackbyrds, Earth, Wind and Fire, the Ohio Players, the various incarnations of George Clinton's Parliament-Funkadelic empire (which included James Brown alumni bassist Bootsy Collins, saxman Maceo Parker, and trombonist Fred Wesley), pioneer rappers Grandmaster Flash and Afrika Bambaataa, and "punk-funk" artist Rick James.

In the sixties, the group that created the most successful fusion of funk and pop was Sly and the Family Stone. Based in countercultural San Francisco, the group was integrated not only racially, like its music, but sexually as well. Between 1968 and 1971, they recorded a series of "Top Ten" pop hits including "Dance to the Music" (1968), "Everyday People" and "Hot Fun in the Summertime" (1969), "Thank You (Falletinme Be Mice Elf Agin)" (1970), and "Family Affair" (1971), which united the funk and rock cultures in a way that no other artists had been able to accomplish. After 1971, the group's popularity began to decline, owing primarily to Sly's drug-induced personality changes and irregular personal appearances.

Another black artist who embraced the hippie counterculture was a rhythm and blues guitarist from Seattle named Jimi Hendrix. Hendrix was a virtuoso guitarist who started as a teenager in the 1950s as a sideman for acts like the Isley Brothers. But he never found an audience for his early American guitar playing, so he went to England, where he developed a caricatured sexual image and a more extravagant guitar style. Guitarist Eric Clapton described his rise to popularity: "He had the whole combination in England. It was just what the market needed, a psychedelic pop star who looked freaky, and they're also hung up about spades and the blues thing was there. So Jimi walked in, put on all the gear, and made it straight away. It was a perfect formula."[74]

Hendrix brought his English success back to the United States, where he made millions of dollars selling millions of albums, virtually all in the white market. Toward the end of his career, he tried to reorient his music, but the business interests surrounding him pressured him not to change his commercial, psychedelic, oversexed black-man image. The situation drove Hendrix not only to chemical excesses, but also to his Electric Ladyland studios, where he logged some eight hundred hours of tape exploring fusions of jazz, rhythm and blues, and contemporary rock styles with musicians like Miles Davis, John McLaughlin, and other avant-garde jazz notables. None of these tapes was released during Hendrix's lifetime and he never attracted a black audience to the music with which he was identified.

The young whites who idolized Hendrix were "turning on, tuning in, and dropping out," at a time when the black community was becoming more militant and directed in its political activity. While Hendrix was surrendering to the siren call of strawberry fields, James Brown was being courted by the political establishment as ambassador to the street. In 1970 he was quoted in *Rolling Stone* as saying: "Me and Nixon don't get along. He asked me to go along to Memphis in the campaign. I don't want to be his bullet proof vest. I didn't want to protect him from my people, deceive them. Make them think he's with me and I'm with him."[75] But Brown's sympathies soon changed. In 1972 he endorsed Richard Nixon for the presidency. The move hurt his credibility in the traditionally Democratic black community. Soul Brother No. 1 became, in the eyes of his critics, Sold Brother No. 1. Later, changes in popular taste associated with the rise of disco nearly brought his career to a halt. His last pop hit of the decade was, ironically enough, "Papa Don't Take No Mess" (1974).

James Brown had been wooed by the political power structure long before his endorsement of Nixon. On 4 April 1968, the day Martin Luther King was assassinated, he was booked into the Boston Garden. Faced with potentially uncontrollable racial tension, the city made it possible for the show to be broadcast on public television, which kept Boston cool—at least for one evening. He was also flown to Washington, D.C., in 1968, to appeal to rioting youngsters there. Growing black militance had focused the attention of government and the business community on the music industry as one desirable structure for coopting black revolt. The appeal the Nixon administration held for Brown was the president's endorsement of "black capitalism."

The idea of black capitalism has long been kicked around in political circles as a palliative for the inequities in the distribution of wealth and power in the United States. In those areas where blacks are traditionally allowed to achieve (precisely because they are fields penetrated by individuals, not masses of people) such as sports and entertainment, the idea is a particularly persistent one. But, as we have already seen in the example of Motown, black capitalist solutions to the plight of black artists are often a mixed blessing. Success may be won for a few individuals, but often at the price of artistic constraint and economic exploitation, with little or no economic benefit to the black community as a whole. The advancement of the black capitalism strategy in the music business in the late sixties followed a similar pattern. There ensued a flurry of rhetoric and action over the next few years that ultimately produced far more in the way of headlines than anything resembling long-term change in the internal structure of the industry.

In May of 1969 New York Senator Jacob Javits gave a speech before a Recording Industry Association of America (RIAA) conference wherein he expressed the "hope that the industry ... will move forward ... by striking a resounding vote for black capitalism."[76] At the 1969 convention of the National Association of Television and Radio Announcers (NATRA) that same year, Stan Gortikov, then president of Capitol, publicly accused the industry of being "too damned white."[77] Employing a variety of tactics that ranged from cajoling to rational appeals, various parts of government and big business seemed willing to support a program to make the music business a model of integration. *Billboard* wrote editorials urging the industry to hire more African Americans. The Federal Communications Commission notified radio stations that they would have to integrate at the disc jockey and executive levels. In 1969 Stax-Volt, which at this time was owned by Gulf and Western, announced an outreach program aimed at recording black acts. By 1971, Warner and Capitol had followed suit, opening recording studios in ghetto areas. In the early seventies another breakthrough of sorts came in black films. Movies like "Shaft," "Superfly," and "Troubleman," the so-called blaxploitation flicks, were musically scored by Isaac Hayes, Curtis Mayfield, and Marvin Gaye respectively.

Perhaps the boldest step during this period was taken by United Artist (UA) records, which turned to FM radio stations to market their black artists. United Artists had distinguished itself with a roster of extremely talented and successful black acts (for example, War, Ike and Tina Turner, and Bobby Womack) that it claimed to market with its white rock artists rather than in the more limited rhythm and blues network. The most spectacular of the UA success stories was War. With five platinum albums and more than $33 million in record sales, War was another important exception to the rule that it is necessary to cater to white audience tastes in order to generate significant album sales in the popular market. *Billboard* magazine attributed the group's success to a young and more sophisticated black record-buying public. This analysis is limited, however, since any album selling multimillions of units has to be selling in the white market as well. United Artists claimed credit for their nondiscriminatory marketing technique. It is difficult to explain the staggering success of the band, but there is some evidence that UA was not all that it claimed to be. In 1974, War initiated legal proceedings to buy their way out of their contract with the company, presumably because of its very low royalty rate. Another of UA's major artists, Bobby Womack, who had a million-selling single with "Understanding," said: "I think my company stinks. . . . They say, 'Hey man, Don Mclean is the one,' and I say, 'Yeah, man, but look how long he's been holding the ball and y'all done thrown the sink on him and everything, shit on him, and this nigger's still selling with nothing. You gave me what you give him in terms of promotion and Bobby Womack would be a superstar.' "[78]

Many record companies also experimented with black promotion men during this period and kept them when they found they sold better to hip FM disc jockeys than their white counterparts. In 1970 Mario Medious was an undistinguished black employee in the sales department at Warner; by 1972, he was the "Big M," with a full-page story in *Rolling Stone* devoted to Warner's new crack promotion man. These innovations in the promotion of records were not planned in advance by the major, white-controlled record companies, but evolved as a better procedure for marketing new records. Although black promotion men were used to push records, the main avenues of talent promotion, the concert circuit and radio, were still fully run by whites.

In 1972, four years into the "back to black capitalism" movement, artist Jerry Butler complained that there were only three veteran black concert promoters in the entire country: Teddy Powell in New York, Regal Sports in St. Louis, and Henry Winn in Atlanta. The promoter system that operated in the 1970s grew out of the white psychedelic ballroom circuit of the late sixties, moved into colleges, and then developed into a commercial network of concert halls and coliseums. The black community did not have enough money to sustain an entirely separate concert circuit, and many white promoters complained of racial tension when they presented black acts. As a result, many booking agencies developed a standing policy of not packaging black and white acts together. Because of audience and promoter racism, many black artists were effectively excluded from the dominant concert network.

Radio in fact marched backward from the late sixties through the early seventies. Despite all the industry pronouncements about affirmative action in hiring black deejays on pop stations, there was little if any increased representation of African Americans in radio. Further, there was actually a cutback in the proportion of black music that was played on radio. In 1969 *Billboard* announced: "Soul Cut on Top 40 Stations." Commenting on the decision among many AM stations to limit black music, Jerry Wexler said: "Radio stations who were serving their audience, or so they thought, didn't want to burden them with the sound of breaking glass in Watts or the sirens coming from Detroit, which was what R&B music meant at the time. In their opinion, R&B would be disturbing to their middle-class listeners, so they took most of it off the radio."[79]

As the more radical elements in the black community were systematically neutralized, there was a corresponding decline in the popularity of the more militant-sounding rhythm and blues from the Deep South. Reflecting the "quieter" mood of the early 1970s, the black popular music that came to the fore was the "soft soul" sound pioneered by the Philadelphia-based writer-producer team of Kenny Gamble and Leon Huff, and producer-arranger Thom Bell. Joining forces with Sigma Sound Studios in Philadelphia, they developed a style in the late 1960s which they described as "not as bluesy as the Memphis/Muscle Shoals stuff, not as pop as Detroit." Working with artists like Jerry Butler, the Intruders, and the Delphonics, Gamble and Huff parlayed a seven hundred dollar bank loan into thirty million-selling singles in a five-year period, with twenty-two records on the charts in 1968 alone. In 1970 Gamble and Huff grossed over one million dollars. The Delfonics' classic 1968 hit, "La La Means I Love You," was a harbinger of sounds to come. But the Philadelphia enterprise did not hit its stride until 1971, with the formation of Philadelphia International Records (PIR) and a distribution deal with CBS. Employing lush orchestral arrangements over a polite rhythmic pulse, groups like Harold Melvin and the Blue Notes ("If You Don't Know Me By Now"), the O'Jays ("Back Stabbers," "Love Train"), the Stylistics ("You Make Me Feel Brand New"), and the Spinners ("Could It Be I'm Falling in Love") set the standard in black pop for the next few years. Other artists, like the Chicago-based Chi-Lites ("Oh Girl") and the ever-changing Isley Brothers ("That Lady") soon followed suit. Even southern soul yielded the velvety smooth Al Green ("Let's Stay Together," "I'm Still in Love with You"). Of course, the pop Motown sound of artists like the Supremes and the Temptations continued to be popular.

Once this softer, pop-oriented, and less "disturbing" black music came to dominate the market, black artists skyrocketed to 44 percent on the year-end singles charts in 1972 and experienced a steady increase in numbers on the album charts, peaking in 1975 with an unprecedented 28 percent. As has often been the case during periods of repression, however, other developments in black music were occurring underground. The next major trend would surface as disco.

From Disco to Rap:
High Technology Meets the Streets

With significant influences from the gay and Latino communities, early disco must be understood primarily as part of the continuing development of black dance music. As journalist Barbara Graustark pointed out: "At the start, disco was an amalgam of pirated songs. In black, Latin and gay all-night clubs on Fire Island, in New York City and San Francisco, disc jockeys would create nonstop dance music by weaving together twenty-minute medleys of tunes by Diana Ross, Barry White, The Temptations and Marvin Gaye."[80] During this underground phase, disco was simply called "party music." As it began to evolve into its own musical genre, its sources of inspiration came from far and wide. Early on it seemed like self-contained funk bands such as Kool and the Gang ("Funky Stuff," "Jungle Boogie," "Hollywood Swinging"), the Ohio Players ("Skin Tight," "Fire"), and Earth, Wind, and Fire ("Shining Star") would make a major contribution. But, as disco developed into a more "upscale" trend, the "cruder" sensuality of post–Sly, James

Brown-inspired funk was eventually eclipsed by the smoother, sleeker sounds associated with Philadelphia and the more controlled energy of what came to be known as Eurodisco.

Most of the early disco releases in the United States were by black artists. Among those which made the rare crossover from clubs to radio were "Soul Makossa" (1973), an obscure French import by Manu Dibango, "Rock the Boat" (1974) by the Hues Corporation, and George McRae's "Rock Your Baby" (1974). Perhaps the first disco hit to reach the charts *as disco* was Gloria Gaynor's 1974 release, "Never Can Say Good-bye," reportedly one of the first records especially mixed for the discos. The widespread popularity of Donna Summer's "Love to Love You Baby" (1975) moved disco closer to the surface. And by 1975 Van McCoy and The Soul City Orchestra had established the Hustle as the most important new dance craze since the twist.

Even at this level of success, disco was largely ignored by the established recording industry. Reported Andrew Kopkind in the *Village Voice*:

> [T]he record companies seemed bewildered by what they had and promo people continued their quirky disregard of the disco category in their portfolios. Instead, they inflated passing fancies into seismic cultural events: Peter Frampton, reggae, and punk, for example. Not that some of those sounds or stars lacked merit; certainly Springsteen, Bob Marley, and the best of the New Wave deserve seats high in rock and roll heaven. But disco would soon swamp them all, and nobody was watching.[81]

With no promotional support forthcoming from the record companies, disco had little hope of gaining access to the airwaves. The one exception to the rule was New York's top black station, WBLS, where deejay Frankie Crocker, remembered as the Alan Freed of disco, was responsible for crossing over many of the early disco hits from clubs to radio. But WBLS was clearly an exception. For the most part, disco was systematically excluded from radio. Forced to remain underground in this way, it continued to receive its primary exposure in clubs popularized only by the creative genius of the disco deejays:

> [T]he club DJs prided themselves on psyching out a crowd and then programming them into an ecstatic frenzy, slip-cuing records into a continuous sequence and equalizing them for dancing by boosting the bass. The top DJs became taste-making alchemists-engineers with cults that followed them from club to club.[82]

Like the music they played, these turntable wizards were initially shunned by the record companies. The labels did not supply the club deejays with records in the same way that they would serve a radio station. Instead, the club deejays were expected to make the rounds to each label individually in order to get records. Consequently, the deejays organized themselves into record pools, central distribution points where music could be discussed and new tastes created. Through this network of record pools and nightclubs, disco quickly developed an alternative to the airplay marketing structure of the business. It represented the first time since early rock 'n' roll that the music industry had been taken by surprise.

Disco's fanatical following turned out to be not only an underground party culture but also a significant record-buying public. Disco deejays, it turned out, could break hits from the dance floor. Such hits were capable of selling tens of thousands of copies in New York City alone with virtually no radio play, an outstanding achievement in an industry that had committed billions of dollars to the airplay system of marketing. As early as 1976, the year-end pop charts were bursting with disco acts like The Silver Convention ("Fly, Robin, Fly," "Get Up and Boogie"), Hot Chocolate ("You Sexy Thing"), Wild Cherry ("Play That Funky Music"), K.C. and the Sunshine Band ("Shake Your Booty"), Rhythm Heritage ("Theme from S.W.A.T."), Sylvers ("Boogie Fever"), Johnny Taylor ("Disco Lady"), Maxine Nightengale ("Right Back Where We Started From"), and, of course, Donna Summer. It is worth noting that most of these acts were black.

During the next year and a half or so, disco continued to demonstrate its commercial potential from the bottom up. Artists such as the Emotions ("Best of My Love"), Thelma Houston ("Don't Leave Me This Way"), Rose Royce ("Car Wash"), Brick ("Dazz"), Hot ("Angel in Your Arms"), Taste of Honey ("Boogie Oogie Oogie"), Peter Brown ("Dance with Me"), Yvonne Elliman ("If I Can't Have You"), Chic ("Dance, Dance, Dance"), and Heatwave ("The Groove Line") swelled disco's ranks on the year-end singles charts. Again, in the absence of sustained national exposure via radio, many of these disco releases achieved hit status on the basis of regional sales. And, again, most of the performers were black.

In keeping with the popular music tradition of black innovation and white popularization, it was not until a white supergroup—in this case the Bee Gees—came to dominate the scene that the disco juggernaut finally took on the mantle of respectability. Commenting from the vantage point of 1979, culture analyst Andrew Kopkind observed: "This past year has seen several disco stars achieve the necessary 'crossover' effect, bringing the music out of the subcultural ghettoes into mainstream life. The Bee Gees were crucial to that passage; they made disco safe for white, straight, male, young, and middle-class America. What Elvis Presley did for black rhythm and blues, . . . the Brothers Gibb have done for disco."[83]

Given the unprecedented success of the movie "Saturday Night Fever" ($130 million gross in its initial U.S. run) and the sound track of the same name (15 million copies sold in the United States; 30 million worldwide), disco became impossible to ignore any longer. Artists of all persuasions jumped on the disco bandwagon. Cher's Casablanca entry, "Take Me Home," reached no. 8 on the pop charts. Dolly Parton contributed "Baby I'm Burnin'." Even jazz flutist Herbie Mann had a disco hit, with "Superman." Perhaps the most noticeable disco converts were the Rolling Stones, whose "Miss You" sold two million copies, and Rod Stewart, who scored the best-selling single of his career with "Do Ya Think I'm Sexy?" With such guaranteed hit-makers as these on board, radio and television soon followed suit.

The full commercial potential of disco was realized when WKTU, an obscure "soft rock" station in New York, converted to an all-disco format. Within months, WKTU went from a dreary 0.9 percent share of the market to an unprecedented 11.3 percent share, making it the most listened to station in the country. That was in December 1978, and by March 1979 there were some two hundred disco stations broadcasting in almost every major market from Miami to Los Angeles. Syndicated television programs like "Disco Magic" and "Dance Fever" brought the dancing craze to the heartland.

Disco had clearly taken over. Different sources estimated that disco accounted for somewhere between 20 percent and 40 percent of *Billboard*'s chart action. Disco records captured eight of the fourteen pop Grammy awards in 1979. Some thirty-six million adults thrilled to the musical mixes of eight thousand professional deejays who served a portion of the estimated twenty thousand disco clubs. In the process, the phenomenon spawned an industry with annual revenues ranging from four to eight billion dollars.

The music business may have been slow to catch on to disco

but, always hungry for a new trend, it soon replicated the successful
120 beat-per-minute formula ad nauseum. The entire disco apparatus was harnessed in the service of industry profits. Record pools,
first organized as a collective response to industry indifference, now
served as indispensible marketing tools, supplying the record companies with crucial demographic data. Everything from Glenn
Miller's "Chattanooga Choo-Choo" to Beethoven's "Fifth Symphony," to the theme from "Star Wars," fell prey to the relentless
disco thumping. Percy Faith even recorded a disco version of "Hava
Nagila." In the hands of the industry, disco seemed to sweep up
everything in its wake.

Many black artists began to complain that they had no alternative
but to submit to the demand for disco. "We're in a period of
McDonald's of music, where it's mass-marketed like junk food,"
lamented Melba Moore, who had a "Top Forty" disco hit with "You
Stepped into My Life," "I don't know what *good* is any more."[84]
In a given week, as many as forty of *Billboard*'s "Hot 100" were
disco releases. With the market saturated to this degree, there was
bound to be a backlash. And given disco's particular history, it
was bound to have racial overtones.

The most visceral anti-disco reactions came from the hard rock/
heavy metal axis of popular music. FM rock radio followed its
audience almost instinctively by initiating anti-disco campaigns.
Slogans like "Death to Disco" and "Disco Sucks" were as much
racial epithets as they were statements of musical preference. Even
after disco as a distinct musical style began to collapse under its
own weight, the racism associated with the anti-disco sentiment
was simply generalized to other forms of black music. As explained
by *Los Angeles Times* critic Robert Hilburn:

> Where young rock fans traditionally find identity or strength in the
> communal celebration of specific genres of rock (punk, heavy metal),
> much of the energy in the mid- and late 70's was suddenly directed
> against something. "Death to Disco" became a rallying cry. In its
> enthusiasm, a large percentage of this white audience equated anything
> black with dance floor trend.
>   Rock-oriented radio stations could have educated this young audience
> on the historical link between rock and black music by programming
> classic Motown-Stax-Hendrix tracks or the rock-oriented tracks by such
> contemporary black stars as Stevie Wonder, Prince, Donna Summer, and
> Rick James. Eager to be culturally in tune with their listenership,
> however, the stations carelessly picked up on the anti-disco sentiment

and fell into racist programming policies: They simply stopped playing all black records.[85]

Following the lead of consultant Lee Abrams, who conceived the radio format known as Album Oriented Rock (AOR), rock radio reasserted its primacy (and its racism). Black-oriented radio was forced to move in the direction of a new format—Urban Contemporary.

Urban Contemporary, it must be admitted, is an interesting concept in that it was designed as a multiracial format. In its original conception, black artists in the soul, funk, and jazz categories, such as Stevie Wonder, Donna Summer, Rick James, Third World, Funkadelic, Quincy Jones, and George Benson remained central to a station's playlist and white acts that fit the format, like David Bowie or Hall and Oates, were added. For a time the UC stations proved to be quite successful, surpassing even the AOR outlets in some instances. Still, in its historical context, there is a sense in which Urban Contemporary simply institutionalized a process of "reverse crossover" that had begun during the heyday of disco radio. While UC provided greater access for white musicians on what had been black-oriented stations, black performers did not gain any reciprocal access to rock radio. From this perspective, Urban Contemporary may well have proven to be a net loss for black artists. By the end of 1982 black artists had plummeted to 16 percent on the year-end pop singles charts (their lowest showing since 1956) and an even more dismal 11 percent on the album charts.

The rock press simply continued its systematic lack of coverage of black artists. From 1978 to 1982 *Rolling Stone*, for example, pictured only one black musician on its cover—vocalist Donna Summer. Publisher Jann Wenner made clear the racial dimension of this practice when his magazine finally ran a cover story on Prince. "My circulation department certainly wasn't asking me to put Prince on the cover," explained Wenner. "They know the issue of color works against him. It's a fact of life that the stars of 'The Jeffersons' aren't going to sell as well as Tom Selleck."[86] If the industry was moving in the general direction of narrowing access for black artists, the practice of excluding them almost completely emerged as a full-blown policy in the creation of the most powerful music outlet ever to be developed—MTV.

MTV, the first twenty-four-hour music video cable channel, was launched on 1 August 1981, by Warner Communications and The American Express Company. With less than 40 percent of the country wired for cable, MTV, the fastest growing cable channel in history, was soon reaching some 15 million subscribers and was unquestionably the most effective way for a record to get national exposure.

MTV's music videos were to be programmed strictly on the basis of extensive market research designed to target the musical preferences and buying habits of the young rock 'n' roll audience. For its advertisers, MTV claimed to deliver the perfect consumers: "85 percent of its viewers are between 12 and 34 years old."[87] Described by MTV Marketing Vice President Marshall Cohen as "the most researched channel in history," MTV stands as a testament to the racist implications of the pseudoscience of demographics, or as Chief Executive Bob Pittman calls it, "psychographics." In 1983 *People* magazine reported that "on MTV's current roster of some 800 acts, 16 are black."[88] MTV executives defended this practice on the basis of the channel's format, claiming that few black artists recorded the kind of rock 'n' roll that MTV was programming. This argument is, of course, circular: if the channel is formatted according to the tastes of a largely white, suburban audience in the first place, then the format can not be used as a way of explaining away the racial bias. The format is precisely the *cause* of the racial bias.

Perhaps the most blatant act of racial exclusion was MTV's rejection of five Rick James videos at a time when his album *Street Songs* had sold almost four million copies. An MTV spokesperson gave the standard reply: "We play rock and roll. We don't play Rick James because he's funk."[89] The response was particularly unconvincing in this instance because MTV was playing Prince heavily at the time. Trying to split musical hairs between Prince ("Little Red Corvette," "1999") and Rick James ("Super Freak") as a way of setting limits on one's definition of rock 'n' roll was at best an exercise in futility. One possible explanation for this seemingly irrational distinction was the fact that Prince recorded for Warner, one of MTV's parent companies, while Rick James appeared on Motown. In any case, as of 1983, MTV had yet to air a Rick James video.

It was Michael Jackson and the incredible success of the *Thriller* LP that finally destroyed MTV's format argument. With sales estimated at thirty-three million copies worldwide, *Thriller* had become the largest selling album in history; its crossover appeal was readily apparent. But even with this kind of acceptance, MTV was initially reluctant to air the video of "Billie Jean." Whether it was the overwhelming popularity of the record that changed MTV's mind, or the widespread, but officially denied, rumor that CBS Records threatened to pull all of its videos from MTV unless they aired the Jackson tape, the fact is that "Billie Jean," soon followed by "Beat It" and "Thriller," became some of the most popular videos ever aired on MTV.

While the obvious acceptance of the Michael Jackson videos relaxed the color line on MTV somewhat, the situation for black artists did not get appreciably better. In July 1983 *Rock & Roll Confidential* reported the following statistics based on a tally of *Billboard*'s MTV listings for the week of 16 July:

— Number of black artists with new videos added: zero
— Black artists in Heavy Rotation: 2 (neither by U.S. artists)
— Medium Rotation: 1 (not by a U.S. artist)
— Light Rotation: 1 (that old category-stomper, Donna Summer)
— Number of black performers with MTV concerts or specials in the history of the channel is still zero.[90]

Far from taking its cue from Michael Jackson's success and using the occasion of his acceptance to showcase other black acts, MTV devoted a significant portion of its airtime to breaking white rock acts from other countries. Australia's Men at Work, for example, owed their American success completely to MTV exposure. Beginning in 1982 with Adam Ant, MTV showcased so many English groups, including Eurythmics, Billy Idol, Duran Duran, Culture Club, and Def Leppard, among many others, that it contributed significantly to what can only be described as the Second British Invasion. By the mid-eighties, a number of new music video outlets had formed in reaction to MTV's restrictive programming policies. Black Entertainment Television (BET) and the long-standing Soul Train have provided the primary video exposure for black acts.

Throughout this period, black artists continued to move in different directions. The more traditional soul artists like Smokey Robinson, Stevie Wonder, and Diana Ross began to reappear on the pop charts. Some black artists, most notably Prince and Tina Turner, moved in a rock-oriented direction. And a whole new style of black music, known as rap, was finally unleashed on the public.

Rap music must be understood as one cultural element within a larger social movement known as hip hop, which also included break-dancing and graffiti art. The movement was nothing short of a whole way of life. According to critic Tim Carr: "Hip Hop is to funk what bebop was to jazz . . . a new strain of an old form, stripped down and revved up, rejuvenated. The Young Turks challenging the old masters. Just as bebop replaced still collared swing orchestras with Zoot-suited combos . . . so has hip hop emerged as a musical style with a brand new way of walking, talking, dancing, and seeing the world."[91]   With its roots in the gang cultures and ghetto communities of the South Bronx and Harlem, hip hop originated at the same time as disco but the movement developed in almost complete isolation for more than five years. As British chronicler David Toop explained: "Since nobody in New York City, America, or the rest of the world wanted to know about the black so-called ghettos—the unmentionable areas of extreme urban deprivation—the style was allowed to flourish as a genuine street movement."[92]

As was the case with disco, the early culture heroes of hip hop were deejays. As early as 1973 pioneer, Bronx-style deejays, like Kook Herc, soon followed by Afrika Bambaataa and Grandmaster Flash, had already begun to distinguish themselves from their disco counterparts. They played more hard-core funk material, like Jimmy Castor's "It's Just Begun," "Apache" by the Incredible Bongo Band, and James Brown's "Get on the Good Foot." More importantly, they handled the records differently. While the disco deejays concentrated mainly on segueing smoothly from one cut to the next, Herc, for example, began to experiment with playing only the hottest, most percussive portion of each record—the "break." Identified by these sustained peaks of dance beats, this technique of musical collage came to be called "break-beat" music, and the young "b-boys" and "b-girls" who danced to it came to be known as "break" dancers.

Hip hop deejays also tried to outdo each other by spinning outrageous combinations of records. In addition to James Brown, Sly and the Family Stone, and the Jackson Five, one of Bambaataa's sets might also have included the theme from the *Pink Panther*, the Beatles, the Rolling Stones, Grand Funk Railroad, Kraftwerk, and the Monkees. "Hip hop," said David Toop, "was the new music by virtue of its finding a way to absorb all other music."[93]

By 1976 the deejays had introduced technical innovations like "scratching" (back-cueing a record with the sound system turned on) that continue to be a defining characteristic of the music.

The best Bronx-style deejays quickly outgrew the small house parties where they had started and moved into clubs like the Hevalo and the Black Door, into community centers like the Bronx River Community Center, and finally into the Audubon ballroom, which could accommodate up to three thousand people. In these larger venues the deejays began to use members of their "crews" as "MCs" whose job was to provide some sort of vocal entertainment as a means of crowd control. Like the deejays and breakdancers, however, the MCs soon developed their own sophisticated styles— eventually called "rapping"—and around 1978 they began to surpass the deejays in cultural importance.

Like breakdancing, "MC'ing," as it was first known, started in the streets as a solo art; there would be one DJ and one MC. Among the first solo MCs were Eddie Cheeba, DJ Hollywood, and later Kurtis Blow. But their style was more disco-oriented. The first Bronx-style MC was, again, Kool Herc. Then Grandmaster Flash expanded the idea to include whole groups of MCs. Soon rap groups were popping up all over the Bronx and Harlem with names like Double Trouble, The Treacherous Three, and The Funky Four Plus One. Flash started the Furious Five, one of the best-known rap groups. Afrika Bambaataa worked with a number of rap groups, including the Jazzy Five, the Cosmic Force, and finally, the Soulsonic Force.

Although the style of these groups clearly evolved spontaneously, it is important to note that, according to David Toop, the roots of rap could be traced through the Caribbean islands all the way back to West Africa. In this country elements of rap could be found in prison songs and competitive urban word games like the "dozens," in the street rhymes of Muhammed Ali and the verse of the Last Poets, and in the lyrics of artists such as James Brown and Gil Scott-Heron. Two records that illustrate some of these influences are "Hustler's Convention," an album recorded by Lightnin' Rod, who had been the leader of the Last Poets, and James Brown's "King Heroin." Rap came from the streets and, as a result, its themes were often quite topical, as was clear in the case of titles like "How We Gonna Make the Black Nation Rise" by Brother D, "Problems of the World" by the Fearless Four, and "White Lines (Don't Do It)" by Grand Master Melle Mel and the Furious Five.

Bronx-style rapping had been around since 1976, but it was not put on record until 1979. Prior to that time it existed only in live performance or on the homemade cassettes which blared from "ghetto blasters" in the streets of the Bronx. It was surprising, therefore that the first two rap records did not come from the Bronx. "King Tim III (Personality Jock)" was recorded by the Fatback Band, a Brooklyn group, and the classic "Rapper's Delight" was made by the Sugar Hill Gang, whose label was based in New Jersey. The phenomenal success of "Rapper's Delight" also attracted other outsiders to the hip hop scene. The first rap record to reach No. 1 on the pop charts was "Rapture" by the white new wave group, Blondie.

More than five years after the subculture had come into being, hip hop was "discovered" in turn, by the music business, the print media, and the film industry. Though the first wave of the movement had long since peaked, hip hop was accorded all the flash of the new "in thing." It soon entered the downtown New York club scene. Like other well-known hip hop deejays, Afrika Bambaataa was invited to spin at the Mudd Club, the Ritz, the Peppermint Lounge, Negril, Danceteria, and finally the Roxy, where he brought in crowds of up to four thousand people every Friday night. In such fashionable nightspots hip hop attracted a large new white audience. It also attracted more white performers, managers, and producers like the Tom Tom Club, Malcolm McLaren, and Trevor Horn.

This kind of exposure is, of course, a mixed blessing. Particularly through films like the low budget *Wild Style* and the blockbuster *Flashdance,* followed by *Breakin'* and *Beat Street,* hip hop was brought to the attention of a mass audience. But the mass media have a way of ripping any cultural phenomenon out of its historical context. *Flashdance,* for example, made it appear as though break-dancing techniques had been invented by Jennifer Beals (or her double). And even though Blondie's lead singer (rapper?), Debbie Harry, was credited in some circles with being respectful of rap style, it would be difficult to trace her musical roots back to the Last Poets let alone the Yoruba. Still, during this period some of the best Bronx-based rap records were produced. Two of the best-known are "The Message," by Grandmaster Flash and the Furious

Five, and "Planet Rock" by Afrika Bambaataa and the Soulsonic Force, both released in 1982.

In the mid-eighties, rap music was taken over by a second generation of artists such as Whodini, The Force MDS, The Fat Boys, and Run-D.M.C., who recorded the first gold rap album, *Run-D.M.C.* (1984). At about this time, debates began to surface as to whether or not rap would continue. In the final analysis, such debates were largely irrevelant. Hip hop style had already infected other cultural forms—ranging from ballet and modern dance to fashion design and studio art to pop, rock, funk, soul, and jazz. Commenting on the music of 1984, critic Stephen Holden wrote: "Last season's synthesizer-pop has been dressed up and rhythmically charged with elements of "hip hop," the New York-originated dance music style that embraces rapping, scratching, breakdancing, and harsh, electronic sound effects. In fashion industry terms, the mood for these records might be described as one of elaborate severity, in which high technology meets the streets."[94]

By 1985 all of the trends that would define the decade were already apparent. The widespread appropriation of hip hop styles transformed rap from a passing fad into a cultural mainstay. The phenomenal pop successes of artists such as Michael Jackson, Prince, Tina Turner, Lionel Richie, and Whitney Houston established black American artists as international superstars. A number of cross-racial, pop-oriented duets featuring artists such as Stevie Wonder and Paul McCartney ("Ebony and Ivory"), Michael Jackson and Paul McCartney ("The Girl is Mine," "Say Say Say"), Michael Jackson and Eddie Van Halen ("Beat It"), Diana Ross and Julio Iglesias ("All of You"), and James Ingram and Kenny Rogers ("What About Me") brought a new dimension to the very term "crossover" and set the stage for further cross-racial collaboration. Michael Jackson's and Lionel Richie's "We Are the World" (1985)—the ultimate crossover recording—ushered in the era of "charity rock." At least in quantitative terms, 1985 was a good year for black artists. While maintaining a respectable 28 percent of the year's "Top Pop Singles," black artists rose on the year-end pop album charts to an all-time high of 38 percent in 1985.

Similar trends continued over the next couple of years, with black artists scoring eight of the top twelve pop singles in 1986 alone. Chiefly responsible for these successes were the pop-oriented sounds of artists like Whitney Houston, Lionel Richie, Anita Baker, Luther

Vandross, and Janet Jackson, and the continuing appeal of cross-racial pairings such as Dionne Warwick and Friends ("That's What Friends Are For") and Patti LaBelle and Michael McDonald ("On My Own") in 1986, and Aretha Franklin and George Michael ("I Knew You Were Waiting For Me") and Linda Ronstadt and James Ingram ("Somewhere Out There") in 1987. In addition, however, a new wrinkle appeared in black music: rap, which had always been based on twelve-inch singles, made the transition to albums. In the relative absence of radio play, even—indeed, especially—on black radio, rap artists such as Run-D.M.C., UTFO, L. L. Cool J, Whodini, Heavy D. & the Boyz, Salt-N-Pepa, and the Fat Boys made significant inroads into the album and cassette market. Eight of *Billboard*'s top thirty black albums for the week of 28 November 1987 were rap albums.

Even a cursory look at rap's audience made it clear that something of a generation gap had developed in black music. Nowhere was this separation more apparent than in the programming on black radio. *Billboard* maintains charts that distinguish between sales and airplay for the top forty black singles. Of the twenty-eight rap songs that reached the top forty sales chart in the first forty-six weeks of 1988, only sixteen registered on the airplay chart.[95] Rap was not receiving airplay commensurate with its sales. Explained by Tony Gray, Program Director at WRKS in New York: "Those records appeal to a specific demographic, primarily 12-to-18-year-olds, or perhaps 12-to-24-year-olds. The battle that [black] radio stations have is that they do need to play popular music, but for marketing reasons they have to be concerned with the 25-plus listeners as well. You don't want to alienate those listeners because that's where the bulk of your revenue comes from."[96]

Black radio has often been caught between "rock" and a hard place in the struggle for a viable listenership. But in these instances, black stations were exhibiting a reluctance to play cuts that were clearly outselling other selections on their playlists. Beyond a simple generation gap, the split between rap and other forms of popular black music may also be an indicator of the increasing importance of class divisions within the black community. Put rather bluntly by Bill Adler, publicist for Run-D.M.C., L. L. Cool J, and Public Enemy, among others: "Black radio is run by 'buppies' [black urban professionals]. They've made a cultural commitment to a lifestyle that has nothing to do with music on the street. . . .

This music very rudely pulls them back on the street corner, and they don't want to go."[97]   The artists themselves often identify "bourgeois blacks" as the main source of resistance to rap.

To be sure, rap's detractors have had no lack of issues to point to.   From different quarters, rap has been roundly chastised for being bigoted, violent, and/or sexist.   Cries of anti-Semitism directed at Public Enemy's Professor Griff reached a peak when the former Minister of Information (who was subsequently fired and then rehired as liaison to the black community) claimed in an interview with the *Washington Times* that Jews were responsible for "the majority of wickedness that goes on in the world."[98]   The confrontational stance and uncompromising lyrics of groups like Public Enemy ("Fight the Power") and N.W.A. ("---- the Police") have fueled the notion that rap promotes violence.   As to rap's sexist tendencies, Harry Allen offered a pointed summary in *Essence:*

> When Ice-T releases a record called "Girls, Let's Get Buck Naked and Fuck" ("Girls, L.G.B.N.A.F." on the album cover), when 2 Live Crew on a cut called "S & M" calls to women to bring their "d--k-sucking friends," when Ultramagnetic M.C.'s Kool Keith on "Give the Drummer Some" talks about smacking up his bitch in the manner of a pimp, sisters understandably scream.[99]

"Hip-hop is sexist," concludes Allen.   But, he is quick to add, "It is also frank."

One wonders if rap would be as upsetting as it seems to be were it not for its frankness.   While rap should not be let off the hook for its sexism, it should be noted that sexism has never been a stranger to any genre of popular music or, for that matter, any aspect of life in America.   "As an unerringly precise reflection of the community," continues Allen, "hip-hop's sexist thinking will change when the community changes."[100]   Similarly, rap's other shortcomings should be considered in context.   Critic Jon Pareles, who correctly berated Professor Griff for his misguided prejudices in the *New York Times,* also acknowledged that Public Enemy's "overall message is one of self-determination for blacks."[101]   Brian Turner, president of Priority, defended signing controversial artists to his label as follows: "What impressed me about N.W.A. and Eazy-E was that these guys lived the things they talk about.   All I was hearing on the news was the perspective of the police and outsiders—you never get the perspective of the actual guy they're talking about. When I saw what these guys wrote, it really hit me that their side of the story is important to tell."[102]

That violence has occurred at some rap concerts is undeniable. It is an issue that rappers themselves have addressed head-on. Following the leadership of Nelson George, a number of rap groups, including Stetsasonic, Boogie Down Productions, and Public Enemy, among others, initiated the Stop the Violence Movement aimed specifically at black-on-black crime. As one of their projects, these groups contributed their time and talent to "Self-Destruction," the all-star rap recording that became the anthem of the movement. It is a potent declaration against violence. It is a positive step.

A good deal of rap's appeal comes from its speaking positively to real issues. "Any examination of rap's lyrical content," writes David Nathan, "reveals a very high percentage of anti-violent, anti-drug messages, many aimed at improving self-esteem, encouraging the youth of the '80s to continue their education and approach adulthood with a positive approach."[103] This can be contrasted with the current lyric vacuity of most other forms of black pop. Writing for a *Billboard* special on "The World of Black Music" in the Summer of 1989, Dan Stuart pointed out that "today it's virtually impossible to find a non-rap song in the black top 40 that contains lyrical content that deals with any topic besides dancing and romancing."[104] "Self-Destruction," for example, sold nearly five hundred thousand units and never even registered in the black airplay top 40.

The turmoil surrounding rap may have presented a problem for black radio, but major recording companies were quick to recognize the financial potential of this phenomenon. While few majors signed rap acts directly, buy-ins and distribution deals with successful rap indies (independent labels) soon became commonplace. Columbia Records was the first to bank on rap's potential when it concluded a custom label deal with Def Jam (L. L. Cool J, Oran "Juice" Jones, the Beastie Boys, Public Enemy) in 1985. Jive Records (Whodini, Kool Moe Dee, Steady B., D. J. Jazzy Jeff and the Fresh Prince, Boogie Down Productions) entered into distribution arrangements with both RCA and Arista. Cold Chillin' Records (Marly Marl, Roxanne Shante, Biz Markie, M. C. Shan) signed a distribution deal with Warner Bros. in 1987. Warner Bros. also bought a piece of the action at Tommy Boy (Stetsasonic, Force MDs, De La Soul, Latifa, Black By Demand). Delicious Vinyl (Tōn Lōc, Def Jef) has a national distribution deal with Island.   National distribution for Priority (N.W. A., Eazy-E) is handled by Capitol.

The majors, by and large, have been intelligent enough to leave creative functions at street level.   And in providing the rap indies with superior distribution, they have considerably increased rap's access to mainstream outlets.   Rap often gets more support on pop radio than on black radio.   Even MTV, that bastion of resistance to black music, has a rap show.   Initially buried in a late-night weekend slot, Yo! MTV Raps is now aired every weekday in the after-school slot and has become the channel's single most popular program. As a final indicator of mainstream acceptance, the National Academy of Recording Arts and Sciences (NARAS) added a rap category to the Grammy awards in 1989.   The death of rap has been predicted again and again by the critics.   If anything, however, the music has grown stronger, its artists have become more socially engaged, and its audience has expanded significantly.

Conclusion

When the music industry first confronted the issue of black rhythm and blues artists selling pop in the 1940s, their work was still listed as "race" music.   As the music began to cross over into the white market, however, it was decided that a more palatable term was needed.   Record companies toyed with labels like "ebony" and "sepia" for a while, but these, too, were obviously distinctions of color, not musical style.   Eventually "rhythm and blues" became the accepted term.   The rhythm and blues charts were actually discontinued altogether for a brief period in the sixties and shortly thereafter replaced by the term "soul." In some ways, the industry has now come full circle.   The term currently used in *Billboard* is "black" music.

Here we must distinguish between black music as a cultural tradition and black music as a marketing category.   While there is no question that the rich musical tradition that grows out of the African American experience should be accorded a special cultural status, the problem is that, in practice, the category "black music" is often used to slot black artists, at least initially, into a limited market.   Recently a number of black artists—pop superstars such as Michael Jackson, Lionel Richie, Whitney Houston, Anita Baker, and others, "alternative" black artists like Living Colour, Tracy Chapman, Terence Trent D'Arby, and Robert Cray, and gold and platinum selling rappers such as Run-D.M.C., Public Enemy, D. J. Jazzy Jeff and the Fresh Prince, Salt-N-Pepa, and N.W.A.—have begun to break out of the mold. Employing a variety of styles that can be traced back through various strands of the African American experience, these artists have been successfully marketed through pop outlets without abandoning a connection to the black audience. These gains, however, have been offset to some degree by white artists such as Madonna and George Michael coming to be regarded as innovators in the field of black music. Even black personnel within the industry defended Michael's winning "Best Black Male Vocalist" at the American Music Awards in 1989.

All of the major record companies continue to maintain separate divisions or subsidiaries for "black music," which is to say, for black artists who sell primarily to a black audience. These departments generally operate with inferior production and promotion budgets. Radio formats are designed to target particular demographic populations that are fragmented not only along lines of musical taste, but along racial and cultural lines as well. Booking agencies still maintain a tacit standing policy of not packaging white artists and artists of color on the same bill. To this day there is a touring circuit for black acts known as the "chitlin' circuit." Finally, black music is invariably underreported in the music press.

As black musicians achieve greater acceptance in the mainstream market, they are confronted by an infrastructure that is fully owned and operated by whites. Pressure is exerted on them to sever their ties with the attorneys, agents, managers, booking agents, and promoters who may have been responsible for building their careers in the first place. The question thus remains: Is the presence of black superstars an indicator of change in the way the industry does business or are these successful black artists simply the individual exceptions who will serve to get the rest of the industry off the hook? As long as market research takes precedence over cultural development, audiences for popular music are likely to remain fragmented, in part along racial lines. To the extent that African Americans are not represented in all facets of production, the image of African Americans in music is likely to remain a split image.

1. Steve Chapple and Reebee Garofalo, *Rock 'n' Roll is Here to Pay: The History and Politics of the Music Industry* (Chicago: Nelson-Hall, 1977), chap. 7.

2. Eileen Southern, *The Music of Black Americans: A History* (New York: W.W. Norton, 1971), 353.

3. Russell Sanjek, *American Popular Music and its Business: The First Four Hundred Years: Vol. III, from 1900 to 1984* (New York: Oxford University Press, 1988), 176.

4. Nat Shapiro, *Popular Music: An Annotated Index of American Popular Songs: Vol. 2, 1940-1949* (New York: Adrian Press, 1965), 6.

5. Nelson George, *The Death of Rhythm & Blues* (New York: Pantheon Books, 1988), 10.

6. Leroi Jones, *Blues People* (New York: William Morrow, 1963), 160.

7. George, *The Death of Rhythm & Blues*, 9.

8. Ibid., 11.

9. Charlie Gillett, *The Sound of the City: The Rise of Rock and Roll* (New York: Outerbridge and Dienstfrey, 1970), 9.

10. Jones, *Blues People*, 171.

11. See Erik Barnouw, *The Golden Web: Broadcasting in the United States: 1933-1952* (New York: Oxford University Press, 1968), 204.

12. Johnny Otis interviewed by author, Cambridge, Massachusetts, 1974.

13. *Billboard*, 3 January 1953, 3.

14. Arnold Shaw, *Honkers and Shouters: The Golden Years of Rhythm and Blues* (New York: Collier Books, 1978), 213.

15. Saul Bihari quoted in "World of Soul," *Billboard*, 23 June 1967, 26.

16. Ahmet Ertegun interviewed by Steve Chapple, New York, N.Y., July 1974.

17. Lee Eliot Berk, *Legal Protection for the Creative Musician* (Boston: Berklee Press, 1970), 177.

18. Fred Parris interviewed by author, Cambridge, Massachusetts, 1974.

19. *Billboard*, 22 December 1956, 10.

20. Christopher Small, *Music of the Common Tongue: Survival and Celebration in Afro-American Music* (New York: Riverrun Press, 1987), 371.

21. Leonard Chess quoted in *Rolling Stone*, 18 January 1973, 38.

22. Gillett, *The Sound of the City*, 96–97.

23. George, *The Death of Rhythm and Blues*, 68.

24. Chuck Berry interviewed in the Taylor Hackford documentary, "Hail! Hail! Rock 'n' Roll," 1987.

25. Michael Lydon, *Rock Folk: Portraits from the Rock 'n' Roll Pantheon* (New York: Dell, 1968), 20.

26. Milt Gabler quoted in Shaw, *Honkers and Shouters*, 64

27. John Storm Roberts, *Black Music of Two Worlds* (New York: William Morrow, 1974), 189.

28. Hettie Jones, *Big Star Fallin' Mama* (New York: Dell Publishing Co., 1974), 41.

29. Roberts, *Black Music of Two Worlds*, 190.

30. Ray Charles quoted in *Rolling Stone*, 18 January 1972, 18.

31. Kwabena Nketia quoted in Roberts, *Black Music of Two Worlds*, 190.

32. Ibid., 182–83.

33. Small, *Music of the Common Tongue*, 201.

34. Ibid., 25.

35. *Billboard*, 11 December 1954. Cited in Nick Tosches, *Country: Living Legends and Dying Metaphors in America's Biggest Music* (New York: Charles Scribner's Sons, 1985), 52.

36. *New Musical Express*, 21 September 1956. Quoted in Gillett, *The Sound of the City*, 328–29.

37. Sam Phillips quoted in Peter Guralnick, *Feel Like Going Home: Portraits in Blues and Rock 'n' Roll*, (New York: Outerbridge and Dienstfrey, 1971), 140.

38. Elvis Presley quoted in Gillett, *The Sound of the City*, 36.

39. Margaret McKee and Fred Chisenhall, *Beale Black and Blue: Life and Music on Black America's Main Street* (Baton Rouge, LA: LSU Press, 1981), 9.

40. Jerry Lee Lewis quoted in Guralnick, *Feel Like Going Home*, 150-91.

41. Carl Perkins quoted in Lydon, *Rock Folk*, 32.

42. Johnny Otis interviewd by author, Cambridge, Massachusetts, 1974.

43. Tosches, *Country*, 55.

44. Shaw, *Honkers and Shouters*, 497.

45. Ibid., 215

46. George Lipsitz, *Class and Culture in Cold War America: A Rainbow at Midnight* (South Hadley, MA.: J. F. Bergin Publishers, 1982), 224.

47. Russ Sanjek interviewed by Steve Chapple, New York, 1974.

48. Russ Sanjek, "The War on Rock," lecture given at the New School for Social Research, New York, N.Y., 11 February 1971.

49. Gillett, *The Sound of the City*, 360.

50. Emmanuel Celler quoted in Sanjek, "The War on Rock," 11.

51. Frank Sinatra quoted in Sanjek, "The War on Rock," 14–15.

52. Vance Packard quoted in Sanjek, "The War on Rock," 15.

53. Chapple and Garofalo, *Rock 'n' Roll is Here to Pay*, 247.

54. Gillett, *The Sound of the City*, 127.

55. Sanjek, *American Popular Music and its Business*, 444.

56. Arnold Shaw, *The Rockin' '50s'* (New York: Hawthorn Books, 1974), 56.

57. *Rolling Stone*, 11 May 1968, 19.

58. Gillet, *The Sound of the City*, 127.

59. Ortiz Walton, *Music: Black White and Blue* (New York: William Morrow, 1972), 35.

60. Martha Reeves quoted in *Rolling Stone*, 23 May 1974, 25.

61. Smokey Robinson quoted in *Rolling Stone*, 28 September 1968. 14.

62. Martha Reeves quoted in *Rolling Stone*, 23 May 1974, 26.

63. *Rolling Stone*, 13 May 1971, 17.

64. *Rolling Stone*, 21 December 1968, 20.

65. *Rolling Stone*, 11 November 1971, 18.

66. Martha Reeves quoted in *Rolling Stone*, 23 May 1974, 28.

67. Marvin Gaye quoted in Ben Fong-Torres, *Rolling Stone Interviews*, vol. 2. (New York: Simon and Schuster, 1973), 388.

68. George, *The Death of Rhythm and Blues*, 85.

69. Ibid., 86.

70. Otis Redding quoted in *Rolling Stone*, 20 January 1968, 15.

71. Guaralnick, *Feel Like Going Home*, 332.

72. Jones, *Blues People*, 41.

73. Robert Palmer, "James Brown." In Jim Miller, ed., *The Rolling Stone Illustrated History of Rock & Roll* (New York: Rolling Stone Press, 1976), 136.

74. Eric Clapton quoted in *Rolling Stone*, 11 May 1968, 21.

75. James Brown quoted in *Rolling Stone*, 11 January 1970, 10.

76. Senator Jacob Javits quoted in *Billboard*, 17 May 1969, 34.

77. *Billboard*, 17 July 1969, 11.

78. Bobby Womack quoted in *Rolling Stone*, 4 April 1970, 11.

79. Jerry Wexler quoted in *Billboard*, 20 November 1971, 103.

80. *Newsweek*, 2 April 1979, 59.

81. *Village Voice*, 12 February 1979, 11.

82. *Rolling Stone*, 19 April 1979, 29.

83. *Village Voice*, 12 February 1979, 16.

84. Melba Moore quoted in *Newsweek*, 2 April 1979, 58.

85. *Cape Cod Times*, 16 July 1983, 12.

86. Jann Wenner quoted in *Los Angeles Times Calendar Section*, 4 September 1983, 3.

87. *Newsweek*, 18 April 1983, 98.

88. *People*, 4 April 1983, 31.

89. Ibid.

90. *Rock and Roll Confidential*, January 1984, 2.

91. *Rolling Stone*, 26 May 1983, 22.

92. David Toop, *The Rap Attack: African Jive to New York Hip Hop* (New South Wales, Australia: Pluto Press, 1984), 14.

93. Ibid., 154.

94. *New York Times*, 23 September 1984, 78.

95. *Billboard*, 24 December 1988, R-8.

96. Tony Gray quoted in *Billboard*, 17 June 1989, B-12.

97. Bill Adler quoted in *Billboard*, 24 December 1988, R-21.

98. *New York Times*, 10 September 1989, Arts and Leisure, 1.

99. *Essence*, April 1989, 117.

100. Ibid.

101. *New York Times*, 10 September 1989, Arts and Leisure 33.

102. Brian Turner quoted in *Billboard*, 24 December 1988, R-16.

103. *Billboard*, 24 December 1987, R-5.

104. *Billboard*, 17 June 1989, B-12.

Part Two

MAKING MOVIES BLACK:
THE FILM INDUSTRY

3 FILM

THOMAS CRIPPS

As we have seen in the Introduction, all of the contributors to this book have been drawn to a conflict-model as a means of accounting for the changing place of African Americans in various media of communication. The history of blacks in movies has been no exception to this pattern, except for one trait. Although all media in the twentieth century have been intensively capitalized oligopolies of a few sellers serving hordes of buyers, movies, because of their nature as entertainments offered in a broad national market supported directly by ticket sales, have offered a window of access to blacks. Unlike broadcasting and advertising, movies were fueled by direct payments from consumer to producer; unlike the press, movies aspired to national scope, and for prices higher than pennies; unlike broadcasting, the equipment for filmmaking and for viewing was accessible; unlike music recording, movies were less hedged about by the intricacies of copyright and marketing. This meant that there were fissures in the system which, particularly in times of social crisis, allowed for a "play" in the wheels of commerce that enabled African Americans to protest their treatment through direct advocacy, penetrate into the classical Hollywood system, or make their own movies independently.

This is not to say that having an impact on movies at their source has been an easy matter for blacks. Hollywood movies have always exhibited a sort of cultural politics in their treatment of ethnicity, but their usages of African Americans have always seemed more resistant to change, even under the pressure of social crises. The reason for this inertia derived from the circumstances of their production. By the teens of this century, moviemaking had been rationalized, first into a cartel of patent holders, then of filmmakers, producers, and eventually corporate studios—all serving a distributive system that played to audiences whose expectations had been shaped by normalizing forces such as advertising, journalistic reviewing, lush picture palaces, a system of promoting stars, and particularly a studio system that routinized production into a classical cinema of surefire, risk-free, cost-effective products that fulfilled audiences' anticipations of style, texture, and satisfying happy endings.

As Dates and Barlow have argued in the Introduction, recent critics have confirmed the efficacy of movies for purveying ideology to the point of suggesting that powerful psychic, anthropological, and social forces embedded in the experience of moviegoing itself have enhanced their capacity. Along with the smoothly accessible style of Hollywood movies—with their unruffled, narrative flow, familiar cutting patterns "sutured" over any disturbing contradictions, all resolved in a satisfying "closure"—these extratextual forces assured easy acceptance by a receptive audience. Unavoidably, the resulting films affirm the social status quo (and the place of blacks in it), at least according to T. W. Adorno and other Marxist critics of this generation. Other critics have followed the French psychiatrist and critic, Jacques Lacan in holding that apparently authorless Hollywood movies, consumed in a dreamlike state in darkened rooms, recapitulated the child's course toward adulthood, thereby serving as unchallenged purveyors of the ideology of a dominant class. Some critics, Lacan included, have carried this argument into semiology, the branch of linguistics that studies language as a system of arbitrary signs that "signify" meanings. For them it has been a predictable step to regard movies as a language and their audiences as a group susceptible of study by anthropological methods, as though they shared a sort of universally coded mentality derived from moviegoing and through which they received a collective ideology.[1]

As well as these cultural critics, a school of Marxist critics has reinforced a general leftist consensus that Hollywood commercial movies have served as an ideological conduit for the ruling class. All the worse for blacks, Hollywood's dominance coincided with the arrival on the American urban scene of a ready-made proletariat in the form of waves of European immigrants and of southern black fugitives from life on the bottom rung of an exhausted agrarian system.   The world wars accelerated the black drift into a half-century-long rising tide.   According to Marxists, movies were the principal means the capitalist system used to integrate both groups into the economy as tractable workers; in return, the movies gave moviegoers an illusory sense of power derived from heroes on the screen with whom they identified.   Moreover, so ran the argument, such noncoercive suasion rested not on the mendacity of a capitalist cabal; rather, movies had become part of an infrastructure linked to capitalism but driven by its own energies applied toward providing pleasure for moviegoers and earning profits for the studios.[2]

The challenge for African Americans would be to battle against such apparently ironclad determinism by protest, intervention in Hollywood, and indigenous filmmaking of their own.   Indeed, some critics admitted of the possibility.   As Jeremy Morton Paine wrote, movies can only "half create the environment they are half created by."[3]   In fact, one school of criticism, led by Andrew Sarris, had arisen by asserting as a virtue certain filmakers'—*auteurs*, Sarris called them—skills at circumventing the wills of their masters in the studio front offices by insinuating their own persona and politics into their movies.

This is not to wave aside Lacan's extension of Freud into the process of moviegoing, nor of Claude Lévi-Strauss's view of film as the unconscious bearer of a deeply running group sensibility, nor even of Adorno's certainty that popular culture can only ratify the social status quo.   Rather, it must be asserted that, no matter how similar blacks are to other Americans, they also reside behind a veil created by, as W. E. B. Du Bois observed, a "twoness" of American life.   Lacan's idea of self-development derived in part from the child's sense of difference from patriarchal authority.   How does this translate into poor, black moviegoing communities, where one-parent families headed by a lone woman are the norm, or what is Oedipus's role in a matriarchate?   In such a neighboorhood the entire spectrum of posturing, dressing, and acting the "bad nigger" or "hardman" may arise from rebellion against a matriarchy in which no man is ever present.   Or to put a reverse spin on the query, if a black youth rebels against a hustling dude of a father, will the outcome be a black square in a gray flannel suit?   Who is the father and who the mother in "the rough theater of the street" in black Philadelphia, where every household seemed to an anthropologist to be "in motion," sloughing off members, taking on new ones. The anchor in this rough sea is not the family, but Tele-machus's jackleg garage, where life is an unending round of hustling, baiting, "woofing," signifying—each a verbal challenge that might end in violence. The evidence of a larger order outside the street itself is the radio, each receiver in the street tuned to WDAS, the soul station, each addressing its own "bubble of musical sound" to a single listener whose significant male "other" can only be Tele-machus, a scratchy radio voice, or hazing, ragging peers.[4]

Clearly, in such a setting the father has been replaced by the cool, often incipiently violent, sharply dressed "bad dude" whom Hollywood learned to portray in *Super Fly* and other "blaxploitation" movies of the 1970s, and by Run Run Shaw and his circle of martial arts moviemakers in Hong Kong.[5] Rather than ratifying a capitalist order, these characters exalted the physical license that a half-century ago John Dollard, in *Caste and Class in a Southern Town* saw as one of "the gains of segregation." In such a community, praise went not to the dutiful worker but to the quick-to-anger dude indifferent to any consequences; here, the highest praise for conduct might be Richard Pryor's line, "That nigger's crazy."

In contrast, white culture (which included the many African Americans who knew street life only as the distant core of memory that provided a source of selves) seemed buttoned-down or uptight. But here, too, particularly in times of crisis, blacks found channels of access to white circles of power. Here, where Alexis de Tocque-ville, Henry James, and others had observed a curious absence of established order that had resulted in rendering every decision open to bargaining and lobbying by, as the economist John Kenneth Galbraith called them, "countervailing powers," the "play" among the forces allowed blacks occasional moments of compelling influ-ence over public affairs.[6] That such an arrangement seemed to promise only an endless tale of half-loaves won by a few elite blacks was not lost on Marxist critics, particularly those in the Frankfurt circle who, with Herbert Marcuse, regarded such liberalism as no more than "repressive tolerance."

But at least one thinker, Antonio Gramsci, a founder of the Italian Communist party who spent much of his life in Mussolini's jails, revised Marx to admit of the prospect of an alliance of workers across class lines, thereby challenging the vulnerable superstructure of capitalism and forcing negotiations toward outcomes that would fall short of revolution but lead to new cultural arrangements to which workers might consent. Moreover, he suggested that this might be accomplished by raising up "organic intellectuals" from among oppressed peoples themselves, rather than passively awaiting the arrival of professional Marxist-Leninist cadres.[7] Independently, James K. Feibleman, in his *Theory of Culture*, all but arrived at an Americanist case of this phenomenon. During wars, he argued, adversaries grow cohesive, in "much the same" way as Gustav LeBon had described mobs. "That is why wars," he wrote, "despite all the evil they entail, have the good effect of drawing together people of divergent views and interests," an outcome he found in "the rise of the Nazis in modern Germany [which] placed renewed emphasis upon the racial problem."[8]

In fact, as we shall see, World War II provided the seminal event that anticipated the strategies of the postwar civil rights movement. Blacks joined the war effort while insinuating their own goals into it—William G. Nunn of the *Pittsburgh Courier* would call for a "Double V," a victory over both Nazism *and* racism. As a propaganda of unity took shape around catchwords like "brotherhood" and "tolerance," Walter White of the NAACP managed to give it life by holding his annual convention on the doorstep of Hollywood, cultivating allies in the Office of War Information (OWI), and lobbying to distribute racially angled War Department movies to civilian audiences—all of this while Germany edged toward a so-called final solution to the "Jewish question": genocide. In other words, blacks and their liberal allies acted in concert in a pluralistic setting much as Gramsci had described Sicilians in search of "nurturing class alliances."[9]

If such intervention were possible in lesser crises than world war, then we should expect blacks to enjoy a lively movie history, protesting pejorative stereotypes, lobbying for legislative or judicial relief from them, campaigning in Hollywood for more varied fare, and, as though between the cracks of the industry, making their own movies. Nowadays, as a critical vocabulary of "postmodern" criticism has emerged, black intellectuals readily demand a break with Hollywood's "encoding" of racial stigmata and a weaning of audiences away from the linear narrative that has seemed to such critics a too-glib bearer of bourgeois ideology. But long before such formulations had grown into a canon, a place for it had been prepared by black activists in search of a way out, through censorship, direct action, and moviemaking. True, they might not have known they were warring against, as Kobena Mercer put it, "dependent expressivity" while searching for a "diaspora culture" free from, as Clyde Taylor wrote, "the repressive doctrine of [Western] aesthetics," but their goal was nonetheless clear.[10]

The contemporaneous jargon aside, every alert moviegoer knows that Stepin Fetchit appeared in movies as a figure apart, intended to set off the heroism of the white hero and to refute the image of blacks as brutes; and some may know that he described himself in precisely those terms, as a charming scamp who played ambassador between the estranged races. For similar reasons, many moviegoers annually watch *Gone with the Wind* with its celebrated black roles—Hattie McDaniel's Mammy and Butterfly McQueen's Prissie—that served to punch up, set apart, and contrast with the white principals.

Black movie history, then, is the account of nagging at the heels of this imagery in order to bring about a change in the "horizon of expectations," the audiences' anticipation of what black characters were supposed to be. This ambition would, of course, have been an empty one without the fortuitously changing circumstances arising from various wars, depressions, and other cultural crises, the new "particular cultural conditions" that Gerald Mast thought might "influence, if not dictate" the qualities of movies.[11] The goal: nothing less than a break with Hollywood's codification of black as apart or even absent, different from, or even inferior to the milieus of standard American movies, and in its place a duty, as James Snead wrote, to "coin unconventional associations for black skin within the reigning film language."[12] This is not to claim such a thing as a black shot or cut. Rather, over almost a century of African American and movie history, blacks have campaigned for a Hollywood alertness to seismic changes in black circumstances that dictate an end to outmoded conventions—that is, an end to anachronistic usages of shots, cuts, smoothly flowing narratives, and happy endings—a disjuncture with the past. It was not the shot, but the uses to which it had been put that defined its blackness.

At the risk of seeming too glibly to dismiss a generation of carefully worked out theories of films and their meanings, and of seeming too bent on asserting a historical basis for black film and its theories, I wish to emphasize that this is my specific intention. In Lacan's psychiatry, Lévi-Strauss's deconstructionist anthropology, Saussure's semiology, and the film theories that have spun off from them, there seems to be scant room for history to play its part. Indeed, among the best historians who have been touched by their work—Ferdinand Braudel in his *Wheels of Commerce*, Emmanuel Roy Ladurie in his *Carnival* and *Montaillou*—there has appeared to be a preference for history as broad canvas, in which individual will or effort or authorship had no place. In contrast, for blacks (as for Jews or any minority set apart) history is everything. Besides, few students have with certitude studied black psyche, language, or anthropology. Indeed, among the folk, "deep down in the jungle," as Roger Abrahams slyly put it, at first glance all theories seem to be reversed. The head of the household is a woman. Language indeed seems a system of random signs: it changes at a dizzying pace, as hep becomes hip becomes hip-hop; naming girls rests purely on the arbitrariness of richly sibilant sounds such as Nichelle, Ta-Tanisha, and Kaleesha, while boys' names range from sharp plosives like Derek to two-beat sounds like LeRoy, LaVon, DeRon. And anthropology has been wrested by the tribe away from the anthropologists who, even as they search for African survivals in African America, are confounded by black inventions of new ones such as Kwaanza, an Africanesque holiday cut from whole cloth as a black variation on the mainly Teutonic celebration of Christmas.[13]

Thus, out of African American history has emerged a black cinema that is itself rooted in history—a history, first, of struggles of a weak minority for a protective censorship, then a century-long campaign to affect Hollywood movies at their source, and finally a parallel line of race movies. Sometimes these trends have coalesced into genres of black film complete with a distinctive idiom, sometimes religious in tone, at others pastoral and southern, and, at still others, urban, cool, jiving. Often, much like a college newspaper that includes a glossary of the latest slang for the benefit of the freshmen, black films have taken on the mode of an anatomy of black life. As surely, for example, as Arthur Hailey's *Hotel* is both fiction and an anatomy of the inner workings of a hotel, so Melvin Van Peebles's *Sweet Sweetback's Baad Asssss Song* was intended as an anatomy of a ghetto that many blacks (and almost all whites) saw only at a safe distance. Such movies will, of course, set about constructing heroes whose deeds will ever be debated, as in the case of, say, Sidney Poitier's sweet-tempered Homer Smith in *Lilies of the Field* (1963), for which he won an Oscar but for which he drew fire from black critics who found his character yet another in a long line of too accommodating black males. Nonetheless, the goal remained a constant—to relocate black figures toward the center of the frame and the action, to share the closeups and two-shots, as well as eyeline contact from shot to shot which established their centrality in the stakes, and to recast a black mythic presence, either pastoral as in *The Autobiography of Miss Jane Pitman* and *Nothing But a Man*, or urban, as in *Sweetback* or *Friday Foster*. But this has carried us far ahead of the story—the history.

The black political columnist G. James Fleming liked to think that African Americans, by their mere presence, altered the substance of American politics. To formulate the idea most starkly: if there had been no blacks there would have been no Civil War. The early days of movies were no exception. Arriving as they did on the urban scene at the end of the nineteenth century, movies could not help but take into account the fact that blacks fought in the nation's wars, faced the cruel excesses of post-Reconstruction terrorism, and moved in droves to northern cities. In six years beginning in 1898 (the year of the Spanish-American War), African Americans appeared in Thomas Edison's reportorial *Colored Troops Disembarking* (1898), while a similar film, *The Colored Invincibles*, was described in a distributor's catalogue as showing blacks fighting with "as much zeal as their white brothers." Then in 1903, Edwin S. Porter's film of *Uncle Tom's Cabin* which, at fifteen minutes, was one of the longest films made up to that time, provided a faithful if sentimental rendering of Harriet Beecher Stowe's abolitionist tract. And a year later Biograph released *A Bucket of Cream Ale* (1904), in which a black servant, angered by a rude Dutchman who has thrown a glass of ale in her face, turns about and dumps an entire tin bucket on *his* head.

None of these films had been a response to black pressure, yet all were signs of a black presence venturing into formerly lily-white preserves. Black soldiers had been on the frontier since the 1860s and were among the first to serve in Cuba during the Spanish War, mainly because someone in the War Department had thought them immune from tropical diseases. Perhaps the appearance of Stowe's *Tom* as a movie was an urban, progressive revival of its social message after generations of road show dilutions of it. And perhaps *A Bucket of Cream Ale* was pure reportage: blacks in northern cities had seemed not only quicker to anger than their southern brethren but also were led by an ever more militant "talented tenth," as W. E. B. Du Bois had labeled them. In any case, such movies signified an end to a white southern monopoly on racial ideology that was at the bottom of so many early movies such as *Chicken Thieves*, *A Night in Coon Town*, and *Interrupted Crap Game*. Even so, these two genres of racial movies, by the fact of their clashing imagery (which catalogers reported as necessary data to their distributor-customers), suggested that white people *knew* that a new black person had arrived on the urban scene and stood apart from older stereotypes. Two such movies were contrasted according to their racial portrayals, one of them about "two bad coons," the other whose "darkies are of the 'Old Virginny' type."

Of all these primitive films, Biograph's *The Fights of Nations* (1907) most clearly signaled the arrival of blacks on the urban scene as well as a pioneering instance of structuring the film so as to evade suggesting the problematic future of urban blacks. Composed as a string of vignettes purporting to show how various ethnic groups fight, it particularly hazed Irish drunkenness, Jewish glibness and avarice, and black inclinations toward dancing and fighting with razors. Almost subliminally, the film anticipated the persistence of segregation: in a final tableau in which Uncle Sam and John Bull shake hands and an Indian enters the circle, all of the groups reappear for a sort of curtain call—all save the blacks, yet a reviewer wrote that all were "well represented": in other words, the only good blacks were *absent* blacks.

By this time, at the height of both the great wave of European immigration and the urban progressive movement, black efforts on their own behalf had only just begun. James Weldon Johnson (he and his brother Rosamond were the authors of "the Negro national anthem," *Lift Every Voice*) wrote two movies that were so poorly done that he swore off them for the rest of his days; the first black producer, Bill Foster, began the making of race movies; Lester Walton, critic on the black *New York Age* and later Minister to Liberia, called for a black protest that never came against a lurid movie about a lynching; and Bert Williams made two short films of his more famous routines which, however, failed to engage film-bookers. But at least these men had played out their roles as the organic intellectuals who might help set the terms of future negotiated detente.

This uneven and fitful contest for nominal influence over movies reached combat pitch between 1910 and 1915, not so much because conflicting ideologies were more sharply at issue then, but because history itself was at work in the form of the golden anniversary of the Civil War. Unfortunately for African Americans, the memory of the war had settled into a wistful aching for a lost pastoral heritage that coincided with the southerners' collective reverence for "the lost cause" of southern independence (a mentality that reduced the racial basis of the war to a sidebar). At the same time, Democrats, including their southern wing returned to Washington in full cry, a mood often masked as a love feast between the veterans of the war, and one captured on film at least once, when President Taft in 1909 addressed a joint encampment of Confederate veterans and the Grand Army of the Republic.[14] Coincident with this shift in national politics was a political development in the movie industry where directors began to exercise a formerly unthinkable degree of control over their crews, partly because of a migration of filmmaking away from Eastern cities, and partly because a cartel of patent holders had only just broken up and no alternative corporate structure had emerged.[15]

One of these commanding figures was David Wark Griffith, a Kentuckian raised up on Victorian culture, especially the version of it that had held sway in the plantation South. Together, he and his collaborator, Thomas Dixon, a preacher, courthouse politician, and racist ideologue who laced a series of lurid novels with his own brand of white supremacy, produced The Birth of a Nation (1915), the capstone of scores of lesser movies that celebrated the Old South and the slavery that underwrote its way of life. The difference between their movie and The Empty Sleeve, Hearts and Flags, A Slave's Devotion, and its other forebears lay in the boldness of the producers' portrayal of African Americans as at once slavish and vicious, sexless and lustful, corrupt and loyal.

More than any single cultural event, The Birth of a Nation galvanized blacks into seeking coalitions across ethnic lines, with the result that the NAACP with its white, Jewish, urban, philan-thropic, socially conscious elite, used the movie as the occasion for a boom in its national influence. Not only did the movie play on every convention of southern racial lore, its specific intention was articulated by Dixon at the opening of the 1906 stage version: "My object is to teach the north . . . what it has never known—the awful suffering of the white man during the dreadful reconstruction period

. . . to demonstrate to the world that the white man must and shall be supreme." For African Americans yet another cause for astonishment was the ease with which the message played in the North. Blacks for the first time struck back with every available tactic: they lobbied in state houses for laws banning racial slander, pressed Griffith for softer treatment, and before the year was out began to cultivate Chicago financiers and California moviemen with an eye to making their own film rebuttal.

So shrewdly did *The Birth of a Nation* pluck at the strings of racist conventions that even the blacks were taken in by them. In one instance a black soldier ever so diffidently proposes marriage to a virginal white girl, who shies away, bolts with him in pursuit promising no intent to harm her, and finally throws herself off a cliff—an incident that was used as the excuse for forming the Ku Klux Klan. In all of its protests the NAACP referred to the sequence as "the chase" or, less frequently, "the rape," but never as "the courtship scene"; that is, all viewers, black and white, had been raised on black images burdened with meanings linked to sexuality and bestiality (Dixon had written that the soldier scuttled "crabwise"). Such scenes were pointedly used to argue that mulattoes, by their nature as light-skinned *mischlings*, owed allegiance to no group but only to their overweening ambition to join the dominant group in their society. Oddly, such rhetoric not only reintroduced southern sexual politics to northern audiences but anticipated one of Hitler's arguments for dealing with "the Jewish question." In any case, *The Birth of a Nation* thrust upon Americans a full-blown cultural crisis that roused blacks and their allies to prod legislatures to write laws against racial slander, campaign to force Griffith to palliate such scenes as the chase and to add an epilogue designed to show black progress under freedom, and finally to create movies of their own, among them a sprawling, outsized epic to be known as *The Birth of a Race*.[16]

Only such an ambitious project could shake the credibility with which Dixon had clothed *The Birth of a Nation* when he managed, through an old classmate, Woodrow Wilson, to present a showing both to the president and his guests and to the entire United States Supreme Court. As a counterweight, blacks and their white "angels" plunged into *The Birth of a Race*, which was at first a loosely collaborative effort of Emmett J. Scott, Booker T. Washington's secretary at Tuskegee Institute, and the NAACP, along with movie figures led by the scriptwriter, Elaine Sterne, and Carl Laemmle, who had only just opened an imposing studio in California on land he had named Universal City. Once again, a national cultural crisis loomed, this time in the form of the Great War, but it was not entirely to the benefit of the African American minority. As the war grew into the worst sort of calamity, in which whole armies were slaughtered in a few days by the cruelest of modern weapons, as in the case of the British at the Somme campaign in 1916, the Americans, already having reelected Wilson because "he kept us out of war," seemed receptive to a pacifist tract. So John W. Noble's crew, shooting in Tampa, far from the eyes of Scott (Washington had died in November 1915 and the NAACP had lost interest), slowly drifted away from an epic of the black contribution to civilization and toward pacifism. Then, abruptly, the Americans entered the war and jogged the filmmakers toward reworking the material into a subtheme endorsing American belligerence. Sadly, by then the mainstream angels, such as Julius Rosenwald, the first Jewish vice president of Sears and Roebuck and a lifelong philanthropist on behalf of black causes, had withdrawn, and the project had fallen into the hands of vaudeville promoters and stockbrokers like Giles Corey of Chicago who eventually was convicted of fraud.

Nonetheless, the race angle, couched in a rhetoric of universal brotherhood, survived in snippets—Simon the Cyrene helping Jesus to bear the cross, head shots of the races of the world, Lincoln and emancipation, and other oddments—and, in the final reel, in a marvelous sequence that must have provided the first-ever visual argument for racial integration: a black and white farmer are working their field when they hear the nation's call to arms, whereupon they dissolve from overalls into military uniforms and march off toward the camera and out of the frame, thus integrating the forces a quarter of a century before the army itself would. Unfortunately, cinematic merit did not survive the rigors of production, and audiences, after a splashy first night in Chicago's Blackstone Theatre, stayed away in droves.[17]

From this point on, the American moviemaking system achieved worldwide dominance by filling the world's theaters with American movies, thereby filling a gap left by the wartime ruination of European studios. Unavoidably, as the system grew into the massive Hollywood institution that shaped films from script to screen, blacks might have come to expect less satisfying treatment. In fact, the decade following the war was a golden age of race-moviemaking, as though blacks sensed that in good times with only echoes of crisis little could be expected of Hollywood. Even so, within the narrow range of black portrayal in Hollywood movies, a few socially interesting images survived. Indeed, thenceforward the fineness of black performance and imagery would in fact dance on the fringe of consciousness and echo the past while trying out new futures. Reinforcing this corporate scaffolding was the so-called Hays Office, an institutional form of self-censorship in 1922 designed to placate a rising voice for legislative censorship of sexuality on the screen. But into the bargain went a certain amount of political censorship. The combination of politics and sex as bases for control of the screen created a template against which all black performance was tested, and much of it except for comedy was indeed found wanting and so helped to define blacks as the absent Other on the fringe of white life.[18]

Not that there was no grain of verisimilitude in the Hollywood version of American life. Although in cities everywhere blacks had become more of a presence—protesting, voting, joining bohemias like Greenwich Village, appearing in the odd all-black Broadway musical, filling slots in the national burlesque and vaudeville circuits—and had become the subjects of Broadway dramas such as Paul Green's highly praised *No 'Count Boy*, Wallace Thurman's *Harlem*, and Marc Connelly's Pulitzer-Prize fable, *The Green Pastures*, they still remained apart from the institutional and economic life of the nation.

But movies had settled into their corporate, studio-dominated, risk-free, vertically integrated system which, in good times such as the boom years of the 1920s, preferred the surefire rather than the new. Thus a good black role became one that confirmed the enduring system and the place of white people in it, so that any deviant black role leached through to the surface only as a sort of Freudian slip. In such tranquil times Hollywood at least partly earned the reputed power awarded it by theorists in search of the covert means of conveying ideologies. And yet Hollywood's power, even in times of its dominance, must be seen as fissured, remote from its audience's changing beliefs (which the studios almost never bothered to consider), and guided by rule-of-thumb rather than research. It was because of this that the power of the southern box office to affect movies was routinely overrated by the studios' marketeers. More than any other region, the South was the creature of its moribund economy of low-wage cotton mills; dependence upon fickle crops such as cotton, tobacco, and rice; a long hot (and unair-conditioned) summer that drove people out of theaters into dog-tracks, night baseball games, tentshow revivals, and state fairs. If fidelity to racial ideology depended upon pleasing such a volatile society, then it would seem that any crisis, much less a great depression, might destabilize the medium enough for black activists to make an impact upon it.[19]

For the time being, however, before the deluge of 1929, movies seemed monolithic in their racial rhetoric, and blacks felt driven to make their own race movies. For African Americans, movies provided only the hidden delights that came with their ability to read a double code of performance, along with an occasional outlaw movie made by a maverick outside the system and the still rarer overseas movie containing a bit by the charismatic Josephine Baker.

The makers of a half-century-long cycle of *Tarzan* movies, for instance, were never able to tame Africans into a negative subspecies of Tarzan's pale ethnic superiority. Whenever they played it as Edgar Rice Burroughs had written it, the hordes of natives gone amok seemed dangerously close to the "bad niggers" of Southern racial lore. Besides, the NAACP having successfully lobbied in several states on behalf of censorship of stereotypes and with the Hays Office taking form early in the decade, the industry inched toward inventing substitutes for black heavies—shifty-eyed Arabs in peacetime, fascist spies in wartime. In the ensuing vacuum of black roles, each gemlike bit was admired by black audiences in search of representation on the screen. Stepin Fetchit boasted that in *In Old Kentucky* (1926) he and Carolynne Snowden played the first ever on-screen black romance. Snowden, as a result of such roles, won more than a year of song-and-dance dates at Sebastian's Cotton Club, did a dance number in Von Stroheim's *The Merry Widow*, went to all the cast parties, hired a maid, and bought a roadster, all of which the black press lovingly reported as though to say a black woman had won some points in a heretofore lily-white game. Fetchit enjoyed a similar fame, which he enhanced by stenciling "Fox Contract Player" on the door of his car. Other facets of black imagery broke through the surface of all manner of movies, ranging from yet another faithful rendering of *Uncle Tom's Cabin* to Edna Ferber's famous *Showboat* with its striking, if silent, role of Joe (played by Paul Robeson on the stage), and its dramatic encounter over miscegenation.

Whenever a movie lapsed into hoary racial cant, there was always a black critic either to challenge it, to steer audiences toward race movies, or to overpraise the good stuff. "All through it the Negro is shown to splendid advantage," said Calvin Floyd of *Uncle Tom's Cabin*, and even white people applauded "each time a slave scored a point."

At times toward the eve of the "great crash," those few movies made in the modern temper found fresher uses of black roles. The hoboes of William Wellman's movie of Jim Tully's *Beggars of Life* (1928) included Mose (played by Edgar Washington, a Los Angeles policeman and father of eventual UCLA football player, Kenny Washington), an ally in hobo-jungle scraps and a train-wise forager for food. In celebrations of American history such as Cecil B. DeMille's *Old Ironsides* and Wellman's *The Rough Riders*, blacks appeared in their appropriate roles on the gundecks or in the ranks of the cavalry in Cuba. And always they served as arch indicators of a fallen white status: in *Manslaughter*, when the heroine is sentenced, the audience knows that an ominous black jailbird will be among the first icons of her new situation.

The Great Depression brought yet another opportunity for blacks to use movies as a wedge with which to intrude into the social fabric. The crisis, as it surfaced in movies, unavoidably made the point that the onset of the depression thrust blacks and whites into closer proximity, if only to stand in the same breadlines. At the same time, for a fleeting moment a rumor spread through black circles that early recording equipment reproduced black voices with greater fidelity than white. The two events helped blacks to renegotiate their circumstances under the heat and pressure of economic depression.

However, this turn of events must not be taken as a sign that America suddenly had been transformed into a like-minded, harmonious, *gemeinschaft*, communal love feast. While it is true that cultural crises such as massive, nearly uniformly felt catastrophes do draw the attention of nations inward toward shared commonalities, they become no more single-minded than in more stable times when, as Althusser and others have asserted, the ideology of a dominant group appeared to hold a critical hegemony over their society. Rather, as Feibleman has suggested, threats to collective well-being tend to draw peoples together into unaccustomed fellow feeling akin, he argued, to Gustav LeBon's anatomy of the psyches of mobs.[20] Even so, new mentalities were not necessarily unanimous, but were more like categorical differentials that marginally distinguished one ethos or ontology from another. And in America, movies provided one expression of the half-formed new frame of mind that it had itself been half-formed by.

At first, technology mattered more than politics. With the coming of sound, blacks were accorded an opportunity to strut their best stuff—their legendary, seemingly natural musical flair which, along with the rumor that black voices recorded better than white, conferred upon them a momentary hegemony over the medium. As early as 1929, only months after sound film had become practicable, a team composed of a New York director and devotee of Harlem life, Dudley Murphy, and a group of blacks led by the singer Bessie Smith, the composers J. Rosamond Johnson and W.C. Handy, the dancer Jimmy Mordecai, and others, shot a brief two-reeler of Handy's *St. Louis Blues*, with Smith singing the title song and Mordecai as her reed-slim, dancing dandy. So on-the-nose was their little gem that censors averted their eyes from its erotic bits, regarding them as merely anthropologically correct, while *Variety* interviewed a Harlem nightspot manager to confirm its authenticity. Within a year, Murphy followed with the evocative *Black and Tan Fantasy* (1930), a "half savage, half tender" visualization of a Duke Ellington composition. Finally, in 1933, Murphy capped his short burst of creative energy by shooting John Krimsky and Gifford Cochran's movie of Eugene O'Neill's *The Emperor Jones*. Yet this was more than a revival of O'Neill's play, which depicts a Pullman porter with a sort of Jungian collective memory of prior savagery who flees jail, reaching a Caribbean island where he sets up as a tinpot emperor ruling over a half-savage people. Murphy, with consulting help from black intellectuals and staging guidance by the theaterman, W. C. DeMille, gave Paul Robeson (as Jones) motives in a dense black back-story, thereby humanizing (and blackening) the drama. Thus, in less than four years Murphy demonstrated the richness which sound film could bring to African American themes. Indeed, in 1934 Duke Ellington pulled off an astonishing coup by recording on film an entire symphony (*The Symphony in Black*) in four moody movements, a sort of narrative, visual tone-poem that carried blacks from Africa through their arrival in Harlem. A productive cycle of similar musical two-reelers quickly followed.

Of course, too much might be inferred from individual triumphs. When the Hollywood producer Ernest Lubitsch praised black actor Clarence Muse's direction of *Run Little Chillun*, Muse insisted that "Hollywood's not prejudiced; they'll buy anything that's successful." And even James Weldon Johnson guessed that whites might pick up black material because of a "reluctance [on the part of black writers] to see what they consider lower phases of Negro life."

Perhaps Hollywood's most startling depression-induced break with its past was a drift toward collective, broadly social themes along with resolutions of dramatic conflict that coincided with solutions to social problems. For African Americans this trend took two forms: a short-term willingness to use all-black material and a generalized inclusion of blacks in urban "problem pictures." The former case resulted in a mere half-dozen efforts, all of which would have been unthinkable in the Republican boom years of the 1920s. For blacks, they opened a running debate over what to show the white folks. In *Hearts in Dixie* (1929), for example, surely the earthen, folkish community of sharecroppers is given its quiet dignity, but of them all only one kid seems smart enough to go north and become "a big doctor." In *Hallelujah!* (1929), it is not a lone black preacher who is tempted by the wiles of Nina Mae McKinney; it is all black males who run wild when they reach the big city. And despite a pious claim to anthropological objectivity following the main titles, *The Green Pastures* (1935) seemed to be about all of African America and its uncritical, shrill, emotional folk religion rather than about an isolated Southern hamlet. It was as though no amount of Hollywood good intentions could prevent the bedrock of racial cant from breaking through the surface, as though it were a shard of Lévi-Strauss's universal memory or a white Freudian self winking at the presumption of blacks—the eternal Others—in claiming the screen for themselves. But, on balance, black critics leapt at the chance to praise small favors. The *Amsterdam* commended Clarence Muse in *Hearts in Dixie* for his "sterling work . . . in putting over the moral that nothing the colored man has was obtained without hard work." Oscar DePriest, the lone black congressman, told the Harlem first-night audience that *Hallelujah!* revealed "how far our race has progressed culturally and artistically since the Emancipation Proclamation." And Ralph

Matthews in the *Afro-American*, thought *The Green Pastures* "a disgrace" only because Warners' failed to use the original Broadway cast. By the end of the decade, Sol Lesser reached for similar density of black cultural expression by engaging Muse and Langston Hughes to write his own B-movie black musical, *Way Down South* (1939).

As for the "social problem" movies, it was not so much that they displaced the standard racial fare, but that they contrasted with it and by their presence challenged it. So, although *The Littlest Rebel* and *The Little Colonel* persisted, a few old stereotypes changed with their times, new black roles emerged, and African Americans joined the ranks of America's "problems" to be solved in the last reels of scores of movies. In *The World Moves On*, for example, Stepin Fetchit played a conventional servant, but one who followed his employer into the French Army in World War I where he was wounded at the front. Jungle movies—not the B-movie level, of course—more than ever used real locations and real Africans, as in Metro's *Trader Horn* and Fox's *Rhodes of Africa* with its chieftain played by "a genuine Matabele warrior." And every genre seemed to find a place for blacks: the convicts in *Hell's Highway* and *Ladies They Talk About*; the gamblers in *Smart Money* and *Bullets or Ballots*; Paul Robeson instead of Stepin Fetchit in the remake of *Showboat*; Muse's rebellious slave in *So Red the Rose*; Slim, the black gunman in Duke Mantee's gang in *The Petrified Forest*; the Haitian doctor in the movie of Sinclair Lewis's *Arrowsmith*; Bill Robinson's black policeman in *One Mile from Heaven*; the uncommonly blunt drama of "passing" at the center of John M. Stahl's movie of Fannie Hurst's *Imitation of Life*; the ever more flippant servants, such as Hattie McDaniel in *Alice Adams*; the intercuts to "the Harlem crowd" during the fight sequences of *Golden Boy*; the blacks scattered among *The Boy Slaves* and *Wild Boys of the Road*; and so on. Moreover, moviegoers noticed. Black students in Greensboro, North Carolina, for example, boycotted theaters that had refused to book *One Mile from Heaven*; black critics winnowed wheat from chaff, praising Muse, for instance, while chiding Fetchit for his "low comedy;" and liberals discussed the rush of new images. "Have you seen 'Slave Ship'?" wrote the critic Carl Van Vechten to his friend James Weldon Johnson. "This goes a little further in the direction of realism than most movies on this subject." In fact, so much was on stage, screen, and page that he predicted in 1935, "This is likely to be a NEGRO WINTER."[21]

But the depression also raised another issue of black's social and political identity that African American thinkers had rarely debated. For the first time in decades the depression and the second of the world wars that followed it cleared a national place for black political issues that they had not held since Reconstruction. Beginning with the Mississippi constitutional convention of 1890, and capped by the *Plessy vs. Ferguson* decision by the Supreme Court, racial politics had become a local matter all but totally removed from federal jurisdiction. Not only hundreds of lynchings but major civil strife such as the Wilmington, North Carolina, riot of 1898 were all reckoned to be local matters. So profound was the plight of blacks in the ensuing decade that it precipitated a massive migration northward, not to abate for a half-century, an era which the historian Rayford Logan called "the nadir" of black fortunes in America. Ideologically, in black circles this calamity had revived an old debate between assimilationists and cultural nationalists that was a central issue in the making of race movies between the wars.

At first, in the years following *The Birth of a Race*, most race movies took the path of bourgeois liberalism as defined by Booker T. Washington's Tuskegee Institute: education was designed to train blacks in marketable skills so that, as DeFoe said of his countrymen, each man could become "the complete English tradesman." After all, Jesse Binga's bank in Chicago, Charles Clinton Spaulding's North Carolina Mutual Insurance Company in Durham, and Phil Payton's Afro-American Realty Company in Harlem seemed to offer stark evidence that the way out of victimization at the hands of southern terrorists was through skill and enterprise. Early black movies were full of the ideology of capitalism. Even the first draft of *The Birth of a Race* was based on Washington's *Up from Slavery*, which had equated "Dr. Washington's personal strivings [with] the strivings of the race climbing up."[22]

A typical title in the pioneer days of race movies was the Lincoln Motion Picture Company's *The Realization of a Negro's Ambition*, a film that is now lost but whose evocative title suggests why the firm screened it before the 1916 convention of the National Negro Business League, a group founded by Booker T. Washington. The theme? A young African American seems thwarted and denied by racism until he learns to prospect for oil and thereafter wins a fortune and the hand of his best girl. For a time the black press joined in encouraging support of such films as "one of the great vitalizing forces in race adjustment." Sometimes editors simultaneously urged "sensible support of Negro producers like (Oscar) Micheaux" coupled with "organized protest" against Hollywood movies. Late in the decade, the Colored Players firm of Philadelphia produced the finest race movie of its time, *The Scar of Shame* (1927), a film that pointedly reached for a bourgeois ideological mode that might reach a mass audience. The movie calculatedly set class against class by portraying the hero and his set as being in search of "the finer things," in contrast to the lower-down blacks, whose environment held them back. Clearly, as in all race movies by their nature as all-black expressions, both the black plight and its resolution were in black hands. And because the dramatic conflict pitted black against black, the eventual denouement would inevitably be resolved on behalf of the black good guys, thereby defining heroism as being a brave individual rather than performing a collective act. And yet, as one of the characters points out as he reads the fallen heroine's suicide note, "our people have much to learn," by which he means a black version of classical liberalism: individual striving toward personal goals in a laissez-faire society.[23]

The Great Depression, as it had done to general American mentalities, changed all of this. On the debit side, the coming of sound-film raised the stakes of moviemaking, thereby shutting out some prospective black filmmakers and reducing others, such as Oscar Micheaux, to penury and the necessity of borrowing from white angels. Unavoidably, as black critic Romeo Daugherty observed, black moviegoers were drawn to Hollywood technical facility and "well-trained stars" rather than to the "strained acting, poor staging, and poorer scenery [which] discloses that another shoestring [black] article is on its way." But, more hopefully, the "new conditions," as President Roosevelt described the depression at his inaugural, set in motion a fitful revival of African American cultural nationalism that had begun back in the days of the Lincoln company, when filmmakers had put on film the works of Paul Laurence Dunbar, Charles Waddell Chesnutt, and other black writers. During the depression years such filmmakers broadened their range to include a parody of Marcus Garvey's movement, Micheaux's attempts at urban themes such as *The Girl from Chicago*

(1932) and his autobiographical *The Exile* (1931), Bill Robinson's flawed celebration of black musical performance in *Harlem Is Heaven* (1932), and Jack Goldberg's *The Unknown Soldier Speaks*, a tribute to black soldiers in World War I.

Although most of them improved on techniques only marginally and often contented themselves with echoes of Hollywood genres such as Westerns, musicals, and gangster movies, a few of them tempered their formulas with infusions of politics. Micheaux's *Underworld* (1937) and Bert and Jack Goldberg's *Double Deal* (1939), nominally about gambling in cities, paused to celebrate black individual and group aspiration. Ralph Cooper, the most prolific star of the black gangster genre, phrased the new formula most explicitly in his *Am I Guilty?* (1940) in which he played a physician who dreamt of opening a free clinic but was dragged by circumstances into a moral dilemma when criminals retained him as their specialist in gunshot wounds. Edgar G. Ulmer's *Moon over Harlem* (1939) played a similar angle, but with a note of environmentalism that called attention to how poverty breeds crime and in-group violence. The hero counters with a plea for solidarity. "When they stoop to chiseling poor colored folk they're steppin' on my toes," he says. "I sure like the way you talk," says one of his allies. "It makes us *all* feel like men." The best of them, *Paradise in Harlem* (1940), used the gangsters versus Harlem formula as the motive for a community fundraising effort marshaled around a black jazz version of *Othello*. But by then on the eve of World War II, the movement all but ended, having fallen victim to its own failure to attain consistently competent B-movie standards and to the fact of Hollywood's gradual incorporation of palatable black roles into its own depression-era movies. Besides, the rigors of competition thrust most of the black firms under the control of white angels on both coasts, led by Bert and Jack Goldberg's International Road Shows in the East, Ted Toddy and Alfred Sack in the South, and Harry and Leo Popkin's Million Dollar Productions in Los Angeles, in addition to threatermen like Frank Schiffman in Harlem and David Starkman in Philadelphia, who sponsored race movies as a means of filling their own screens. In any case, race movies had all but expired by 1941.[24]

World War II, more than any other single event, demonstrated the likelihood of the impluse of national unity against foreign danger drawing the members of a normally pariah caste into formerly lily-white corridors of power and influence. In the bargain, it also temporarily drew blacks away from group nationalism and toward a revival to achieve full egalitarian citizenship. Indeed, even before the war the spirit that would inform racial propaganda was already afoot in white liberal circles. As though anticipating their wartime fellowship, as early as 1939 Eleanor Roosevelt had joined with blacks in a demonstration of future changes. The black singer Marian Anderson had been denied a gig at Constitution Hall, a theater owned by the Daughters of the American Revolution, of which Mrs. Roosevelt was a member. Not only did Mrs. Roosevelt resign, but together with Secretary of the Interior Harold L. Ickes, she offered Anderson the Lincoln Memorial as an arena, to which she drew an Easter Sunday crowd of fifty thousand. Moreover, not only had Mrs. Roosevelt demonstrated a racial liberalism long absent from Washington, but the Gallup poll reckoned that a majority of Americans agreed with her stance. With such straws in the wind on the eve of an impending foreign war against nations that included racism in their policies, blacks seized an opportunity to demonstrate that their own social goals and the nation's had very nearly become one. In the following year, for example, A. Philip Randolph, founder of the all-black Brotherhood of Sleeping Car Porters, enlisted Mrs. Roosevelt in his campaign for a federal commitment to equal opportunity for black workers in war industries. His threatened march on Washington quickly resulted in a presidential order integrating war-related industries. Meanwhile, Carlton Moss, a young radio scriptwriter and Morgan College alumnus, had formulated such discrete events into a staged "Salute to the Negro Soldier" designed as a propaganda primer expressing an evolving mentality.[25] In other words, even before the Japanese bombing of Pearl Harbor, African America had begun severally to assert the oneness of its own social goals with a general American need for unity against a foreign enemy.

Predictably, the bedrock of Hollywood output, the various B-movie genres, seemed untouched by the onset of the war. But as we have seen, national crises precipitate new terms that minorities may bargain for and consent to. As early as 1940, coincident with the opening of a struggle between the British and the Italians for control of North Africa, the Suez Canal, and perhaps even the oil fields of Persia, two apparently random events took place: Walter White of the NAACP began to cultivate friendships with Hollywoodians, one of whom, Walter Wanger, had purchased *Sundown*, Barre Lyndon's *Saturday Evening Post* serialized African potboiler. Gradually, under the influence of White's suasion and the rising drama of the African war, Wanger changed his movie to include a war whose aims were only gradually embracing such high-flown goals as anticolonialism. Not only was black Africa treated with uncommon fidelity to its culture traits, but the outcome of the plot included a vague hint of postwar changes in the African status quo. In the case of movies over which White held little influence, such as *In This Our Life*, Warner's film of Ellen Glasgow's Pulitzer Prize novel, he was quick to write congratulations to the stars for their liberal treatment of its black aspects. So effective were these Hollywood liberal gestures on the eve of war that, when David O. Selznick insisted that in his *Gone with the Wind* blacks "come out on the right side of the ledger" and that in these "fascist-ridden times" the Ku Klux Klan episodes of Margaret Mitchell's book not survive to reach the screen, black filmgoers actually enjoyed and appreciated his gestures (despite the continuing survival of Hollywood's hoariest black stereotypes).[26]

With the actual onset of war, the trend accelerated, with blacks and their liberal allies in Hollywood and in the Office of War Information playing their roles as agents of a new mentality thrust into prominence by the nature of a struggle between fascism and liberal democracy. Always, however, they worked on changing sensibilities—not overt behavior. Moreover, even ideology was treated gingerly and unevenly. Zanuck's Fox took the plunge; Y. Frank Freeman's Paramount held back. The Pentagon inched toward changed racial relations in the ranks; field-grade officers fought it. And so on. But the new conditions significantly altered the implicit ideology of movies; the rhetoric of war-borne unity and brotherhood necessitated a new racial rhetoric.

In turn, the new ideology raised two separate issues: not only what Hollywood was to show the nation but who was to teach it to Hollywood. Walter White already had tested his links to Hollywood, but as lone wolf. After Pearl Harbor, however, he had become one of Gramsci's organic intellectuals in the van of changes that needed no prodding from revolutionary cadres. The imperatives of national unity themselves not only gave White his opportunity but also thrust him into alliance with government agencies and Hollywood "moguls" whose collective embracing of the goal of national unity assured

White and the NAACP of access to formerly unthinkable power and influence. In staccato cadence White opted to hold the NAACP convention in Los Angeles, on the doorstep of the studios; the Office of Defense Transportation waived rules against needless travel; Wendell Willkie, chairman of Fox and special counsel to the NAACP, gave the keynote address; in a round of luncheons, White exacted promises from the moguls to include blacks in a wider range of roles in proportion to their numbers in society and to link them to the war effort; Hollywood liberals began writing suitable material (or, as in the case of *Sundown*, rewriting the old); the Office of War Information and the Department of the Army took up the idea of making *The Negro Soldier* and other propaganda reflective of the new conditions; and finally, near war's end the NAACP successfully lobbied to compel the government to give its surplus prints to schools, trade unions, and other communicators.[27]

The new African American presence was everywhere. In *The Maltese Falcon* (1941), Sam Spade stops at a mail drop where we see a neatly dressed black couple in the frame. Why black?—unless someone, moved by the changing climate, specifically *ordered* them from Central Casting. In *Tarzan's Desert Mystery* (1941), the Africans fight the Germans. Why?—Sol Lesser recalled that the State Department asked him to work it in. A black soldier is a central figure in Metro's *Bataan* (1943). Why? A leftist writer thought he belonged there; the producer kept him in over the objections of the front office; and when a subsequent writer wrote him out, a young black actor hired as part of the new sensibility informed White; White successfully lobbied for his reinstatement. *Crash Dive* (1943) featured a black sailor in a submarine crew, a machine gunner in a night landing on an enemy beach. Why? The black press reported that he had been modeled on Dorie Miller, a black messman who turned machine gunner in the heat of battle at Pearl Harbor. Not all war movies boasted such clear-cut evidence either of White's hand or of the spirit of the times. Yet their range embraced a tribute to black show business in *Stormy Weather*, an all-black Broadway musical in *Cabin in the Sky*, jazzy bits in *Star Spangled Rhythm* and *This Is the Army*, Canada Lee's stoker in *Lifeboat*, Paul Robeson's imposing figure in *Tales of Manhattan*, Rex Ingram's Sudanese soldier in *Sahara*, Hattie McDaniel's modernized, wartime model domestic servant in *Since You Went Away*, not to mention the dignified, bourgeois, soldierly black extras who turned up in crowd scenes of all sorts.

Not only were these movies appearing, but moviegoers noticed them and quickly learned to expect each new film to attain a higher sensibility. The decade had begun with overt propaganda worn on the sleeves of public events such as Moss's New York revue *Salute to the Negro Soldier* or the collective authors—Hughes and Henry Blankfort, with music by Ellington and Billy Strayhorn—of *Jump for Joy*, which had drawn broad audiences ranging from "middle-class ofays" to "dicty Negroes." "All the sketches had a message for the world," recalled one of the chorus girls. But after these heady days, criticism among liberals sharpened, even grew barbed, as they pressed for still greater levels of racial revisionism that followed from the rhetoric of official propaganda. Blacks, sometimes in concert, wrote letters of praise or complaint to the studios. More rarely, the NAACP attacked specific films while they were in production, hoping to alter them *before* release, which resulted in at least one gutted film, Metro's biography of Andrew Johnson, *Tennessee Johnson*. Newspapers either complained, as the Richmond *News-Leader* did of the cameraman on *Cairo* who "hunted . . . out" Ethel Waters "to the exclusion of the other actors" or, as the *New York Times* did, praised *In This Our Life* for its "one essential component," its "brief allusion to racial discrimination." The weeklies were even more pointed, complaining that the fad for black material was "obscene" in its "rush" to embrace black themes, or that *Stormy Weather* so failed to live up to its own hopes that a critic quipped "Rain! No game!" The calibrations grew so fine that the *Amsterdam* carefully praised the psychological Western, *The Ox-Bow Incident* as a "rare opportunity," while carping at its black actor, Leigh Whipper, for playing his role in "servile fashion." There seemed to be Negro cultural committees or better films committees everywhere, and their members wrote both to Hollywood and to White, once to the latter praising a *Dr. Kildare* B-movie for its "United Nations" mood, but hazing its failure to include a black doctor. The veteran critic Lester Walton not only caught the drift of the movies but, as Feibleman might have done, attributed it to a changed ontology. Of Hollywood he wrote: "They are tired as we are of these [lingering] caricature[s]," and therefore "there is no excuse for any of us" to play the old roles.[28]

As both commentator on and formulator of the emerging racial ideology of the war, William G. Nunn, publisher of the *Pittsburgh Courier*, along with his cartoonist, created his famous "Double *V*" campaign. In cartoons (showing a *V* for victory shaped by two hands, one black and one white), editorials, and gimmicks such as "Miss Double *V*" contests, he promoted the idea among readers that the time was ripe for pressing a quid pro quo, a bargain in which blacks agreed to serve in exchange for assurances of an improved status following the war to be grounded in the wartime slogans of "brotherhood" and "tolerance."[29]

For its part, the army entered into the spirit of the times only gingerly, bound by a 1940 selective service act not to discriminate in drafting troops, but equally bound by military custom to segregate black troops into separate, often noncombatant, units under white officers. But soon after the war began, the army's own civilian advisers, acutely aware of the new mood, along with Judge William Hastie, the War Department's civilian aide for racial matters, joined with the NAACP and Hollywood liberals in the service of the Signal Corps, to make movies that might give voice to the "Double *V*" while tiptoeing through the thickets of army conservatism.

The result was a place in Frank Capra's production schedule at the makeshift Signal Corps center on Western Avenue in Hollywood. There, Moss, the black writer, Stuart Heisler, a Hollywood journeyman director, script doctors Ben Hecht and Jo Swerling, along with a large cast of black soldiers, turned out *The Negro Soldier* (1944) and a spate of similar liberal propaganda vehicles, ending with two of the most explicit, even insistent, titles: *Teamwork* and *Don't Be a Sucker*. At the prodding of civilian advisers Donald Young and Charles Dollard, the army had set out to make a training film designed to introduce black soldiers to their contribution to American military history and white troops to the fact of a black component in their army.

The movie was completed and approved for viewing by the troops in January 1944. The finished film revealed a quality of Hollywood style that promised much for a black future in movies: that is, the classical idiom and all of its rhetorical strategies were turned to the task of recreating and redefining African Americans on film (and in society), much as Gramsci and Feibleman in their separate arguments had anticipated. Crisis had begotten both a new order and a new black place in it as a result of a national crisis that had drawn Americans together across formerly unbridgeable lines. It opened with Moss, the writer, playing a preacher who refers to a flurry of iconic expressions of the nation's will to integrate blacks into the nation.   Gold and white banners speckled with the blue stars symbolized men in military service.   One sequence centered on Joe Louis's heavyweight boxing match with Max Schmeling, the German champion who had once defeated Louis.   Moss pointed out that the victory by an "American fist" had come to have greater social moment, in that each contender was serving in his nation's army in "a far greater struggle" between fascism and democracy. He read directly from *Mein Kampf*, linking its references to world conquest to those in which Hitler referred to Africans as "born half apes" whom no amount of training could convert to lawyers or doctors.   Then, in a classically edited sequence of both reenactment and documentary, Moss traced the history of black military service to the country, ending with a concocted moment when a studio prop cairn commemorating black service in France in World War I is shown with marching German boots supered over it, as in an abrupt cut the Germans blow up the symbol of black former glories. Finally, the last half of the movie shrinks to a human scale by following the career of a young black officer candidate through basic training to his graduation.   And in a coda that shows blacks (considerably overrepresented) in various aspects of army life, including West Point, Moss graphically hinted at the Double V that Nunn's *Courier* had advocated.

Black leaders quickly saw the transformation in the treatment of blacks, and after a preview in the Pentagon for black journalists, a series of test-viewing by samples of soldiers, and a final battery of tests by the Office of War Information, the film went into civilian release.   The result was a national debate over the film and its prospective impact.   On the left, the National Negro Congress thought it "the best ever done," while the seasoned critics of the center thought of it as so conventional as to "sugar-coat" the racism that it purported to treat.   Moss weighed in with a prediction that the film might "mean more to Negroes than most white men could imagine."

Moreover, these African Americans quickly leapt to use the influence of their newly filled seats of power.   Joining with celebrated figures from politics and show business, the NAACP and other activists successfully lobbied to thwart the release of *We've Come a Long, Long Way*, a race movie compiled by Jack Goldberg and narrated by the black evangelist Elder Solomon Lightfoot Michaux. Together, Roy Wilkins of the NAACP, Truman Gibson who had replaced Hastie, and Thurgood Marshall, legal counsel of the NAACP, assembled lists of white liberal allies, religious figures, and celebrities, filed an *amicus curiae* brief on behalf of *The Negro Soldier* as the only practicable medium for dissemination of racial "facts," and prodded a Hollywood writers guild into endorsing the film as a "real contribution to national unity" and a rebuttal to "racist lies." By the spring of 1944, the movie had enjoyed a Los Angeles premiere sponsored by the mayor's Committee on Civic Unity, appeared in a series of films shown at the Museum of Modern Art in New York, become available to schools, libraries, and trade unions, had gone into release in Latin America, Haiti, and other foreign countries, and had been reviewed in the metropolitan press ranging from the *New York Times* to the "People are Talking About" column of *Vogue*. Soon afterward, the same machinery was turned toward broad distribution of its bolder sequel, *Teamwork*.[30]

The point here, of course, is that crisis, dislocation, and shifting ways of speaking to the ethnic dimension of American nationalism had conspired to introduce into movies a thread of black advocacy, oddments of black culture, dramatic heroes who acted in the name of the group, bits of the anatomy of black life, and most of all the vague promise of integration into the daily round of national life. In Hollywood movies as well as in federal propaganda, black roles had moved toward the centers of both the frame and the action. In the last reels of several movies, blacks had been part of resolution in the form of both a political and dramatic closure. In fact, many race-angled wartime movies, borrowing some of their texture from prewar social problem movies, had resulted in a new genre of films— the "message movie," which endorsed some liberal sentiment by codifying it into the rhetoric of image, structure, and action.[31]

The question for black activists in 1945 was how to sustain the drive once the crisis of war had abated. At first, such an ambition seemed readily obtainable. The new place of blacks in the movies had already helped to drive black viewers toward the mainstream— at least as long as it flowed with bits of black life. Many of the filmmakers who had worked on wartime projects brought to peace-time Hollywood some of their sensibility. Other filmmakers contributed to a boom in, as the historian James T. Shotwell put it, the "thinking picture," or films that took up social themes, a trend that in turn helped shape a documentary film culture which fed on a nontheatrical audience in unions and schools. The NAACP, indeed dozens of activist groups, regularly issued filmographies designed to spread the news. And audiences seemed ready for the new era. On the documentary side, more institutions than ever owned 16 mm projectors, while on the theatrical side, Hollywoodians had concluded that audiences were ready for meatier fare, that soaring costs and slumping revenues required more sophisticated material, and that the old studio system itself was crumbling and on the verge of reshaping into a more independently minded world of filmmakers.

To take only one instance of this liberal drift, the Hollywood director Mervyn Le Roy, producer Dore Schary, writer Albert Maltz, singer Frank Sinatra, and a small RKO crew shot *The House I Live In*. The title came from a popular wartime liberal anthem that celebrated a sort of old-neighborhood ethnicity to which the war had given new, nationalistic meaning. The two-reeler began with Sinatra as himself, taking a break from a recording session, only to come across a gang of kids who have cornered a lone boy in an alley. He is their chosen victim because, as one of them says, "We don't like his religion." Sinatra at first brands them as "Nazis," then persuades them not only to lay off the kid but to take him into their group. How? His rhetoric is lifted right out of the late war and its central metaphors, the wartime random distribution of blood plasma without regard for the race of donors (albeit a late development in the black case) and a legendary story, told in flashback, of the bombing of a Japanese battle cruiser by an airplane piloted by Colin P. Kelly and guided by bombardier Meyer Levin. The little homily about racial and ethnic harmony won an Oscar for its year, played theaters, and then went into widespread distribution in schools, churches, and union halls.[32]

Along with the OWI's wartime releases like *The Negro Soldier*, *Teamwork*, and *Don't Be a Sucker*, a film commissioned by the Army from Paramount as a propaganda warning against German divide-and-conquer tactics, such movies held out the hope for a postwar liberal cinema. But, at the same time, the war's end also raised the question of the permanence of war-born social change; after all, African Americans with long memories might have remembered that World War I had ended in the Red Summer of 1919, during which no less than two dozen race riots around the country spoiled the return to peacetime. Ever since the French Revolution political theorists had analyzed the phenomenon of "Thermidor," the period of exhaustion that follows violence and terror. Thermidor has seemed not only the window of opportunity for men of the right, the men on horseback, but also the time when the urge for order is stronger than the resolve to preserve the fruits of revolution.

The end of World War II, at least as far as African Americans were concerned, at first seemed no exception to this pattern. Certainly Hollywood movies seemed less forthright in their portrayal of the racial issues that had surfaced as a result of the war. But this impression was only partly true. In Hollywood, the caution arose more from a particular fear of perilous economic times, especially for the future of Hollywood, and from a general fear of racial material that story editors were only just learning to appraise. Nonetheless, by 1947 Harry Truman's government revived wartime issues with its release of *To Secure These Rights*; moreover, Gallup polls uncovered an at least marginal willingness on the part of white citizens to accept such egalitarian measures as a peacetime extension of Roosevelt's fair employment executive order. If Hollywood seemed at first too timid to play to this sensibility, the gradual breakup of the studio system, which was brought on by a pluralizing of American tastes and interest, suburbanization, which thinned formerly dense markets, the weakening of censorship arrangements, and the judicially imposed requirement that the corporate chain of integration of movies from script to screen must be broken, all provided ample reason for caution in a perilous fiscal world. But at least as important in shaping postwar ideology were persistent survivals of liberal propaganda campaigns.

Gradually, Hollywood moviemakers rejected avant-garde means of presenting African Americans to postwar audiences and settled for civilian versions of the blacks who had been redefined by wartime needs for a unified nation. Thus the inevitable Thermidorean reaction resulted not in a regression to former ideals but an integration of crisis-inspired images of war into a peacetime society. Just as the formula for wartime movies required a lone black to be introduced cautiously and manageably into a white microcosm—a platoon or submarine crew—so the postwar "message movies" created a special Negro whose entry into the center of the frame required whites to deal with his presence and, incidentally, to be made better by the experience.

Beginning in 1948, most major studios bought properties from which to develop the new blacks: Louis De Rochemont's *Lost Boundaries*, Metro's *Intruder in the Dust*, Fox's (and Zanuck's) *Pinky* and *No Way Out*, and Stanley Kramer's Columbia release, *Home of the Brave*. In each case black characterization was only incidental to the dramatic core, which more centrally reflected the postwar world and how the presence of lone blacks affected the white circles into which they had penetrated. The blacks in Walter L. White's *Reader's Digest* book, *Lost Boundaries*, are "passing," and the movie is about how a white village comes to accept a remarkably talented black doctor and his family. *Pinky*, too, is passing but is made more pointedly "black" in that her passing has stemmed from childhood inadvertence; and eventually, as an adult, after she has become a nurse, she rejects her white status, embraces her black identity, and struggles to open a clinic and daycare center for black children. Black Lucas, in William Faulkner's and Clarence Brown's *Intruder in the Dust* is unique by virtue of his inheritance of land, a rarity for Mississippi blacks, and his undaunted willingness to flaunt his singularity. He wears a black fedora, carries a pistol, pays his bills, uses a gold toothpick, and refuses to "play the nigger" for a local white boy struggling to come to terms with such a rare and self-possessed black man. In *No Way Out*, Sidney Poitier played the first of his paragons of black virtue who spent three decades using some special talent—medicine, teaching, carpentry, social work—as a device for teaching white people to become better for having encountered him.

Of them all, *Home of the Brave* most pointedly proclaimed its wartime origins. Kramer and his writer, Carl Forman, had both worked in the Signal Corps film unit; Robert Rossen, the director, and George Glass, his publicist, were Hollywood leftists; and as though in tribute to their roots, Forman named the main black character "Mossy" in honor of his association with Carlton Moss, the author and star of the army's *The Negro Soldier*. The movie is about the impact made on a squad of soldiers when a black volunteer is thrust into their midst. Each soldier, of course, represents a predictable response from a menu of white American responses— withdrawal, animosity, barbed hatred, cool professionalism, and warm, if limited, liberal openness. For the first time ever, racism is presented as a form of social pathology and the heavies as sociopaths. Unfortunately, when Mossy undergoes a hysterical paralysis caused by his leaving his buddy to die on a Japanese-held island, the flashbacks that form the narrative of his therapy add up to an unintentional conclusion that he, the black victim, has induced his own hysteria because of feelings of difference from whites. Thus his "cure" is to come resolutely to regard himself as being like everyone else, despite racist laws and customs that have told him otherwise. Not that Hollywood liberals played blacks false here. Rather, in the first years following the war, as they searched for a rhetoric expressive of their hoped-for changes in black status, liberals shed Israel Zangwill's "melting pot" as a simile for their goals and espoused historian Kenneth M. Stampp's idea that "Negroes *are*, after all, only white men with black skins, nothing more, nothing less."[33]

If this seems a less than earthshaking formulation of the liberal, black future, it must be remembered that American racial politics were in flux but shifting distinctly to the left, sometimes nudged by the half-gestures of movies. Several lines of development ran parallel to Hollywood's message movies. First, race movies declined, unable to stand against the new Hollywood, except for a string of rhythm and blues revues that survived until 1955. Second, even the most arcane African Americana, although embedded only in a few independent films, often drew crossover audiences. For instance, Gjon Mili's *Jammin' the Blues* (1944) was not only the finest example of jazz ever made on film, it also was *Life's* "Movie of the Week, " while *The Quiet One* (1947), the creation of a cell of New York intellectuals led by Janice Loeb, Sidney Meyers, Helen Levitt and James Agee, reached mercilessly into the depth of urban poverty and yet enjoyed a strong run in the nation's new "art houses." Third, B-moviemakers joined the trend either by exploiting racial tensions or by celebrating accessible black heroes. Harry and Leo Popkin, for example, who had begun the war making race movies of relatively good quality, made *The Well* (1951), a low-budget, tightly wound reenactment of an event in which a black girl fell into an abandoned well, polarizing a town into black and white adversaries and nearly sparking a riot. Joe Louis, Jackie Robinson, and the Harlem Globetrotters (or at least Abe Saperstein, their founder) were among the subjects of B-movie "biopics." Finally, now and again the oddly interesting black film came through customs from abroad. Italian "neorealists" sometimes used Dots Johnson or John Kitzmiller or other black soldiers who had arrived with the 92d Infantry during the war in *Paisan, Senza Pietà*, and other films which blacks took politically pointed roles. In *Paisan*, for example, Dots Johnson played a GI whose boots are stolen by a Neapolitan waif whom he has befriended; later after catching the kid as he is looting an army truck, the soldier angrily tries to return him to his parents only to find that he is orphaned and lives in a crowded cave—an epiphany scene from which the audience is supposed to assume that the world's oppressed are linked by the thread of their common plight. The most sensational of the foreign movies was Jean Paul Sartre's *The Respectful Prostitute*, which elicited such hoots from black audiences amused by its off-the-mark portrayal of American race relations that exhibitors tried to market it as a "sexational" import. The most disappointing film was Richard Wright's own *Native Son* with the author himself as his ill-fated hero, Bigger Thomas; his book had been a bestseller before the war but by 1951 seemed curiously old-fashioned because of its stiff Marxism, one-dimensional heavies, and garbled mise-èn-scène caused by interrupted shooting in Chicago, Buenos Aires, and elsewhere.[34]

But what of Stampp's "white men with black skins"? Sidney Poiter's enduring career assured Columbia and his other employers, as well as his audiences, that for a quarter of a century the screen would formulate race relations and black life in terms set forth by Stampp and enacted by Poitier. In other words, Poitier's era—and clearly it deserves no other label—marked the higher ground on which African Americans consented to be ruled. As Kenneth Spencer's preacher in *Bataan* had shown, he could be a great demolition man; as *Pinky* had shown, she could fight for legacy in white people's court and convert it to black uses; so Poitier's Dr. Brooks in *No Way Out*, his egalitarian but fiery black convict in *The Defiant Ones*, his tragic Kimani in *Something of Value*, his East End teacher in *To Sir With Love*, his Homer Smith the carpenter in *Lilies of the Field*, thence to the beau ideal of the era, *Guess Who's Coming to Dinner?* in which Poitier's saintly United Nations' physician is made to seem, as a result of his outsized virtues, eligible to marry a rich white woman. Each of his roles was a calculated marvel of precise, already won political goals. His powers were in the sense of limits, and a cool restraint that masked a banked fire whose unseen heat and flames must be inferred. Almost always, in liberal fashion, his color seemed weightless in the plot—indeed invisible in *The Slender Thread* and *A Patch of Blue*; in the former he was just a voice on a suicide hot-line; in the latter, befriender of a blind girl.[35]

Many movies offered their own versions of Poitier's paragons: Juano Hernandez in *Intruder in the Dust*, *The Breaking Point*, and *Young Man with a Horn*; Ossie Davis's title role in *Purlie Victorious*; Bernie Hamilton's prim suitor in *One Potato, Two Potato*; Maidie Norman's sane maid in *Whatever Happened to Baby Jane?*; Woody Strode's and Hernandez's soldiers in *Sergeant Rutledge*; and even Sammy Davis's hip convict in *Convicts Four*. All together they seemed to ratify the status quo, but at least it was a recently *achieved* status quo that had arisen from pressures applied by blacks themselves beginning in 1942.

In addition, Poitier's era, due in part to his own success, opened the screen to various tests of the limits imposed by the actor and the keepers of his image. Gene Persson and Anthony Harvey's production of Leroi Jones's *Dutchman* so theatened to dispel the mood that New York City agencies withheld cooperation and it was finished in London. Shirley Clarke's *The Cool World* (1964) provided the most acid yet reportorial drama of the black slums since *The Quiet One* but also suffered from scant bookings. When Darryl Zanuck determined to bring Alec Waugh's anticolonialist novel *Island in the Sun* (1957) to the screen, he cautiously removed the Poitier role, a crisp, politically assertive lawyer, reallocating his lines to other characters, among them a wooden, tethered labor leader played by Harry Belafonte. One interracial love affair was chilled by removing it from the Caribbean off-camera to London, and another (Belafonte's with Joan Fontaine) was rendered platonic, thereby earning a nationwide hazing from critics who knew the book and expected more.

Meanwhile from 1954 onward the civil rights movement warmed to its task. More importantly, as it grew more urban, more threatened by overreactive police, and more sophisticated in its use of television, the movement gradually grew from desultory local protests to a nationally televised melodrama. The result was America's first cultural crisis that reached a daily, national audience even as it happened. Moreover, not only did television provide a visual urgency, it effectively created a new black hero, the former victim, who daily rose to the occasion at lunch counters in Greensboro, bus stops in Montgomery, and dozens of other small town encounters with southern police. So "profoundly constructive" was its effect, according to Clarence Mitchell of the NAACP, that one television producer labeled his medium "the chosen instrument of the black revolution."[36]

Willy-nilly, television by the mid-1960s had produced a hero whose images contrasted sharply with Poitier's cool style. Coupled with congressionally created agencies that monitored equal opportunity, the increasingly angry mood led to an expanded black presence on both television and movie sets and to a search for redder meat than had been provided by Poitier's vehicles. So in 1968 the *Los Angeles Sentinel* headlined a story: "TV Is Black Man's Ally." Soon the network serial dramas reflected the search for new material. *I Spy, Mod Squad, The Outcasts,* and other prime-time network programs featured spies, rebellious cops, and truculent former slaves in prototypes of "bad" black roles that Hollywood either could not abide or would not distribute. From soap opera to Public TV magazine and talk shows, even the staffs included blacks and were, as in the case of *Black Journal,* even bossed by them. "Black is the color of our new TV," reported one magazine. Futhermore, critics rushed to keep up. When, for example, the producer of *Julia,* a serial about a black widowed nurse, ingenuously described the show as the sum of "a lot of hopes and dreams," a few weeks later a white critic censured the show as "this well-meaning program [that] would contribute to the castration theme in the history of the Negro." In keeping with the angry black voices in the streets, television struggled to maintain its own pace of change. "Encounter television," William Greaves of *Black Journal* called it. *Variety,* the show-business trade paper, summed up the trend as "an emerging multi-media stereotype: intensely brooding, beautiful black rebel."[37]

Movies, on the other hand, spoke either through Poitier's harmonious voice or with the foreign accents of Michael Roemer's *Nothing But a Man* (1964), Melvin Van Peebles's French-made *The Story of a Three Day Pass* (1968), and Costa-Gavras's *The Battle of Algiers* (1967). In no case did the films drawn from outside of Poitier's sphere reach mass audiences. Their subtlety, the play of their little satires, their homage to group solidarity, all remained inaccessible to the audiences in the ghetto grindhouses. Yet it was they who spoke to the changing times before Hollywood got around to it. Costa-Gavras, in a mode that came to be his signature-style, not only portrayed war-torn Algiers as a combat zone but introduced viewers to the ideas of the black, Martiniquain psychiatrist Franz Fanon. Echoing Lévi-Strauss, the film spoke for using indigenous culture as a weapon against the French occupying army, as in the instance of Algerian Muslim women concealing grenades in the folds of their traditional robes and veils. At the same time, each unanswered stroke of native violence either discredited the French or drove them to excesses of cruel reprisal that belied their claims to colonialist paternalism. The texture of advocacy, the anatomy of a culture, the throngs of urban outlaws who cared not a whit for personal safety all forecast eventual American versions.

At a more humorous level, Van Peebles's movie was also about black male assertiveness, but expressed from within American culture. His hero is, in fact, an American soldier courting a young French woman. On the one hand, this is seen by his superiors as a reason for harassing him, but also as a sign that the soldier himself has embedded in his psyche the same taboos against interracial sex, the audience is allowed access to his fantasies. The importance of a date with his white lover is comically seen as he dresses with flair, as "The March of the Toreadors" plays on the sound track. And, as he encounters his girlfriend, he fancies himself a sort of jungle prince, swinging through the vines in pursuit of her.

Of the three filmmakers, the German Roemer came closest to a film version of the combative black presence in the streets and on the TV screen; in fact, James P. Murray in *Black Creation* magazine called *Nothing But a Man* "the greatest of black motion pictures."[38]

But for all its merits as a faithful, pastoral rendering of ordinary life in the black South, it spoke little to urban strife. Its hero took pride in quiet resistance to southern insult. When the idea of leaving for northern cities crossed his mind it was always as a last measure and one dampened by the memory of his father's sodden, defeated death in the city. Back home, he maintains certain standards: he prefers gandy dancing on the railroad but will change flats and pump gas if need be, while at the bottom of his scale and only when driven to it will he consent to pick "other people's cotton." Besides, he must modulate his resistance because of his wife's condition: daughter of a preacher, she pours coffee at church socials, teaches school, and is quite pregnant—and none of this can be put at risk by an uppity husband. Thus, Roemer's movie was solid social drama in a European realist mode, but far from the jangle of the new black machismo of television drama. Later in the decade the majors not only clung to Roemer's pastoral model but put more distance between their movies and current events by choosing material set in former times, as in the cases of Martin Ritt's depression-era pastoral, *Sounder*, and Gordon Parks's auto-biographical *The Learning Tree.*[39] And with good reason: by averting their eyes from the action in the nation's streets filmmakers were able to personalize and humanize black plight and rage, thereby rendering them palatable for crossover audiences. Why risk fragmenting the aggregate audience by playing to the emotional pitch reported on the nightly news? Why not escape it instead?

The mounting pitch of the civil rights movement as recorded on the nightly news might have been crisis enough to force a veering off toward blacker movie material, much as William Greaves and other black television workers had precipitated such a shift in *Black Journal* and other TV programs. But the assassination of Martin Luther King, Jr., in the spring of 1968 not only accelerated the trend but gave permission to violent *revanchists* in the movement to break out of whichever of his nonviolent constraints had been holding them in check. Certainly, black drama and other expressions had signaled such a drift. Even as the Black Panther party and other paramilitary groups took up weapons both as props and as defenses, Leroi Jones (by then Amiri Baraka) wrote a series of plays, such as *Jello*, in which "Rochester" ritually murders Jack Benny; Jimmy Garrett wrote *We Own the Night*, in which the action takes place behind the barricades of an urban insurrection; and Sam Greenlee turned out his angry novel, *The Spook Who Sat by the Door*, an anatomy of the workings of the CIA, from which black defectors learned techniques of guerrilla warfare and then took them back to their neighborhoods.

Clearly, as the movement reached crisis stage, African Americans had already begun to respond to it in volatile terms that had so far eluded movies. At the same time, Melvin Van Peebles, sometime expatriate in Europe and a prospective filmmaker, having been shut out of Hollywood, contrived to make a movie in France that he brought to the San Francisco Film Festival as the "French" entry. Van Peebles proved to be the perfect catalyst that set in motion almost a decade's-worth of, as *Variety* called them, "blaxploitation movies." More than any other black figure in the business, he carefully fabricated a personal legend as an urban outlaw, thereby creating in a single forthcoming film *Sweet Sweetback's Baad Asssss Song*, a genre of films that redefined black filmmaking and even saved a couple of studios from bankruptcy.

Van Peebles's accomplishment consisted of his facility for synthesis. By folding elements of legendary black outlaws such as Staggerlee into the title role of Sweetback, and by playing it himself after having cultivated his own legend as an outlaw, Van Peebles managed the improbable—the creation of a black genre in a single film. Most critics of genre film have argued that a film genre, or type, evolves over time and derives from elements drawn from familiar traits, audience preferences, expectations created by advertising, and the tastes of characteristic filmmakers. The result is a genre: the Western, the musical, the John Ford movie, and so on. Van Peebles, by mixing his own personal legend with that of his central character, foreshortened the process into a single archetypal film. He sported a tattoo on his neck that said: "Cut on the dotted line." He wore the blue denim of the movement, smoked thin cigarillos, and peppered his rap with street talk (his solution to racism: "Take names and kick ass"). When the dedication of his associates flagged, he refocused their attention by banging their heads on the floor or hanging them out of an upper window. Or so he said.

The result was that the black Other strode to the center of the frame and of the action. His jangling music by Earth, Wind, and Fire, his choppy cutting, saturated coloring, his portrayal of white policemen as irredeemable gargoyles fit only for execution seemed to violate and overturn every precept of Hollywood's smoothly flowing narrative tradition. Into the bargain, he recodified black from feckless comedy or winsome song-and-dance into ominous threat, who in the last reel promised a vengeful return. A measure of his success finds testimony in the young black urban audience's half-decade search for sequels in a steady stream of "blaxploitation" films that echoed, rehearsed, and played variations on several shared themes and moods: a lone black hero (albeit played against a rhetoric urging black unity), an anatomy of black ghetto life and culture, a celebration of black history and style, an advocacy of a black future free of "the man" (a generic term with a range of meaning, from white oppression to European culture), an *aesthetique du cool* or a cool, insouciant style of walking and talking.[40]

This is not to argue that Van Peebles invented the code; rather, he synthesized its elements, much as Griffith had done in combining Victorian fiction, American road-show melodrama, and cinematic devices already introduced by various pioneers. As early as 1967, for example, Herbert Danska had filmed John A. Williams's *Night Song*, a biographical novel about jazzman Charlie Parker, with Dick Gregory in a tour de force performance. Poorly distributed and recut by its eventual owners, it nonetheless earned praise from critics in search of breaks with Hollywood convention. In Hollywood itself (or at least Culver City, home of MGM), Gordon Parks and Joel Freeman produced *Shaft* from Ernest Tidyman's script. Its hero recodified black imagery merely by inserting a magazine model, Richard Roundtree, into a Dick Powell role as though in *Murder My Sweet* or other 1940s *films noirs*, and by retailoring the lingo, dress, and body English to fit the new black circumstances. Other Hollywood productions borrowed a tactic from the white music industry and "covered," or made their own versions of, white genres, as in *Blacula* (*Dracula*), *Cool Breeze* (*The Asphalt Jungle*), *Abby* (*The Exorcist*), *The Lost Man* (Carol Reed's Irish rebellion film, *Odd Man Out*), *Up Tight* (John Ford's 1935 Oscar-winner, *The Informer*). More rarely, black sources were the foundation for a movie as in the case of Chester Himes's black cops in *Cotton Comes to Harlem*. Others ranged from productions of black companies such as Belafonte's *The Angel Levine* (by Czech director Jan Kadar), the British *Leo the Last*, and some, like *The Bus is Coming*, which amounted to no more than interesting home movies.[41]

Unfortunately, the genre flagged by the 1970s, losing its creative energy and its young black audience to Chinese martial arts movies imported from Hong Kong and Singapore. They were almost operatic in their outsized revenge stories in which, typically, an innocent but superbly trained monk witnesses the violation of his sister at the hands of a bloated mandarin drug dealer. Only at the extremity of realizing the enormity of these crimes does the monk surrender to the urge for revenge and turn his martial arts upon the hapless minions of the mandarin, who himself is dispatched in the last reel. Not that the genre died completely. Football stars like Fred Williamson and Jim Brown, fugitives from other genres such as Carl Weathers, the black adversary in *Rocky*, Jim Kelly, a martial arts devotee; and others kept it alive in grindhouses and drive-ins well into the 1980s.[42]

But what remained of African American life in the ensuing years of filmmaking? More than at any other moment in black American history, black intellectuals had perceived a threat that would have occurred to few observers during, for example, the nadir years at the beginning of the century, when black images were recodified into new modes of behavior that hovered on the verge of assimilationism. For example, Brock Peters's precisely etched performances as a terribly victimized sharecropper in the movie of Harper Lee's *To Kill a Mockingbird* and as a sly Harlem criminal in Sidney Lumet's *The Pawnbroker* were really about the coming of age of two white children and the rebirth of a Jew's soul after his stunting existence in a Nazi concentration camp, respectively. The viewer is grateful for Peter's work and for the filmmakers' wise use of it, but it served only to illuminate a white story. Even "blaxploitation" movies rarely did more than gloss the African American culture they pretended to serve. *Claudine* sketched (too comically) life on welfare; *Five on the Black Hand Side* satirized certain fissures in black family life while glibly papering over them in the last reel; *Kongi's Harvest* reduced the complexities of African nationalism to Hollywood conventions of good and evil; *Lady Sings the Blues* and *Leadbelly* were little more than "biopics" of the singers Billie Holiday and Huddie Ledbetter.

Moreover, this cultural neutralization, however well intended as a means of access for white audiences into the arcana of black life, also disallowed the making of any movie that might be more narrowly focused, culturally complex, or politically aggressive. Even when a movie reached for a blackened angle as, for example, Michael Schulz's *Carwash*, reediting and cutting dogged them into release. And no amount of black admixture to the Hollywood formula could alter the ambivalent place that women hold in black life, a place so deeply embedded as to have linguistic roots. The famous African American *portmanteau* word, *motherfucker*, for example, catches the ambiguity, in that its meaning has ranged from "fighting word" that speaks with contempt of matriarchy to a superlative term describing, for example, a "bad dude" (or, synonymously, "bad motherfucker"). Suffice it to say that this linguistic history, and its sources in black family histories, has left black women with a range of portrayal almost as narrow as it had been when McDaniel won her Oscar in 1940. She had grown only from Mammy to "my old lady" and from *Carmen Jones* to "black-bitch" (uttered as though one word). That the ambiguity persists may be seen in the vibrant protests against the treatment of women in Norman Jewison's movie of *The Color Purple.*

Unavoidably, then, almost any piece of work made for a mass audience offended the minority that served as its topic or angle. That is, the extent to which Hollywood spoke to ethnic matters was the extent to which the majority expressed lingering hegemony. In this sense Marcuse was correct: majority rule unconsciously carried with it the threat of dominance, and therefore the equally unconscious tendency to endorse the status quo.

Therefore, no amount of black presence or personal success in Hollywood can promise the faithful rendering of black history and life. Necessarily then, Oscar Micheaux and his cohorts had been prescient: even as his career atrophied after 1940 in the face of Hollywood's crisis-based embracing of African American material, he had written to the Office of War Information begging for a chance to work in the war effort for fear that white filmmakers who had not experienced a lifetime of playing to black audiences would misread the codes, garble what black images signified, and worse, lapse back into Hollywood stereotypes. In other words, an age when Hollywood devoted an overweening attention to black material might be precisely the age in which blacks should wish for a black cinema.

In any case, following on the heels of the "blaxploitation" era, and to some extent inspired both by it and by the revivified black television image, young black, often academically based, filmmakers emerged. They came from all directions: William Greaves came to Public TV by way of the National Film Board of Canada; St. Clair Bourne sharpened his tools making documentaries for Public TV, the most famous among them *Let the Church Say Amen;* Warrington Hudlin made *Black at Yale* and *Streetcorner Stories* while fretting his way through the experience of Ivy League campus life. Moreover, through a Black Filmmakers Foundation, Third World Newsreel, Tony Gittens's Black Film Institute in the University of the District of Columbia, and other indigenous agencies, these filmmakers have managed to reach an international black audience in a line so direct that they speak to their constituency more efficiently than Hollywood speaks to its. In a way, the threat of being swallowed by a larger culture has provided them with a nagging culture crisis that gives them a reason for being as well as assuring them an eventual place in history.

At this writing, the work of these filmmakers has carried them toward a goal only dimly seen by Oscar Micheaux and the other independents between the world wars: freely created films derived from African American sources and distributed to a large crossover audience whose tastes only slightly mediate between maker and consumers.   More than any other figure so far, Spike Lee, a resident and celebrant of Brooklyn, sometime student, and advocate of the Black Filmmakers' Foundation, has succceeded in realizing this pluralistic ambition.   His films have tickled the edges of black courtship rites (which, luckily for his distributors, seemed startlingly parallel to white customs) in *She's Gotta Have It*, probed, often acerbically into black "Greek letter" societies on campuses in *School Daze*; and sketched the most politically and socially complex anatomy of cross-cultural and cross-racial relations ever seen on film, in *Do the Right Thing*.   Unlike his forebears, from those who made *The Birth of a Race* to *Sweetback*, Lee has been tolerant of ambiguity, even cultivating it in his work; this has provided him with a distinctive voice that has coincided with the tastes of urbane black audiences who have learned to live with ambiguity, as well as of white audiences for whom, too, racial matters have grown less starkly black-and-white. *Do the Right Thing*, for example, has no heavies, only an entire cast that have misplaced their anger, set out to defend empty forts, and celebrate vacuous commercial celebrities and music as "their" own, and allowed themselves to be led into battle by the most unprepossessing people in the ranks.   The result is a tour-de-force probe into how slights and hurt feelings escalate into reasons to attack "others."[43]

Lee's success has promised much.   Everyone in black film circles knows of an African American filmmaker suddenly invited to Hollywood to "do lunch" and talk "product." *Vogue*, as it had done for Moss in 1944, tried to enshrine a reluctant Lee as an icon of fashion.   Foreigners honored his work, as well as that of members of his circle in New York and of other black circles on the West Coast.   And he made the cover of *American Film*.[44]

More than any other figure in African American filmmaking, Lee has calculatedly linked himself with the history of black independent filmmaking, has self-consciously reached for a black audience, and used a rhetoric (of both filmmaking and marketing) that has rendered his work accessible to crossover audiences without compromising the inner values of his work.   St. Clair Bourne's *Making 'Do the*

Right Thing' (1989) might have been yet another cream puff in the self-promotional genre of movies about the making of bigger movies, but it shrewdly caught the sense of Lee's work by editing together several set-piece interviews with the principals along with journalistic footage of life on the location in the Bedford-Stuyvesant sector of Brooklyn. "We owe a lot to Oscar Micheaux," he says, promising to "pick up the torch." In another homage, he trotted out Melvin Van Peebles, framed in a violent fragment from his *Sweetback*, and recorded him praising Lee for not segregating himself from the black "community." At the same time, in assuming this black posture, he neither cheapened nor dismissed the sensibilities of Danny Aiello and the rest of the white cast. Along the way, Lee draws upon an eclectic memory that ranged from an old *Hitchcock Presents* TV show to a recent *cause célèbre* murder of a black youth by a white mob in Howard Beach, a neighborhood only minutes from Lee's Brooklyn locations.

At the end of *his* film, Bourne effectively provides a coda that sums up *Lee*'s film. He uses the climactic scene of *Do the Right Thing*, a fire which destroys a pizzeria as the black neighborhood chants, "Howard Beach, Howard Beach," to assert a black consciousness; but allows Lee to scoff at the "bullshit" implicit in overpraise of black filmmakers and to insist on the need to "learn your craft."[45] He quotes a disc jockey in Lee's film as he asks, "Are we gonna live together?" but also ends with a block party at shooting's end in which everyone toasts Lee's ironically named company, "Forty Acres and a Mule," thereby ending with the riddle at the root of all African American filmmaking—whether it can succeed in reaching a broad audience without losing its historic identity.

1. A critical history and analysis of recent trends in movie criticism may be found in, respectively, Norman F. Cantor, *Twentieth Century Culture: From Modernism to Deconstruction* (New York, et al., 1988), and Noel Carroll, *Mystifying Movies: Fads and Fallacies in Contemporary Film Theory* (New York, 1988).

2. The weight assigned to ideology extends over a wide range. See John Fiske, "Television: Polysemy and Popularity," *Critical Studies in Mass Communication,* 3 (Dec. 1986): 394, in which the Frankfurt school is cited for its unremitting portrayal of "the people" as "cultural dupes," as opposed to (p. 400) Fiske's analyzing the implicit ideological thread in a popular television private-eye show, *Hart to Hart.* In general, more recent Marxists have tried to move away from a sort of reductionist,

monocausal Marxism, and even from Lacan and extensions of his work in Louis Althusser which have argued that ideology, willy-nilly without forethought, is conveyed from various "signifying practices" and the highly receptive position in which moviegoers find themselves. See, for example, Lawerence Grossberg, "Strategies of Marxist Cultural Interpretation," *Critical Studies in Mass Communication,* 1 (1984): 409–10.

For Hollywood as the manufacturer of the stuff of such an ideological rhetoric grounded in circumstances of production see, for example: Robert C. Allen and Douglas Gomery, *Film History: Theory and Practice* (New York, 1985), 84–87; David Bordwell, Janet Staiger, and Kristin Thompson, *The Classical Hollywood Cinema: Film Style & Mode of Production to 1960* (New York, 1985), 250, in which they argue that the studio system "defined the range of practical possibilities" of filmmaking; and, for the notion of Hollywood as a form of "state apparatus," Robert Sklar, "Oh! Althusser! Historiography and the Rise of Cinema Studies," *Radical History Review* 41 (1988): 10–35.

3. Jeffrey Morton Paine, *The Simplification of American Life: Hollywood Films of the 1930s* (New York, 1977), 8 (quoted).

4. Jack Katz, *Seductions of Crime: Moral and Sensual Attractions in Doing Evil* (New York, 1988), 225–36, on "bad niggers," "badasses," their "bitches," and the mores of the "hardman;" Dan Rose, *Black American Street Life: South Philadelphia, 1869–1970* (Philadelphia, 1987), 58, 60, 171; ("bubble"), 215.

5. See for example, Thomas Cripps, "*Sweet Sweetback's Baadasssss Song* and the Changing Politics of Genre Film," in *Close Viewings,* ed. Peter Lehman (Gainesville, Fla., 1990); and on Chinese martial arts movies as an alternative cinema for black youth, see Verina Glaessner, *Kung Fu: Cinema of Vengeance* (New York, 1974), 14.

6. John Kenneth Galbraith, *American Capitalism: The Concept of Countervailing Power* (Boston, 1952), passim.

7. On Gramsci and his links to Frankfurt through common sources in idealism, see Cantor, *Twentieth Century Culture,* 201–203; and on the man and his ideas, John Hoffman, *The Gramscian Challenge: Coercion and Consent in Marxist Political Theory* (New York, 1984), 18, 20, 51; and particularly on the idea of "organic intellectuals," see Walter L. Adamson, *Hegemony and Revolution: Antonio Gramsci's Political and Cultural Theory* (Berkeley, 1980), 100–101, 148–49, 168–70. For a black application, see Kobena Mercer, "Diaspora Culture and the Dialogic Imagination: The Aesthetics of Black Independent Film in Britain," in Mbye B. Cham and Claire Andrade-Watkins, eds., *Blackframes: Critical Perspectives on Black Independent Cinema* (Cambridge, Mass., 1988), 50, 59.

8. James K. Feibleman, *The Theory of Culture* (New York, 1946, 1968), 7, 43, 96, for the quotations on LeBon, wars, and Nazis.

9. For two essays on African Americans and World War II, see Thomas Cripps, *Slow Fade to Black: The Negro in American Film 1900–1942* (New York, 1977), xiii and John Morton Blum, *V Was for Victory: Politics and American Culture During World War II* (New York, 1976), vi.

10. Mercer and Taylor, quoted in Cham and Andrade-Watkins, *Blackframes,* 11 and 13, respectively; "encoding" and "narrative" taking up in James A. Snead, "Recoding Blackness: The Visual Rhetoric of Black Independent Film," *Whitney Museum of American Art: The New American Filmmakers Series,* program no. 23, 1–2.

11. Gerald Mast, *A Short History of the Movies,* 4th ed. (New York, 1986), 5 (quoted); and Allen and Gomery, *Film History,* 84.

12. Snead, "Recoding Blackness," 1.

13. For an anatomy and a brief history of *Kwaanza*, see Gossie Harold Hudson, "Kwanzaa (sic): It's That Time Again," *Morgan Bulletin*, 1 (Dec. 18, 1989): 2.

14. This account is drawn from Cripps, *Slow Fade to Black*, i and ii.

15. Bordwell et al., *Classical Hollywood Cinema*, xi, makes the case for rising directorial control after 1909.

16. Cripps, "The Reaction of the Negro to the Motion Picture 'The Birth of a Nation,'" *Historian*, 25 (May 1963): 244–62.

17. Cripps, "*The Birth of a Race* Company: An Early Stride toward a Black Cinema," *Journal of Negro History*, 59 (Jan. 1974): 28–37; and Cripps, "*The Birth of a Race:* A Lost Film Rediscovered in Texas," *Texas Humanist*, 5 (March/April 1983): 10–11. A print of the rediscovered film is in the Library of Congress. See also *Image as Artifact* (Washington, 1988), an American Historical Association videotape produced by John E. O 'Connor, which makes use of both paper documents and parts of *The Birth of a Race* itself.

18. It was at this moment that Hollywood movies came to dominate a Europe drained by war and susceptible to American imported films. At the same time, as a vertical oligopoly that affected film from script to screen, Hollywood grew into a manufactory that rationalized its own system of production. In such a setting the theories of Louis Althusser seemed irrefutable. Movies easily seemed to be conveyors of an imaginary world, and ideology, "precisely that which signifying practices manufacture," as Lawrence Grossman in "Strategies of Marxist Cultural Interpretation," *Critical Studies in Mass Communication* 1 (1984): 393–421, wrote of Althusser and Stuart Hall. Indeed, according to Althusser, the system itself, in the way that it located "omniscient" viewers in darkened, dreamlike states outside the action yet linked to it, set an ideological agenda. See also Stuart Hall, "Signification, Representation, Ideology: Althusser and the Post-Structuralist Debates," *Critical Studies in Mass Communication* 2 (June 1985): 91–114, in which he analyzes Althusser's idea that any institution, such as Hollywood, by its nature joins society's superstructures, which serve as "ideological state apparatuses" manufacturing "systems of representation."

19. Cripps, "The Myth of the Southern Box Office: A Factor in Racial Stereotyping in American Movies, 1920–1940," in *The Black Experience in America: Selected Essays*, ed. Lewis Gould and James Curtis (Austin, 1970), 116–44. It is in times when a society perceives itself as going well that Louis Althusser's notion of cinema as state apparatus seems compelling. Movies are formed by codifications of what movies are supposed to be, then monitored in their degree of success by censors, critics, and audiences, under social conditions that seem sanguine. Perhaps, then, as D. N. Rodowick argues in *The Crisis of Political Modernism: Criticism and Ideology in Contemporary Film Theory* (Urbana, Ill., 1988), 76, a film is most starkly "refracted through the ideology" and most pointedly records the "world of the dominant ideology." Or, as Bordwell, *Classical Hollywood Cinema*, 82, put it, as the medium evolved in the nutrient broth of profit and was polished by its formulas, the resulting "principles reinforce dominant ideological positions."

20. Feibleman, *Theory of Culture*, 7.

21. The narrative of the era between the wars is drawn from Cripps, *Slow Fade to Black* vi–x; for Van Vechten's quotation, see 289.

22. Emmett J. Scott, quoted in Cripps, "*The Birth of a Race* Company," 30.

23. This account of "race movies" is drawn from Cripps, *Slow Fade to Black*, vii, xii. A surviving fragment of *The Scar of Shame* is accessible in many libraries, among them the Library of Congress and the Enoch Pratt Free Library in Baltimore. See also, Cripps, "'Race Movies' as Voices of the Black Bourgeoisie: *The Scar of*

Shame (1927)" in *American History/American Film: Interpreting the Hollywood Images*, ed. John E. O'Connor and Martin A. Jackson (New York, 1979), 39–56.

24. Cripps, *Slow Fade to Black*, xii.

25. Brochure loaned to the author by Carlton Moss.

26. Cripps, "*Sundown* (1941): World War II as a Cultural Crisis That Shifted American Racial Dominancy and Ideology," paper read before the 14th Annual Florida State University Comparative Literature Conference (1988); on *In This Our Life*, see Walter White to Olivia DeHavilland and Jack Warner, 1941, in NAACP Records, Library of Congress, Washington, D.C.; and Cripps, "Winds of Change: *Gone with the Wind* and Racism as a National Issue, " in *Recasting: "Gone with the Wind" in American Culture*, ed. Darden Asbury Pyron (Miami, 1983), 137–52.

27. Cripps, *Slow Fade to Black*, xiii.

28. Cripps, *Slow Fade to Black*, xiii.

29. Derived from a survey of the *Pittsburgh Courier*, January–April 1942; Blum, *V Was for Victory*, 208.

30. Thomas Cripps and David Culbert, "*The Negro Soldier* (1944): Film Propaganda in Black and White," in *Hollywood as Historian: American Film in a Cultural Context*, ed. Peter C. Rollins (Lexington, Ky., 1983), 109–33.

31. The foregoing changes, although unthinkable before the war, must not tempt us to see them as the mere inexorable acting out of Gramsci's or any other theory. In sum, they happened because of the direct social action of African Americans and their liberal-leftist allies who were moved by the urgency made manifest by a national crisis that seemed to have a bearing on black fortunes. For the specific tactics of these movements, see: Thomas Cripps, "Movies, Race, and World War II: *Tennessee Johnson* as an Anticipation of the Strategies of the Civil Rights Movement," *Prologue: The Journal of the National Archives* 14 (Summer 1982): 49–67; Thomas Cripps, "*Casablanca, Tennessee Johnson,* and *The Negro Soldier*—Hollywood Liberals and World War II," in *Feature Films as History*, ed. K. R. M. Short (London and Knoxville, 1981); and Thomas Cripps, "Racial Ambiguities in American Propaganda Movies," in *Feature Films as History*.

32. A copy of the script is in the Albert Maltz Papers, Twentieth Century Collection, Mugar Library, Boston University; the story is told in fragments in Mervyn LeRoy, *Mervyn LeRoy: Take One,* as told to Dick Kleiner (New York, 1974), 156, 163–64; and Kitty Kelley, *His Way: The Unauthorized Biography of Frank Sinatra* (Toronto, 1986), 106–7, 271, 516.

33. Kenneth M. Stampp, *The Peculiar Institution: Slavery in the Ante-Bellum South* (New York, 1956, 1964), vii.

34. Thomas Cripps, "*Native Son* in the Movies," *New Letters* 28 (Winter 1972): 49–63; reprinted in David Ray and Robert Farnsworth, eds., *Richard Wright: Impressions and Perspectives* (Ann Arbor, 1973).

35. Poitier's life was not all crystal stairs. At the apogee of his career he began to feel the press of black critics who found him too accommodating to white interests. Yet he resented being blamed for Hollywood's reluctance to opt for "a variety of positive images." Of one of his black critics who had done a piece for the *New York Times*, "Why Do White Folks Love Sidney Poitier So?" Poitier wrote; "What I resented most about Clifford Mason . . . was his laying of all the film industry's transgressions at my feet." Sidney Poitier, *This Life* (New York, 1980), 337.

36. For an instance of black protest against television portrayals, see Thomas Cripps, "*Amos 'n' Andy* and the Debate over American Racial Integration," in John

E. O'Connor, ed., *American History/American Television: Interpreting the Video Past* (New York, 1983), 33–54; and for a sketch of the impact of black protest on TV programming, see Thomas Cripps, "The Noble Black Savage: A Problem in the Politics of Television Art," *Journal of Popular Culture* 8 (Spring 1975): 687–95.

37. The standard history of African Americans in television is J. Fred MacDonald, *Blacks and White TV: Afro-Americans in Television since 1948* (Chicago, 1983); quotations from Cripps, "The Noble Black Savage," passim.

38. Cripps, "Sweet Sweetback's Baadasssss Song," in Lehman, *Close Viewings*; quotation from Thomas Cripps, *Black Films as Genre* (Bloomington, Ind., 1978), 49.

39. Cripps, *Black Film as Genre*, vii, "*Nothing But a Man.*"

40. Cripps, "Sweet Sweetback's Baadasssss Song," in Lehaman, *Close Viewings*; see also Melvin Van Peebles, *Sweet Baadasssss Song* (New York, 1971), for a script draft and some accounting of its making and exploitation.

41. Cripps, *Black Film as Genre*, 48–51.

42. Marilyn D. Mintz, *The Martial Arts Film* (South Brunswick, N.J., 1978), 145–46, says, "They depict a certain range of rebellion and pose possible alternative behaviors that appeal to the suppressed . . . (as a) fantasy and a forerunner of change."

43. *Sun* (Baltimore), 5 Jan. 1989, for the *Vogue* story in which Lee was asked for a light piece on fashion but put a biting spin on it that clashed with the editor's hope for a "cool" piece. *American Film*, July/August 1989, for one of several covers which Lee attained during the summer of his success. See also Spike Lee, *Do the Right Thing* (New York, 1989), a journal and script.

44. The literature on African American film continues to grow. In addition to the works cited in this chapter, the reader will wish to consult the following works (and their bibliographies): Donald Bogle, *Toms, Coons, Mulattoes, Mammies & Bucks: An Interpretive History of Blacks in American Films* (New York, 1973); Martin Dworkin, "The New Negro on the Screen," *Progressive* 24 (October–December 1960): 39–41; Daniel J. Leab, *From Sambo to Superspade: The Black Experience in Motion Pictures* (Boston, 1975); Richard Maynard, *The Black Man on Film: Racial Stereotyping* (Rochelle Park, N.J., 1974); Lindsay Patterson, *Black Films and Filmmakers: A Comprehensive Anthology from Stereotype to Superhero* (New York, 1975); Charles D. Peavy, "Black Consciousness and the Contemporary Cinema," in Ray B. Browne, *Popular Culture and the Expanding Consciousness* (New York, 1973); Jim Pines, *Blacks in the Cinema: The Changing Image* (London, 1971); Henry T. Sampson, *Blacks in Black and White: A Source Book on Black Films* (Metuchen, N.J., 1977); James R. Nesteby, *Black Images in American Films, 1896–1954: The Interplay Between Civil Rights and Film Culture* (Washington, D.C., 1982); Edward Mapp, *Blacks in American Film: Today and Yesterday* (Metuchen, N.J., 1972); and Gladstone L. Yearwood, ed., *Black Cinema Aesthetics: Issues in Independent Black Filmmaking* (Athens, Ohio, 1982).

Useful compendia include: Marshall Hyatt, ed., *The Afro-American Cinematic Experience: An Annotated Bibliography & Filmography* (Wilmington, Del., 1983); Phyllis Rauch Klotman, *Frame by Frame—A Black Filmography* (Bloomington, Ind., 1979); David Meeker, *Jazz in the Movies: A Guide to Jazz Musicians 1917–1977* (London, 1977); Anne Powers, ed., *Blacks in American Movies: A Selected Bibliography* (Metuchen, N.J., 1974); Allen L. Woll and Randall M. Miller, eds., *Ethnic and Racial Images in American Film and Television: Historical Essays and Bibliography* (New York, 1987); J. William Snorgrass and Gloria T. Woody, *Blacks and Media: A Selected, Annotated Bibliography* (Tallahassee, Fla., 1985).

45. See Bourne's film, *Making 'Do the Right Thing'* (1989), in general video release. In a sense Lee, like many black filmmakers of his generation, works as a practitioner rather than a theorist, as Stuart Hall said of Antonio Gramsci, a "political intellectual and social activist [in] . . . organic engagement with his own society." See Stuart Hall, "Gramsci's Relevance for the Study of Race and Ethnicity," *Journal of Communication Inquiry* 10 (Summer 1986): 5–27.

Part Three

SOUNDING OUT RACISM:
THE RADIO INDUSTRY

4 COMMERCIAL AND NONCOMMERCIAL RADIO

WILLIAM BARLOW

Blackface Radio (1920–39)

The advent of radio broadcasting in the United States coincided with the cultural ferment of the Roaring Twenties, the decade of the fabled Jazz Age. The "flappers" and "flaming youth" of America's white bourgeoisie were in open revolt against the lingering puritanical and Victorian moral codes that were the foundation of their parents' culture. In their efforts to break away from this stifling heritage and its outmoded morality, these cultural rebels turned to African American music and dance. Jazz, blues, and the Charleston became synonymous with the cultural life of the 1920s' obstreperous young adults and symbolic of their defiance of the older mentors of the established social order.

This expropriation of African American song and dance by rebellious elements of the nation's white middle class had contradictory results. On the one hand, American commercial entertainment was infused with new African American musical and performing styles—often subversive of the dominant culture—which fed the rebellion of white American bourgeois youth against their parents. However, the price paid for this cultural transaction was a misguided and condescending dilution of the original art form, because once they entered into the mainstream of American culture, African American song, dance, and humor were appropriated either by white entertainers and/or white businessmen who tailored them to their own liking and reaped the profits from their sale. Black artists and performers, the inheritors of these art forms, discovered not only that they were exploited financially by the entertainment industry but that they were also forced to compromise their art, and often their integrity, in order to gain entrance into show business. The repercussions of these cultural contradictions, which came into sharp focus during the 1920s, were to play a decisive role in determining the form and content of African American participation in radio broadcasting up until World War II.[1]

Black dance music, known as jazz, was an early staple of local and eventually network radio programming in the twenties. But, invariably, it was the prominent white dance bands that received the lion's share of prime-time airplay. The orchestras of Vincent Lopez, B. A. Rolfe, Ben Bernie, and particularly Paul Whiteman, were familiar to regular radio listeners. Meanwhile, the pioneering African American bands of the era—for example, King Oliver's band in Chicago, Bennie Moten's in Kansas City, and Fletcher Henderson's in New York—were rarely heard on the airways. Likewise, such white singers as Sophie Tucker, Al Jolson, and Rudy Vallee were network radio's major performers of African American songs, including the blues, during the Jazz Age. At the same time, the era's greatest African American blues vocalists, Ma Rainey, Bessie Smith, Lonnie Johnson, and Leroy Carr, were seldom featured on local radio outlets and they were never heard on network radio; hence they were unknown to a large, influential nationwide listening audience.[2] The lone exception was Deford Bailey, a black harmonica player who appeared on the Grand Ole Opry. But, in general, the blues and jazz featured on the radio airways in the 1920s were white cover versions of the African American originals.

In addition to promoting the popularity of white vocalists and dance bands performing their versions of African American music, the advent of commercial broadcasting in the United States also gave a number of white vaudeville entertainers still doing blackface comedy routines a new lease on life. In fact, they were the first performers to portray African American characters on network radio. The most famous blackface minstrels on the airways prior to World War II were "Amos 'n' Andy," played by two white comedians, Freeman Gosden and Charles Correll. Gosden was a Virginian with close cultural ties to the antebellum South. His grandfather had been a Confederate soldier who continued to wage guerrilla warfare against the North even after the South had officially surrendered. Young Freeman had been raised in Richmond, Virginia. An African American female housekeeper took care of him from his infancy into his teens. His closest childhood friend was a black youth called "Snowball," who lived in his household while the two boys were growing up. Later, during his career as network radio's foremost virtuoso of "Negro dialect stories," Gosden credited "Snowball" with being the source of much of his humor. Charles Correll, on the other hand, came to blackface humor through his association with, and career in, vaudeville. He was born and raised in Peoria, Illinois, where his father was a construction worker. Young Charles took up show business to escape the drudgery of his father's working-class vocation and life-style. He played the piano in nickelodeons while also developing his skills as a soft-shoe dancer. He then hired on as a traveling vaudeville director with the Joe Bren Company, which staged variety shows in small towns in the Midwest with the aid of local amateurs. It was while working for Joe Bren that Correll got to know a fellow employee with similar interests and ambitions named Freeman Gosden.[3]

While working and rooming together in Chicago in the mid-1920s, Gosden and Correll developed their first blackface minstrel team for radio, called "Sam and Henry." According to vaudeville composer and pianist Eubie Blake, they modeled their act after the black comedy team of Miller and Lyles, who starred in "Shuffle Along" on the New York stage.[4] The early comedy routines were aired on WGN, a local Chicago station without network affiliation. They moved next to WMAQ, where they changed their program's name to "Amos 'n' Andy" and began to record their shows for syndication to other radio stations. The name change was necessary because WGN still owned the rights to the "Sam and Henry" title. The syndication of the new "Amos 'n' Andy" series attracted the attention of NBC, and by 1929 it was airing the show from 6:00 to 6:15 P.M. six nights a week on its "Blue" network, which was one of its two national radio linkages. At that juncture "Amos 'n' Andy" became a national radio phenomenon. The blackface characters Gosden and Correll fashioned into Amos 'n' Andy were fairly typical of the prevailing minstrel stereotypes in American show business. Amos was a classic "Tom" stereotype. As the authors described him: "Trusting, simple, unsophisticated. High and hesitating in voice. It's 'Ain't dat sumpin'?' when he's happy or surprised, and 'Awa, awa, awa' in the frequent moments when he's frightened or embarrassed."[5]

Andy, at the other extreme, was cast as a "coon" stereotype.

The same authors described him as: "Domineering, a bit lazy, inclined to take credit for all Amos's ideas and efforts. He's always 'working on the books' or 'resting his brain' upon which (according to Andy) depends the success or failure of all the boys' joint enterprises. He'll browbeat Amos, belittle him, order him around, but let anyone else pick on the little one—look out!"[6]

Gosden and Correll cleverly manipulated these stereotypes by playing them off against each other and situating them in Chicago's Southside ghetto trying to earn a living from a broken-down taxi operation, "The Fresh Air Taxicab Company of America, Incorpulated." They epitomized the gullible African American "country rubes" from the rural South, comically aspiring to fame and fortune in the "big city" even while being habitually victimized by the same urban milieu. Moreover, they were happy and hapless losers content with "playing the fool," whatever the occasion.

The techniques Gosden and Correll used in fashioning their comedy routines are evident in their many recorded scripts. In addition to juxtaposing a "Tom" and a "coon" stereotype, other blackface-inspired representations were incorporated into the program's cast. The most famous of these characters were Sapphire, a bossy, shrewish "mammy" figure, and the infamous Kingfish, a blustering, shiftless, conniving variation on the "coon" stereotype even more outlandish than Andy. A second technique constantly relied on was all the characters' misuse and misunderstanding of the English language and, by extension, of the American way of life. The following excerpt from a 1928 commercial phonograph record demonstrates this characteristic. The topic was the upcoming presidential election:

> *Amos:* What's de difference between a Democrat an' a Republican, Andy?
>
> *Andy:* Well, one of 'em is a mule an' de other one is a elephant. Dat's the way I gets it.
>
> *Amos:* I don't know either to be a Democrat or a Republican.
>
> *Andy:* Well, where wha' your ancestors?
>
> *Amos:* My aun' didn' have no sisters.
>
> *Andy:* No, no your ancestor, your . . . never min'.
> I believe you ought to be a Democrat 'cause you look more like a mule more than anythin' I know.
>
> *Amos:* How you know who to vote for in dis election, Andy?
>
> *Andy:* Look up de record. Look at Presiden' Coolidge. What did he do durin' his admiration?

Amos: He's been fishin' mos' of de time, ain' he?

Andy: Listen, Coolidge is a Republican an' fo' de' las' fo' years or so he's done had Hoover locked up waitin' to put him in office.

Amos: What you mean he done had Hoover locked up?

Andy: Well, I was readin' in de paper right after Hoover was nomulated dat Coolidge was gettin' ready to take Hoover out of de cabinet.

Amos: He better get out an' get some fresh air if he's gonna be Presiden' I'll tell you dat. Now you tell me—why can't there be a Democrat and a Republican Presiden' at de same time? Why not let Hoover be Presiden' one week an' Al Smith be Presiden' de nex' week. Ain't no use in havin' alotta hard feelings.

Andy: Amos, de Presiden' of de country don't have nothin' to do now. De trouble wif dat is de Republicans would get everything messed up fo' de Democrats and vice versa.

Amos: And what?

Andy: Vice Ver-sa.

Amos: He ain't runnin' is he?
       Now tell me dis. How many votes does it take to elect a Presiden'?

Andy: Well, one of 'em has got to have de majority and de other one has got have de pleurisy.

Amos: Both of 'em is bad, isn' dey? My grandpa had de pleurisy, but I ain't heard of nobody havin' dat other thing.[7]

The frequency of the malapropisms in the above scene highlight the characters' lack of education and, ultimately, their lack of intelligence. Moreover, it contributes to the message that lurked behind blackface humor. What lies at the core of this comedy routine is the idea that a typical African American is grossly ignorant of the American political system; hence, to allow the Amoses and Andys the right to participate in the political processes of voting, running for office, supporting candidates, and so on would be tantamount to making a mockery of American democracy.

It is evident that the "Amos 'n' Andy" formula relied on racial stereotypes, malapropisms, and recycled comedy formats taken from vaudeville and minstrelsy. Not surprisingly, it was the first network program to develop a mass appeal among a national listening audience during the depression. Blackface humorists had been amusing white audiences for over a hundred years; Gosden and Correll were simply cashing in on a venerable tradition in American show business. What made them different from their predecessors was the large number of people they reached with their comedy, including some African Americans. At the height of its popularity, the fifteen-minute daily comedy was listened to by 53 percent of the nationwide radio audience, which in the early 1930s was close to forty million people. "Amos 'n' Andy" sparked a boom in the sale of radio sets when it began to attract a mass audience, and it generated a number of spin-off commercial products, like phonograph records, a feature-length film, comic strips, toys, and even a candy bar. Gosden and Correll became overnight cultural sensations. They were the highest paid actors on radio in the country and were invited to perform at the White House for President Herbert Hoover. With the advent of success and celebrity status, their radio show spawned a host of imitators, who flooded the airways with "Amos 'n' Andy"-inspired caricatures, like "Watermelon and Cantaloupe" on the "Corn Cob Pipe Club," WEAF, New York; "Molasses and January" on "Showboat," NBC; and "Moonshine and Sawdust" on the "Gulf Show," NBC.[8]

The African American response to the "Amos 'n' Andy" soap opera and the hoopla surrounding its sudden notoriety was varied. At one extreme, their comedy was defended as being both "true to life" and "clean-minded"—that is, they were praised because they never used the epithet "nigger" in their routines. Moreover, Gosden and Correll were active in supporting African American charities, and they had consulted with a number of African American community leaders in Chicago while in the process of developing their radio show. Robert Abbott, editor of the *Chicago Defender*, was an open supporter of the two comics and wrote glowing accounts of their service to the African American community in his newspaper. Yet the racial stereotypes and a reliance on bad grammar for laughs eventually caught up with "Amos 'n' Andy," bursting the bubble of adulation surrounding them. The catalyst for the African American protest against the program was Robert Vann, editor of the *Pittsburgh Courier*, a weekly black newspaper that rivaled the *Chicago Defender*'s nationwide appeal. The *Courier* had a circulation of two hundred fifty thousand in forty states in 1931 when Vann launched an editorial offensive against the "Amos 'n' Andy" show. He objected to the program's demeaning characterization of African Americans and was particularly indignant at the fact that two white men were getting rich from their second-rate interpretations of African American life and humor. The editorial barrage from Vann's typewriter also noted that the "Amos 'n' Andy" theme song was taken directly from D. W. Griffith's "Birth of a Nation," a film known for its racist depiction of black people. In the final analysis, the editorials stressed that the soap opera was detrimental to African Americans' self-respect and that it should be forced off the air. Vann's criticism provoked a flood of supportive replies to the *Courier* and other black newspapers around the country. A woman in Los Angles even expressed her objection to the program in verse:

> American Negro, wake up! wake up!
> Show radioland you must be treated fair.
> So get ready to join the mighty force
> To push old "Amos 'n' Andy" off the air.[9]

The public outcry against the soap opera reached its height with a petition campaign to terminate the program, sponsored by the *Courier* in 1931. Over seven hundred forty thousand signatures were gathered and turned over to the National Association for the Advancement of Colored People (NAACP), which in turn presented them to the Federal Radio Commission (FRC), along with a formal request that the FRC remove "Amos 'n' Andy" from the airways. The commission ignored the petitions and the NAACP request, in effect refusing to take a position on the issue. The protest then slowly dissipated, but not before opening up the possibility of future protest actions against negative portrayals of African Americans in broadcast programming.[10]

Blackface minstrelsy's twilight years were spent on network radio from the late 1920s up through the 1930s. In addition to Gosden and Correll, a number of other white entertainers made their living on radio by performing the old minstrel routines. "Amos 'n' Andy's" closest rivals were the "Two Black Crows," played by George Moran and Charlie Mack, two comedians from New York City. The "Two Black Crows" launched their radio career on CBS in 1927, after having spent years on the vaudeville circuit and having rerecorded a number of "coon" songs and skits for the Columbia Record Company. Even as late as 1939, "Pick and Pat," a white comedy team doing blackface humor, was listed among the top five half-hour comedy shows on network radio by the Crosely rating service.[11] These old minstrel stereotypes, like the racism they encouraged, were slow to die out.

African American women were also initially portrayed by white actors on the radio. Marlin Hurt, a white male, was responsible for creating the well-known female character "Beulah." She was a domestic worker molded on the "mammy" servant stereotype: fat, matronly, domineering, loyal to her white employers, and so on. Likewise, Tess Gardella, a white actress, was the first person to portray the most famous of the "mammy" stereotypes, Aunt Jemima, on Victor Records and network radio in the late 1920s. One white actor named Jimmy Scribner actually developed twenty-two separate characters for a soap opera on African American life called "The Johnson Family," which was aired on the Mutual Broadcasting System.[12] In all these cases, the white entertainers were inclined to rely on recycled racial stereotypes inherited from blackface minstrelsy.

Black performers attempting to gain access to radio broadcasting jobs encountered the same sort of discrimination and racial dilemmas as had their precursors in minstrelsy, vaudeville, and the record industry. They were exploited economically and artistically, while also being coerced and/or seduced into roles and styles not of their own choosing. Bert Williams's blackface humor was not only highlighted at the Ziegfeld Follies between the set changes, beginning in 1922, it was also broadcast over WHN, a local New York radio station that at times featured black vaudevillians. In Washington, D.C., that same year, African American radio pioneer Jack L. Cooper was forced to emulate Bert Williams's comedy routines in order to secure employment on a variety show featured on station WCAP. Cooper played four different African American characters on the program. His talents as a ventriloquist enabled him to make the claim that he was "the first four Negroes on radio."[13] Prime-time or network programs, like "Plantation Nights" on KFI Los Angeles in 1932, all were conceived by white advertising men, who modeled them on the familiar minstrel stereotypes inherited from show business. "Plantation Nights" was a variety show set on a southern plantation, with African Americans cast as slaves singing, dancing, and joking for "massa" and "missus." "Showboat" featured two African American comics, Ernest Whitman and Eddie Green, doing a "coon" act, while Hattie McDaniel was cast in the role of a "mammy" figure. To add insult to injury, some African Americans had to study their own dialect as it was perceived and then taught to them by white scriptwriters. Lillian Randolph spent three months learning dialect from a white vocal coach before she was able to get a part on the "Lulu and Leander" series on WXYZ in Detroit, Michigan. Johnny Lee, an actor who got a part on the

"Slick and Slim" program, said, "I had to learn to talk as white people believed Negroes talked in order to get the job."[14]   This practice persisted well into the 1940s.   Wonderful Smith, an African American comic with the "Red Skelton Show," was dropped from the series because, as he put it, "I had difficulty sounding as Negroid as they expected."[15]

The onset of the depression ended the promise of diversity and cultural pluralism many thought to be inherent in the technology of radio broadcasting in the 1920s.   The realities of the capitalist marketplace forced almost 90 percent of the two hundred or so educational radio stations off the air.   Most of these stations were owned by colleges or churches that could not afford to pay for their upkeep and had no alternative sources of funding.   In addition, many of the smaller, independent commercial stations without network affiliation also failed financially.   Only the two networks, NBC and CBS, as well as their affiliates, prospered as radio became the "national pastime."   Moreover, the networks' hegemony over radio broadcasting during the depression years tended to work against the interests of African Americans.   They were totally excluded from the business and the technical operations of the radio industry and played only a token role, at best, in network programming.

Three of the major radio shows hosted by African Americans that were aired by the networks during this period illustrate this point. In 1933, the "Ethel Waters Show," sponsored by Amoco, was dropped by NBC shortly after its debut because of a threatened boycott of the program by the network's southern affiliates.   This tactic was used successfully by southern radio-station owners and managers on a number of occasions in the 1930s and 1940s.   Even with a sponsor—Fleischman's Yeast—the "Louis Armstrong Show," aired on CBS in 1937, seemed doomed to failure from its inception.   The program was produced by a white advertising agency that had Armstrong doing comedy routines and singing Tin Pan Alley standards instead of highlighting his prodigious musical talents by playing the trumpet.   It was scheduled in the same time slot as the top-rated "Jack Benny Show" on NBC, therefore did poorly in the ratings, and was quickly canceled after a thirteen-week run.   Cab Calloway's "Quizzicale" on NBC suffered a similar fate.   In the words of the host: "it was impossible for Negroes to get a regular commercial sponsor in those days.   In fact, the problem didn't change until recently.   Even in the fifties, Nat King Cole's variety show was cancelled when the sponsor pulled out and just about admitted that it was because of pressure from Southern affiliates, who didn't like the idea of a Negro show."[16]

The most successful African American actor on network radio during the 1930s was Eddie Anderson, who played Rochester on "The Jack Benny Show." Rochester was Benny's valet and chauffeur; he also had strong predilections toward drinking, shooting craps, chasing women, and "totin' a razor." This clever and at times contradictory mixture of the "faithful servant" and the urban "coon" stereotypes produced an updated blackface character tailor-made for the national listening audience. As a comic foil for Jack Benny, Rochester was allowed to be smart and sassy with his boss, even as he also mothered Benny, a die-hard bachelor. This led one historian to argue in retrospect that: "The pair became, in fact, the oddest racial couple in American culture. They shared intimacies and domestic arrangements on radio and television that went far beyond the typical employer-employee association. In developing a symbiotic relationship, they reflected subtle changes occurring in American society that would ultimately alter the stereotype of the black male."[17] At the other pole was Eddie Anderson himself, who became so defensive about the stereotype issue that he denied its very existence.

> I don't see why certain characters are called stereotypes. . . . The Negro characters being presented are not labelling the Negro race any more than "Luigi" is labelling the Italian people as a whole. The same goes for "Beulah," who is not playing the part of thousands of Negroes, but only the part of one person, "Beulah." They're not saying here is the portrait of the Negro, but here is "Beulah."[18]

The major tendency of the commercially sponsored network show prior to World War II was either to exclude African Americans from its programming or to allow them to play only stereotyped characters. However, African Americans interested in radio broadcasting were never content with this situation, and they were constantly trying to develop viable alternatives. In New York City in the fall of 1927, Floyd J. Calvin produced the first radio program devoted to "negro journalism." The hour-long show was sponsored by the *Pittsburgh Courier* and broadcast on WGBS. In the late 1920s, actor/writer Carlton Moss launched an African American drama series, "The Negro Hour," on another New York City radio station. The radio series was short-lived, but the dramatic group that formed to act on it evolved into the highly acclaimed Lafayette Players, who were involved in black radio drama in the 1930s. In 1929, the Harlem Broadcasting Corporation was founded; it was the first independent African American radio venture of its kind. The company operated its own radio studios on the corner of Lenox Avenue and 125th Street. It also leased broadcast time on WRNY, a local radio outlet, and ran an artist bureau for African American radio talent. A radio extravaganza produced by the Harlem Broadcasting Corporation in 1930, called "A Rise to Culture," was staged at Harlem's Union Auditorium. Over one hundred performers, including W. C. Handy, donated their talents to the event.[19]

The depression eventually forced the Harlem Broadcasting Corporation out of business, but while it lasted it served as a prototype for future independent African American ventures into radio broadcasting. In 1926, Jack L. Cooper left Washington, D.C., for Chicago, where he worked in advertising and sales for the *Chicago Defender* until launching his first radio venture on WGBC in 1927. WGBC was a low-power "ethnic" radio station that sold airtime slots to German, Polish, Lithuanian, Greek, Italian, and now African American entrepreneurs, who in turn produced ethnic-language radio shows as a vehicle for soliciting advertising dollars from small businesses in their respective communities. Cooper's show, initially called "The Negro Hour," was a pioneering achievement in black radio history; it was a breakthrough program that set important precedents for what would follow. For example, Cooper featured first and foremost, the latest recordings of the leading black dance bands of the era, such as those headed by Duke Ellington, Earl Hines, Fletcher Henderson, Andy Kirk, Count Basie, Jimmy Lunceford, and Chuck Webb, as well as famous vocalists like Bessie Smith, Ella Fitzgerald, Louis Armstrong, and Fats Waller. This enabled him to build up a loyal black audience, as he was the only person on the air in Chicago playing the popular black music recorded on the race labels. In addition, he developed the first regular black newscast, utilizing material gathered from the *Chicago Defender*, and other black publications. Later, he created the Missing Persons Program to help itinerant black migrants locate their kinfolk in the city. By 1949, Cooper was a millionaire who owned his own broadcast studio and advertising agency; the latter employed as many as ten staff writers and a team of satellite DJs to program the forty hours of airtime on four different radio stations under contract. Jack Cooper's mastery of the urban brokerage system in ethnic radio paved the way for other African Americans hoping to break into commercial radio; some of the more successful were Ed Baker and Van Douglas in Detroit, Eddie Honesty and Jack Gibson in Chicago, Hal Jackson in Washington, D.C., and Norfley Whitted in Durham, North Carolina. Together, they set the stage for the unusual postwar ascendancy of the African American disc jockey.[20]

As the depression grew worse in the 1930s, African Americans continued to make some modest inroads into the commercial radio industry, but resistance to their presence on the airways also grew stronger. For one thing, more African American musicians began to be heard on local and even network radio. These included Duke Ellington, Cab Calloway, Maxine Sullivan, Fats Waller, Jimmy Rushing, Stuff Smith, the Mills Brothers, the Golden Gate Jubilee Quartet, the Southernaires, and Billie Holiday. Only a select few of these musicians had their own shows; usually they appeared as guest artists on local and network variety programs or dance concerts. Moreover, the white "swing" bands of the era, such as Guy Lombardo's Royal Canadians, the Casa Loma Orchestra, the Dorsey Brothers, Artie Shaw, Glen Miller, and Benny Goodman— the so-called King of Swing—still dominated the network airways as far as dance music was concerned. For example, the popular NBC late-night dance program "Fitch's Bandwagon" maintained a strict color line when hiring musicians up until 1939, at which time it finally gave in to a wave of criticism and booked the Count Basie Orchestra. That same year, the first integrated jazz group to be heard on network radio, the Benny Goodman Quartet, performed live on CBS. White clarinetist Goodman and drummer Gene Krupa were joined by African American musicians Teddy Wilson on piano and Lionel Hampton on vibraphone.[21] The networks seemed to be slowly yielding to the continuous barrage of complaints and con- demnation emanating from the African American press and a handful of sympathetic supporters in the radio industry.

African Americans had a harder time gaining access to commercial radio's dramatic and public affairs programming than to its music and variety offerings. At the local and the network levels, they often encountered outright censorship when trying to voice their opinions, especially with regard to racial issues. Threatening phone calls canceled a program series on "The Catholic Church and the

Negro Question," scheduled to be aired on WMC in Memphis, Tennessee, in 1935. The Catholic church was the sponsor of the aborted series.[22] In Baltimore, Maryland, an NAACP special program to be aired on WCAO in 1939 was terminated after management learned that among the issues to be discussed was segregation at the University of Maryland.[23] The situation was much the same at the network level. The Southernaires gospel show on NBC always featured a guest speaker until Major Arthur Springarn, the NAACP national president, diverged from his "blue-penciled" script to deliver a blistering attack on racism in American society. NBC abruptly canceled the guest speaker segment of the program permanently.[24]

Racial censorship even reached the network soap operas. White scriptwriters Sandra Fand and Peter Michael found their references to African Americans routinely deleted from their scripts for the NBC soap "Lone Journey." The line "Negro blood is just the same as ours" even brought a reprimand from their superiors, who claimed it would offend southern listeners.[25] The argument that southern white listeners—that is, the southern radio market—would be alienated both by African American participation in radio programming and by any candid appraisal of the nation's racial conflicts allowed network radio neatly to sidestep both issues while blaming the recalcitrant southerners and their segregationist policies for their absence. Here was a classic example of the dictates of the radio marketplace perpetuating racism in the radio industry.

The two giant networks, however, were not completely monolithic when handling racial questions related to their operations. Countervailing forces, like the African American press and African American radio talent seeking more challenging and respectable roles in the radio industry, served to prick the consciences of a select number of network producers and executives. As a result, some programming portraying African Americans in a more positive light began to make its way onto the networks. Most often, these were "sustaining" programs without commercial sponsors: they were paid for by the networks. The first African American hero to be heard on network radio was Juano Hernandez's portrayal of "John Henry: Black River Giant" in a series broadcast by CBS in 1933. Hernandez was allowed to conceptualize his character as "a powerful, bad ladies' man" and was given the freedom to portray John Henry in that manner during the series.[26] Other radio programs that transcended the typical African American stereotypes included a scattering of locally produced efforts like "A Harlem Family," a dramatic series that dealt with the trials and tribulations of an ordinary African American family living in Harlem during the depression era. The series was aired on WMCA in New York City in 1935 and was sponsored by the city's board of education.[27] The U.S. Office of Education also attempted to fill the void by sponsoring a series of special radio programs on African American life, including an ambitious tribute to Booker T. Washington in 1935. The broadcast emanated from Atlanta and featured Tuskegee College president Dr. Frederick Douglass Patterson and the Tuskegee student choir. NBC aired the tribute as a sustaining program on one of its two national networks.[28] In 1937, WKY in Oklahoma City initiated a public affairs show directed toward the city's African American population, called "Afro-America Speaks." It was the first ongoing radio program in the country to address racial and social issues from an African American perspective.[29]

One of the most dramatic programs on network radio during the 1930s that involved African American talent was the 1939 broadcast of the highly acclaimed "Ballad for Americans," featuring Paul Robeson. It was on CBS's experimental sustaining program "Pursuit of Happiness," which aired on Sundays and was produced and directed by the award-winning radio dramatist Norman Corwin. "Ballad" was a patriotic anthem glorifying the history of the United States as a sovereign republic. The lengthy hymn championed the ideals of brotherhood and the democratic spirit, while castigating prejudice and racial intolerance. It was a call for all Americans to live up to the nation's cherished creed of "freedom, justice, and equality" for all of its citizens. This overriding theme was encapsulated in the following verse stanza:

> Man with white skin can never be free
> While his black brother is in slavery
> Our country's strong, our country's young
> And her greatest songs are still unsung.[30]

Paul Robeson's sonorous baritone voice was the ideal vehicle for "Ballad for Americans," as was the man behind that voice. He had previously brought the folk songs of his people alive on network radio, and he had also dramatized their African heritage in special presentations enacted on prime-time offerings like NBC's "Shell Chateau." In addition to his prowess as a vocalist and an actor, Robeson was also a political leftist, active in the struggle against both fascism and colonialism. Through "Ballad," and then an upsurge of similar programs, he was able to help rally the American people against the threatening forces of facism and nazism in Europe and Asia.

The Middle Passage (1939–49)

On the eve of World War II, commercial radio in the United States was given a new mandate. There was a need for unity, and especially racial harmony, to facilitate the successful mobilization of the American people for the war effort. Network radio was viewed by government leaders and broadcast industry executives as a ready-made conduit for propaganda to encourage the mobilization. But in order to project in audio the mass image of a unified population arduously engaged in the vast enterprise of retooling American industry, commerce, and culture for total warfare, African Americans would have to be given a more visible and less stereotyped presence on wartime radio. The War Department referred to this as their "intergroup strategy" for the home front. Twelve million African Americans could no longer simply be ignored or trivialized by America's "national pastime." It now became a programming priority to integrate African Americans into prime-time network programs in order to implement the government's special propaganda objectives.[31] As the war clouds gathered over the homeland, the radio industry temporarily abandoned the cold cash logic of the capitalist marketplace and, figuratively speaking, wrapped itself in the American flag.

The radio networks and the United States government worked together as partners in their efforts to promote a more favorable and constructive audio profile for radioland's African Americans during the war years. Both the Federal Security Agency within the U.S. Office of Education, and the Office of War Information in the War Department produced and processed radio propaganda packages to be aired on the networks and overseas free of charge. The Federal Security Agency's "Freedom's People" series aired its initial program on NBC only ten days after Pearl Harbor was bombed. It was intended to "dramatize Negro participation in past wars." The thirty-minute special included a drama about a World War I African American soldier decorated for valor, "The Battle of Henry Johnson." In addition, musician and composer Noble Sissle, along with Colonel West A. Hamilton, Commanding Officer of the 366th Infantry Regiment, reminisced about James Reese Europe's famous black military band, which had been attached to Colonel Hamilton's unit during the war.[32] The "Freedom's People" series would continue to highlight African Americans' contributions to the nation's many previous wars on NBC during the early 1940s.

On the international front, the United States government took the lead in promoting racial solidarity among the allies. Paul Robeson not only spoke out for the war effort on network radio at home, but he also made propaganda broadcasts for the War Department that were sent via shortwave radio transmission to Europe, Africa, and the Middle East. One of the more notable worldwide broadcasts during World War II was a special program commemorating the one hundred and thirty-fifth birthday of Abraham Lincoln.[33] Moreover, the War Department set up its own worldwide radio network, the Armed Forces Radio Service (AFRS), to reach the troops stationed abroad. By and large, the AFRS maintained an open-door policy toward including African Americans in its programming, which was consistent with the new mandate in domestic broadcasting. Wonderful Smith, who had endured stereotyped roles on network radio in the 1930s, was delighted when he was allowed to do his own music show for AFRS in Calcutta, India.[34] The AFRS was in competition with the early "Tokyo Rose" radio broadcasts to U.S. troops stationed in the Far East. The latter not only played the best American popular music—including jazz—available on records, but also made direct appeals to African American troops, questioning why they would want to fight for a country that kept them in a segregated, second-class status within its armed forces. At the time, the U.S. military had a policy of segregation in its ranks.

Back on the home front, the networks launched a variety of efforts to improve the visibility of nonstereotyped African Americans and to confront the issue of race relations in American society. CBS enlisted the services of radio's most famous soap-opera producers, Frank and Ann Hummert. They, in turn, introduced black characters into the plots of their two most popular soap operas.

The first appeared in "Our Gal Sunday" in the summer of 1942. He was "Franklin Brown," a clean-cut, patriotic young African American in military training. In the "Romance of Helen Trent," the patriotic and educated black character was a doctor working as a staff physician in a war factory. There was a good deal of discussion about the "capabilities of the Negro people" when the doctor was involved in the plot.[35] CBS also produced a special series dealing with ethnic and racial diversity in the military entitled "They Call Me Joe." The theme of the program stressed that such diversity was the sign of a vital democracy. As if the point had not already been made, the CBS network in 1945 broadcast a series entitled "The Negro at War," which continued to glorify African Americans' service in the nation's wars.[36]

Both networks responded swiftly to the national crisis in race relations provoked by the 1943 Detroit race riot. The conflagration left six whites and twenty-nine African Americans dead; hundreds were injured or arrested, and close to a million-dollars-worth of property damage was reported. While the local police aggressively quelled black looters on Hastings Street, killing seventeen African Americans in the process, white mobs were allowed to indiscriminately attack black citizens on Woodward Avenue, the city's racial dividing line. Order was restored only when federal troops were dispatched to Detroit by President Roosevelt. A month after the riot, CBS broadcast "An Open Letter on Race Hatred." Written and directed by the award-winning dramatist William Robsen, this radio docudrama assailed racism on the home front by linking it to fascism abroad. The white gangs of "kluxers, cowards, and crackpots" that wantonly attacked African Americans in Detroit were likened to the "gangs of German youth armed with beer bottles and lead pipes" whose assertion of "mob rule" had put Adolf Hitler in power. In a postscript to the program, former Republican presidential candidate Wendell Willkie stated bluntly:

> Two-thirds of the people who are our allies do not have white skins. And they have long hurtful memories of the white man's superior attitude in his dealings with them. Today the white man is professing friendship and a desire to cooperate and is promising opportunity in the world to come when the war is over. They wonder. When the necessities of war cease to make cooperation valuable to the white man, will his promises mean anything? Race riots in Detroit, Los Angeles and Beaumont, Texas do not reassure them. . . . Fascism is an attitude of the mind, an attitude which causes men to seek to rule others by

economic, military, or political force or through prejudice. Such an attitude within our own borders is as serious a threat to freedom as is the attack from without. The desire to deprive some of our citizens of their rights—economic, civic, or political—has the same basic motivation as actuates the fascist mind when it seeks to dominate peoples and nations. It is essential that we eliminate it at home as well as abroad.[37]

"An Open Letter on Race Hatred" won the prestigious Peabody award for broadcasting excellence in 1943; that same year, *Time* magazine called it "one of the most elegant programs in radio history."[38]

Shortly after the Detroit race riot, Paul Robeson appeared on NBC's "Labor for Victory," a program produced by the American Federation of Labor and the Congress of Industrial Organizations during the war years. Robeson frankly acknowledged that the cause of freedom had been set back by the Detroit incident but added that freedom was still obtainable for African Americans in the country, hence they should continue to support the war effort. NBC followed this program up with "Let's Face the Race Question" on "America's Town Forum"; it featured a panel of prominent African Americans, including poet Langston Hughes, who discussed strategies for ending racial discrimination in American society. CBS's "Peoples' Platform" series aired a discussion entitled: "Is the South Solving Its Race Problem?"[39] Never before in the history of network broadcasting had racial issues been probed so openly on the national airways.

But even as global victory was at hand, the discussion of race relations and the emphasis on black programming was disappearing from the American airways. Moreover, military decision makers took the lead in reversing their own wartime policies. The War Department and CBS cosponsored a series on veterans adjusting to civilian life called "Assignment Home." A script on the employment problems of black veterans entitled "The Glass" was scheduled by CBS but was rejected by the War Department because it was not a "military" matter. The black press and the NAACP protested the cancellation.[40] Another program, "The Story They'll Never Print," created by the American Negro Theater for WNEW in New York City, was submitted for the AFRS series "This Is the Story." The script was drawn from case studies of factory integration conducted by the Urban League, and it dramatized the fact that black and white workers could coexist in the same factory without racial antagonism. This program was not flagged down by the War Department, but a colonel at the AFRS headquarters in Hollywood, California, destroyed the AFRS's copy of it with the explanation that "no nigger-loving shit goes out over this network!"[41]

Commercial radio also slowly returned to business as usual when the war ended. However, a few special African American programs continued to be aired by the networks, and they continued to generate controversy. CBS produced an extravaganza in honor of National Negro Newspaper Week on 24 February 1946. The lineup included Frank Sinatra, Rex Ingram, Dr. Charles Drew, Joe Louis, Jackie Robinson, Ella Fitzgerald, the Ink Spots, Paul Robeson, and a special message from President Truman.[42] In the summer of 1946, NBC launched "The Nat King Cole Show," while CBS introduced "Night Life," featuring a black master of ceremonies named Willie Bryant and broadcast live from Harlem. The show had a racially mixed cast, which caused an outcry from some of the network's southern affiliates that still had the clout to get it dropped from the schedule. Later in the decade, the Mutual Broadcasting System aired a four-part series entitled "To Secure These Rights." The programs dramatized the findings of President Truman's Commission on Civil Rights. A number of southern radio stations refused to broadcast the series, and a coalition of southern politicians demanded and got rebuttal time from Mutual. Other black radio ventures that proved to be short-lived included a Mahalia Jackson gospel show on CBS and "The Jackie Robinson Show" on the fledgling ABC network. Lack of commercial sponsors and recalcitrant southern broadcasters again forced their early demise.[43] Meanwhile, "Amos 'n' Andy" was expanded into a half-hour comedy series, while Beulah on "The Fibber McGee and Molly Show" and Rochester on "The Jack Benny Show" continued to thrive as the nation's favorite blackface radio comics.

As in the past, African Americans and their allies in the radio industry continued to protest against racial discrimination and stereotyping in commercial broadcasting. The more blatant stereotypes, like Aunt Jemima, the trademark of the Quaker Oats Company, became the targets of criticism; in this case, the company was threatened with a product boycott. The Ohio State University Institute for Education by Radio's 12th Annual Conference featured a panel discussion on African Americans in radio programming in May 1946. One of the panelists was William Robson, author of

"An Open Letter On Race Hatred." He criticized the miscasting of African Americans as "Uncle Toms and Aunt Jemimas" because it led to reinforcing "white racial supremacy." A second panelist, *Billboard* magazine editor Lou Frankel, stated candidly: "Radio is not contributing a damn thing to better race relations. With few exceptions, radio still handles the Negro in the same old Uncle Tom, crap-shooting minstrel tradition. Jack Benny's Rochester is a good example."[44]

By the end of the decade, however, domestic "cold war" tensions were having an adverse effect on the struggle against racial barriers and stereotyping in the radio industry. The House Committee on Un-American Activities (HUAC) held a series of controversial hearings on suspected Communist subversives and sympathizers in the Hollywood entertainment industries. The networks broadcast the proceedings live to the nation. In the aftermath of these hearings, a small group of ex-FBI agents began to compile their own dossiers on suspected Communist sympathizers in radio, film, and television. They published a newsletter, and then in 1950 a book called *Red Channels*, listing these individuals and citing their alleged pro-Communist activities. It was virtually a roll call of the most progressive people in the entertainment industries, including those most active in the struggles for civil rights and racial equality. Among those listed were producer Norman Corwin, conductor Leonard Bernstein, playwright Lillian Hellman, and actor Phillip Loeb, who was cited for sponsoring the "End Jim Crow in Baseball Committee." Also mentioned was William Robson. Both Loeb and Robson soon found it impossible to find employment in the broadcasting field. Being cited in *Red Channels* was often tantamount to being blacklisted by the networks, which even imposed their own loyalty oaths.[45]

A number of distinguished African Americans in show business were also listed in *Red Channels*. Once again, they were individuals in the forefront of the struggles for racial justice, and their careers were often adversely affected. Among those listed were Paul Robeson, actor Canada Lee, pianist Hazel Scott, writer Shirley Graham, vocalist Lena Horne, poet Langston Hughes, writer Theodore Ward, actress Fredi Washington, and folksinger Josh White. In the case of White, he was so distraught because of the accusations made against him that he appeared as a "friendly" witness at the HUAC hearings, where he distanced himself from the leftist cultural politics of Robeson and Lee, in particular. Robeson was especially vulnerable to red baiting attacks because of his long-standing support of communism and the Soviet Union. During World War II, he had been a key American spokesman for racial tolerance and solidarity among allies around the world, a black champion of the nation's cherished ideals of democracy, freedom, and justice for all. But with the onset of the cold war, he was harassed by government investigations, vilified in the media and the press, blacklisted from employment in show business, and even denied his passport thus effectively curtailed from making appearances abroad. By the end of this ordeal, Robeson could be called the most hounded black casualty of the Communist witch-hunts conducted at the height of the cold war era.

The chilling effect of cold war red-baiting made it more perilous for African Americans to criticize racism in the radio industry openly. Nevertheless, many continued to do so, even under the threat of being blacklisted. In New York, the "Committee for the Negro in the Arts" sponsored a conference on "Television, Radio, and the Negro People" in June 1949. The committee's report to the conference on the state of radio documented the exclusion of African Americans from industry jobs as executives, producers, directors, sound-effects technicians, and commentators. In addition, it was critical of the continuing stereotypical portrayal of African Americans on network radio. In conclusion, the report stated:

> The truth about the American Negro is not held a fit subject for radio. The Negro is isolated and misunderstood and not allowed to communicate. Radio today has posed for each of us the question: Is the greatness and humanity of Negro America—of Crispus Attucks, Frederick Douglass, Marion Anderson, Paul Robeson and Jackie Robinson to be presented over the radio channels forever in terms of Amos 'n' Andy and Beulah?[46]

Among those members of the committee who signed their names to the call for the conference were Shirley Graham, Theodore Ward, and Fredi Washington—all of whom were listed in *Red Channels*. The following month, actor Canada Lee echoed the criticisms of the committee's report in an interview printed in *Variety* magazine. Lee was also suspected of holding leftist political beliefs, which might account for his stating—no doubt with a certain sense of irony—that an "Iron Curtain" prevented African Americans from entering the field of broadcasting. As a consequence, blackface stereotypes like "Amos 'n' Andy, Beulah and Rochester" dominated the portrayal of African Americans on the network airways, while their real life stories and characters were ignored.[47]

Canada Lee was not only an outspoken critic of racial discrimination in the radio industry, he was also a central figure in one of the most provocative and innovative black radio series of the postwar era. "New World A-Coming," adapted from Roi Ottley's well-known book on African Americans of the same name, premiered in 1944 on WMCA, a local New York City outlet not affiliated with either of the major networks. It was a weekly half-hour program broadcast from 3:00 to 3:30 P.M. on Sundays and sponsored by a Harlem civic committee. Roi Ottley wrote many of the scripts and also narrated a few of them; Michel Grayson was the producer and director of the series; Duke Ellington wrote the theme song for the program; Canada Lee served as the narrator for much of the series and acted in many of the dramatic productions. In its thirteen-year history, "New World A-Coming" featured a wide spectrum of programming, from dramas to documentaries, from live broadcasts of famous entertainers to special tributes to prominent black movers and shakers. The radio documentaries mostly dealt with local or race issues and concerns. There were specific programs on housing, hospitals, and health care in Harlem, as well as more generalized soundscapes like "Harlem: Anatomy of a Ghetto." There were special programs on black orphans, nurses, and churches in New York, as well as a groundbreaking exposé of the plight of Puerto Ricans in the city, which won a coveted Peabody award. Other documentary programs of note included "The Story of Negro Music," "Hot Spot USA," a look at housing discrimination in U.S. war industry centers, and "Apartheid in South Africa," which also won a Peabody award. In "The Story of Negro Music," Canada Lee's narration traces the evolution of African rhythms and songs into slave spirituals and secular songs, which then evolved into the blues, ragtime, and jazz. Examples of the music's evolution are provided by a local gospel choir and an all-star jazz band featuring pianist Art Tatum and vocalist Billie Holiday.[48]

Many of the factual stories told in documentary style on "New World A-Coming" could be more aptly described as "docudramas," in that almost all the historical events were recorded dramatically. This practice of restaging history for public consumption was used extensively in film newsreels like The March of Time during this period. It was even less complicated to remake history in the radio medium, where voices, music, and sound effects were all that one needed to create the desired audio imagery. The docudrama technique is evident in "The Story of the Vermont Experiment," a program in praise of a church project that placed black youths from Harlem with white farm families in Vermont for a few weeks in the summer. The project was alluded to in the New York's black press as a model for building good race relations. In the radio show, the two ministers responsible for the project, Adam Clayton Powell in Harlem and Richard Lowe in Vermont, play themselves; they restage a series of conversations with each other that highlight the progress of the experiment. In addition, there are a series of short vignettes which dramatize the interactions between the black youths and the white families; apprehensions are expressed on both sides, racial barriers are broken down, new bonds of friendship and understanding begin to emerge. At the end of the program, narrator Canada Lee proclaims: "The Vermont Experiment is a significant development in the progress of good race relations in this country, a milestone on the road to a New World A-Coming!"[49]

In "Negroes in the Entertainment Industry," two-thirds of the show is given over to a fictitious docudrama. After an introduction that critically alludes to the underemployment of African Americans in the entertainment field, the program is devoted to a dramatic sketch of a typical young black musician named Sonny who wants to become a concert pianist. Unfortunately, economic realities compel him to forego his youthful ambition and join a dance band in order to make a living. After enduring low pay, long hours, and racial discrimination while traveling with the band on the road, the young man returns home to contemplate quitting music altogether and going to work as an elevator operator, like his father. But in the end, his mother admonishes him, "Get some fight back in you!" The theme music rises to a crescendo and Canada Lee states: "Sonny's story is the story of thousands of Negroes in the entertainment field today. Traditionally, it was supposed to offer real opportunities for Negroes, but the spectre of race prejudice pursues the Negro entertainer wherever he turns. What an irony it is, when much of the music that identifies America to the world rose from the voices of American blackmen."[50] To punctuate the program, pianist Hazel Scott is introduced; she recounts how she also had ambitions to be a concert pianist as a young girl but was eventually forced to play on the nightclub circuit in order to survive. Then, as if to prove her point, she proceeds to play a jazzy version of a Rachmaninov composition to end the show.[51]

The dramatic programs staged for "New World A-Coming" were either based on original radio scripts or on adaptations of previously written plays, novels, or short stories. Examples of the last include Dorothy Parker's short story "Arrangements in Black and White" and Howard Fast's epic novel about the Reconstruction era, "Freedom Road," which was presented in two parts on successive Sundays. Parker's story, scripted for radio by Roi Ottley, becomes a cautionary tale on race relations for white people. The action takes place in a fashionable East Side New York penthouse where a concert is being given by a famous black concert vocalist named Walter Williams. A frivolous white female guest named Mrs. Burton asks the hostess of the recital to introduce her to Williams, in the process revealing an appalling naïveté with respect to black people and their culture. After having met the concert singer, Mrs. Burton exclaims to the hostess: "I haven't any feeling at all because he's a colored man. Wait until I tell Burton [her husband] that I called him Mister!" There is a sharp musical sting, then narrator Ottley concludes:

> Yes, she called him mister. Obviously, there's nothing world-shaking about this, and you may rightly say I know no such person. But this woman, like thousands, is the victim of the popular misconceptions about Negroes. Too often has she seen Negroes in motion pictures and radio caricatured as lazy buffoons, naive childen, and faithful servants enchanted by their white masters. Thus, when the races meet much embarrassment follows, for well-intended meetings may hurt, even anger Negroes. Today's presentation was offered as a sort of guide of what not to do in similar circumstances. The truth is people like Mrs. Burton become fewer in number as democracy is extended in American life.[52]

The fictitious deconstruction of the infamous Mammy stereotype is the driving force behind the drama entitled "The Mammy Legend." Narrator Canada Lee introduces the program by stating:

> If there is one thing that irritates Negroes today it is the Mammy legend, often romanticized in song and story. Yes, of course the Mammy did exist once. For at least two centuries she was an institution of the Old South. But today the Mammy has become largely a fiction, a museum piece of slavery days. Yes, it is true that Mammy doesn't live here anymore. Yet you still hear people say. . . .[53]

There follows a collage of white voices making stereotypical remarks about female black maids and domestic workers. Lee concludes his introduction by saying that the persistence of such racist attitudes can in these days lead to conflicts between employers and their hired help. What then unfolds is a story about one such black maid, named Martha, and her white employers, the Milburns. Martha has worked for the Milburns for ten years and has practically raised their son, Junior; her own son, Charlie, is in the armed forces training to be a pilot. When Charlie shows up for an unexpected visit, he gets into a discussion with the Milburns and their guests about segregation in the armed forces. Charlie argues that segregation is antidemocratic and therefore incompatible with the country's professed ideals. This makes his white audience uneasy. After Charlie leaves, Martha overhears Mr. Milburn tell one of his guests that Charlie's "radical" ideas will get him in trouble in the "real world." Then a bit later that night, she again overhears him, this time lecturing his son, Junior, about the perils of "mixing with colored people." The father is obviously upset because Junior had openly idolized Charlie during his brief visit. This proves to be the last straw for Martha; she confronts the Milburns about trying to pass their racial prejudices on to their son and states that she can no longer work for them in good conscience. Mr. Milburn is apologetic, but the damage has been done. Martha leaves the Milburns' household and goes to work in a parachute factory. In the last scene she is visited by Junior at her new apartment. She is delighted to see him and invites him in. The play ends with her line, "In my house, friends are always welcome!"[54]

A final category of programs experimented with on "New World A-Coming" were the tribute extravaganzas for famous people and/ or special events. During the war years, this included a tribute to D-Day forces shortly after the success of the invasion and a farewell tribute to President Roosevelt when he passed away. After the war, the tributes focused more exclusively on African Americans and their achievements. Typical of this program format was a "Tribute to Canada Lee," staged during his celebrated portrayal of Bigger Thomas in the Broadway adaptation of Richard Wright's controversial novel, *Native Son*. The show was produced in conjunction with the Mutual Broadcasting System, which offered it to affiliates nationwide. Paul Robeson served as the host and master of ceremonies. After his introduction, the program began with a short comedy skit starring Hattie McDaniel and Eddie "Rochester" Anderson broadcast live from Hollywood. (It was strange that Anderson was invited and agreed to participate in the tribute, given Lee's public criticisms of the Rochester stereotype.) The program also featured Bill "Bojangles" Robinson tap dancing on the air, live music by Duke Ellington and his orchestra, W. C. Handy playing the "Saint Louis Blues" on his trumpet, a congratulatory telegram from Joe Louis, and a segment from the *Native Son* play. In addition, Richard Wright was on hand to laud Canada Lee's accomplishments, while Lee himself came forward and thanked everyone at the end of the show. For his part, Paul Robeson sang a special song for the occasion, which he wrote "in the spirit of Native Son":

> Jim Crow
>
> > Lincoln set the Negro free
> > Why is he still in slavery?
> > Why is he still in slavery?
> > Jim Crow
> >
> > This is the land we call our own
> > Why does the Negro ride alone?
> > Why does the Negro ride along?
> > Jim Crow
> >
> > When it's time to go to the polls
> > Why does the Negro stay at home?
> > Why does the Negro stay at home?
> > Jim Crow
> >
> > Freedom for all it is said
> > Freedom to suffer until he's dead
> > Freedom to suffer until he's dead
> > From Jim Crow
> >
> > If we believe in liberty
> > Let's put an end to slavery
> > Let's put an end to slavery
> > From Jim Crow.[55]

Even when staging what was essentially a black radio variety show, "New World A-Coming" managed to sustain a critical cutting edge toward racial discrimination and stereotyping. As a result, it consistently broadcast programs that viewed race relations in American society through the looking glass of African American history and culture. But, unfortunately, the series had only a select local audience in New York City, while the national radio audience continued to tune into the networks to listen to Amos 'n' Andy, Beulah, and Rochester.

The other crowning achievement among independently produced black radio programs during the postwar era was the series "Destination Freedom." It was also a half-hour feature broadcast on Sunday afternoon, in this case over WMAQ in Chicago, and ran from June 1948 to October 1950. The creator and writer of the program was Richard Durham, a talented black author and journalist with some previous experience in radio. In addition to having worked as an editor for the *Chicago Defender* and *Ebony*, Durham had also written radio scripts for two Chicago-based productions, "Democracy USA," a 1946 series on famous African Americans who had made contributions to the struggle for democracy both at home and abroad, and "Here Comes Tomorrow," a soap opera set in Chicago's Southside ghetto. But Durham's greatest triumph in radio came in conjunction with the scripts he wrote for "Destination Freedom." All 105 scripts were meticulously researched dramatizations of black history and culture. They focused on the struggles and achievements of a broad range of African American leaders: lawyers, preachers, doctors, soldiers, scholars, politicans, entertainers, authors, athletes, and artists. To dramatize these "real-life stories," Durham worked with the W. E. B. Du Bois Theater Guild, a local group of socially conscious actors; they included Oscar Brown, Jr., Janice Kingslow, Wezlyn Tilden, Jack Gibson, Fred Pinkard, and Studs Terkel. The first thirteen productions were sponsored by the *Defender*; the remainder were sustaining programs sponsored by WMAQ.[56] Ironically, this was the same station that had launched the Amos 'n' Andy series two decades earlier.

Thematically, "Destination Freedom" resonated with the political and social conflicts that were at the heart of the black experience in American society from slavery to the post–World War II era. The plots confronted and exposed the brutality of southern slavery, Jim Crow segregation, and lynching from the perspective of the victims. Racial discrimination in education, employment, housing, transportation, and public accommodations received critical attention in the scripts as part of the African Americans' ongoing struggle to overturn these injustices. In most instances, the heroes and heroines in Durham's historical dramas were achievers and activists who found themselves constantly at odds with the discriminatory racial practices endemic to American society. The sagas of Crispus Attucks holding firm to his convictions and sense of worth in the face of entrenched racial bigotry, Frederick Douglass challenging the cultural and legal basis of slavery: "We will have no peace until all men are free in public opinion as well as law!", and Ida B. Wells realizing that lynching was not a "moral" issue, but rather "a matter of murder for money and jobs"—all illuminated the clash between democratic ideals and the harsh realities of racism in the U.S.[57] It gave their respective stories a compelling tension and framed the psychological action in each script.

Richard Durham's efforts to reconstruct the heroic in black drama reinforced the radical message in his plays. His quest for the authentic history of African Americans led him to the writings of W. E. B. Du Bois, Carter G. Woodson and John Hope Franklin. Du Bois and Woodson also proved to be valuable protagonists for two of Durham's more provocative scripts. The Du Bois play was entitled "Searcher for History"; it dramatized his contributions to the struggle for racial equality and to the scholarship available on black history and culture. Du Bois sought to illuminate the past because "only in the light of truth and publicity can we begin to dissolve discrimination and race hatred." Likewise, Carter G. Woodson as a "Recorder of History" worked to "uncover the treasures of Negro life so that America's goal of equality and justice may be strengthened by the knowledge of their struggle for freedom in the past."[58] In both episodes, understanding of the past was a precondition for a brighter future.

The panorama of black history gave Richard Durham a rich assortment of heroic figures to draw upon. In particular, it enabled him to venerate an array of rebellious leaders of African descent who were in the forefront of the war against slavery. Scripts were not only devoted to Frederick Douglass, Harriet Tubman, Gabriel Prosser, Crispus Attucks, and Denmark Vesey, but also to the liberators of Haiti, Henri Christope and Toussaint L'Ouverture. The Denmark Vesey docudrama focused on an entire cadre of revolutionaries who plotted the Charleston insurrection. They included Vesey, an ex-slave who had purchased his own freedom; Rolla Hand, a trusted house servant of a prominent white Charleston family; Paul Poyeus, the major black preacher in the city; and Gullah Jack, an African conjurer with a loyal following among the field slaves working on the plantations located in the countryside around Charleston. This diverse lot was brought to life in Durham's script. Each individual brings something different to the group and takes on a specific role in the plot. Their common cause and strong brotherhood bonds symbolize African American solidarity in the face of slavery: none are free until all are free. Denmark Vesey summarizes the cadre's credo when he tells the judge who has just condemned him to death:

> My treachery began when I read the Declaration of Independence. It said all men were created equal. It grew when I read that black Crispus Attucks died to help the colonies become free. Did he die just to free white men or all men? Then I read what Ben Franklin, Tom Paine, Lafayette, and Jefferson had said and their words warmed my blood. They wanted their revolution to make all men free and equal. But they stopped with some men free and some men slaves. I took up where they left off. I found my price when I was a slave. I paid it. If my life is the price I pay to be free—take it. I'll pay it. But until all men are free and equal—the revolution goes on.[59]

The ideological perspective implicit in Richard Durham's "Destination Freedom" not only championed the cause of freedom and equality for all men but also for all women. Long before either civil rights or women's rights were placed on the postwar national agenda, Durham was agitating for both in his scripts. Alongside Frederick Douglass, W. E. B. Du Bois, Jesse Owens, and Walter White were Harriet Tubman, Sojourner Truth, Ida B. Wells, Mary Church Terrell, Mary McLeod Bethune, Marian Anderson, Katherine Dunham, Gwendolyn Brooks, and Lena Horne. These black women were discriminated against because of both their race and their sex; their consciousness was tempered by a fusion of both experiences. As Sojourner Truth says to her captives as they ready to burn her at the stake for her opposition to slavery: "Where half the world is servant to the white man—there is no peace. . . . Burning me will not burn out the right women have to be free, to choose their own ways of life, to be their own masters."[60] Mary Church Terrell also articulates this crucial synthesis of race and sex discrimination while addressing a hostile crowd of white women, in a program called "The Long Road."

> Women! Since when have we needed cowards in bedsheets and masks

and shotguns to safeguard our persons and our homes? The only protection women need is protection by equality under the law. Equality of opportunity and the right to share the benefits of this land alongside men. Equality to choose an associate without fear of intimidation by bigots and the hissing of cowards. That's why I'm staying in the South and getting Negro and white women together. To find their freedom together. In the right to vote and the right to work will freedom be found—for once a white woman bows down to white masculinism—she is ready for slavery.[61]

A final dimension of "Destination Freedom's" ideological perspective made common cause with the anticolonial struggles of colored people in the Third World. The African Americans' struggle against racism and exploitation in the United States made them kindred spirits with those in Africa and Asia who were fighting for their liberation from foreign domination. In fact, Richard Durham perceived African Americans as a "universal people" able to join together with and inspire the downtrodden all over the planet. The longevity of their ordeal in the New World, as well as their resilience in the face of constant oppression, made them ideal advocates for the struggling masses everywhere. In Durham's own words:

It so happens that there has come to be created in America a people whose emotional fabrics and repeated experiences bring them very close to becoming in this atomic age the universal people. While some leaders may have difficulty identifying their lives with this mainstream—a Negro personality undergoing the experiences of segregation and share-cropping—it is instantly recognizable to 500,000,000 Chinese people who have undergone the same experience under imperialism for three hundred years. A Negro character confused by the caste system in the land of his birth is instantly identifiable to the 450,000,000 Indians in Asia and the 150,000,000 Africans in Africa, with Burmese Malayans, with the Jewish people whose identical struggle had led to the creation of a new nation, and with millions of Europeans and white Americans who also want to uproot poverty and prejudice.[62]

Richard Durham's "Destination Freedom" elicited critical acclaim during its two years on WMAQ. It was praised by the governor of Illinois, Adlai Stevenson, and the noted producer Norman Corwin. In addition, it won an award from the Institute for Education by Radio at Ohio State University. But by 1950 the series had run its course. The political climate cooled with the advent of the Korean War, and the black focus of the program became a casualty. After Durham and the Du Bois acting troupe left the series, it was hosted by a fictitious Paul Revere and began to dramatize scripts on American war heroes like Nathan Hale and Dwight David Eisenhower. Only the name of the program remained unchanged.

It was perhaps inevitable that "Destination Freedom" was so short-lived. From its inception, Durham had had difficulties with his NBC supervisors over the portrayal of his characters and the direction of his plots. He defined his purpose in a written intro-duction to the series: "To break through the stereotypes—shatter the conventions and traditions which have prevented us from dramatizing the infinite store of material from the history and current struggles for freedom."[63] But his supervisors would have liked a different approach to the program. Initially, they tried to assign a number of the script proposals to in-house NBC staff writers. Durham was forced to remind them that the program's concept and title were copyrighted under his name. He would take them elsewhere if they did not accept his writing and his control over the final product. Next, the staff director assigned to the program by NBC attempted to change the character of Crispus Attucks in the very first script that was to be dramatized. Durham responded with a lengthy explanation as to why the character should remain as he conceived it. In part, it read:

> What I as a writer am striving to accomplish with certain major Negro characters—and what I had in mind as a purpose when I drew up the idea for the show in the first place—was to portray Negro people as they actually are; as I know them, see them, live with them, as I know they think, react and feel in certain positions and not as they are portrayed or characterized (or sub-characterized) in the movies and on the radio in general. In other words, none of the Negro characters can be portrayed in the stereotyped manner because none of the situations contained in these dramas will be derived from the stereotyped situations. A Negro character will be rebellious, biting, scornful, angry, cocky, as the occasion calls for—not forever humble, meek, etc., as some would like to imagine it. Let me illustrate this: During the table conference before the show, you gave some directions to the actor playing Attucks which went like this: "There must be a certain humbleness in your approach—or else we lose sympathy with your cause—don't talk down to others, etc." The result was that Attucks turned out to be the most insignificant of them all—although he was what the show was all about in the first place. Perhaps the actor went too far in the direction you indicated— nevertheless, I think when you examine the record you'll find him so humble as to be inconsistent with the fiery rebel which he was in real life. A good many white people have cushioned themselves into dreaming that Negroes are not self-assertive, confident, and never leave

the realm of fear or subservience—to portray them as they are will give a greater education to the audience than a dozen lectures on the subject. His place within the play I think should determine his characterization, not what is assumed as his role in society. His role in society and history has been so distorted—so much based on illusion, chauvinism and conjecture—so much a part of a psychological need of a good many whites for some excuses to carry on untenable attitudes—that the first point in the series was to bring up some little known facts of history which would give the audience a new insight on people in general. Back to the portrayal of Attucks. In giving that particular direction what happened was that all of the fight, the anger, the effect of a man who'd give—and gave—his life for freedom—was torn off. Attucks picked his own destination—others didn't pick it for him. Consequently, whether or not people "lose sympathy" with him is beside the question. Your Attucks had somewhat the approach of an intelligent pullman porter. Not the biting, fighting hero which would have carried the audience with him—at least the Negro audience. In other words, these characters are leaders, initiators of historical movements—not accidents. In most cases they were in their time leaders of white groups as well as Negro groups—as was the case with Attucks or Frederick Douglass. For instance, to present Harriet Tubman as a sort of refined version of Aunt Jemima would be criminal. To present her as a sort of religious fanatic would be far-fetched. To present her as so many Negro women are— dauntless, determined, who have a healthy contempt for people who live by race prejudice and who are quick to recognize and extend a warm hand to other humans would be an honest, but for radio, a radical approach. All of what I say is based on my experiences as a Negro and upon the attitudes the average Negro (let alone the above average, as these characters are) has towards his destiny. It's this—and out of this I think you can base and direct certain types of Negro characterizations with unfailing accuracy: Negroes in general believe that their complete, full-scale emancipation is inevitable. No amount of demands for abnormal subservience, segregation or denials can stop it. They take equality as a matter of fact—as most people take the fact that two times two equals four.[64]

In spite of the high quality and relevance of "Destination Freedom," it was, like "New World A-Coming," destined to reach only a limited audience. Not only was it confined to being aired exclusively in Chicago, but, like all other radio broadcasts in major urban centers during this period, it faced new competition from television. In fact, the advent of commercial television led to cataclysmic changes in both the programming formats and the economic structure of the radio industry. The networks abandoned the production of radio programs in favor of television, taking with them radio's most popular entertainers and national advertisers. In effect, the networks, working hand-in-glove with the advertising industry, reorganized the national radio market into a nationwide television market. The same advertising agencies sold the same consumers to the same advertisers. The only major difference was that the medium had changed. If the radio stations affiliated with one of the networks could not afford to switch to television broadcasting, then they were left without their major source of programming and advertising revenues. This sudden shift sent shock waves throughout the radio industry. Local stations were left to fend for themselves without the support of the networks. Not only did they need to find a new source of programming, but also new advertisers and even a new audience. Ironically, these rapid changes in commercial broadcasting inadvertantly led to the establishment of the first black formatted radio stations in the United States.

Throughout most of the 1940s, the brokerage system continued to provide African Americans living in northern cities with their only radio outlets. In Chicago, Jack L. Cooper held onto his position as the city's leading black radio broadcaster, but now there were other contenders in the field, especially Al Benson. Like Cooper, Benson sold his own advertising time to small-scale businesses, delivered the commercial pitches over the airways, and programmed his own music. Also like Cooper, Benson was able to negotiate time slots with three different radio stations in the Chicago market. Unlike Cooper, however, Benson was a former Mississippi preacher who played down-home southern blues, not big band jazz; he spoke over the airways in a southern black dialect, not in proper English; and he catered to the city's burgeoning population of black southern migrants, not to its aspiring black bourgeoisie. By 1948, Al Benson had eclipsed Jack Cooper as Chicago's leading African American radio broadcaster. He would go on to achieve celebrity status not only as a disc jockey, but also as a record producer, concert promoter, TV show host, and outspoken civil rights advocate.[65]

In New York City, many of the stations selling time to ethnic radio programmers found the local black radio market more and more appealing. WCNW in Brooklyn programmed in eight foreign languages, but African American shows were its most lucrative offerings. These included regular weekday programs by "Smiling" Henry Copeland, a blues musican who played guitar and harmonica; Henry Newbie, a folksy commonsense philosopher and raconteur;

and Myrtle McWyte, a commentator on black fashions and society in New York. There was also a smattering of public affairs programs—in particular, "The Voice of the Negro Community" and an antiracism forum hosted by Wilhelmina Adams.[66] In addition to "New World A-Coming," WMCA also broadcast "Tales from Harlem," a musical variety show hosted by Joe Bostic, and "Sleepy Joe," a children's program of B'rer Rabbit folktales. Other New York stations, like WNEW, WWRL, and WLIB, also became involved in broadcasting special African American programs to the extent that, by the end of the 1940s, they all had radio studios located in Harlem. In addition to the music shows devoted to jazz, blues, and gospel, they also broadcast religious programs and public affairs series like "The Walter White Show" on civil rights issues and "The Negro World," a show sponsored by the newspaper of the same name.[67]

In the South, the brokerage system never gained enough foothold to enable African Americans to develop their own radio programs. Instead, white business enterprises with black clientele began to sponsor shows oriented toward their consumers; these shows often featured black performers. One of the first and most influential was "King Biscuit Time," aired on KFFA in Helena, Arkansas, on weekdays from 12:00 to 12:15 P.M. The program was launched in 1941 as a vehicle to promote King Biscuit Flour, which was produced and sold by the Interstate Grocery Company, the actual sponsor of the show. It featured the legendary blues musician Rice Miller, soon to be better known by his radio name, Sonny Boy Williamson. Miller was a masterful blues harmonica player and songwriter well known throughout the Mississippi Delta for his distinctive blues stylings and his flamboyant showmanship. He organized a small blues band that included guitarist Robert J. Lockwood and drummer Peck Curtis. They played on KFFA five days a week at noon and then traveled to evening engagements in the region. From all indications, "King Biscuit Time" was a huge sucess with black radio listeners in the rural mid-South. It developed such a large following that the owner of the Interstate Grocery Company began to market a new product called "Sonny Boy Corn Meal." Each bag of cornmeal featured a picture of a smiling Rice Miller, with harmonica in hand, sitting on a giant ear of corn. "King Biscuit Time" enjoyed a lengthy association with KFFA, even though Miller and Lockwood had moved on by the late 1940s. At that juncture, there was a growing number of other radio programs in the South that featured African American blues and gospel performers. Invariably, they were sponsored by white businessmen hoping to sell their wares to black consumers.[68]

Black-Oriented Radio (1950–65)

The first radio stations to devote their entire formats to black-oriented programming were also owned and managed by white entrepreneurs. They directed specially tailored radio shows and advertising messages toward the African Americans located within the range of their broadcasting signal. By the late 1940s, that audience of fifteen million people was being heralded in trade magazines like *Sponsor* as a lucrative "new Negro market."[69]   There were three principal factors involved in the sudden emergence of this market. The urban migration of African Americans was relocating them in the major metropolitan radio markets. Education and income levels among African Americans were on the rise, as were the numbers of African Americans who owned radio receivers. At the same time, commercial radio was facing bleak economic prospects due to the arrival of television. Given this situation, a number of radio-station owners began to cultivate the new black urban market in order to avoid going out of business. Among those who did so were Bert Ferguson and John Pepper, owners of WDIA in Memphis, Tennessee.

Ferguson and Pepper had purchased WDIA in 1947; it was initially a low-power 250-watt daytime operation. At first, they tried to program classical music, but too few listeners and advertisers responded to the format. They then decided to experiment with programming aimed at the large black population living in and around Memphis and to boost their power to 50,000 watts. To accomplish this, Ferguson approached Nat D. Williams about hosting a regular show and advising them on how best to reorient the station toward a black clientele. Williams had some previous radio experience as a master of ceremonies for a local talent contest that was broadcast live in Memphis by WBHQ. Ferguson worked for WBHQ as an engineer during that time and got to know Williams. It was as a result of this acquaintance that Nat D. Williams was offered a job on WDIA. His first show, "Tan Town Jamboree," debuted on WDIA on 21 October 1948 and was an overnight sensation. He was the first black radio announcer in the mid-South to play the popular rhythm and blues records of the day over the airways. Within six months, WDIA was to make the transition from a classical music station to one appealing exclusively to African American listeners and advertisers.[70]

Nat D. Williams had no illusions about the motives of his employers. In his local *Memphis World* newspaper column he openly discussed the proposition with his readers: "They are businessmen. They don't necessarily love Negroes. They make that clear. But they do love progress and are willing to pay the price to make progress. One of the most neglected markets in the mid-South is the Negro market. And that's true because so many white businessmen take the Negro for granted."[71] Ferguson confirmed Williams's analysis, stating: "The Negro market has become too important to be overlooked or ignored any longer in this day of strong competition for the consumer dollar—and the Negro's money has the same golden color as anyone's."[72] Nat D. Williams pressed ahead with the task of revamping the WDIA format to appeal to a black audience. The replacement of classical music by a musical format that featured rhythm and blues, formerly called race music by the record industry, was his first change.

> We came up with the idea of giving them some blues. Only thing is, the only black record in the station was "Stomping at the Savoy," which became the theme song of my show—and it was by a white singer. We started scrounging around and finally got some records by blues artists—like Fats Waller, Ivory Joe Hunter—and then we had to clean them up. Some of those records were . . . well—suggestive. And the way I cleaned them up was, when they got to be suggestive, I'd just start talking. First thing you know it caught on. The listeners were ready for a different sound, it seemed.[73]

In addition to initiating a new musical format, Williams was also able to launch a wide variety of novel programming at WDIA, as well as to recruit other talented African Americans onto its airways. His first recruits were A. C. Williams and Maurice "Hot Rod" Hulbert; both men, along with Nat D. Williams, were teachers at the local black high school. A. C. Williams hosted two blues shows, "Wheeling on Beale" and "Saturday Night Fish Fry," a gospel show called "Delta Melodies," and a live music review for local black teenagers called "The Teen Town Singers." He would eventually become WDIA's public relations director. Maurice "Hot Rod" Hulbert hosted a popular evening rhythm and blues show for a few years before moving on to Baltimore, Maryland, where he continued to work as a pioneering black disc jockey. Nat D. Williams's most famous recruit, however, was young B. B. King, who took over the evening rhythm and blues slot after the departure of Hulbert. King's career as the country's premier urban blues musician got its initial boost as a result of his radio exposure on WDIA in the early 1950s.

Gospel music, religious programs, and women announcers were as prominent on WDIA as the blues. In addition to A. C. Williams's "Delta Melodies," the station featured regular gospel music shows hosted by Ford Nelson and Theo "Bless My Bones" Wade, the announcer for a religious vocal group called "The Spirit of Memphis." A weekly Sunday morning service was broadcast live from a local black church, as was a daily show featuring a singing country preacher named "Gatemouth" Moore. Black women given a vocal presence on WDIA included Willa Monroe, the "Tan Town Home-maker"; she was the first black female broadcaster in the mid-South. In addition, Starr McKinney, crowned "Miss Bronze Memphis" in 1947, hosted a show highlighting the social and civic activities of black women living in Memphis; and Martha Jean "The Queen" Steinberg hosted her first rhythm and blues music program on WDIA before moving on to become a popular disc jockey in Detroit, Michigan.

The balance of WDIA's black-oriented programming was in the news and public affairs areas. Nat D. Willaims organized a news program that covered stories of special interest to African Americans living in Memphis and the mid-South. There was a daily "Good Neighbor" feature that paid tribute to the good deeds performed by local citizens. There was also a "Missing Persons" program akin to the one Jack L. Cooper had pioneered in Chicago a decade earlier, and a consumer advocacy show named "Call to Action." The most acclaimed public affairs program on WDIA was "Brown America Speaks," a Sunday afternoon discussion show created and hosted by the ubiquitous Nat D. Williams. "Brown America Speaks" addressed race issues from a black perspective. The program won an award for excellence in public affairs broadcasting from the Ohio State Institute for Education in Radio.[74]

Nat D. Williams's central role in the transformation of WDIA into the mid-South's first black-oriented radio station would be hard to overestimate. He single-handedly established the station's rhythm and blues music format, its news format, and most of its best-known public affairs programs. He also recruited most of WDIA's black staff and became the station's most visible black employee. Fortunately for WDIA, Williams was an active and respected community leader who lent credibility to its sudden format change. As a high school history teacher, he was teaching his students about the history of both African Americans and American Indians long before there was any mention of them in history textbooks. Moreover, the material from his history lessons often reappeared in his weekly newspaper column in the *Memphis World*, or as segments on his radio shows. Last but not least, Nat D. Williams was the producer and master of ceremonies of the celebrated Amateur Night on Beale held weekly at the Palace Theater. He initiated this competition in the 1930s and again in conjunction with WDIA in the late 1940s. These performances helped to launch the careers of local luminaries like B. B. King, Bobby Blue Bland, Rufus Thomas, Johnny Ace, and even a young white farm boy named Elvis Presley. Yet in spite of his many contributions to WDIA, Williams never held a formal management position with the station. Throughout its heyday in the 1950s, the owners and the managers of WDIA—the mid-South's first black-oriented radio station—were all white males.[75]

Most of the other radio stations that switched to a format similar to WDIA's in order to appeal to the new black urban market were also owned and managed by white broadcasters. By 1950 they included WEDR in Birmingham, Alabama; WOBS in Jacksonville, Florida; WBOK in New Orleans, Louisiana; WSOK in Nashville, Tennessee; WLOU in Louisville, Kentucky; WCIN in Cincinnati, Ohio; KXLW in Saint Louis, Missouri; WABQ in Cleveland, Ohio; WOOK in Washington, D.C. Some of the southern stations met with resistance to their format changes. WEDR in Birmingham had its antenna tower destroyed by white vigilantes. WDIA in Memphis received threatening telephone calls from irate white listeners when it switched to a black format. For the most part, however, the transition went unchallenged by the local radio audiences. In Washington, D.C., the owner of WOOK was Richard Eaton, a pioneer in ethnic broadcasting who inaugurated a black format in 1948, the same year that WDIA began to make the transition. Hal Jackson was the first African American announcer and disc jockey at WOOK, where he played a role comparable to that of Nat D. Williams at WDIA.[76]

A broadcast ownership landmark was finally reached on 4 October 1949 in Atlanta, Georgia, when a black businessman named J. B. Blayton purchased WERD, a 900-watt AM radio station, for fifty thousand dollars. Blayton had no real experience in radio broadcasting; he viewed his purchase as a commercial venture. His son, J. B. Blayton, Jr., became the station's general manager; young Blayton was living in Chicago when the station was being purchased by his father. He returned to his hometown with a friend, Jack Gibson, who became WERD's first black program director. Gibson was a veteran of black radio in Chicago. He had begun his career as an aspiring film actor but soon switched to radio after being told by several potential employers that he was "too light to play a Negro and too dark to pass for white." His first job in radio came as a character actor in Richard Durham's pioneering black soap opera "Here Comes Tomorrow." After that he was hired as a disc jockey by WJJD, a 50,000-watt outlet in Chicago. At WERD in Atlanta, which he christened "The Good Word Station," Jack Gibson was responsible for developing the new format. Some of his proposed changes were resisted at first by the white staff members who remained with the station after the ownership change. But eventually Gibson prevailed and WERD's programming became oriented toward African Americans living in Atlanta. A few white staff members stayed on, among them Dr. Esther Millner, a sociology professor from Atlanta University who hosted a discussion program on race relations. But most of the old staff left the station and were replaced by Atlanta's first black radio programmers. Gibson did a regular program on WERD and quickly became the station's most popular announcer and disc jockey. Other music programmers of note were pianist and vocalist Graham Jackson, who performed live from his own studio known as the "Little White House," and Roy Sneed, a former Broadway dancer who hosted "Roy Sneed's Music Box." In the areas of news and public affairs, Jack Gibson initiated a daily newscast based on material from Atlanta's black newspaper, *The Daily World*, and a fifteen-minute daily news commentary hosted by Dr. William Boyd, also on the faculty at Atlanta University. There was also a popular children's show hosted by "Uncle Kenny" Knight. Gibson moved on to WLOU in

Louisville, Kentucky, in the early 1950s. WERD proved to be a profitable business venture for J. B. Blayton and his son while they owned it, but it was resold to white buyers later in the decade.[77]

In 1949 there were only four radio stations in the entire country with formats that directly appealed to black consumers. By 1954 there were no less than two hundred stations in this category, and that number rose to four hundred by 1956.[78] However, black ownership of radio properties lagged far behind these figures. In 1956, WCHB in Detroit, Michigan, became only the third black-owned radio station in the entire country to sign on the air. The station was founded and funded by a wealthy black dentist, Harley Bell, who involved himself in a number of other local business ventures in addition to his dental practice. He initiated this venture at the urging of Larry Dean Faulkner, a young black disc jockey from Nashville whom Bell knew socially. After he secured a license from the FCC and had the station technically operative, Bell hired Faulkner as program director. Faulkner, in turn, hired a team of experienced black disc jockeys, including Joe Howard from Houston, Texas, George White from Cincinnati, Ohio, and, later, Martha Jean "The Queen" Stapleton from WDIA in Memphis, Tennessee. The rhythm and blues format they fashioned was successful enough to enable Bell to launch a local FM radio station with a jazz format a decade later.[79]

The dramatic upsurge in black-oriented radio in the postwar era coincided with the emergence of rhythm and blues as a national crossover phenomenon among white teenagers. Radio was the match that ignited this sudden musical prairie fire, but there were earlier cultural precedents. Black music had received some limited airplay in the 1920s, especially live broadcasts of famous blues and jazz artists. Then, in the 1930s with the advent of the radio disc jockey, the race records of some of the best-known black artists were first heard on the airways. The pioneering radio deejays of the depression era were invariably white males who played popular swing band recordings for urban audiences. The best known were Martin Block (WNEW) and Freddie Robbins (WOV) in New York City; Dave Garroway in Chicago and then New York; Gene Norman, Paul Potter, and Al Jarvis in Los Angeles. This group tended to highlight the established white swing bands and vocalists of the day. A second group of white disc jockeys soon began to experiment with a new musical format by playing race records in lieu of the white cover versions. As could be expected, this group attracted a black audience in addition to their white jazz listeners. The most visible in this group were "Symphony" Sid Torin (WHOM) and later Al "Jazzbo" Collins (WNEW) in New York City; "Jumping" George Oxford in San Francisco; Hunter Hancock in Los Angeles; and "Jitterbug" Johnny Poorhall, who did a show on WHBQ in Memphis in the late 1930s. Poorhall apparently had a substantial African American listening audience in Memphis, while Symphony Sid was well known in Harlem. As discussed earlier, there were very few black disc jockeys on the airways before the post-World War II era, the most prominent exception being Jack L. Cooper.[80]

Postwar radio was characterized by both white and black deejays capturing the attention and imagination of a youthful urban audience with the introduction of rhythm and blues formats. As had been the case in similar cross-cultural exchanges in the past, the black innovators set the new styles, in this case pertaining to the performance of the disc jockey, while their white imitators and benefactors reaped the financial benefits. As late as 1947, an *Ebony* article noted that only sixteen black disc jockeys were at that time on the airways throughout the country; the total number of "wax spinners" on the air was at least three thousand.[81] These lopsided figures had begun to change dramatically by the next decade. Moreover, African Americans who took to the airways in the 1950s tended to be both knowledgeable and effective communicators, on the one hand, and rebellious and even extravagant radio broadcasters, on the other—especially if judged by the established decorum of radio announcers. They threw themselves into the medium with an abundance of enthusiasm and lack of professional pretensions. They talked a steady stream of street "jive," using strange-sounding words, some of which were of their own making. They clapped their hands, danced, shouted encouragement, and sang along with the records they played on the air. They assumed zany radio personae like "Doctor Bop," "Daddy Rabbit," "Professor Jive," "Doctor Daddyo," "Poppa Stoppa," "Nighthawk," "Moohah," "Sugar Daddy," "Chattie Hattie," and "Hot Rod." In short, the first wave of black disc jockeys were audio tricksters; the more unique and outrageous their characters and stories, the larger their listening audiences.

This new breed of media rebels included Joe Bostic (WBNX), Willie Bryant and Ray Carroll (WHOM), Phil "Doctor Jive" Gordon and Nipsy Russell (WLIB), Tommy Smalls (WWRL), and Jack Waker "The Pear-Shaped Talker" (WOV)—all in New York City; Sam Evans, Richard Stams, McKie Fitzhugh, Norm Spaulding (WGES), Jessie Owens (WAAF), Daddio Daylie, and Big Bill Hill (WOPA) were in Chicago; Doug "Jocko" Henderson (WHAT) was in Philadelphia; Hal Jackson (WOOK) was in Washington, D.C.; Maurice "Hot Rod" Hulbert (WSID) in Baltimore; Bill Hawkins (WJW), Andy Franklin (WSRS), and Eddie O'Jay (WABQ) were in Cleveland; Larry Dean Faulkner and "Jolting" Joe Howard (WCHB), Bristol Bryant and Ernie Durham (WJLB) were in Detroit; Jessie "Spider" Burks (KXLW) was in Saint Louis; Rufus Thomas and "Moohah" Williams (WDIA) were in Memphis; Bruce Baye and "Tall" Paul White (WEDR) were in Birmingham; Early Wright (WROX) was in Clarksdale, Mississippi; James "Alley Cat" Patrick (WOAK) was in Atlanta; "Daddy Rabbit with the Do Rag Habit" (WOBS) was in Jacksonville, Florida; Chester "Daddyo Hot Rod" McDowell (KCLJ) was in Shreveport, Louisiana; Lavada "Doctor Hep Cat" Durst (KUET) in Austin, Texas; Larry McKinley (WBOX) and Vernon "Doctor Daddyo" Winslow (WWEZ) in New Orleans. In addition to Martha Jean "The Queen" Stapleton on WDIA in Memphis and WCHB in Detroit, the black female deejays who gained some recognition in the 1950s included Mary Dee on WHOD in Pittsburgh, Pennsylvania, "Chattie Hattie" Leeper on KCKA in Kansas City, Missouri, Vivian Carter on WGES in Chicago, and "Louisville" Lou Saxon on WLOU in Louisville, Kentucky. Louisville Lou worked with Jack Gibson at WLOU before he moved on to WMDM in Miami, Florida. Gibson was instrumental in helping to organize the first black disc jockey trade organization, the National Association of Radio Announcers (NARA) in 1955. But under the control of the tightly knit groups of founders known as the "Original Thirteen," the NARA became little more than a social club that held an annual convention; it failed to develop any significant economic or political initiatives in the radio industry.[82]

Within the growing black urban communities, however, African American disc jockeys like "Jockey" Jack Gibson, Maurice "Hot Rod" Hulbert, Daddy-O Dayley, "Jocko" Henderson, Lavada "Doctor Hep Cat" Durst, and Vernon "Doctor Daddyo" Winslow were all instrumental in popularizing a radical new style of black English on their radio shows. Jockey Jack, dressed in a silk jockey outfit, started his program on WLOU in Louisville, home of the Kentucky

Derby, with the traditional Derby bugle call and then the following incantation:

> My father wasn't a jockey, but he sure taught me to ride
> He sat right in the middle, then from side to side.
> Ride Jockey Jack ride![83]

Maurice "Hot Rod" Hulbert was also renowned for his verbal dexterity and rhyming skills; he liked to start his programs with a boast:

> Not the flower, not the root
> but the seed, sometimes called the herb.
> Not the imitator, but the originator,
> the living legend—the Rod![84]

Trumpeter Dizzy Gillespie credits Daddyo Daley for inventing much of the hip argot of the bebop jazz musicians in the postwar era. Lavada "Doctor Hep Cat" Durst recorded a song he wrote called "Hep Cat's Boogie" and published his own dictionary on hipster language, *The Jives of Doctor Hep Cat.* "Jocko" Henderson, a protégé of Maurice Hulbert's, also called himself "The Ace of Space"; he liked to launch his show with the following bit of street poetry:

> Be bebop, this is your Jock.
>   Back on the scene with my record machine.
> Saying hoo poopsi doo, how do you do.
> When you up you up, when you down you down,
>   But when you mess with Jocko, you upside down.[85]

Perhaps the most unusual transmission of black hipster argot was broadcast on "The Poppa Stoppa Show" on WJMR in New Orleans in the late 1940s. Poppa Stoppa was the radio brainchild of Vernon Winslow, an art professor at the local Dillard College. Winslow was raised in Chicago; he attended college at Morehouse in Atlanta and the University of Chicago and earned his art degree from the Art Institute of Chicago. After taking a position at Dillard, Winslow began to write for the local black newspaper on New Orleans nightlife. In 1948, he wrote to two local radio stations about doing a weekly show that would showcase the city's nightlife milieu and music. One of the stations, WJMR, wrote back asking for a script and an interview; it was no longer network-affiliated and was groping for an entré into the "new Negro" market. After listening to Winslow's plan for the show, the white owner asked him suspiciously, "By the way, are you a nigger?" When Winslow replied that he was a "Negro," the owner exclaimed: "Well I'll be damned. Don't get me wrong, you got a good idea there, but I'd tear my station down before putting you behind the microphone."[86] In the end, however, the owner turned around and offered to hire Winslow to teach his white announcers how to sound like the show's black host, whom he called Poppa Stoppa: "Poppa Stoppa was the name I came up with. It came from the rhyme rap that folks in the streets were using in New Orleans. The language was for insiders, most white folks couldn't understand it so it became a unique identity and people were proud of it as a way to show solidarity and brotherhood. I wrote my radio scripts in that language and Poppa Stoppa was my mouthpiece, so to speak."[87] Vernon Winslow trained a succession of "four or five" white radio announcers how to talk like Poppa Stoppa for WJMR; within a year, the program was the most popular new radio show in town. Winslow then left the station to become Doctor Daddyo on WEZZ; he was sponsored by the local Jax Brewery. In addition to his own show out of New Orleans, Winslow traveled around the region promoting Jax Beer and training a new crew of radio announcers to be Doctor Daddyo. The members of this group however, were African Americans.[88]

Following in the voice prints of these innovative black disc jockeys was a deluge of white imitators, Poppa Stoppa clones who played the new rhythm and blues records and spoke hipster slang with great bravado. The newly discovered target audience consisted not only of African Americans but also white teenagers who were tuning into rhythm and blues shows in increasing numbers. White deejays who gained fame and sometimes fortune in the 1950s through their association with black music included Alan Freed, who reached the pinnacle of his career as a disc jockey in New York City; Tom Donahue in Washington, D.C., and Philadelphia; Bill Randle in Cleveland; George "Hound Dog" Lorenz in Buffalo; Phil McKernan in Oakland, California; Bob "Wolfman Jack" Smith in Shreveport, Louisiana; Jack "the Cat" Elliott and Clarence Hamman in New Orleans; Zenas "Daddy" Sears in Atlanta; Bill Gordon and Dewey Phillips in Memphis; and Gene Nobes, John Richburg, and Hoss Allen—all hosts of "Randy's Record Shop," heard nightly on WLAC in Nashville. WLAC was a 50,000-watt, clear-channel radio station heard throughout the Deep South. Randy Wood sponsored the all-night rhythm and blues show in order to build up his mail-order record business. The broadcasts were popular and profitable enough to allow Wood to launch his own record company, Dot Records. The company covered black rhythm and blues hits with white vocalists Pat Boone, Gayle Storm, and Tab Hunter.[89]

Alan Freed was the most successful and controversial of the white rhythm and blues disc jockeys who dominated the airways in the fifties. He began his broadcasting career as a classical music programmer in New Castle, Pennsylvania, after World War II; at the time, he was a trained musician and mechanical engineer who was also in the early stages of alcohol addiction. In 1951 he inaugurated his "Moon Dog" rhythm and blues show on WJW in Cleveland at the insistence of Leo Mintz, the owner of a local record shop specializing in rhythm and blues records. Freed's late-night shows, often broadcast while he was intoxicated, were the rage of Cleveland and catapulted him into the national limelight. He branched out into concert promotions and in 1954 moved to New York City, the largest radio market in the country. Freed continued his Moon Dog show on WINS and promoted interracial rhythm and blues concerts at Saint Nicholas Arena. Both endeavors met with great success, but in the process Freed came under fire from African Americans, who resented his attempts to imitate black deejays. The manager of WINS was invited to a protest meeting at a Harlem YMCA. As he later described it: "The criticism was basically from the Negro community. That he was an outsider, that he was imitating them, and why shouldn't it be a Negro. We were invited to appear and talk the situation out, and explain why a white man was playing this black music."[90]

Alan Freed's downfall began with his concert promotion business. Late in 1954 he was charged with incitement to riot and anarchy in Boston when a concert he was producing turned into a small-scale riot between teenagers and the police. Live rhythm and blues performed by African Americans for white and black teenagers was proving to be a volatile combination. The incident forced Freed's resignation from WINS, and within a year he filed for bankruptcy. The final blow came when he was indicted on payola charges and then income-tax evasion in the early 1960s. He was a penniless alcoholic without a job or a home when he died in 1965.[91]

Alan Freed's tragic demise paralleled the decline of rhythm and blues music on the radio in urban markets throughout the country. In the mid-1950s, "rock and roll", a term Freed himself claimed to have coined, began to replace rhythm and blues as the popular music of the day. Rock and roll was more exclusively for white teenagers and it would be increasingly performed by young white musicians. By the end of the decade, this new rhythm and blues offspring dominated both the radio and the record industries. Black popular music was again relegated to a marginal status in the music business and the urban radio market. It survived only on those stations that continued to target the African American consumer as their major source of income.

Television and newspapers tended to be the major media battle-fields for the racial controversies of the 1960s, but radio was also caught up in the discord. Transistorized portable and car radios, as well as the rapid growth of FM stereo broadcasting, gave radio a new lease on life; the industry was able to fully recover from being replaced by television as the country's favorite pastime. It was able to adjust to its new role as a "secondary" mass media by cultivating new demographic markets for its advertisers. The youth market and the Negro market were now among the primary targets of commercial radio. The enticement they used was the new popular music that came in the wake of the rhythm and blues—rock and roll tidal waves. This new music was still segregated by the radio and the music industries; rhythm and blues was now designated as "soul" music, while rock and roll was shortened to "rock" music. Soul music was heard on the black-oriented stations. Rock was played on the stations targeting white youth.

Black-Controlled Radio (1965–90)

The continual growth of an urban African American radio audience, coupled with the civil rights gains in the 1960s, helped to fuel an upsurge in the number of black-oriented radio stations on the air. In 1965, there were over one hundred commercial stations with black formats, while another five hundred were doing some sort of special African American programming. In a special report on the Negro market in *Broadcasting*, it was estimated that in 1965 expenditures on "Negro radio" reached the twenty-eight-million-dollar mark, which was three times the amount spent on black-oriented radio in 1961.[92] By the end of the decade, the number of these stations on the air had climbed to over the three-hundred mark, while their advertising revenues more than doubled. More and more, the black-oriented stations during this period became music stations. On the average, 70 percent of their programming was secular music, while another 20 percent was devoted to religious broadcasts; only 5 percent of the broadcast time was allocated to news and public affairs. This was considerably less public service programming than had been broadcast in the 1950s on WDIA or WERD.[93]

With soul music enshrined as the programming choice for black-oriented stations, the role of the disc jockey became even more influential. Deejays were now a potent force, not only on the airways, but in the music industry and in their own hometowns. The legendary figures of the 1950s like Nat D. Williams, Al Benson, Hal Jackson, and Jack Gibson were joined by an influx of new black radio talent. In New York City, Del Shields and Bill Williams on WLIB pioneered a progressive jazz format that mixed together a wide variety of jazz, soul, and even salsa, while Dr. Billy Taylor provided knowledgeable commentary on the history and esthetics of jazz in particular and black music in general. Meanwhile, up in Buffalo, WUFO, under the guidance of Eddie O'Jay, became an important breakout station for new soul artists; in addition, a trio of younger disc jockeys, Gerry Bledsoe, Gary Byrd, and Frankie Crocker, cut their teeth as music programmers on the station, before moving on to bigger markets. In Philadelphia, WDAS's new talent pool of black deejays included Georgie Woods, LeBaron Taylor, and Jimmy Bishop. In Cleveland, Ed Wright emerged as the successor to Eddie O'Jay. In Chicago, Purvis Spann and Herb Kent "The Kool Gent" were instrumental in boosting the ratings of WVON among the city's black listeners, while the silky voiced Sid McCoy was the late-night jazz favorite on WGES, and then WCFL.

The most listened to black disc jockey in Houston, Texas, was Skipper Lee Fraizer on KCOH. In Los Angeles, 75 percent of the African American homes within range of the KGFJ signal listened religiously to the Magnificent Monteque. His familiar invocation, "Burn Baby Burn!" used to introduce the "hot" records he featured on his show, inadvertently became the offical battle cry of the 1965 Watts rebellion. In San Francisco, a hip-talking musician named Sly Stone made his debut on KSOL in 1963; in addition to playing records, he also played the organ and sang his own songs on the air. Within a few years, Sly would form his own band and become one of the decade's most imaginative and innovative black musicians. Another Bay Area musician, jazz saxophonist and composer Roland Young, emerged in the late 1960s on San Francisco's new progressive FM outlets, KMBR and KSAN, as the market's most provocative music programmer. His "free form" mix of jazz, salsa, and soul with music from Africa, Latin America, and Asia was a precursor of the world beat music format that emerged on public radio a decade later. Throughout the better part of the 1960s, black disc jockeys not only pioneered radio's more creative formats, they also continued to champion the new socially conscious soul music of Aretha Franklin, James Brown, and a host of others. They were still the ones who introduced the new black records and artists to their listening audiences, and, for the most part, they retained the power to make or break the hits in their respective markets, even in the wake of the payola scandals.[94]

Yet in spite of these apparent gains in the radio industry made by African Americans, they were still excluded from owning commercial radio properties, and hence from any real control over the content and the direction of the overall programming on the black-formatted broadcast outlets. In 1965, there continued to be only a handful of African American–owned radio stations in the country, less than 1 percent of the total. With the onset of the 1970s, there was little change in this percentage, despite the rapid growth in the number of black-formatted stations. Even though there were over three hundred of these outlets in existence by 1970, only sixteen of them were actually owned by African Americans.[95]

The white owners and managers of the black-oriented radio outlets were faced with a built-in conflict in their dealings with the black disc jockeys who programmed the music on their stations. As long as the black music programmers selected the records to be aired on their shows, they collectively controlled three-quarters of the format. More important, this situation allowed them to deal directly with the record industry, in effect passing over management. The owners' strategy for regaining control over the music format was provided by their industry counterparts, the owners of the nation's leading rock radio stations. In the aftermath of the payola scandals, these stations began to adopt a new "Top Forty" radio music format, which was controlled from the top down. A stated purpose of the "Top Forty" radio format, aside from boosting profits for the owners, was to make payola obsolete. It accomplished this goal by establishing a rotating playlist based on the hit records charted in *Billboard*. The program director was responsible for updating the playlist as the pop charts changed. The disc jockeys' job was now confined to following an official playlist and reading the omnipresent commercials. They had no say in what music would be played on the air and there was no chance for them to get involved in the payola racket. When applied to African American–oriented radio stations, the top forty soul format effectively ended the black disc jockeys' control over the content of their own programs, just as it had ended the white disc jockeys' reign over rock-formatted stations. Both groups were no longer allowed to create exciting radio personae or to determine what music should be played and when. This was especially debilitating to black disc jockeys because it curtailed their ability to introduce new music, often produced locally, to their listening audiences. Within the confines of the "Top Forty" format, they were relegated to working an assigned airshift and following the dictates of management if they wished to continue to receive a paycheck. By the late 1960s, the black personality disc jockey was becoming extinct.

In the forefront of this changeover to a "Top Forty" format were five soul radio chains, all owned and managed by white business interests. Rollin, Inc., owned stations in Chicago (WBEE), Indianapolis (WGEE), Newark, New Jersey (WNJR), and Norfolk, Virginia (WRAP). Rounsaville Radio had outlets in Cincinnati (WCIN), Louisville (WLOU), Nashville (WVOL), and New Orleans (WYLD). Sounderling Broadcasting Corporation owned properties in Oakland (KDIA), Washington D.C. (WOL), and even Memphis (WDIA), which they purchased in the late 1960s. Speidel Broadcasters controlled the largest number of stations, all six located in the southeast region of the country. The fifth soul radio chain was the United Broadcasting Company, with stations in Baltimore (WSID), Cleveland (WJMO), and Washington D.C. (WOOK). These stations were well-financed and profitable enterprises located in key urban markets all over the country. Hence, their collective shift to a "Top Forty" soul format set in motion a dominant new trend among black-oriented radio stations.[96]

The soul radio chains' move to a "Top Forty" format generated some protest and organized opposition from their African American employees, who were quick to ally themselves with the interests of the local black communities being served by the stations in question. More often than not, the resulting conflicts centered on employment issues rather than format considerations, because the changes in format had an immediate impact on employment practices. In Columbia, South Carolina, black citizen groups formally complained to the FCC about the employment policies of WOIC, owned by the Speidel broadcast chain. African American disc jockeys were being given titles like public affairs director, community relations director, news director, and music director without commensurate duties, pay, and authority. In reality, their power and status were being decreased as a result of the imposition of a top-forty soul format by management. In Nashville, Tennessee, WVOL, owned by Rounsaville, was involved in a protracted labor dispute with its black staff over similar issues. The Atlanta, Georgia, NAACP, allied with local black broadcasters, spearheaded efforts to open up employment opportunities for African Americans in that city's radio outlets, all of which were again under the control of white business interests after WERD was resold in 1959.

In the nation's capital, WOOK, owned by the United Broadcasting Company, was the target of local protests over hiring practices. When United ignored the protests, the Southern Christian Leadership Conference launched a nationwide boycott of its other radio stations because of the company's discriminatory hiring policies for management positions.[97]

In addition to the protests over employment practices, there were also some sporadic community-based outbursts protesting the lack of meaningful content in soul radio formats. An ad hoc group of African Americans in Kansas City, Kansas, picketed a local soul station in the summer of 1972, demanding that it upgrade its programming and become more responsive to the needs of the local black community. In Newark, New Jersey, that same year, a militant community organization condemned WNJR, part of the soul radio chain owned by Rollins, for doing away with its public affairs programs. Their manifesto, published in a local newspaper, read in part:

> Stations like this feed our communities and our children monotonous music, skimpy news, and very little relevant programming. The only thing our children can aspire to are songs about drugs, getting high, abnormal love affairs, with nothing about what's going on and what

needs to be done to better our community. We are protesting not only against the fascism and racism involved in removing all legitimate community opinion from this radio station, but also against the pattern of paternalistic, mediocre broadcasting that has set in at so-called "soul stations" around the country. Are the Black and Puerto Rican communities to be continually insulted by programming that imagines all we can do is wiggle our backsides and chugalug brew?[98]

Unfortunately, the African American response to continuing barriers in employment and the absence of relevant content in black-oriented radio lacked a cohesive national strategy. The protests achieved some visible gains, but they tended to be uncoordinated and were easily isolated.

The organization that should have been in the vanguard of developing a national strategy for black radio was the NARA. At its 1967 annual convention, Dr. Martin Luther King, Jr. paid tribute to the crucial role of the black disc jockey in the ongoing civil rights conflict, no doubt hoping to galvanize their efforts for the struggle ahead:

I valued a special opportunity to address you this evening for in my years of struggle, both north and south, I have come to appreciate the role which the radio announcer plays in the life of our people; for better or for worse, you are opinion makers in the community. And it is important that you remain aware of the power which is potential in your vocation. The masses of Americans who have been deprived of educational and economic opportunity are almost totally dependent on radio as their means of relating to the society at large. They do not read newspapers, though they may occasionally thumb through *Jet*. Television speaks not to their needs but to upper-middle-class America. One need only recall the Watts tragedy and the quick adaptation of the "Burn Baby Burn" slogan to illustrate the pervasive influence of the radio announcer on the community. But while the establishment was quick to blame the tragedy of Watts most unjustly on the slogan of Magnificent Monteque, it has not been ready to acknowledge all of the positive features which grow out of your contributions to the community. No one knows the importance of Tall Paul White and the massive nonviolent demonstrations of the youth of Birmingham in 1963; or the funds raised by Purvis Spann for the Mississippi Summer Project of 1964; or the consistent fundraising and voter education done for the Southern Christian Leadership Conference and the Civil Rights Movement by Georgie Woods, my good friend from Philadelphia. Tonight I want to say thank you not just to these few, but to all of you who have given leadership to our people in thousands of unknown and unsung ways. We would certainly not have come so far without your support. In a real sense, you have paved the way for social and political change by creating a powerful, cultural bridge between black and white. School integration is much easier now that they share a common music, a common language, and enjoy the same dances. You introduced youth to that music and created a language of soul and promoted the dances which now sweep across race, class, and nation.[99]

At the same time that Dr. King was praising the black disc jockeys, the NARA was facing an internal crisis that would soon destroy it as a viable organization. A year earlier, a group of young politically active members known as the "New Breed" wrested control of the NARA away from the older "Original Thirteen" who had dominated it from its inception. The militant New Breed cadre of African American disc jockeys adopted "black power" rhetoric and made a number of angry demands vis-à-vis the radio and music industries. Soon thereafter, a politics of confrontation emerged, pitting the younger militants against the older members of the NARA and their white allies in the entertainment business. Both of the latter groups soon withdrew their support from the organization amid threats of physical violence and accusations of racism. The New Breed tried to revitalize the NARA on their own, changing its name to NARTA in order to include television announcers and planning their own school of broadcasting, but the damage proved to be irreversible. The organization was never able to overcome the generational schism between the black disc jockeys and ceased to exist as a viable entity after the 1960s. This lack of a cohesive trade organization would seriously constrain the impact of black radio at the national level over the next two decades.[100]

Perhaps the most important new development in black commercial radio during the 1970s was the successful launching of two separate African American radio networks. There had been an earlier attempt to build up a black network in the 1950s, but it had proved to be unsuccessful. Leonard Evans, publisher of the fledgling African American radio trade magazine *Tuesday*, founded the National Negro Network in 1954. Its syndicated programming included news broadcasts, black soap operas "The Story of Ruby Valentine," with Juanita Hall, and "The Life of Anna Lewis," starring Hilda Simms, as well as variety shows with entertainers Cab Calloway and Ethel Waters. The network attracted a clientele by offering its program at bargain-basement prices to black-formatted stations around the country. This strategy won it fifty subscribers, but the network lacked working capital and soon went out of business, as did the trade magazine *Tuesday*.[101]

In 1972, the Mutual Black Network was formed for news and sports syndication under the auspices of the Mutual Broadcasting Network. By the end of the decade, the Mutual Black Network had just over one hundred affiliates and 6.2 million listeners. The Sheridan Broadcasting Corporation, a black-owned broadcasting chain based in Pittsburgh, purchased the Mutual Black Network in the late 1970s; at that time, it was renamed the Sheridan Broadcasting Network (SBN). In addition to the news and sports reports, the network also began to feature live broadcasts of black college sports events and public affairs shows that highlighted African American journalists and political leaders.[102]

The second African American radio network, the National Black Network (NBN), was formed in 1973 by the Unity Broadcasting Company. Established to service the black-oriented radio outlets with short news and sportscasts, this new network was also able to expand its programming as it gained new subscribers. By 1988, NBN had ninety-four affiliates from coast to coast and was offering a wide range of programs. They included a consumer report called "NBN Shorts;" a women's program produced by Marie Haylock entitled "The Action Woman;" a late-night call-in show, "Night Talk," hosted by Bob Law on WWRL-AM in New York; a feature on black entertainers called "NBN Stage Door;" and a regular commentary by journalist Roy Wood, which he named "One Black Man's Opinion." Both black networks provided their affiliates with broadcast quality programs produced from an African American perspective. This was a giant step forward for black programming in the radio industry. The only apparent drawback was that this relatively inexpensive access to news, sports, and public affairs features discouraged similar production efforts on the part of the local stations subscribing to the service. Consequently, news and public affairs staffs at the black-oriented stations, including those owned by African Americans, remained minimal at best.[103]

The 1970s also witnessed a significant upsurge in black-owned and operated radio stations in the United States. While there were only sixteen of these stations in 1970, the number rose to fifty-six in 1976; by 1980, there were eighty-eight commercial stations owned by African Americans. However, because of the rapid rise in the number of commercial outlets overall, those eighty-eight stations were still less than 1 percent of the total number of AM and FM radio properties operating in the country by the end of the 1970s.[104]

Two influential black civic leaders who purchased radio stations in the early 1970s were John Johnson in Chicago and Percy Sutton in New York City. Johnson, the owner and publisher of *Ebony*, bought WJPC in Chicago in 1972. That same year, Sutton, an established political leader in Harlem, founded Inner City Broadcasting in order to purchase WLIB-AM and WLIB-FM. From the outset, it was apparent that Percy Sutton and his associates at Inner City had both an economic and a political agenda for their broadcast properties. In a 1972 interview, Sutton commented on the political agenda: "Communications will form the substance of politics from now on. What we can bring to black people in America in terms of information will determine what black politics will be in the future. Image is part of it, but communicating facts to the electorate may soon be all of it. When you think of how differently the informed person will respond, the potential for change in this country becomes fascinating."[105]

Inner City Broadcasting took over two radio stations that were already established as progressive forces in New York's African American communities. WLIB-AM had a black format that included a highly acclaimed news and public affairs department. A series of shows, produced by the station, on disadvantaged youth in the city won two Peabody awards in 1970. Inner City's first step was to expand the news and public affairs; WLIB-AM became "Your Total Black News and Information Station," offering more news and public affairs programming than any other black-formatted radio outlet in the country. Its informational shows focused on local, national and international issues of concern to New York's black population—everything from housing in Harlem to Shirley Chisholm's presidential campaign to the struggle for independence in Zimbabwe. There were also special bilingual programs in Spanish and French for the city's Puerto Rican and Haitian communities. WLIB's best-known program was a four-hour weekday morning talk show hosted by Judy Simmons. By the early 1980s, its estimated three hundred thousand listeners per quarter-hour made it the most popular local radio program in the country.[106]

Prior to being purchased by Inner City Broadcasting, WLIB-FM had pioneered an innovative music format that highlighted jazz in all of its diversity, from traditional to Latin to bebop to avant-garde. After completing the purchase, Inner City changed the station's call letters to WBLS-FM and hired Frankie Crocker as program director. Crocker was already a popular black disc jockey in New York; his mandate was to transform WBLS into the top-rated station in the market. In order to accomplish this, Crocker narrowed and diluted the jazz format, playing only the most commercially successful jazz releases and mixing them with the back pop music that dominated the Billboard charts. The more a record sold, the more airplay it received. In addition, Crocker's new format featured the latest disco dance tracks popular in local nightclubs. The combination proved to be a gold mine; by the mid-1970s, WBLS, "The Total Black Experience in Sound," was ranked among the top three stations in the market.

However, the popular success of WBLS spawned a host of imitators—all competing for the same audience and advertising dollars. The most successful competitors were WKTU-FM and WKSS-FM. In order to maintain WBLS's momentum and ratings, Crocker added to the playlist white artists who ranked high on the *Billboard* charts and whose style was compatible with the current black popular music—artists like Phoebe Snow, Bette Midler, Elton John, Boz Scaggs, Hall and Oates. "The Total Black Experience in Sound" soon became "The Total Experience in Sound." According to Crocker, this crossover format was an attempt to "increase the percentage of white artists played, and in turn, the number of white listeners, and ultimately, white advertising dollars" without losing the black audience base. The new format was then dubbed "urban contemporary" by the radio industry. By 1980, WBLS was the number one-rated station in the New York market; its overall average of approximately two hundred thousand listeners per quarter was at that time the best in the country. But once again, the new format attracted imitators, and WBLS's reign as number one was to be short-lived. Moreover, this new crossover trend, dictated by the economics of the radio marketplace, encouraged the establishment of a format at WBLS, and then other local black stations, which only paid lip service to the cultural and social diversity of New York's African American population.[107]

A similar cycle of innovation, success, competition, and crossover was evident at other black-controlled stations in large urban markets during this period. In Washington, D.C., the *Washington Post* donated its commercial FM radio license to Howard University in 1971. WHUR-FM signed on the air the next year with a lively jazz format calculated to expose listeners to the great masters of that tradition: Louis Armstrong, Bessie Smith, Duke Ellington, Billie Holiday, Charlie Parker, Ella Fitzgerald, John Coltrane, and Miles Davis. In addition, the musical programming was supportive of local jazz musicians, giving them exposure on the airways. The news and public affairs shows were equally novel for the nation's capital. The "Daily Drum," a full hour-long evening newscast, featured special coverage of the local black community, as well as news from Africa and the diaspora. The public affairs offerings were geared to meet the practical needs of the station's black listeners. There were regular programs on health and nutrition, money management and family relationships. WHUR's first station manager was Phil Watson, a progressive black communications lawyer with a strong commitment to community service.

In the mid-1970s, WHUR changed directions, becoming more market-oriented and professional. When Howard students vociferously protested the shift, which tended to marginalize their involvement in the station, they were awarded a campus cable radio operation as consolation. WHUR's new general manager was Kathy Liggins, the station's former sales manager, who approached radio as first and foremost a business enterprise; her blueprint for WHUR was calculated to make it the number one money-maker in the market. Consequently, the station's progressive jazz format and its extensive public affairs offerings were modified considerably; the jazz all but disappeared and the public service shows were curtailed. WHUR's music playlist gravitated toward the artists appearing on Billboard's black music charts; black superstars were prominently featured, while local talent was largely ignored. To her credit, however, Liggins did provide some opportunities for new air talent at the station. Her biggest discovery was Melvin Lindsay, a former WHUR student intern whom she installed in the night-music slot. Lindsay's show, which he called "The Quiet Storm" after the song of the same name by Smokey Robinson, blended popular black love ballads with mellow instrumental jazz. It not only became the top-rated show in the market for that particular time slot, but its format was also adopted by other black stations around the country, becoming in effect the new black "adult contemporary" format of the 1980s. But overall, WHUR's educational mission was subsumed by its financial one. Even though the "Daily Drum" remained on the air, community service in general now took a backseat to public relations. This trend continued throughout the 1980s, as the station continued to fine tune its "Urban Adult" format as listed in the *Washington Post* in order to compete for top ratings in the market.

The contradiction between WHUR's commercial mandate and its educational mission as a media property of the nation's top black university was nowhere more apparent than during the recent student protests there. In the spring of 1989, Howard University students occupied the administration building on campus, demanding better student services, more support for Afrocentric course offerings, and the removal of Republican National Committee Chairman Lee Atwater from Howard's Board of Trustees. Atwater had just been appointed to the board by Howard University President James Cheek; his acceptance of the position touched off the student uprising. On the morning that marked the height of the conflict, while university administrators and city officials were deciding whether or not to use the city's riot police to clear the students from the building forcibly if necessary, WHUR's morning host, Gerry Bledsoe, was spinning records and giving away free tickets to the Ringling Brothers' Barnum and Bailey Circus, as part of a promotional campaign the station was conducting. The only campus radio coverage of the unfolding crisis was broadcast on WHBC, the student cable station, which had a number of its staff reporting from inside the building. It was only after the crisis had been resolved by the resignation of Lee Atwater, and the withdrawal of the riot squad from campus, that WHUR routinely mentioned the student protest in its evening newscast.

In the 1980s, the number of black-controlled radio stations continued to grow; by 1986, there were one hundred and fifty AM (94) and FM (56) stations owned by African Americans. Most of these stations had only one owner, which indicates the small-business dimension of the operations. As for formats, about two-thirds of the stations are listed as being "urban contemporary" or "adult contemporary," the latter of which targets an older, upscale, racially mixed audience by playing more "oldies" or "classics" from the 1960s and 1970s.[109] The remaining stations have progressive black, jazz, gospel, talk, or some mixture of these more marginal formats. This drift toward urban and adult contemporary formats by black-controlled stations has fueled a heated debate among African Americans in the radio and music industries. On the one side are the entertainment professionals, who argue that such formats are essential because they make it possible for black radio stations to compete with white-owned stations, thus enabling them finally to get a fair share of the advertising pie. Critics of this trend, like music writer Nelson George, contend that such crossover formats are tantamount to "cultural suicide" for African Americans. One reason for this is that the crossover is not balanced; many more white musicians are featured on urban contemporary stations than black artists on rock-formatted outlets. But, more important, this crossover tendency, like the integration policies of the past two decades, assimilates only the most successful and privileged black artists and disc jockeys into the mainstream of corporate America. Hence the crossover phenomenon draws valuable personnel and resources away from the black community, and from the collective task of building a self-sufficient culture for the masses of African Americans who are still relegated to the margins of American society, and have little chance of crossing over into the mainstream.[110]

Black Public Radio (1967–90)

Fortunately for African Americans, the cultural vacuum created by black commercial radio's preoccupation with profits and the rating system was partially filled by the emergence of a number of black public radio stations. There are two major categories in this group, educational and community. The educational stations are owned and operated by black colleges and universities granted public broadcast licenses. Most of these black college stations were an outgrowth of the expansion of public radio funding by the federal government under the auspices of the Corporation for Public Broadcasting and its subsidiary, National Public Radio (NPR). Both agencies were created in 1967 and were the catalyst for the rapid growth of public radio stations over the next fifteen years. It was during this era of federal government support for public radio that most of the noncommercial black college radio stations signed on the air. Before 1967, there were only two black educational outlets in the country; at present, there are forty black public radio stations broadcasting regularly.[111]

In contrast, the community radio stations are most often owned and operated by nonprofit foundations controlled by a local board of directors. They were an outgrowth of an alternative radio movement pioneered by the Pacifica Foundation in the 1950s and then institutionalized with the formation of the National Federation of Community Broadcasters (NFCB) in 1974. Community radio stations primarily rely on listener donations to provide an economic base. They have adopted a wide range of organizational structures and program formats, each tailored to meet the communication and informational needs of a particular community. Nevertheless, all NFCB outlets are united in a collective effort to provide a vital alternative to commercial radio through encouraging innovative programming and grass-roots community participation in the day-to-day operation of their stations. At present, there are just under one hundred stations affiliated with the NFCB; of that number, twelve are classified as black community radio outlets.[112]

The first black-controlled NFCB station was KPOO-FM in San Francisco. Known as "Poor Peoples' Radio," KPOO was founded in 1972 by Lorenzo Milam, the "Johnny Appleseed" of the community radio movement. Milam was the catalyst for a number of community-oriented public radio stations, mostly on the West Coast. Although established to serve San Francisco's inner-city poor and predominantly black population, KPOO was initially staffed and controlled by white community radio activists allied with Milam. This led to a series of conflicts between the white staff and the black volunteers involved with the station. The situation came to a head in the mid-1970s when protests by African American volunteers and listeners forced Milam to turn the station over to a board of directors controlled by the black community; in the process, most of the white staff was replaced. By the early 1980s, KPOO had broadened its base to include San Francisco's Hispanic, Asian, Filipino, and Native American populations, in effect becoming the country's first public multiethnic radio station. At present, the diversity of the station's work force and format tends to reproduce this multiethnic outlook in practice. There are music, news, public affairs, and cultural programs in the native language of each of the ethnic groups involved in the station. Consequently, KPOO has been able to expand its listening audience while forging a coalition of African American, Hispanic, Asian, Filipino, and Native American media activists around the operation of the station.[113]

WRFG-FM, "Radio Free Georgia," began broadcasting in Atlanta, Georgia, in the summer of 1973. It was a low-power 10-watt operation staffed by former white and black student activists once affiliated with the Student Nonviolent Coordinating Committee (SNCC) and the Students for a Democratic Society (SDS). The station was located in a low-income neighborhood called "Little Five Point"; both black and white families lived there. The programming was created to appeal to both audiences. The music format included jazz, blues, and bluegrass shows. The news and public affairs programs emphasized local issues of concern to Little Five Point residents. The core of the news staff had worked for *The Great Speckled Bird*, Atlanta's most prominent "underground newspaper" in the late 1960s and early 1970s. They had valuable experience in covering local political campaigns and the activities of the city's police force, which they translated into insightful investigative reporting. But before it could establish an audience base in the Little Five Point region of the city, the station was undermined by internal divisions, which were then exacerbated by an undercover agent's acts of provocation. The station went off the air for a time in the mid-1970s. When it reemerged, it was almost totally oriented toward Atlanta's black community, but it was also in competition with the more powerful and better endowed WCLK-FM, owned by Clark College. In spite of this handicap, WRFG has survived as a predominantly black community radio station. It continues to be licensed to the Radio Free Georgia Foundation, which is governed by a local board of media and community activists.[114]

In rural Warren County, North Carolina, a black nonprofit community organization called Sound and Print United put WVSP-FM on the air in 1977 after four years of planning and fund-raising. The station began broadcasting from the small hamlet of Warrenton with six paid staff members and a format that emphasized jazz, blues, local news, and public affairs aimed at the county's large African American population, the most poverty-stricken group in the entire state. By 1982, with crucial aid from the federal government, the station had expanded its paid staff to sixteen; it had also developed a cadre of volunteer workers that numbered close to fifty and a sizeable rural black audience because of its cultural orientation and WVSP's active involvement in community issues, such as a campaign to prevent the dumping of toxic wastes in the county. But, at this critical juncture in the station's development, cutbacks in government funding by the new Reagan adminstration forced WVSP to reduce its paid staff to minimal levels. Moreover, the station was slow in cultivating a listener funding base both because of the low income levels of the African Americans living in Warren County and because of the novelty of a rural black station trying to operate noncommercially. As a result, in desperation WVSP moved its broadcast site to the more populous city of Rocky Mount in adjacent Nash County in 1984. The hope was that the station would attract new listeners and financial support from the middle-class black population in Rocky Mount while retaining its original listening audience in Warren County. Unfortunately, this strategy failed; the move to Rocky Mount proved to be disastrous, creating internal divisions and antagonisms. Two years later, after various changes in leadership and operating in the red for a number of months, WVSP went off the air. To date, there are no signs that the station will be revived.[115]

The demise of WVSP sheds light on the built-in structural constraints of the community radio model, especially when it takes root in depressed or poverty-stricken regions—rural or urban. Without some outside funding, it is improbable that such a station will be able to sustain itself financially. Yet, ironically, these are the black communities most removed from the U.S. corporate mainstream, and thus the ones most in need of the empowerment potential of community radio.

The most successful black community radio station established during this period was WPFW-FM, a 50,000-watt outlet launched in 1977 by the Pacifica Foundation in Washington, D.C., after a ten-year legal battle for the frequency allocation, which was contested by a Christian broadcasting group. The Pacifica Foundation was the founder of the community radio movement, having opened its first station, KPFA-FM in Berkeley, California, in 1949. From there it went on to establish stations in Los Angeles (KPFK-FM), New York (WBAI-FM), and Houston (KPFT-FM). While Pacifica always sought to involve African Americans and other minorities in its programming and operations, WPFW was the first station under its auspices that was controlled by African Americans. The local black community in Washington, D.C., has a rich historical presence there; it constituted 70 percent of the city's total number of inhabitants in the 1970s and even had its own name, "Chocolate City." The station was mandated to serve the black population in the nation's capital; hence it recruited much of its leadership and talent from that group.

WPFW signed on the air with Duke Ellington's classic "Take the A Train," performed live from a downtown jazz club. Its musical format of "jazz and jazz extensions" filled the void left when Howard University's WHUR abandoned its jazz format in pursuit of higher ratings. In addition to in-depth excursions into the jazz tradition and its promotion of Washington, D.C.'s local jazz scene, the station also programmed blues, salsa, Caribbean, Brazilian, and African music. Its news and public affairs programming stressed issues of concern to the black community locally, nationally, and internationally. There were weekly programs on the criminal justice system, the city government, the local labor movement, the Congressional Black Caucus, the Caribbean, Latin America, and Africa. Also, there were cultural shows by and for children, teenagers, women, and senior citizens, as well as a poetry program and special dramatic presentations. Moreover, WPFW devoted special days of programming to in-depth explorations of the music of jazz greats like Louis Armstrong, Billie Holiday, and Duke Ellington, or black leaders like Martin Luther King, Jr., and Malcolm X. The same in-depth approach was used to explore issues from local drug abuse to apartheid in South Africa.

In the 1980s, WPFW became the largest and most listened-to black community outlet in the country. It had a paid staff of seven, over one hundred volunteer workers, and an annual budget of three hundred thousand dollars, most of which was donated to the station by its over five thousand listener-subscribers. The station weathered five leadership changes, three changes of address, and a license challenge by a right-wing media watch group. More recently, as WPFW experimented some with a new "world-beat" music format, its hegemony over the local jazz audience was challanged by WDCU-FM, a new black public radio station licensed to the University of the District of Columbia, which signed on the air in 1983 with a jazz format. Over the next few years, WPFW's ratings and income from listener donations fell off, making it necessary for the station to increase its on-air fund-raising activities. In addition, a new management team reinstated WPFW's jazz format in an attempt to regain support from the area's jazz listeners, who generally have an affluent demographic profile. Hence, even in the public radio sector, market factors such as ratings and the demographic profile of listeners play an important role in determining the format of the station.[116]

Black college radio stations came of age in the 1970s because of increased government and university funding. Most often, the stations were part of the academic budget and therefore attached to the academic programs specializing in broadcast communications. They, in turn, determined the station's organizational structure and program format, hired the paid staff, and utilized the operation as a training laboratory for students preparing for careers in the radio industry. However, because they are, with two exceptions, non-commercial outlets, public-service, student, and even community involvement are also built into the operations. Consequently, black college stations model themselves after commercial, public, community, and student stations, or some combination of the four. Before the creation of CPB and NPR in 1967, there were only two black college stations on the air: WCSU-FM at Central State University in Ohio and KUCA-FM at the University of Central Arkansas. The upsurge began in earnest in 1969 when WSHA-FM at Shaw University in Raleigh, North Carolina, went on the air. It was joined in the 1970s by eighteen new black college stations, including WCLK-FM at Clark College in Atlanta, Georgia; KGRM-FM at Grambling College in Grambling, Louisiana; WHCJ-FM at Savannah State College in Savannah, Georgia; WHOU-FM at Hampton University in Hampton, Virginia; WEAA-FM at Morgan State University in Baltimore, Maryland; WAMF-FM at Florida A&M University in Tallahassee, Florida; and WBVA-FM in Harrodsburg, Kentucky, which is affiliated with Kentucky State University.[117]

WSHA-FM at Shaw University in Raleigh, North Carolina, began as a low-power, 10-watt operation with only one paid staff member. In the mid-1970s, its raised its power to twelve thousand watts and then to twenty-five thousand watts. The station is committed on paper to both university and community service, but because of budget restraints it is unable to operate an outreach training program for community volunteers. Most of the manpower needed to keep the station on the air comes from student volunteers, who program most of the music. The students also take advantage of WSHA's internship program, which gives them practical experience and college credits for working as broadcast journalists, production engineers, lower-echelon management, or public relations personnel. WSHA initially modeled itself after the more successful black commercial stations in the market. The station's news and public affairs programming was almost nonexistent. The music format targeted black youth between the ages of fifteen to twenty-five; it featured mostly popular rap and dance tracks. In addition, the student music programmers tended to emulate the "air personalities" of the market's most successful black disc jockeys. More recently, WHSA has revised its format to better emphasize its educational mission and community service. It has expanded its public affairs and news offerings considerably; adding everything from local talk shows to syndicated newscasts from the National Black Network. In addition, the music format now features much more jazz and much less rap and dance music. The change has increased WSHA's listening audience, especially since the only other black public radio outlet in the region, WVSP-FM, went off the air.[118]

From the outset, WCLK-FM at Clark College in Atlanta, made jazz and public service the cornerstones of its programming philosophy. Under the direction of the Department of Mass Communications and a paid staff of six, the station was mandated to develop a format that is "distinctly different from other stations in the market . . . to duplicate other stations' programming is to waste scarce radio spectrum and misuse public money provided to noncommercial stations." Toward this end, WCLK's musical programming is "based on a bedrock of commitment to America's premiere contribution to world culture. Jazz." The station pursues a "proactive role with respect to the nurturing, promotion and development of jazz as a vital and authentic American classical music. . . ." The music format is "broad enough to encompass and encourage the products of new jazz artists who are engaged in the innovative, exploratory realms of the music's development."[119]

WCLK's news and public affairs programming is oriented toward the station's black audience. There is a paid news director responsible for the daily newscast, and WCLK also broadcasts the National Black Network's national and international newscast. Likewise, the public affairs programming is coordinated by a paid staff member; its purpose is to "promote cultural, artistic, educational and economic linkages with the community at large." Student interns work in every facet of the station's operations, and are supervised by both faculty and staff. Black community volunteers also work at the station as programmers. Organizationally, WCLK is modeled on the public radio stations affiliated with NPR, but the station also differs from most NPR affiliates in its extensive use of volunteers and its focus on African American music, culture, and communication.[120]

A third model influencing the organization and formats of black college stations is the community radio model pioneered by the Pacifica stations and the NFCB. A good example of a black college station that has adopted this model is WBVA-FM in Harrodsburg, Kentucky. It is a small 10-watt operation with a strong commitment to the African American population living in Lexington and Fayette counties, where its signal can be heard. The station's news and public affairs programming is tailored to meet the social and informational needs of its black listeners. The music format is a blend of blues, jazz, and gospel. In addition, the station operates a training program for local black residents, putting them in charge of creating and maintaining their own programs. The paid staff members, faculty supervisors, and student interns also working at WBVA give it a healthy mixture of personnel and perspectives. Financial support from listener donations and the university has given the station a modicum of economic stability, enabling it to survive to date in a region that has its fair share of poverty and unemployment.[121]

The student-run black college radio stations are usually low-power, low-budget operations broadcasting in the smaller markets. KPVU-FM at Prairie View A&M University in Prairie View, Texas, is a prime example of this type of outlet. All of the staff positions from general manager down are held by students, who receive internship credits and/or modest work-study stipends for their work at the station. KPVU broadcasts twenty-four hours a day with 2,100 watts of power. Its format is music-heavy, targeting the fifteen to twenty-five-year-old youth market; current rhythm and blues, gospel, reggae, and rap shows are weekly features. In addition, there is a brief daily newscast produced by broadcast journalism students, and some public affairs offerings. Although the overall operation of the station is in the hands of the students, they do receive supervision and input from faculty members of Prairie View's communication department, which in effect oversees

KPVU.[122]   Another category of student-run stations are the cable radio outlets on black college campuses; at present, there are seven of these organizations, all of which are student-intensive operations. The students staff, program, and manage these stations, which are limited to broadcasting via cable to campus buildings and dorms, and therefore do not need an FCC license to operate. Cable radio has a long history on black college campuses, dating back to World War II; the first black college station was a cable radio outlet started at Hampton University in 1940. There was also a campus radio station at Lincoln College in Pennsylvania during that period; it was the station that gave Jack Gibson his start in radio announcing. The format favored by the current black college cable stations is student-centered since they invariably do all the airshifts; popular rap and dance "jams" dominate the playlists, while the news and information is tailored to the student community. Although student-centered, these stations can be valuable in terms of the training and experience students derive from working there, as well as the contacts they are able to make with the industry. Barry Mayo, the first student manager of WHBC, Howard University's cable radio outlet, moved on to become a general manager at RKO's WRKS in New York; he was so successful there that he was recently promoted to vice president in charge of RKO's radio chain.[123]

While there have been impressive gains made by African Americans in the public broadcasting arena over the past two decades, National Public Radio has played a mixed role at best in supporting these gains, particularly in relation to employment practices and black ownership of public radio outlets. The organization began in the late 1960s, professing lofty ideals that implicitly spoke to the special communication needs of minorities in the U.S.A. NPR's mission statement promised to "promote personal growth rather than corporate gain" and "not only call attention to a problem, but be an active agent in seeking solutions." However, during its spectacular growth from a modest college-based public radio network with ninety affiliates to a major national network with three hundred and seventy-seven outlets in all the major markets, a listening audience of 7.3 million, and a budget of thirty-three million dollars, NPR did not incorporate much of an emphasis on, much less a concrete program for African American broadcasters, into its master plan. Hence, even though there are over forty black public radio outlets in the country, only seven of them have qualified for the lucrative CPB Community Service Grants, which are used to buy and upgrade equipment and facilities. This is less than 2 percent of the qualified stations, which number over three hundred. To its credit, NPR has a better employment record: 10 percent of its work force are African Americans. This figure, however, was only recently achieved as the result of an ambitious affirmative action program. As Adam Clayton Powell III, the first black NPR vice president of its news operation, explained: "When I walked in here in July 1987, NPR had no—zero—minority hosts, correspondents, newscasters, directors, executive producers, or senior editors." It was only because of Powell's recruitment efforts that minorities were able finally to gain a foothold in the organization.[124]

In the 1980s, the growth of black-controlled public radio outlets slackened off somewhat because of federal government cutbacks and the fiscal crisis threatening to bankrupt a number of African American colleges. Where gains have been made, funding has usually come from local sources. Yet, despite this lack of funds, a diversified group of black public stations still managed to sign on the air in the 1980s. In Brooklyn, New York, Medger Evers Community College worked out a time-sharing arrangement on WNYE-FM with its license holder, the City University of New York (CUNY) Board of Trustees. CUNY continued to broadcast educational programs on WNYE in the day-time, while the evening hours were turned over to a coalition of faculty, students, and community media activists. They developed a program format inclusive of both the college and the surrounding black community, known as Bedford-Stuyvesant. College events like concerts and lectures are broadcast, as are musical and other cultural events held in the community. The news and public affairs programming focuses on issues and information of concern to Bedford-Stuyvesant residents, and encourages audience feedback through call-ins, letters, street interviews, and visits to the station. At present, WNYE's evening program format continues to address the special communication needs of African Americans living in the Bedford-Stuyvesant community.[125]

WPEB-FM is a low-power, 10-watt black neighborhood radio station started in West Philadelphia in 1982; it is staffed by volunteers and controlled by a local broad of directors. The station describes itself as follows: "WPEB is a neighborhood radio station providing a regular and open forum for members of this area to discuss, debate, and learn about the issues that directly affect them.

The station depends on the community it serves, its residents, and their resources, for program content and operational skills."[126] WAFR-FM in Durham, North Carolina, is a similar low-power, black community operation committed to an open-ended format that mixes local news and public affairs with African American' music and cultural programs. Both WPEB and WAFR have a limited audience base and subsist on a shoestring budget, yet their level of community support is still sufficient to keep them on the air. Although marginal as economic entities, they are important as community organizations because they empower their volunteers and listeners with a voice of their own.

The newer black college radio stations have continued to experiment with their unique blend of public, commercial, community, and student formats and organizational structures. WVAS-FM at Alabama State University in Montgomery, Alabama, gravitated toward the public radio model. It signed on the air in 1984 with four paid staff members and a 25,000-watt signal that reaches into eleven counties in central Alabama. The station features a jazz format and an active news and public affairs department, which is also used as a broadcast journalism lab by students majoring in the field. Faculty from the School of Journalism supervise the local news and public affairs programs produced by ASU students. The audience is made up mostly of middle-class, professional African Americans between twenty-five and fifty-four years old. WVSA is the most listened-to black public radio station in the Montgomery metropolitan market and ranked seventh overall when competing with commercial stations.[127]

In contrast, Saint Augustine College in Raleigh, North Carolina, which initiated WAUG-AM in 1984, not only purchased a commercial license, but also opted for a high-tech strategy in pursuit of profit maximization. The bulk of the station's format is provided by the Satellite Music and News Network, based in Dallas, Texas; it uses the latest in broadcast technology, feeding WAUG, by satellite dish, its prepackaged music and news programming. Although student interns are involved in the operation of the station, its primary goal is to make money for the college. This option may become more and more attractive to black colleges, especially if their financial situation remains desperate.[128]

The most recent college station to adopt a community radio model for an outlet located in a black community is WHCR-FM,

"Harlem Community Radio," a low-powered, 10-watt operation licensed to the City College of New York (CCNY). The station is operated by CCNY's Department of Radio, Video, and Film; it signed on in 1986 with a mandate to both train students and involve the local Harlem community in its programming and training. The first general manager was Vincent Thomas, a veteran media professional with ten years of experience in both black commercial and public radio. He designed a format for the people in Harlem who were left out of New York radio programming. It included a music flow that emphasized traditional jazz and salsa, educational and cultural programs for children, and a community forum and bulletin board for local political and cultural organizations. The last was part of an outreach project to recruit members of Harlem's community organizations to work as volunteers for the station in return for being trained in radio broadcasting. Those recruits would also serve as liaisons between their respective organizations and the station. Moreover, half of WHCR's programming was to be bilingual in order to reach the large Hispanic population living in Harlem.

Unfortunately, Thomas was never able to implement his plan for WHCR; he was fired in January 1987, then sued the college for breach of contract, only to reach an out-of-court settlement. Thomas's dismissal was engineered by Tony Batton, the station's faculty advisor from CCNY's Department of Radio, Video, and Film. The crux of the disagreement was that Thomas tried to set up WHCR as a community radio station, which ironically was favored by a majority of the department's faculty, whereas Batton preferred a "professionally operated broadcast facility." In February 1987, Batton prevailed; he was appointed the new general manager of the station and given free rein to develop it along more professional lines. However, Batton's style of management alienated CCNY students, faculty, and administrators; he, in effect, ran WHCR as a one-man show, while demanding an outlandish increase, 400 percent, in financial support for the station at a time when CCNY was going through a funding crisis necessitating across-the-board cutbacks at the college. The situation slowly deteriorated amid conflicting accusations and claims among the warring parties. Finally, in June 1989, Tony Batton's contract as WHCR's general manager was not renewed by the college adminstration. After three years of factional infighting, turmoil, and institutional indecisiveness, WHCR was given a new lease on life. Currently the plan is once again to develop the station along the lines of a community radio model; a new staff is being recruited and a new format is being developed, with input from Harlem residents.[129]

Conclusion: Crossover Dreams and Racial Realities

By the end of the 1980s, black radio in the United States had reached a new plateau. For the first time in its history there were both network and chain operations controlled by African American broadcasters. Furthermore, there now existed a bona fide national advocacy organization, the National Black Media Coalition, capable of coordinating on a national level the ongoing struggles against discrimination in radio employment and ownership. Consequently, the number of black-owned commercial broadcasting outlets has recently been increasing at its fastest rate ever. Moreover, it continued to be lucrative for advertisers to target the urban black consumer. Education and income levels for African Americans in the urban markets rose considerably in the 1970s, and the trend carried over into and lasted through the 1980s. In addition, research on black listeners during this period indicated that there were more of them as a group, and that they listened to more radio than their white counterparts. Ninety-seven percent of all African Americans listen to radio each week, and they listen to an average of thirty hours per week, 20 percent more than white listeners.[130] This should give African American broadcasters a competitive edge in the urban markets with large black populations. Indeed, it appears that black commercial radio might be able to terminate, or at least minimize, its historical dependency on white broadcasters.

However, there still exist a number of structural factors that are formidable obstacles to the goal of African American independence and self-sufficiency in radio broadcasting. For example, recent demographic patterns in the growing black middle-class population reveal a move to the suburbs, like that of the white middle class before them. The result is a significant fragmentation of the black urban audience, an event that has affected recent programming decisions. Fearing the loss of their most affluent listeners, even the leading black-controlled stations in the large urban markets have adopted crossover urban contemporary or urban adult formats. Some radio industry observers have heralded this as a breakthrough opening up the possibility of a new era of multiethnic commercial formats. But careful scrutiny of the airways reveals that, while the urban and adult contemporary formats have succeeded in allowing white artists greater access to black-controlled stations, African American artists have not gained corresponding exposure on white rock stations, except for crossover superstars like Michael Jackson and Prince. Urban contemporary and its spinoffs allow black broadcasters to anticipate the new demographic realities of the urban market, and in so doing to profit from these changes by converting them into higher ratings. However, this change also tends to undercut African American musicians and their music by narrowing their access to black radio outlets; moreover, those replaced by white crossover acts are invariably those with the least exposure in the first place. As has been the case so often in the past, the structure of the radio industry, its way of doing business, presents African Americans seeking an independent broadcast voice with a conflict of interest. The price of success all too often requires that the specific communication needs of the entire black community be forsaken.

On the other front, the upsurge in public radio in the 1970s and 1980s has opened up new terrain for African American broadcasters. They have responded by establishing over fifty college- and community-based public outlets. While some of the black college stations try to emulate successful commercial stations in their markets, most are engaged in promoting new African American musical talent, preserving African American musical traditions, and providing news and information for the local black populations within reach of their signals. In general, the black public stations, in league with the more progressive black commercial outlets, are on the cutting edge of the movement to establish and maintain a self-sufficient African American presence on the radio airways. The white-controlled radio industry has been forced to open its doors to black employment and even ownership, no matter how reluctantly. Further, the negative images and stereotypes that characterized the portrayal of African Americans in the earlier years of broadcasting have all but vanished from radio's airways. These are important advances in the overall African American struggle to achieve racial equality and cultural self-determination. While black stations still only make up less than 2 percent of the total number of radio outlets broadcasting in the U.S.A. today, they are a crucial 2 percent, strategically located in all of the major black population centers in the country. Although they broadcast to local audiences, collectively they can also be quite effective in mobilizing black people on a national level for political campaigns like Jessie Jackson's bids for the presidency, or the more successful effort to have Martin Luther King, Jr.'s birthday declared a national holiday, or the ongoing campaign in the U.S.A. to end apartheid in South Africa. Black radio has played a vital role in furthering causes of this nature and no doubt will continue to do so in the future.

1. See Robert Toll, *Blacking Up: The Minstrel Show in Nineteeth Century America* (New York: Oxford University Press, 1974); Sterling A. Brown, *The Negro in American Fiction* (New York: Atheneum, 1937); William L. VanDeburg, *Slavery and Race in American Popular Culture* (Madison: University of Wisconsin Press, 1984).

2. Chris Albertson, *Bessie* (New York: Stein and Day, 1972), 48–52; Paul Garon, "Remembering Lonnie Johnson," *Living Blues* 12 (Summer 1970): 7–10; Erik Barnouw, *A Tower in Babel: A History of Broadcasting in the United States* (New York: Oxford University Press, 1966), 1:131.

3. Freeman Gosden and Charles Correll, *All About Amos 'n' Andy* (New York: Rand McNally, 1929); Barnouw, *A Tower in Babel*, 224–31.

4. Al Rose, *Eubie Blake* (New York: Macmillan Publishing Company, 1979), 107.

5. Gosden and Correll, *All About Amos 'n' Andy*, 43.

6. Ibid., 44.

7. Freeman Gosden and Charles Correll, *Amos 'n' Andy: The Presidental Elections* (New York: RCA Victor, 27 September 1928).

8. J. Fred McDonald, *Don't Touch That Dial* (Chicago: Nelson Hall, 1979), 27, 113, 343; Arnold Shankman, "Black Pride and Protest: The Amos 'n' Andy Crusade," *Journal of Popular Culture* 12, no. 2 (Fall 1979): 238–47.

9. Shankman, "Black Pride and Protest," 240.

10. Ibid., 243–46.

11. Erik Barnouw, *The Golden Web: A History of Broadcasting in the United States* (New York: Oxford University Press, 1968), 2:110; Dorothy Morrison, "All-Colored Radio Review May Launch a New Cycle," *Washington, D.C. Afro-American* (25 April 1939), 15.

12. MacDonald, *Don't Touch That Dial*, 344–46.

13. Estelle Edmerson, "A Descriptive Study of the American Negro in U.S. Professional Radio, 1922–1953" (Master's thesis, UCLA, 1954), 34-37.

14. Ibid., 67, 89.

15. MacDonald, *Don't Touch That Dial*, 331.

16. Cab Calloway, *Of Minnie the Moocher and Me* (New York: Thomas Crowell Company, 1976), 180.

17. Joseph Boskin, *Sambo: The Rise and Fall of an American Jester* (New York: Oxford University Press, 1986), 179.

18. Edmerson, "The American Negro in U.S. Professional Radio," 76.

19. Norman Spaulding, "History of Black Oriented Radio in Chicago 1929–1963"

(Ph.D. diss. University of Illinois, Urbana: 1981), 23. *New York Herald Tribune,* 10 September 1930, 8.

20. Spaulding, "Black Oriented Radio in Chicago," 71-5; Arnold Passman, "The Jack L. Cooper Show" (unpublished paper, Berkeley, California, 1984), 4.

21. Lionel Hampton, interview by the author, 8 September 1983; *Chicago Defender,* 8 May 1939, 6.

22. *Chicago Defender,* 10 June 1935, 14.

23. *Baltimore Afro-American,* 2 April 1939, 4–5.

24. *Chicago Defender,* 16 February 1938, 15.

25. Ibid., 14 April 1939, 8.

26. MacDonald, *Don't Touch That Dial,* 349.

27. *New York Herald Tribune,* 12 November 1935, 12.

28. *Program on the Education of Negroes* (Washington, D.C.: U.S. Department of Interior, Office of Education, 19 October 1935).

29. *Chicago Defender,* 15 March 1937, 5.

30. *Ballad for Americans* (New York: RCA Victor, 1939). Reissued on Vanguard Records, 1945.

31. Barnouw, *The Golden Web,* 196.

32. Press Release, Washington, D.C.: Federal Security Agency, U.S. Office of Education, 17 December 1941.

33. Barnouw, *The Golden Web,* 197.

34. Edmerson, "The American Negro in U.S. Professional Radio," 87.

35. Barnouw, *The Golden Web,* 180.

36. MacDonald, *Don't Touch That Dial,* 348–49.

37. William Robson, "Open Letter On Race Hatred," *Radio Drama in Action,* ed. Erik Barnouw (New York: Farrar and Rinehart, 1945), 76–77.

38. William Robson, "Recollections," hosted by John Hickman, WMCA (New York), 13 August 1945.

39. MacDonald, *Don't Touch That Dial,* 347–48.

40. *Chicago Defender,* 15 September 1945, 9.

41. Barnouw, *The Golden Web,* 196–97.

42. *Chicago Defender,* 24 February 1948, 14.

43. MacDonald, *Don't Touch That Dial,* 357, 359–60.

44. *Chicago Defender* 13 May 1946, 13.

45. Barnouw, *The Golden Web,* 269–71, 280–81.

46. *The Daily Worker,* 29 June 1949, 9.

47. *Variety,* 13 July 1949, 33.

48. Roi Ottley, "The Story of Negro Music," *New World A-Coming,* WMCA (New York), 14 October 1946.

49. Roi Ottley, "The Vermont Experiment," *New World A-Coming,* WMCA (New York), 16 November 1946.

50. Roi Ottley, "Negroes in the Entertainment Industry," *New World A-Coming,* WMCA (New York), 25 February 1947.

51. Ibid.

52. Dorothy Parker, "Arrangement in Black and White," *New World A-Coming,* WMCA (New York), 8 May 1946.

53. Roi Ottley, "The Mammy Legend," *New World A-Coming,* WMCA (New York), 12 March 1947.

54. Ibid.

55. "Tribute to Canada Lee," *New World A-Coming,* WMCA (New York), 10 February, 1945.

56. J. Fred MacDonald, "Radio's Black Heritage: Destination Freedom, 1948–1950," *Phylon* 39, no. 1 (March 1978): 66–73.

57. Ibid., 70, 72.

58. Ibid., 69.

59. Richard Durham, "The Story of Denmark Vesey," *Destination Freedom*, WMAQ (Chicago), 18 July 1948.

60. Richard Durham, "Truth Goes to Washington," *Destination Freedom*, WMAQ (Chicago), 15 August 1948.

61. Richard Durham, "The Long Road," *Destination Freedom*, WMAQ (Chicago), 7 August 1949.

62. Hugh Cordier, "A History and Analysis of Destination Freedom" (Master's thesis, Northwestern University, 1949), 25.

63. Ibid., 27.

64. Ibid., 28–30.

65. Mark Newman, "Capturing the Fifteen Million Dollar Market: The Emergence of Black Oriented Radio" (Ph.D. diss. Northwestern University, 1984), 23–28.

66. *Amsterdam News* 28 November 1941, 11.

67. MacDonald, *Don't Touch That Dial*, 365–66.

68. Robert Palmer, *Deep Blues* (New York: Viking Press, 1981), 173–98.

69. *Sponsor*, October 1949, 3.

70. Newman, "Capturing the Fifteen Million Dollar Market," 81–89.

71. Margaret McKee and Fred Chisenhall, *Beale Street Black and Blue* (Baton Rouge: Louisiana State University Press, 1981), 93.

72. Newman, "Capturing the Fifteen Million Dollar Market," 103.

73. McKee and Chisenhall, *Beale Street Black and Blue*, 94.

74. Newman, "Capturing the Fifteen Million Dollar Market," 121–23.

75. A. C. Williams, "The Role of Nat D. Williams and WDIA in Blues Promotion," paper presented at Smithsonian Institution Program, Washington D.C.; 19 April 1983, 1–14.

76. Newman, "Capturing the Fifteen Million Dollar Market," 131.

77. Jack Gibson, interviewed by the author, 5 February 1986.

78. Newman, "Capturing the Fifteen Million Dollar Market," 98.

79. Mary Bell, wife of Haley Bell, interviewed by the author, 2 April 1988.

80. Arnold Passman, *The DeeJays* (New York: Macmillan Company, 1971), 47–48, 62–63, 67–68, 122–23, 150, 166, 175, 183, 186; McKee and Chisenhall, *Beale Street Black and Blue*, 35–36.

81. "Disc Jockeys: Sixteen Sepia Spielers Ride Kilocycle Range on Twenty One Stations," *Ebony*, November 1947, 44–8.

82. Passman, *The DeeJays*, 184–86; Nelson George, *The Death of Rhythm and Blues* (New York: Pantheon, 1988), 43, 112–13.

83. Jack Gibson interview.

84. Passman, *The DeeJays*, 225.

85. David Toop, *The Rap Attack: Jive to New York Hip Hop* (Boston: South End Press, 1984), 38.

86. Vernon Winslow, interviewed by the author, 25 March 1988.

87. Ibid.

88. Ibid.

89. Passman, *The DeeJays*, 166, 175. George, *The Death of Rhythm and Blues*, 54–55.

90. Passman, 202.

91. Ibid., 200–4, 221–24, 237–40. Peter Fornatale and Joshua Mills, *Radio in the Televison Age* (Woodstock, N. Y.: Overlook Press, 1980), 38–40, 45–46, 49–51.

92. "The Negro Market: A Special Report," *Broadcast*, 7 November 1966, 76–82.

93. Richard S. Kahlenberg, "Negro Radio," *The Negro History Bulletin* (Fall 1965), 127.

94. George, *The Death of Rhythm and Blues*, 90–91, 129. Spaulding, "Black Oriented Radio in Chicago," 84–85, 97; Passman, *The DeeJays*, 259, 272–74.

95. Fred Ferretti, "The White Captivity of Black Radio," *Columbia Journalism Review* (Summer 1970), 35–39.

96. Ibid., 37.

97. Ibid., 39.

98. "Station WNJR Brings out the Realities of Community Control," *The African World* (28 October 1972), 10.

99. Dr. Martin Luther King, Jr., "Transforming a Neighborhood into a Brotherhood," *Jack The Rapper* 13, no. 666 (11 January 1989): 1.

100. George, *The Death of Rhythm and Blues*, 127–28. Steve Perry, "Ain't No Mountain High Enough: The Politics of Crossover," Simon Frith, ed., *Facing the Music* (New York: Pantheon, 1988), 53, 61.

101. "Away from the Blues," *Newsweek*, 18 January 1954, 51; MacDonald, *Don't Touch That Dial*, 367.

102. Lon G. Wells, "NBN and SBN: Network Radio in the Black," *Dollars and Sense* 7, no. 4 (October/November 1984): 35–39.

103. Ibid., 38–39.

104. "Black Owned Radio," *Media Line* 3, no. 2 (February 1983): 20–21.

105. "Percy Sutton: Power Politics New York Style," *Ebony*, November 1972, 172.

106. Mark Schulman, "Neighborhood Radio as Community Communication" (Ph.D. diss., Union for Experimental Colleges and Universities, New York, 1985), 342–43; Fornatale and Mills, *Radio in the Television Age*, 70.

107. Fornatale and Mills, *Radio in the Television Age*, 127–31.; Ken Barnes, "Top Forty Radio: A Fragment of the Imagination," in Frith, ed., *Facing the Music*, 19.

108. Phil Watson interview by the author, 30 April 1985; Robert Taylor, former WHUR general manager, interviewed by author, 9 September 1986. George, *The Death of Rhythm and Blues*, 131–33.

109. John Downing, "Ethnic Minority Radio in the USA," *Howard Journal of Communications* 2, no. 3 (June 1990).

110. George, *The Death of Rhythm and Blues*, 183–86, 200.

111. Lo Jelks, executive director, Black College Radio Association, interviewed by the author, 2 April 1987.

112. Lynn Chadwick, executive director, National Federation of Community Broadcasters, interviewed by the author, 29 October 1989.

113. Schulman, "Neighborhood Radio as Community Communication," 318.

114. Paula Mantabane, former staff member of WRFG-FM, interviewed by the author, 18 July 1986.

115. Valerie Lee, former general manager of WVSP, interviewed by the author, 3 August 1986.

116. Data and information on WPFW was gathered while the author worked as a volunteer there from 1977 to 1990.

117. Lo Jelks interview.

118. Bishetta Meritt, former faculty advisor of WSHA-FM, interviewed by the author, 5 May 1986. The author has also monitored WSHA on trips to Raleigh, North Carolina.

119. Howard Myrick, "Programming Philosophy for WCLK," "Goals for WCLK," *The WCLK Program Guide* (May 1983), 1.

120. Howard Myrick interviewed by the author, 15 July 1986. "The Jazz of the City," *The WCLK Program Guide* (April 1986), 2.

121. Schulman, "Neighborhood Radio as Community Communication," 319.

122. "Spotlight on KPVU-FM," *Black College Radio News* 9 (January 1988): 3.

123. Lo Jelks interview.

124. Marc Fisher, "The Soul of a News Machine," *The Washington Post Magazine*, 23 October 1989, 18–19, 221. CPB, *To Know Ourselves: A Report to the 101st Congress on Public Broadcasting and the Needs of Minorities and Other Groups Pursuant to PL 100–626* (Washington, D.C.: CPB, 1989), 40–49.

125. Schulman, "Neighborhood Radio as Community Communication," 366.

126. Ibid., 321.

127. "The Voice of Alabama State University Signs On," *ASU Today* 1, no. 9 (15 July 1984): 1–2. "There's Something Going on in the Levi Watkins Learning Center," *ASU Today* 2, no. 6 (15 March 1985): 3.

128. "Saint Augustine College's WAUG-AM Begins Operation," *Black College Radio News* 9, no.1 (January 1989): 1.

129. Vince Thomas, interviewed by the author, 21 July 1986. Mark Schulman, chairman of CCNY's Department of Radio, Video, and Film, interviewed by the author, 29 October 1989.

130. John Downing, "Ethnic Minority Radio in the USA," *Howard Journal of Communications* 2, no. 3 (Spring 1990): 138.

Part **Four**

**FLY IN THE BUTTERMILK:
THE TELEVISION INDUSTRY**

5 COMMERCIAL TELEVISION

JANNETTE L. DATES

American commercial television is a clear reflection of the split in the African American image in popular culture, and of empowered groups' rigid control of most images presented on the television screen. As a nonempowered group, African Americans continued the checkered pattern, noted in earlier chapters, of resistance and accommodation to the system. This chapter will describe the dominant images and their effects, as well as the images that African Americans attempted to negotiate past the industry's gatekeepers. We shall see how these gatekeepers, in one way or another, invariably disallowed continuous presentation of images they did not develop, particularly if the images were foreign to their experience.

As noted earlier, many people fail to realize that the African American experience in society differs from the average American's experience because prejudice and discrimination have profoundly affected almost all Americans of African ancestry. Therefore it is reasonable to expect that televised persons from this group will reflect aspects of that unique experience, including the needs, interests, concerns, or perspectives written by, for, or about the group. In fact, however, the mainstream values and beliefs of African Americans seen on primetime commercial television have not revealed unique African American experience but rather the perceptions of white producers, sponsors, writers, and owners.

What was the collective ideological thinking of white decision makers who developed the images of African American people as they appeared on American commercial television between 1949 and 1989? To discover this we can, as scholars Hall, and Jefferson suggest (see Introduction), decipher the patterns implied by the behavior of such decision makers through the years, or we can deconstruct the language and behavior of the actors in the mythologies to discern the patterns of ideological thinking that were inscribed in the images. To do both, let us look at five selected categories of selected primetime, commercial television programs: drama, comedy, variety shows, miniseries, and soap operas, as well as look at supplier/production companies.

Drama

For the forty years that commercial television has been used to depict America's symbolic images, the overwhelming major depiction of African Americans in primetime, network, weekly programming has been nondramatic. Since the black presence in society was not ignored in other television formats, it is probable that television's white decision makers believed that the general populace would not watch programming featuring serious black people or thought that audiences would not want to watch serious issues concerning them. Occasionally, however, some serious programs were aired for short periods of time; but as they had little support and marketing, they usually died quietly.

To be sure, early television in general ignored serious social issues, featuring happy people with happy problems. In this context, shows with black characters or themes about black people's concerns might not be considered appropriate. As perceived at the time, even African American characters in general-interest, dramatic programs would raise unhappy, divisive social issues in the minds of viewers. Industry advertisers courted viewers and tried to keep them happily tuned in to the sponsored programs so they would purchase the products advertised during commercial breaks. Only on rare occasions in television's early years, therefore, were African Americans seen in dramatic programs during primetime (for example, Sidney Poitier in an anthology series such as "Philco Television Playhouse").[1]

From the early years through the middle years to the most current television offerings of serious dramatic programming, African American talents have most often been showcased on occasional specials and miniseries, and as adjunct themes to a mainstream storyline within a series ("Baretta," "Mod Squad"), and daytime serials ("All My Children," and "One Life to Live").

Thus, in forty years only thirteen weekly dramatic programs that featured African Americans, carried a black focus to viewers, and had significant impact or received critical acclaim were shown on television. Over the years, six of the thirteen dramas aired for less than a year, while six of them were on for just a year. The final series, scheduled for a second season in the fall of 1989, was "In the Heat of the Night." (See the complete listing in table 5.1). Included among the group of thirteen were "East Side, West Side" of the early 1960s, "The Outcasts" of the late 1960s, "The Young Lawyers" of the early 1970s, "Harris & Company" of the mid-1970s, "Palmerstown, U.S.A." of the early 1980s, and "In the Heat of the Night" of the late 1980s.

A hard-hitting drama, "East Side, West Side" presented problems to be resolved by its white hero, Neil Brock (George C. Scott), sometimes within the framework of an enabling social agency. Brock's secretary, Jane Foster (Cicely Tyson), who is African American, offered drama of her own, with her sharp-edged professional demeanor and "Afro" hairstyle. Though Foster was depicted as strong and resourceful and many of the stories involved social problems found in black inner cities, the restoration of order and resolution of problems was the exclusive preserve of the white hero in the series. The show's creators thus continued the tradition (noted in the Introduction) of framing thoughts about the world that said strong, white males solve the problems generated by social disorder and human bungling, whether the victims are black or white.

"The Outcasts," a nonstandard Western, teamed a Virginia aristocrat (turned gunman and drifter, then bounty hunter) with a freed slave (turned bounty hunter). Set in the period following the Civil War, the series portrayed the uneasy relationship between these partners as they tracked down wanted criminals. They had frequent arguments and fights. Their consistent animosity and emotional conflicts reflected 1970s social issues and concerns, and focused on problems and moral issues such as racial injustice. In this case, television's white decision makers went against the trend of not addressing serious, social issues involving blacks, gambling on the hope that the rhetoric of civil rights leaders such as Martin Luther King, Jr. and Whitney Young, Jr., had established a more receptive

Table 5.1   African American-Focused Primetime Commercial Programs

Program	Network	Year
Drama		
"East Side, West Side"	CBS	1963–64
"The Outcasts"	ABC	1968–69
"The Young Lawyers"	ABC	1970–71
"Tenafly"	NBC	1973–74
"Get Christie Love"	ABC	1974–75
"Paris"	CBS	1979
"The Lazarus Syndrome"	ABC	1979
"Harris & Co."	CBS	1979
"Palmerstown, U.S.A."	CBS	Spring 1980 and spring 1981
"Gideon Oliver"	ABC	1988
"A Man Called Hawk"	ABC	1988–89
"Sonny Spoon"	NBC	1988–89
"In the Heat of the Night"	NBC	1988 to present
Comedy		
"Beulah"	ABC	1950–53
"Amos 'n' Andy"	CBS	1951–53
"Julia"	NBC	1968–71
"The Bill Cosby Show"	NBC	1969–71
"Barefoot in the Park"	ABC	1970–71
"The Flip Wilson Show"	NBC	1970–74
"Room 222"	ABC	1969–74
"Sanford and Son"	NBC	1972–77
"Good Times"	CBS	1974–78
"That's My Mama"	ABC	1974–75
"The Jeffersons"	CBS	1975–85
"What's Happenin?"	ABC	1976–78
"White Shadow"	CBS	1979–81
"Benson"	ABC	1979–85
"Diff'rent Strokes"	NBC	1979–85
"Gimme A Break"	NBC	1981–86
"Webster"	NBC	1983–86
"The Cosby Show"	NBC	1984 to present
"227"	NBC	1985 to present
"Charlie & Co."	CBS	1985
"Amen"	NBC	1986 to present
"Frank's Place"	CBS	1987
"A Different World"	NBC	1987 to present

Table 5.1   (cont.)

Program	Network	Year
Miniseries		
"Autobiography of Miss Jane Pittman"	CBS	1974
"Roots"	ABC	1977
"King"	NBC	1978
"A Woman Called Moses"	NBC	1978
"Roots: The Next Generation"	ABC	1979
"I Know Why the Caged Bird Sings"	CBS	1979
"Backstairs at the White House"	NBC	1979
"Beulah Land"	NBC	1980
"The Marva Collins Story"	CBS	1981
"Benny's Place"	Syndicated	1982
"Sister, Sister"	NBC	1982
"Sadat"	(Syndicated "Operation Primetime")	1983
"The Jesse Owens Story"	Syndicated	1984
"Roots Christmas"	Syndicated ABC	1988
"The Women of Brewster Place"	"Harpo Productions, Inc." and "Lichen, Inc"	1989
Variety Shows		
"The Billy Daniels Show"	CBS	1952
"The Nat King Cole Show"	NBC	1956-57
"The Leslie Uggams Show"	CBS	1969
"The Flip Wilson Show"	NBC	1970–74
"The New Bill Cosby Show"	CBS	1972
"Cos"	ABC	1976

climate for such programming. They were wrong. Either the image of an independent, angry, young, black male was not readily acceptable to many viewers, or the white decision makers lost faith in the endeavor and withdrew their support. "The Outcasts" limped through one season.

"The Young Lawyers," a drama set in Boston, focused on cases and courtroom defenses of David Barrett (Lee J. Cobb), a senior lawyer in a neighborhood law office that served as a legal aid service. One of his two protégés, who were university law students, was played by Judy Pace, an accomplished black actress. The cases were reality-based and used the urban neighborhood as a background for the addressed problems and issues. The black characters seen in the series were eager participants in the system as it is. They rarely questioned the social order, helping others—including the weekly viewer—to adjust to society by upholding the law, thus following society's rules and codes.

According to Stanley G. Robertson, the African American executive producer of the short-lived series "Harris & Co.," this series was a special endeavor for him and all the persons involved in its production. Robertson, the first black movie executive and the first black network television executive, poured immense energy and time into maneuvering "Harris & Co." past the complex series of hurdles familiar to all who have attempted to put a series on network television. When the series was canceled after just four episodes, Robertson was devastated. He believed it should have been allowed time to build an audience and that eventually American viewers would have found and loved it. "Harris & Co." realistically approached problems facing a poor black family as seen through the eyes of Mike Harris (Bernie Casey), a widowed Los Angeles auto mechanic raising five children. The black actor/director Ivan Dixon directed some episodes with the same burning intensity he exhibited in his acting roles. Although the series had a short life, it seemed to have had a powerful impact on African American viewers, many of whom recalled, years later, that the compelling first episode had left them in tears. The show's creators wanted to project new images of African Americans in order to introduce a different perspective, a framework for thinking about black people that was based on their own African American inspired vision of black reality. As we know, such a perspective was missing from network television's myths and rituals. These creative people were disappointed at not being able to carry out their mission.[2] "Harris & Co." is a clear example of a failed attempt to establish on commercial television African American inspired and created images of black people in resistance to the dominant culture's regular pattern. Though the creators were unsuccessful in keeping the series on the air, its short-lived presence on the network again demonstrates the split in perceptions surrounding the image of the African American.

Alex Haley, an African American writer, and Norman Lear, a highly successful white producer of many network television series, after the phenomenal success of Haley's miniseries "Roots I" and "Roots II" (to be discussed later in this chapter), aired in the late

1970s, worked together to produce what was referred to as "Roots"—
the continuing series. (Lear's participation in the establishment of
comic televised black images will also be discussed later in this
chapter.) "Palmerstown, U.S.A." was a dramatic series set in the
Tennessee of 1935. Using numerous black artists, such as directors
Ivan Dixon, Georg Stanford Brown, and Gilbert Moses, the series
presented a view of life in a small town where white and black
townspeople coexisted in order to survive. Seen through the eyes
of two boys, one black and one white, who struggled to remain
friends despite the disapproval of others, the series aired in the
spring of 1980 and in the spring of 1981. The perceptions of the
two boys created an opportunity to fuse the split image so often
discussed in this book. Both the white and the black perspective
on a given issue was developed and resolved, even if only on
television. Just seventeen episodes long in the two seasons, in
which eight and nine programs, respectively, were aired a year apart,
"Palmerstown, U.S.A." did not have time to build an audience, nor
did NBC use marketing and positioning strategies to assist in that
process. After its cancellation, many believed that no dramatic
series about the African American experience could survive as a
network television series, particularly if the considerable clout of
Norman Lear and Alex Haley could not pull it off.

Not until seven years later were African Americans seen in
dramatic series on primetime network commercial television. During the 1988–89 season, four African American-focused dramatic
programs premiered. Only one was scheduled for a second season.
"In the Heat of the Night" had been a successful film of 1967,
starring Sidney Poitier as Virgil Tibbs, a Philadelphia homicide
detective, and Rod Steiger as Chief of Police William Gillespie. Set
in the town of Sparta, Mississippi, the movie allowed Gillespie and
returning city-son Tibbs slowly to work out their differences about
racial issues and moral rights and wrongs. In the television series,
with Howard Rollins as a thoughtful, consistent, but less commanding Tibbs, and Carroll O'Connor as a softened Gillespie, the
protagonists resolved their differences within the allotted sixty
minutes each week, with varying degrees of credibility. During
the first season, O'Connor had a heart attack and Rollins had to
carry much of the weight of each episode. The series maintained
steady, high ratings and was usually found among the top twenty
programs each week. With O'Connor returned to good health in

the 1989–90 season, the series seemed destined to have a good run. Rollins's strength in pulling in viewers while the recuperating O'Connor held a lesser role was an important but unheralded milestone in network television. For the first time in its forty-year history, African Americans and their issues were being addressed in a serious framework with a strong, black male characterization, and viewers were watching in large numbers. It was a moment to be savored.[3]

Researcher Bishetta Merritt notes in her discussion of the African American male on primetime television that during the 1988-89 season two other series featured members of the group. In addition to "In the Heat of the Night," there was "Gideon Oliver," with Lou Gossett and "A Man Called Hawk," with Avery Brooks. Merritt believes these three law enforcement officers fit the mold, described by social scientist Cedric X. Clark, as the black male peace keeper for society who helped condition black minds into being regulated toward approved behavior patterns. Merritt notes the striking differences between the Tibbs in the 1967 film and the Tibbs of television. The original Tibbs was intelligent, shrewd, slow to anger or to jump to conclusions, and knowledgeable about black folkways. He was an excellent cop who faced racism and unwarranted suspicions, yet he managed to uncover a murderer's identity and win the admiration and friendship of a bigoted, white southern sheriff. In the television series it was the Chief, not Tibbs who was shrewd, intelligent, slow to anger or to jump to conclusions, and who was considered to be the good and fair cop. His bigotry and shortsightedness had disappeared. Tibbs even needed instructions from Chief Gillespie on how to function with his own people in his home town, since Gillespie appeared to have established a greater rapport with them. Merritt contends that "A Man Called Hawk" was the series with the more well-rounded character: he had roots in the city, a strong sense of his African American heritage, many friends and some enemies. Black people in Hawk's world owned businesses, some were professionals, and some were hoodlums. According to Merritt, however, the physically attractive Hawk, like most other African American males on dramatic television through the years, was neutered by conventions. Though women surrounded him, Hawk had no romantic life; thus his sexuality was denied. In essence, American televised drama has not yet showcased an African American hero who is strong and multidimensional.[4]

Comedies

Televised comedies helped Americans adjust to the social order as transmitted myths and ideologies reinforced society's implicit rules and codes of behavior. In their portrayal of African American images, these comedies picked up threads of the established pattern of white superiority and black servitude, and continued to weave them back into the popular culture. As we have seen in earlier chapters, the pattern had been established by the minstrel shows and continued by the film, radio, and recording industries. These industries, on the one hand, used African American talents (music, cultural nuances, and jargon), while, on the other hand, they consistently denied those of African heritage opportunities to act as fully respected participants and to reflect their culture in their own way.

Researchers such as Matabane, Sklar, Clark, Moore, MacDonald and Signorelli have developed theories that shed light on the reasons television's decision makers allowed very few dramatic programs yet a proliferation of comic ones for framing African American life. These researchers see this phenomenon as indisputably linked with previous eras of racial stereotyping in American popular culture. Moreover, like Althusser and Hall, they suggest that such restriction of racial roles and dimensions was used as a means to reinforce social dominance and control with respect to preferred social relations between the races. Moreover, they believe that characters in restricted roles had fewer life opportunities, fewer resources, less power, lower status, and a greater likelihood of victimization. In addition, these researchers believe that such predominant reliance on the comedy format for representing African American life patterns also restricted the themes and types of values open to exploration within plot structures. Further, comedic settings coerced viewers into believing that they should not become emotionally involved in the plot on a serious level because it was, after all, just a comedy, supposedly a light-hearted look at life.[5]

Television's comic African American characters, unlike their counterparts in some film comedies, failed to illuminate the black experience or speak to African American concerns. Rather, the video medium, with few exceptions, created characters who were black in physical appearance but were most often stereotypical. The characters, stereotypical and otherwise, had views, values, and beliefs that were largely mainstream American. For example, in early television, African Americans who appeared on "The Beulah Show" (1950–53) included seasoned professionals from the film, theater, and radio industries. The Beulah character had originated as a supporting role on radio's "The Fibber McGee and Molly Show" and featured a white male speaking in black dialect. (See chapter 4 for more details.) The setting was a "good," white Anglo-Saxon Protestant neighborhood in a middle-class American suburb where the husband-father went to work, and the wife-mother took care of the child at home with the help of her conscientious maid, Beulah. This setting idealized the image of middle-class American life. The solid, comfortable living-room furniture, the knick-knacks carefully placed on tables, the Grant Wood-type picture hanging over the mantel, the clean, well-groomed youngster, were all symbols of the upwardly mobile, white middle class of the early 1950s. The series usually opened by establishing a problem situation, continued with misunderstandings and confusion that resulted in inappropriate actions on the part of a main character, and ended with the resolution of the initial problem. Beulah was central to the plot in that she guided the family to a safe conclusion, as she alone restored balance and normalcy to the household.

This setting and plot structure coincided with life in the real world of that era. It was the time of the silent generation, when President Dwight D. Eisenhower and Vice President Richard Nixon were the chief executives, when blue-collar workers had gradually moved to the suburbs and adopted the ways of the middle class, and when most white Americans believed that life would continue to get better and better for each generation. At this point, African Americans, feeling a liberal momentum that the war against the Nazis had generated, started demanding better conditions for themselves. In keeping with the new, more militant tone heard across the land, the black middle class, in particular, felt compelled to voice firm opposition to Beulah's lower-class origins and her focus on white people's problems. Moreover, they believed that the series reinforced numerous stereotypes for the large number of viewers, who chuckled knowingly, for example, at Beulah's attempts to persuade the consistently lazy, noncommital Bill to marry her. While some viewers could justifiably note that the "slippery suitor" is typical of most groups of people, in this setting Beulah was the black female servant with little social life of her own. Unable to obtain a commitment from the "significant other" in her life, she seemed destined to nurture and clean up after others. Despite this bleak future, Beulah was content, even happy, about her life and willing to go to great lengths to help others with their problems.

As identified in the 1930s by the great black poet and critic, Sterling Brown, two categories of black stereotyping are: the comic Negro and the contented slave/servant. Beulah, both comic and a contented servant opened the television program, talking directly to the camera about the problem or situation that she and her white family, the Hendersons, were facing that given week. She concluded the opening with a facetious remark such as "Beulah, who spends most of her time in the kitchen but never seems to know what's cookin'." Throughout the thirty minutes of each episode, Beulah conscientiously worked to remedy the family's current problem. She usually enlisted the help of Bill, who was also the handy man for the Hendersons, and her close friend (another maid), Oriole. The Aunt Jemima image discussed in the chapter on the film industry is strongly evident in television as well. Unlike the mammy, who was domineering, strong-willed, and bossy, Aunt Jemima was kind, generous, caring, and sincere. These qualities were typical of the performances of the maids on this show.

The maids among these characters were not scripted to question the system that placed them in the servant's role, and they consciously relegated their own lives to secondary status. Viewers could not conceive of Beulah wanting to be anything but what she was or of her fighting for her children to have a life more self-fulfilling than her own. The characters consistently reflected the values and beliefs of mainstream America. For example, in a 1951 show, Beulah orchestrated a ceremony for the Hendersons to renew their wedding vows because she believed they were drifting apart. This was scarcely a concern about others' lives that typically generated energy in real-life African Americans, who were more often totally involved in their own families' basic survival, especially because prejudice and discrimination had often forced these families to the bottom of the nation's socioeconomic scale.[6]

From viewing black male television characters as developed by white writers and producers, and using theories suggested by Althusser and Hall, we can decipher the ideological basis for character development. A conclusion can be drawn that white producers of black-oriented comedies carefully crafted the style of leading male characters, hoping to increase their palatability to the dominant culture. For example, in the 1950s series "Amos 'n' Andy," Kingfish had no power: usually he was unemployed, and often he just skirted the edges of the law in some nefarious moneymaking scheme. The humorous plots and appealing characters saved the series from unabashed minstrelsy, but Kingfish's weak power position made him merely an acceptable caricature, and thus acceptable to dominant-culture viewers.

"The Amos 'n' Andy Show" was comparable to Jackie Gleason's "The Honeymooners" (1955–71) in story line and theme. Except for Sapphire and Amos, the performers usually spoke in rural black dialect and showed a lack of control over events affecting their lives. They often demonstrated a general lack of knowledge and education, wore unusual clothing such as derbies and flashy suits, and behaved "with exaggerated, hat in hand diffidence and cunning obsequiousness."[7] When a more educated person appeared in the series (Sapphire's sister, Hortense, in a 1951 program), though she had "book learning," the character lacked common sense. She was odd, sexless, and unable to attract males. Moreover, Kingfish was not in charge in his home as Ralph Kramden was in "The Honeymooners." For example, in the episode "Sapphire's Sister," Kingfish did not want Hortense to come live with them and flatly refused to sleep on the couch so that she could share his wife's bed. He was overruled by his wife on each count. Subsequently, he lost all control of his home. He did not get to use the bathroom for hours in this episode because the women all pushed him aside. Throughout the series, Sapphire attempted to "refine" Kingfish and his "no-good friends" by making them more like good folks—the good folks of middle-class white America. This was the standard that "good folks" used and against which they measured themselves and others.

The rural black dialect, malapropisms, mispronunciations, and misinterpretations found in the "Amos 'n' Andy" radio series (noted in chapter 4) are also evident in the television series. For example, in the following excerpt, Kingfish tries to get Andy and his sister-in-law, Hortense, together:

KF: Well Andy lak I tol ya Hortense is a school teacher and she been teachin kids in the 4th grade. Now in order to make an imprint on Hortense I got ta bring ya'up to da intelligince level that she bin accustomed to.

A: Yeah, Dat's da thing ta do all right, but (uh) how we gonna do it?

KF: Well, uh, Hortense is always spoutin' poetry and so I brought a poetry book here. Now Andy, I want ya to mesmerize some of it and when you talk to er I want ya to thow in some a' them, uh, little bits of wisdom. You know, like bon matza and all that stuff.

A: Right.

KF: Well Andy, you better start off on this heah. A-read dat.

A: *The Legend of Hiawatha* by Henry Wadsworth Longfellow. Uh. Took three fellows to write this, huh?

KF: Andy, dat's a long poem. Read that first credenza right dere.

A: Oh, yeah. On the shores of itchy gooma.

In this episode it is obvious that Andy cannot read well. Moreover, Hortense, a professional educator, fails to notice that Andy does not know the poem when she talks with him, although it is supposed to be her favorite. This excerpt demonstrates the dialogue that white writers used to draw laughs at the expense of the black "predicament"—implicitly, that black people want to be white or, at the least, to act as they believe white people act. However, blacks are depicted as obviously ill-equipped to achieve that end. The series was seen by middle-class black professionals as a slap in the face. They were furious about being cast in this role. The driving force behind their fury lay in the knowledge that "Amos 'n' Andy" was the only series on network television that focused on African American culture and that it followed the pattern set in minstrelsy, which they feared seemed destined to continue ad infinitum. The NAACP helped to force the series off the air in 1953. Not until fifteen years later was another comedy featuring black leading characters added to a network lineup.

Except for African American performers seen on variety shows (discussed later in this chapter), who managed on some occasions to infuse some performances with their own interpretations, the African American cultural experience was seldom the focus of network entertainment until the civil rights era of the 1960s heated up. By 1968, the networks felt pressure from within, and from many outside forces, to increase African American participation in the industry. Their new policy was based on and went beyond the

1964 Civil Rights Act. The civil rights movement, coupled with these other pressures, helped push the networks toward producing and airing series that featured African Americans. Thus, the situation comedy "Julia" premiered in 1968. "Julia" was seen by many as an accommodationist program, where the skin color of the lead characters was the only difference between this program and others on the air. It was seen by many critics as too middle-class in orientation, and as a fantasy similar to the Doris Day-type movies that were then very popular. In "Julia," Diahann Carroll played a widowed nurse with a gruff, but liberal boss. Carroll wore designer clothes and had few problems that were typical of African American women living in that period. In a carryover from early television and in keeping with the trend of shows such as "Ozzie and Harriet," Julia's world focused on "happy problems," such as explaining where babies came from to her insistent seven-year-old son. The program lasted for three seasons.

In the 1970s, issue-oriented entertainment was severely snubbed by the vast majority of Americans. The death of relevancy helped to ensure the stifling of television programs or stories treating serious issues affecting African Americans. Ironically, this occurred at a time when blacks, somewhat more than other Americans, placed faith in television as the most credible source of information and as the medium that most effectively reflected African American concerns and issues. As American television moved away from relevant issues, African American participation in television series shifted. The few dramatic roles for black actors that had begun to open up almost totally disappeared, while comedies, purporting to be newly satirical, flourished. Actually, the comedies revived the minstrel stereotypes that had all but disappeared during the 1960s.[8]

Flip Wilson dominated network comedy during the 1970s. Though Wilson's comedy/variety show had high ratings and was generally viewed as hilarious, his negative images of black culture (for example, charlatan preacher, female impersonator) caused many African Americans to shudder. Wilson was criticized for his portrayal of "Geraldine Jones," a wise-cracking, hip-swinging woman of the world. For creating this character, Wilson was accused of encouraging effeminacy in young black males who, some believed, would use him as a role model.

Les Brown, the television critic, wrote that Flip Wilson was appreciated by all for the originality and distinctiveness of his material, which had "no credible coordinates in white society," and because he did not sentimentalize black culture but mocked it. In the final analysis, however, Brown believed Wilson "substantiated a racist view of blacks,"[9] which was a part of his appeal for whites. On the other hand, Wilson was just as popular with African American viewers. His crossover appeal had an antecedent in the early days of minstrelsy. The African American minstrel Billy Kersands had used characters for his routines from African American folklore. (See Introduction for more details.) He often had animal tricksters ingeniously gain the upper hand over powerful "others," while Wilson had his characters "outsmart" others through verbal exchanges. Both Kersands and Wilson struck a responsive chord among African Americans, who understood each performer's meaning and intent in a different way from those who were uninitiated. Black audiences understood, for example, that Kersands often "poked fun" at whites, just as Wilson did years later.

Nevertheless, Flip Wilson's comedy/variety show was different from earlier variety shows in which African Americans had played key roles (for example, "The Billy Daniels Show" in 1952, and "The Nat Cole Show" in 1956, which will be discussed later in this chapter), in that Wilson had more control over his image and a larger budget than the earlier performers had had. Like Daniels and Cole, Wilson's show came directly from characters he had developed in his nightclub acts as a stand-up comedian. Moreover, Wilson's Clerow Production Company controlled aspects of the production of the series. At this period in history, American viewers responded to Wilson's vision of the African American experience. It was soon after the height of the civil rights marches and the numerous calls for affirmative action. Because of the tone set by the White House during the administrations of Presidents Kennedy and Johnson, the media decision makers probably thought the average American believed he was liberal, and that he should be. It appears that "The Flip Wilson Show" was scripted to appeal to this liberal slant among average viewers.

In the early 1970s, producers Norman Lear and Bud Yorkin believed that America was at last ready for racial comedy with themes and story lines that sometimes focused on the African American's unique experiences in society. At this point, both Yorkin and Lear had established careers as television writers/producers. Lear, for example, had written material for "The Ford

Star Review" and the "Colgate Comedy Hour" and had served as writer/director for "The Martha Raye Show," the "Tennessee Ernie Ford Show," and "The George Gobel Show." As the principal writer/producer of "All in the Family," Lear had solidly established himself as a major force in television comedy. "All in the Family" featured the bigoted, but lovable(?), Archie Bunker, whose wife, daughter, and son-in-law labored, by example and by cajolery and trickery when necessary, to change Bunker into a more tolerant person. From time to time, Lear also included in the cast of characters the owners of a small cleaning establishment in the neighborhood, an African American family: the Jeffersons. Bunker frequently had negative interactions with various members of this family because of his bigotry and racism. Subsequently, the series entitled "The Jeffersons" was a spinoff from "All in the Family." Lear's comedies were very popular, but they sparked controversy during their years on network television. Indeed media critic Michael Arlen saw series such as "The Jeffersons" as a part of the crop of television programs that connected to nothing except the assumption of being connected to something.[10]

As readers will recall, television's world of the 1950s and 1960s had featured happy people with happy problems. When "All in the Family" and "The Jeffersons" aired, they generated issues and aroused emotions, often by using racial epithets, that were new to network television and were not fashionable in polite society. In a 1974 research study of reactions to "All in the Family," Vidmar and Rokeach found that prejudiced persons and unprejudiced persons ascribed different meanings to the intent and outcome of episodes in this series. They concluded that unprejudiced and minority viewers perceived and enjoyed the show as satire, while prejudiced viewers perceived and enjoyed the show as one of the few that was "telling it like it is!" Vidmar and Rokeach believed the show reinforced prejudice and racism and that, by making Archie Bunker a lovable bigot, a disservice was done to race relations and social harmony.[11]

In any event, Lear's programs were leaders in popular culture, as they brought ethnic humor and wrenching social comment to nationwide television audiences. Lear has said that he felt a strong concern for human values and that he wanted his programs to cause viewers to debate issues, confront problems, and disagree whenever necessary until they were able to work them through. But he also argued that he was not trying to change the world with his television series, noting that "if the Judeo-Christian ethic has had no effect on prejudice over the past 2,000 years, I'd be an awful fool to think we could do it in a half-hour of comedy."[12] With his work, however, Lear created a unique set of television families, which in that decade included more than ten network comedies in which most characters were not afraid to show anger and confusion, and to use earthy language. This set of television families included African Americans as starring characters in "Sanford and Son," and "Good Times," as well as "The Jeffersons." Lear also wrote and produced a pilot for a comedy series about a black congressman entitled "Mr. Dugan." The show never made it to the CBS network as planned. Lear withdrew it as a result of the strong negative reaction it received from African Americans, including members of the Congressional Black Caucus, who previewed it. Still, Lear was justifiably called the czar of network television comedies of the 1970s. He set the tone and charted the course that was followed by numerous television comedies for many years after.

Lear's "Good Times," particularly, attempted an honest portrayal of the concerns and problems facing black people, which were different from those faced by middle-class white people. Rarely before had viewers seen conscientious, entertaining attempts to portray unique aspects of this part of American life. With encouragement from the producers, black contributors to the candid portrayal of black cultural jargon included the performers, as well as a few black writers, who used their cultural heritage to address issues usually left unaddressed on American television. Conventionally silly television fare, "Good Times" basically was about a family's search for economic stability. At various points, it rose to focus on social/civil rights issues, such as an unemployed father, parents unable to use credit cards because of a poor credit rating, rent parties to raise rent money, racism as it affected various family members' earning power, and the like. The series was essentially an "outsider" creation in that it attempted to tell the majority population about the minority, as opposed to "insider" creations, which are designed for the minority group to contribute to its own culture and identity and to allow it to express its unique worldview.[13]

Television viewers' perceptions about African Americans changed during the 1960s as the civil rights story unfolded at dinnertime each day. Moreover, law and order and the "silent majority" were much discussed by those in the Nixon White House of the late 1960s and early 1970s. Then, between 1972 and 1979, Richard Nixon was forced to resign as president of the country, Gerald Ford served out Nixon's term, and Jimmy Carter was elected to a single term in office. When "Good Times" first aired at this point, the civil rights era was drawing to a close. The series was introduced to American viewers by its producers as a sympathetic, "authentic," and realistic portrayal of the black man's plight. The setting in the series established the environment as a lower-class, housing projects apartment, where the frugal, conscientious mother, Florida (played by Esther Rolle, who was formerly the maid on "Maude"), used curtains behind which she hid clothes and household items. One room served this family as the entrance area, living room, and the dining-kitchen area. The three bedrooms were out of most camera shots, as large windows allowed suggestions of daylight or nighttime into the living room-kitchen area. A desk and chair in one corner were surrounded by boxes, probably used to store family belongings. When the series premiered, Esther Rolle was the star. As the scripts developed, however, Jimmie Walker (J.J.), the older son, eclipsed Rolle (Florida) and John Amos (James), as he caught on with teenage viewers who often influenced their parents' viewing patterns.

Though the setting was a lower-class, poor neighborhood, the values and beliefs expressed in "Good Times" were from middle America. In the segment "J.J.'s Eighteenth Birthday," for example, the worldly character Willona, with snapping fingers and "I know the score" glances, stated, "When I was twenty-five, I decided to blow out the candles, freeze the cake, and stop the clock," as J.J.'s parents manipulated their plastic money to try to give him a worthy eighteenth-birthday celebration. Willona, established as good-hearted, represented a lower-class figure, but in her the writers created a contradictory image. Viewers were never quite sure whether she was a swinger or a middle-class striver fallen on bad times, who was forced to live in "the projects." The "J.J.'s Eighteenth Birthday" episode could have evolved into an authentic vignette about black culture at the lower socioeconomic level, but instead the plot developed in the "usual" (white, middle-class) style. For example, for this celebration everyone came in changed clothes, "dressed up" for the occasion, and helped prepare J.J.'s favorite foods. After eating, they "moved to the living room," which was two steps from the kitchen table, for coffee and cake. Few people would act this way in this setting.

The comedy of "Sanford and Son" was based on the assumption that the characters lacked intelligence. It was a modern version of "Amos 'n' Andy," featuring outlandish (though often funny) plots and one-dimensional clown characters. Redd Foxx was a well-known stand-up comedian from the nightclub circuit. He had built up a strong following among black audiences. His material often featured racy, off-color humor with much profanity. Like Nipsey Russell, a comedian who played minor roles in other television programs and was Foxx's contemporary, and Richard Pryor, another major comedian from television and film, Foxx had used racial incidents as a basis for much of his satirical humor. When he was signed to play Fred on "Sanford and Son," black viewers anticipated and received the type of performances from Foxx that they expected, with some important alterations.

Fred Sanford was a stubborn bully who dominated others with his sharp tongue and ever-present anger. Sanford seemed to be angry at anyone who intruded on his turf, from his dead wife's sister to any nonblack who entered his domain, a junkyard where he and his son acquired and recycled society's discards. This series was not original to America, however. The story concept was imported from a popular British series entitled "Steptoe and Son." The American story lines were sometimes infused with African American cultural nuances, but the basic themes were created by white producers and writers, based on the British model. Again, viewers saw African American characters whose values and outlook were shaped and designed by outsiders to their culture.

As noted earlier, "The Jeffersons" began as a spinoff from "All in the Family." George Jefferson was cast in the mold of the freed, corrupt, black legislators of the film "Birth of a Nation," who were depicted as arrogant and idiotic. The audience is asked to laugh at Jefferson's antics and his basic insecurity without unconsciously making an association with his blackness. Obviously this is a difficult feat to accomplish. "The Jeffersons" dealt with middle-class strivers who happened to be black. When it was orginally broadcast, the theme celebrated the arrival of the nouveau riche black middle class. George Jefferson, characterized by producers as a loudmouthed braggart, spoke a great deal about "honkies" and "whities," while Louise, his wife, tried to appease him and smooth the ruffled feathers of others. Usually, the plots centered on George's attempts to climb the social ladder or make more money, with some note made of how difficult it was for those of African descent to move up in American society. The humor and warmth of the show often came from Louise's methods of controlling George and the problems he caused. Louise Jefferson, though submissive to a degree, exercised great influence over George because, no matter what the conflict, George was never right. Even in the early episodes, though George was recognized as having exceptional business acumen, those skills were never transferred into his personal family relationships. This family was seldom portrayed as engaging in group activities or working toward a collective goal. In a 1983 article in the journal *Channels*, columnist William Henry noted that "The Jeffersons" appealed to white Americans because they represented African Americans who had "made it." "The Jeffersons" was the fulfillment of the American dream. Henry thought that viewers "yearned to believe that a social revolution had been won," and that this somehow freed white Americans from redressing any more grievances which African Americans might have said were due. He went on to argue that though George Jefferson was a counterpart to Archie Bunker, the distinct difference between the two men's situations made George a palatable character to white viewers. He noted that Archie was the master in his own home while George was not ("George's wife outmaneuvered, out foxed and out whoofed him, constantly"). Archie was taken seriously whereas George was not (other characters tried to reason with Archie about his bigotry, while George was ignored or laughed at), and Archie had the respect of his household, while George did not. For example, George constantly battled with his maid over who was really master.[14] In the early years of "The Jeffersons," Lear developed George's character in the manner described above in an attempt to bring to viewers' consciousness some of the same social issues generated by the Archie Bunker character, seen this time through the eyes of a counterpart in the black community—George Jefferson. The Jefferson character, like Bunker, was a flawed person who tried to live life on his own terms, marching to his own drummer and subject to insecurities and human frailties. Lear thus attempted to make viewers empathize and identify with a black person similar in human strengths and failings to themselves. He succeeded with both characters, by touching the pulse of an America that had become jaded by post-Vietnam blues—partially because of ambivalent feelings about the conflict itself and partially because of their loss of faith in the country's leadership.   Americans were no longer idealistic about the nation.   Thus, Lear's comedies reflected a "tell it like it is" philosophy of life that featured imperfect characters and realistic problems.

A 1974 article by Eugenia Collier, a college professor and writer, entitled "Black Shows for White Viewers," compared two of the highly rated television series featuring African Americans in prime time.   She concluded that "Sanford and Son" was appealing because viewers could laugh *at* weak people in order to feel good about themselves, whereas viewers of "Good Times" laughed *with* strong survivors.   She argued that "Good Times" had appeal because of the universal attractiveness of protagonists pitted against strong outside forces that make courage, resourcefulness, and intelligence essential to survival.   She believed that viewers were enriched, made wiser and more humane, by their experiences with "Good Times" but were diminished by their experiences with "Sanford and Son" because the latter program focused on the baser instincts—trickery, ignorance, naïveté, and mental aberration.[15]

"Benson" fit the pattern that scripted African American male characters as innocuous true-believers in the system, who supported, defended, and nurtured mainstream, middle-class American values, interests, concerns, and even faults.   Benson was thus an emasculated, nonthreatening, "acceptable" black male.   A spinoff from the highly successful series of the seventies, "Soap," the "Benson" series featured Robert Guillaume as Benson Dubois, a witty and quietly subversive but dependable confidant of the governor of some mythical state.   Benson began the series as the head housekeeper but was later promoted to a position of Lieutenant Governor.   According to sociologist Herman Gray, Robert Guillaume was "attractive and likeable, cool under pressure, and perhaps the quintessential black middle class professional."   The Benson character was the apex of all the servant and helping roles that black actors had played historically in television and the movies.   There was, however, one major qualification—"Benson was uniquely modern—sophisticated, competent and arrogant!   He openly maintained his integrity and his pride week after week [though] . . . the posture of servitude was maintained." In this sense, Gray believed, Benson represented the culmination of a white view of acceptable African American males.[16]

The adoption of black male children into middle-class white American homes on television allowed creators opportunities to send conscious and subconscious messages to viewers about molding and controlling the minds and hearts of young African American males, possibly to make them more acceptable to whites. In the situation comedy "Webster," Emmanuel Lewis played the black adopted son of a white couple in a cross between a kid show and a family comedy. Like "Different Strokes," the hit NBC series with a similar theme, the subliminal message the "Webster" series sent out was that black people did not involve themselves with their own people's children when their parents died. This circumstance could be seen as an advantage since white foster parents could then socialize the youngsters into the "real" American way. Even visits from grandparents or cousins, or any evidence of their concern about the youngsters' welfare, were not central to the theme of either of these two series during their first seasons. Beginning with the second season, Ben Vereen was featured as Webster's uncle, who vainly attempted to adopt the youngster and visited with him on occasion. In reality, however, the black extended family often had black women who reared generation after generation of other people's children—grandchildren, cousins, nephews and nieces, and so on—"because their own folks were gone or dead."[17]

"The White Shadow," an earlier series that had aired from 1979 to 1981, had featured a white basketball coach/physical education teacher and his predominantly black high-school team. "The White Shadow," "Webster," and "Different Strokes" each treated the issue of race as peripheral, as the frame of reference for addressing other issues where race was simply another individual difference rather than a social or public issue. Race as a central theme of concern in American society was ignored or broken down into simplified components and then resolved with ease. Like early television series such as "East Side, West Side," usually the problems raised on television, even those involving African Americans and particularly evident in these programs, were resolved by a white male problem-solver.

The domestic family comedy "Gimme a Break" (1981) seemed to reflect a Reagan-inspired return to the Eisenhower era. The series continued the theme started by the proud but servile, cocky but nurturing, loyal mammies in the many Hollywood film classics and carried into the Eisenhower era by television's "Beulah." The star of "Gimme a Break," Nell Carter, first captured national attention in 1981 when she won four major awards (including a Tony) for her electrifying performance in Broadway's "Ain't Misbehavin'." From there, Carter landed a role as the rambunctious Sergeant Hildy Jones in the television series "Lobo," which was quickly canceled. She had a continuing role in the daytime serial "Ryan's Hope" and played parts in three films—"Hair," "Back Roads," and "Modern Problems."

On "Gimme a Break," Carter seemed cognizant of the parallels between her character and other maids' roles black women had played when there were few options open to them if they wanted to practice their craft. She parodied Butterfly McQueen's role in "Gone with the Wind" in one episode and defended her mammy-like role to a visiting friend (Addie, played by Telma Hopkins) in another episode. Nonetheless, she continued in the role because it was a hit with crossover markets and because roles for African American women, scarce in all forms of mass entertainment, were especially hard to find in network television in the early 1980s. It was an achievement for an African American woman to land the lead role in a hit series, but there were a number of factors that prevented African American viewers from feeling comfortable with Carter's performance in the series. The opening song focused on the show's theme. Its lyrics, sung by the star, included the lines "Gimme a break. I sure could use it. I've finally found where I belong!!" Some asked if these words implied that African American women belonged in someone else's home, caring for other people's children, and neglecting their own lives?

In the series, Carter played a dominating mammy to the white children. As she was so ill-tempered and viewers might have been offended by her physical abuse of the white youngsters on the show, it appears that a decision was made to include Addie, as a foil for Nell's temper. Thus, on numerous occasions, Nell insulted Addie, yelled at her, and slapped her around. Addie often ducked when no punch was thrown because she was so used to the abuse. In one program, Nell went to court to beg the judge not to take "her babies" since she had promised their dead mother that she would raise them as her own. The judge decided against the children's aunt and in Carter's favor when Nell fell to her knees, crying and beseeching the judge to let her keep "her" children. For a young African American woman to fall to her knees obsequiously begging to continue in a servant's role on network television in the 1980s was astounding— particularly after the country had experienced the civil rights movement in the 1960s and 1970s, which had engendered much soul-searching about racial issues among thoughtful people, black and white.

Nell noted in one episode that Jonathan, Julie's new husband, had broken an irreplaceable knickknack that had been handed down to Nell by her grandmother, who had *immigrated* to this country on a slave ship. One cannot conceive of any thoughtful African American allowing such themes and lines to remain, as they obviously distort historical facts.[18]

"Gimme a Break" followed the pattern set by a majority of African American comedies before it: it reflected mainstream beliefs and views, African American culture was not addressed, and the lead character was often irresponsible and childlike. Like "Beulah" from the 1950s, the mammy of "Gimme a Break" lacked the European-oriented sex appeal typical of American television, did not question her role as a servant, put her own life second as she fretted about the problems of her white employers, and could not be viewed as a fighter against the "system," who would want more for African American children than she had.

Carter's own strong personality was quite evident in the program, for Nell, the performer and character, was always in control. Even when the children's father, "the chief," was alive and actively involved in the story lines, Nell the character dominated him and everyone else. Loud, bossy, and "in charge" from the moment each episode began, Nell's own ethical code was obvious, but was juxtaposed to a wide amoral streak that allowed her to lie and cheat when it suited her purpose, as the audience roared with laughter. The producers developed Nell as a person who was pragmatic, competitive, and manipulative but likeable and endearing, who was absolutely sure of her values—which were, of course, mainstream America's values. As with the African American comedies of the 1950s and 1960s, the producers did not allow the attention of viewers to stray to events related to racial problems. Nell was made to turn a deaf ear and a blind eye to the biggest issue evident at many turns in the series—the potential social devisiveness of the racial issue. Like most television programs of the period, this series brought no civil/social rights problems to weekly viewers. Nell nurtured and loved the white youngsters left in her care. The manipulations and domineering attitude were used only to help them in some way.

It appears, however, that Nell the performer exerted great influence during the production of the series. Her sense of timing, eye contact with viewers, number of shots focused on her body language, and the camera angles themselves showed a carefully planned and executed delivery of her personality to the audience. It is hard to believe that the producers and writers could have perfected this delivery without Carter's active, detailed involvement. Nell's flawless pacing and pregnant silences, accompanied by a telling glance, allowed viewers to share a secret with her at numerous points in the average show. Thus, although the producers, directors, and writers shaped the Nell character to their mainstream experiences, Nell was able to control aspects of her performances to convey a slightly different message from what was probably written on paper as the original intent. Had she chosen to do so, because of her powerful position, Carter could have infused more African American tradition, experience, and sense of pride and dignity into the series. Not just the star, she also had control over the unconsciously perceived meanings that went beyond the show's dialogue. Carter elected instead to maintain her distance from racial/social issues. Many black viewers were, at best, ill-at-ease with their feelings toward the series, for they viewed Nell Carter as very talented, but misguided. In fact, many middle-class African Americans made it a point never to watch the series.[19]

Starring Marla Gibbs (formerly Florence, the maid on "The Jeffersons"), the series "227" of the mid-1980s developed a multidimensional, black female television presence. This family comedy had responsible leading characters, despite the trend of the preceding decades that had seen development of irresponsible leads for most African American comedies. Marla played Mary, an urban apartment house tenant, whose husband and children formed a background for many of the show's plots. Usually Mary and her female neighbors interacted in story lines that followed themes of concern and interest to many women in the 1980's, regardless of race. Like Mary Tyler Moore of the 1970s, the "227" Mary represented everywoman, or what everywoman would like to be. Married to Lester, a construction company supervisor, a steady, reliable husband, and a devoted father, she was the mother of a typical teenage daughter.   Mary was slim, well-groomed, and full of the wry wittiness that had endeared her to viewers of "The Jeffersons."

In "227" Jackie Haree's character, Sondra, was developed as one-dimensional in most episodes.   The one joke surrounding her scenes involved her chasing or being chased by all types of men.   However, Mary, Pearl, Rose, and even Sondra, at some point, had some scenes that showed different dimensions of their characters.   Various episodes focused on serious concerns that the women addressed within the context of their friendships with each other.

Mainstream culture was reflected in most of the plots in the series as the women resolved their problems.   For example, Rose and Pearl played supporting roles to Mary and Sondra, who were reminiscent of Mary and Rhoda of the "Mary Tyler Moore" show. Both Marys were straight, middle-class, somewhat do-good types. Sondra and Rhoda were both mavericks.   They overtly refused to conform to the straight rules that guided the lives of their respective Marys, though they each recognized the norms and codes of society. In the episode "The Anniversary," for example, Sondra flirted with Mary's father and father-in-law and offered to bring a few extra men to the party as door prizes.   She carried such acts off jestingly, suggesting that she was only half-serious and that she recognized how others were responding to her.   She obviously enjoyed the attention she received, just as Rhoda enjoyed the responses she received to her unconventional ways of dealing with life.   For the most part, although the show featured an all-black cast, "227" did little to reflect aspects of African American culture.   Thus it appealed to both mainstream and African American viewers, who rated it among the top twenty-five shows most weeks.

"Amen" premiered during the 1986–87 fall season.   Sherman Hemsley (formerly George of "The Jeffersons"), cast as Deacon Ernest Frye of First Community Church, traded barbs with the young, attractive minister, Reverend Rueben Gregory, played by Clifton Davis (formerly the son, Clifton, on "That's My Mama"). Deacon Frye, a practicing attorney who appeared in court to defend clients from time to time, was a softened version of the strutting, posturing, loudmouthed character Hemsley had played on "The Jeffersons." The main references to black culture were the music played during the opening and at transitional points in the show, the skin color of the characters, and the body language and jargon of some of the characters.   Frye, for example, used the ghetto walk typical of many young men in the black inner city when he strutted about. He also bantered frequently with the sisters who served in numerous capacities in the church. On the other hand, the Reverend, often the straight man for Frye's witticisms and caustic remarks, exuded mainstream values. Much of the humor in the series was based on Frye's unconventional interactions with others. His irreverent attitude toward the Reverend and the sisters, for example, caused the audience to roar with laughter.

"A Different World" premiered in the fall of 1987. Created and produced by Carsey-Warner Productions, in cooperation with Bill Cosby, it originally featured Lisa Bonet, a young woman who had played one of Cosby's daughters in the series "The Cosby Show" (discussed later in this chapter). Set in a historically black college atmosphere, the series developed the sparkling, bright-eyed talents of college-age youngsters in an ensemble format. The show was placed on the network schedule to follow the number one–rated Cosby show. Thus, it immediately found its way to the list of top ten primetime television programs during the first part of the 1987–88 season. Concerned about Lisa Bonet's willfulness, Cosby brought in Debbie Allen as producer-director. Allen was remembered for her pithy, brief role in the movie "Fame." Moreover, she had played roles on television in shows like "Good Times" and in television commercials for Excedrin, Nice 'N Easy, and Final Touch. She also had appeared on Broadway in "Purlie" and in road shows of "Raisin," "Guys and Dolls," "The Music Man," and " Sweet Charity." Her versatility and skills were demonstrated again and again as she danced and sang on television programs ("Stompin at the Savoy" with Ben Vereen) and played brilliant dramatic parts, such as her roles in "Roots" on television, and "Ragtime" in film.

When Debbie Allen burst into American homes in the key role as Lydia in the televison series "Fame," American audiences immediately liked her strong-willed, no-nonsense but sensitive, caring character. For a change, American television viewers saw a young, attractive, black female professional in the lead role in a continuing series that featured drama as well as music, dance, and comedy. When Cosby and Carsey-Warner tapped Allen as producer-director, it was one of the first times that an African American woman reached the decision-making level in network television, particularly with a primetime top ten-rated series. Allen took "A Different World" in new directions. Musical sequences, dancing, dream sequences, and the like figured in the new twists in the series. Her keen sense of what was authentic to the black collegiate atmosphere and to black culture was used to control plot development. (Allen had graduated from historically black Howard University in 1976.) One episode, for example, featured a "Step Show," where fraternities and sororities competed before an appreciative audience as they sang and danced in syncopated, African culture-based rhythms. Such events were a regular part of African American undergraduate sorority and fraternity social activities.[20]

Bill Cosby: A Special Case of Comedy

In a discussion of network television comedies, William H. (Bill) Cosby, Jr. deserves special attention. Bill Cosby's television offerings through the years were most often in situation comedies. He began working on network television in the 1960s, however, as a stand-up comedian frequently featured on late-night talk shows. In 1965, when producers were looking for a costar for Robert Culp for the action-adventure series "I Spy," they chose Cosby. Cosby accepted after determining that he would not be the faithful sidekick to the hero but an equal partner.

"I Spy" offered viewers a black American as a visible feature character who was inoffensive. Cosby's character did not usually address his blackness or another character's whiteness, and, like other shows with black characters on primetime television, he was portrayed in an atmosphere where being black merely meant having slightly darker skin. Bill Cosby and Robert Culp played Central Intelligence Agency (CIA) agents who traveled the world from one dangerous assignment to the next. Cosby played the role of a suave, resourceful, and highly educated, but sensitive and humane character. During the three years of "I Spy" 's primetime existence, Cosby emerged as the partner who spoke many languages fluently and was reliable, competent, effective, and efficient. At the same time, he displayed a strong self-respect, coupled with a sense of comic timing that appealed to many viewers. Moreover, Cosby seemed to not take himself or the world very seriously at a time when there were very serious concerns about social and civil rights on many minds. Thus, he made people feel comfortable with his presence and somewhat forgetful of his African heritage. Cosby was an all-American to most people.

Cosby's part in "I Spy" can be compared with roles played in films by Sidney Poitier during the same period. Some argued that the black superhero was so far from the average person's reach that the character's value as a role model or as a source for identification was lost. After all, the stoic, self-effacing, moral, fair, self-righteous superhero is not easily emulated. Although some critics argued that the superhero was a reversed stereotype and an unrealistic anachronism, most agreed that the roles played by Poitier and Cosby were a welcome relief from the minstrel characters of early films and television.

From 1969 through 1971, the situation comedy series "The Bill Cosby Show" featured Cosby as Chet Kincaid, a high-school coach and bachelor. Though black militancy was in vogue at the time, Cosby played Kincaid as black, proud, and nonmilitant. The series was moderately successful. A few years later Cosby and CBS joined forces in a television experiment, "Fat Albert and the Cosby Kids," a cartoon comedy series for children. Robert Wood, then president of the CBS-TV network, noted that the "Fat Albert" series "was an attempt (a very successful one, as it turned out) to fuse entertainment and education, in a mixture of laughing and learning." "Fat Albert" set the course for television in the vital new area of ethics, values, judgment, and personal responsibility. By the end of its three-year run, the "Fat Albert" animated television series had inspired a number of new directions in children's television. Subsequently, many other Saturday morning programs began to include clarification of values and to deliver "messages" as they entertained, and they continued this trend for years after.

In the 1972–73 season, Cosby starred in "The New Bill Cosby Show," a comedy-variety series. Cosby's Jemmin Company produced the shows, allowing the star to have more artistic control over productions. Cosby made great use of talented, creative black artists in this series. The show lasted one season. For a few months in late 1976, because of his success as a regular guest on the PBS educational series "The Electric Company" where he demonstrated his skill at working with and entertaining youngsters, ABC had Cosby host a primetime hour-long variety series oriented toward children. "Cos" did not catch on with viewers, however, in its time slot opposite "60 Minutes" and "Wonderful World of Disney," and it was canceled after a few months.

Eight years later, in the fall of the 1984–85 season, Cosby's NBC entry, entitled "The Cosby Show," featured Cosby as Cliff Huxtable, an obstetrician living with his wife and four children in a New York brownstone. Their fifth child, away at college most of the time, appeared sporadically in featured parts. The show put black images on the screen that people could admire. The characters on "The Cosby Show" seemed authentic, representing a real African American upper-middle-class group rarely presented on American television. That the characters were good-looking, witty, charming, and conscientious about their love and respect for each other helps to explain why viewers enjoyed visiting with them each week.

The executive producers and other media moguls were aware that Cosby had obtained excellent "Q" ratings from audiences through the years, which meant he was perceived as extremely likeable. They thought his show was worth risking money on even though situation-comedy formats were on the decline in the early 1980s. NBC originally guaranteed Cosby just six shows. The series was number one in the ratings book the first week it aired, received wide acclaim from viewers and critics throughout the season, and finished third for the year. The strength of the show as a smash hit surprised the NBC executives and even Cosby himself. It was the number one show in the country from its second through its fourth season.

"The Cosby Show" demonstrated the skills of a craftsman and artist who had polished his art through years of hard work and careful study. Cosby's comedy reflected an ability to generate a pace, a control of thought patterns, a control over other people, and the use of subtleties to make a point. His style embraced a kind of comedic humanism. "The Cosby Show" had the Bill Cosby stamp on it in many small details. There were references to black culture, paintings by African American artists on the walls in his home and office, and a general attitude that focused on comic perceptions about the universality of the human condition seen within the framework of a strong, proud, African American, upper-middle-class family. To viewers the show's style seemed effortless and impromptu, but in reality it reflected Cosby's years of studying himself, his audiences' reactions to his brand of humor, and his strong sense of how to be a humane humorist rather than merely a funny guy.   Critics compared Cosby to Mark Twain, Charlie Chaplin, and Will Rogers rather than to other live comedians because he appealed to many age groups, racial groups, and cultures, and because he brought a gentle whimsy to his work.   People tended to like the show, as they liked Cosby, because of these factors. Cosby was particularly pleased, and surprised, at his phenomenal success.   He happily noted that many marketing experts insisted that American viewers were racists who could not accept anyone who failed to fit marketers' misconceptions of what America wanted to see from black actors.   He was elated that the viewers had proved them wrong.

Bill Cosby led the television industry into uncharted waters with his series.   Though "The Cosby Show" was like other programs that starred African Americans in reflecting mainstream values and beliefs, American viewers were allowed to see a rarity for television: a wealthy, strong, black male star who was a sexy, loving husband and a conscientious, responsible father.   This strong black man showed strength of character and noble spirit, but he could also be silly at times.   The character was developed as multidimensional rather than as a cardboard figure, as many characters tended to be in television comedies.   His show opened up new opportunities for many African Americans.   For example, Cosby sought black artists for cameo roles on the show who had not been seen on network television in years (for instance, Dizzy Gillespie, the world-renowned trumpet player, and Judith Jamison of the Alvin Ailey Dance Company and the Broadway show "Sophisticated Ladies").   Cosby included black writers among his creative staff and by the third year insisted on using a black director for some of the episodes. Conscious of the need to lead the networks toward more equitable treatment of blacks, he used his position to require that more doors be opened for African Americans.   Thus, Cosby's programs, including "A Different World," can be viewed as contributions to a fusion in the split image of African Americans.

With the Cosby influence, the 1980s more than any other decade in history saw a change in the way African Americans were involved in network comedy on commercial television.   "The Cosby Show" taught mainstream viewers elements of the African American experience in subtle ways.   The Martin Luther King Day celebration, for instance, evoked a reminiscence by the two older generations in the family about their participation in the historic March on Washington in 1963. Few mainstream television series would or could have addressed the historic march in this manner and made it entertaining. Probably none could have had the leading characters talk about why the march was so important to black people while maintaining credibility as entertainment. Mainstream viewers were thus subtly sensitized to the unique problems and concerns that African Americans experienced even when they were as mainstream in outward appearance as the Huxtable family seemed to be. Those same viewers got consistent doses of the family's appreciation of jazz music, artistic works by African American artists, the earthy music of James Brown, and the street dance craze—all part of African American cultural contributions to mainstream American popular culture.

"The Cosby Show" also sensitized network executives to the idea that American viewers might be ready again to respond to warm, witty, family comedies, including those about African Americans, despite the view that had surfaced in the 1980s that situation comedies were no longer marketable on network television. More situation comedies premiered in the years following the success of "The Cosby Show."[21]

Variety Shows

The dominant image of black people on television in the fifties was that of "the entertainer." In the earliest American television programs, black people were employed with some degree of dignity by Ed Sullivan, Arthur Godfrey, Milton Berle, Steve Allen, and a few others like them who frequently used African American performers in their variety shows without consigning them to stereotypical roles or to the rigidity of white models. It took courage and strength of conviction for these white men to decide to include black people in this way in those days, because the prevailing argument of the time—borrowed from the radio and film industries—nearly dictated that television bow to the southern market, which many believed violently objected to Negroes being cast in any role other than stereotypical ones. Black performers entertained on variety shows as singers, musicians, and dancers. On some occasions, integrated entertainer groups such as "The Mariners" were featured on such shows as "The Arthur Godfrey Show."[22]

Lorenzo Fuller, one of the first black people to host a televised musical variety show, performed regularly on all the major television networks between 1947 and 1953. His work also included his accompaniment of singers like Juanita Hall and Ethel Waters. Fuller was best known as the accompanist on "Arthur Godfrey's Talent Scouts," where he once was requested to sing and subsequently won first place in the show for that night. He developed musical arrangements for Kate Smith, "The Today Show," and "Hallmark Hall of Fame," and for numerous other television programs that aired in the 1950s and 1960s. In 1952, Rybutol began sponsorship of "The Billy Daniels Show," a fifteen-minute musical variety series. This, one of the first network television series hosted by an African American, enjoyed a thirteen-week run.

Many believed that the appearance of Negroes on television was a sign that barriers were coming down. Some believed that the Federal Communications Commission (FCC) and advertisers, because of their responsiveness to social forces, would lead the way to opening up television as a strong medium of black expression. This belief increased among black viewers because of black-oriented publications. Black people involved with television even in minor ways were often featured in publications like *Ebony* magazine and the *Afro-American* newspaper. Unfortunately, the awesome breadth and scope of original black talent failed to penetrate the television medium, despite the emergence of an era of integration (between 1947 and 1965) that had resulted from the liberal momentum of the war years. As it turned out, for the most part what African Americans did on television in the late forties and early fifties was often unoriginal and unimpressive, for blacks had always been singing and dancing for white America, first in slavery, later in minstrelsy and vaudeville, and then in films. They merely continued their performances before television cameras, often imitating whites who were imitating them. Moreover, because they believed that in order to be accepted they had no choice, they usually failed to show different aspects of the reality of African American life.[23]

Cab Calloway and Pearl Bailey were frequent performing guests on early variety shows. A look at *Jet* magazine listings for the decade of the fifties reveals that they both appeared on network television variety programs more than sixty times combined. Calloway was a song-and-dance man who led his own band for many years, appearing in stage shows across the country. While on radio after World War II, he had his own show on NBC entitled "Cab Calloway's Quizicale." His Hollywood films were usually inserts in largely white musicals where his band backed featured performers such as Lena Horne. Often the plot allowed for a musical interlude at a night spot or some big event where "Negroes" could perform without disturbing the main plot. His television appearances usually featured him singing and dancing or conducting his own compositions. Those for which he was best known were "Minnie, the Moocher," and "Hi De Ho." In addition, he popularized the term that Bill "Bojangles" Robinson had coined for "everything's wonderful"; when all was fine and dandy Calloway said it was "copacetic." Calloway's clowning acts as he sang and danced eclipsed the public's realization that he had a strong baritone voice and great musical abilities. The true extent of his talents was never seen, for like many other black entertainers of this period he had to keep the majority audience comfortable with his presence, so he clowned around. Calloway became a master at pleasing audiences of all colors in his many appearances on shows like "Songs for Sale," "Toast of the Town," and "The Steve Allen Show."

Pearl Bailey had been pleasing audiences ever since she and her brother Bill started in show business in the forties. Called Pearlie Mae by her friends, Bailey had numerous Broadway shows, a few Hollywood films, and many, usually white, nightclub appearances to her credit when she began appearing on network television. She quickly became a favorite with variety show hosts, such as Milton Berle and Ed Sullivan. Sassy, sarcastic, and witty, Bailey's artistic skill made viewers of both races respond to her unique style. She sang and talked when she "pitched" a song. For example, her rendition of "Tired" included her singing:

> Tired of the life I lead, tired of the air I breathe,
> Tired of the things I do.
> Gonna lead the life of Cindy Lou, gonna do the things
>   that I know she'd do.
> Cause I'm tired, mighty tired of you.

Then, Bailey would talk for three to ten minutes—depending on her preset plans and her perception of the audience's mood—about men and the problems women had handling relationships with them. Her pungent comments made men laugh at themselves and women laugh in recognition of evoked feelings. Calloway and Bailey were warmly accepted by white viewers, while they each also pleased black viewers. Though both these entertainers had experienced race-related problems, and solved them in public in some instances, like their white counterparts they brought no social issues to America's television viewers of the forties and fifties. Thus viewers could be entertained by black performers such as these, content in the confidence that everything was "copacetic" for the happy African American stars who appeared before them so frequently on other people's shows.

In the 1950s Nat "King" Cole seemed a sure shot for having his own network variety television series because of his immense popularity. Four of his songs were number one hits between 1944 and 1957, and thirteen were among America's top ten at some point during the period. Between 1940 and 1955, Cole had records on Billboard charts for 274 of the 780 weeks. He was a frequent performer on such TV shows as "The Steve Allen Show," "The Milton Berle Show," "Songs for Sale," "The Perry Como Show," "Toast of the Town," and many others. "His popularity exceeded that of Frank Sinatra, Doris Day, Tommy Dorsey and Dinah Shore."[24] Therefore, in 1956, when NBC agreed to give Nat Cole a fifteen-minute series of his own, many believed he had a good chance of surviving and eventually doing well. As it turned out, however, though he had respectable ratings at various points, Cole was unable to continue the series beyond a year (fifty-nine weeks) because advertisers were afraid to sponsor an African American on television. Sponsors feared hostile southern markets and the possibility of a nationwide rejection of their product, which might have been labeled "Negro" products.[25]

Lena Horne and Harry Belafonte were frequent entertainers on other people's variety shows during the 1960s. Unlike African American entertainers in these early years of television who were treated respectably but not royally, Horne and Belafonte both received the royal treatment. Each handled television appearances with conscientious dignity, and they fiercely controlled their performances according to their own creativity, interpretations, and perceptions. Black viewers were justifiably proud to see them on the occasional specials in which they starred.

Lena Horne had started out, at the age of sixteen, singing with bands at the "Cotton Club" in Harlem. She had become a star in Hollywood because of her appearances in movies such as "Panama Hattie" and "As Thousands Cheer." Her most important movies, "Cabin in the Sky" and "Stormy Weather," characterized her as an exotic siren rather than a prostitute, the typical role assigned attractive black women in that era. Horne had carried herself with such grace in her roles that she epitomized traditional middle-class values.

In the 1950s, like other movie stars of the day Horne sought opportunities to be seen on the popular small screens of network television. Horne was one of the entertainers blacklisted by *Red Channels*, the publication that listed those who were "thought" to have Communist sympathies. At one point, she was unable to make any television appearances at all. When she began appearing on network television with the assistance of Ed Sullivan, who had been instrumental in helping to clear her name, she came across as aloof, controlled, and ladylike. Variety show hosts and audiences seemed enamored of Horne's television persona. With the help of her husband, white bandleader Lennie Hayton, she polished her singing style and delivery, accentuated her strengths, and minimized her weak points. Sullivan, Perry Como, Steve Allen, Milton Berle, Frank Sinatra, and others invited Horne for numerous appearances. Black viewers saw her as sophisticated, "just like middle-class white women," while white audiences found her protestant reserve and control appealing. However, when Horne sang songs like "The Lady Is a Tramp" she insinuated that viewers might not believe merely what they were allowed to see.

On the variety shows, Horne usually appeared alone onstage, sitting on a stool or standing, rather than plastered to a pillar as she had been in her many Hollywood film feature roles. On the Perry Como shows, Horne and Como sang frequent duets, as Como totally ignored taboos about interracial touching or emotionally involving lyrics. There were few criticisms from viewers about his "transgressions." Such was not the case with the widely acclaimed singer Harry Belafonte when he touched the arm of Petula Clark, a British singer, after a particularly emotion-rending duet the two had performed on her television show, "Petula," sponsored by Chrysler in 1968. After the sponsors made a big issue about the incident, Belafonte vowed to use his creative energies in other media and rarely returned to network television. This outcome would not have been predictable at the beginning of Belafonte's network appearances, for he had been one of the "darlings" of television in the fifties and sixties.

When he was discovered at the Village Vanguard Club in New York City, Belafonte won wide recognition as a folksinger. Middle-class women of all races flocked to see him with his shirt open to the tight leather belt that merely adorned his hip-hugging pants, as his songs evoked a feeling of nostalgia for a way of life and a moral system that was a part of the past. Belafonte was a native New Yorker of Jamaican/West Indian background. His music represented years of research, for he had been intrigued by American folk music and had spent many hours playing Library of Congress records in preparation for building a repertory of old and modern folk ballads. In addition, he had acquired old and unusual folk songs sung by prisoners, field workers, and riverboat men. When he sang, he evoked deep feelings as he told a story.[26]

Though Horne and Belafonte controlled certain aspects of their specific performances, power to direct their appearances (words spoken, placement on the set, lighting, time placement in the program, camera angles) was largely in the hands of the decision makers—the white producers, directors, writers, and, most importantly, the sponsors of the shows—as had been the case with blues singers in the music industry of the 1920s (see chapter 1). As can be seen by the previous instances, white decision makers of the 1960s allowed more sexually oriented freedom to black females, while restricting such freedom for the black male in network television appearances. Thus, the dominant group helped to maintain the practice, enculturated by other media through the years, of channeling and controlling the behavior of African Americans, particularly males.

Numerous African Americans appeared as performers in other people's variety shows through the years and, as noted earlier in this chapter, Bill Cosby and Flip Wilson each starred in his own variety show on network television during the 1970s. Wilson's show was among the last variety programs to star an African American host on network television, as the variety show format declined in popularity.

Miniseries

During the last week of January 1977, ABC-TV telecast one of the first made-for-television movie miniseries. "Roots I," and later "Roots II," broke all previous records for high ratings for any program and for national attention paid to the subject of African Americans. Most critics agreed that the overall impact of the two series was beneficial to African Americans. They projected sympathetic portrayals of black Americans as positive protagonists of indomitable spirit locked in admirable struggles with the problems of life, where racism constrained most facets of their existence. On the other hand, some critics argued that "Roots" on television failed to show how African Americans were used as human capital to support a fledgling industrial order in the South, where for two hundred and fifty years black Americans literally built America and received minimal rewards for their efforts. Critics believed that this major flaw in "Roots" reflected reality, particularly because the African American typically had negative perceptions about himself and was usually unaware of his people's vast contributions to the nation's success.

Critics also questioned the authenticity of "Roots" as black drama because it failed to include either a writer or director of African American heritage, with the exception of two episodes of "Roots II," directed by Gilbert Moses and Georg Stanford Brown. Some believe that the storyline of Haley's book was acceptable to the establishment mainly because the book failed to question the system that lay behind the unrelenting series of problems that befell the characters even though most of them had a racial-conflict orientation.

There was a strong plea from African Americans for more representation of their own interpretations of their experiences in American history (like the Reconstruction era, or the Marcus Garvey movement, or the Compromise of 1877), and for programs about the harsh existence of field hands in slavery, for a story based on Ralph Ellison's Invisible Man, or for a story about Malcolm X or Nat Turner. There is, apparently, an audience for authentic African American stories. Moreover, some contend that during slavery and Reconstruction, black Americans did not merely accommodate the will of the dominant group but very often resisted in a variety of ways. For example, African Americans lamented that "Roots" missed an opportunity to portray blacks and whites actively engaged in the struggle to destroy the slave system. To some, "Roots" was an admixture of helpless African Americans and brutal whites reminiscent of *Uncle Tom's Cabin*. The "Roots" projection of black Americans was seen as a regression to a less heroic, less dignified black image than the one advanced during the 1960s, and many believe that much of the struggle during the civil rights period was geared to destroy the slave mentality so graphically resurrected in the "Roots" series. Ultimately, the experiences of Americans of African descent deserved a fuller and more honest treatment than they were given in "Roots." For, here again, the commercial television industry had used African Americans for its purposes without allowing black people to share in deciding how those images should be developed.[27]

The wave of black dramatic miniseries that followed "Roots I" was a promising break in the dull trend of African American images usually seen in television broadcasting. However, issues concerning the integrity of some of those productions were raised. Programs such as "Roots II" and "A Woman Called Moses" depicted valiant efforts by ordinary people to survive despite great adversity. In both programs the courageous *individual* was pitted against evil outside forces and each individual's ultimate victory was seen as a singular act of survival. The "system," which caused a large measure of the suffering undergone by these characters, was not questioned by the television characters, nor by extension the viewers, and the African American "hero/heroine" was presented in each instance as "a victim." Moreover, the story lines were often altered from the original text to make them more palatable to white viewers. I believe that the African American story *also* must[28] be told to viewers from the African American perspective rather than always through a filter of (admittedly, very often, quite sympathetic) whites who, nevertheless, usually have a different perspective and objective.

After the success of "Roots" and "Roots II," many believed that the impressive acting talents and abilities of the black performers from the two series would be in high demand. However, roles for African Americans in drama on commercial television were almost as scarce after "Roots" as they had been before. Many began to believe more strongly that white America could not take a consistent, serious look at the African American in a way that would allow black people to share their view of their culture and partially define their own image. Thus, success with a dramatic commercial television series featuring African Americans still eluded black creative talents.

The 1980s were the Ronald Reagan era in American history. Reagan was elected president in 1980 and in 1984. The conservative former governor of the State of California, Reagan set a tone of leadership for Americans which galvanized doubters about affirmative action and anti-civil rights and women's rights groups into action. Begun in the Kennedy-Johnson era, affirmative action was designed to give minorities opportunities to move into the mainstream of American society in areas such as education and the workplace. The Reagan administration officially ignored the movement for equality of minorities and women, and the push for equal rights for all became a thing of the past for many Americans. Media moguls fell in step with the nation's leaders by producing and airing programs that fit the new conservative mood of the country. For example, in early 1980, NBC-TV contracted with David Gerber Productions, in association with Columbia Pictures, a multimillion dollar venture to produce a six-part miniseries entitled "Beulah Land." Many African Americans who were offered roles in the miniseries turned them down because, in an attempt to capitalize on the phenomenal success of "Roots," the series focused on a romanticized white version of the slavery period in American history. There were approximately fifteen speaking roles for black people in "Beulah Land." Most of the roles were negative and perpetuated the image of the slave as either ignorant, oversexed, utterly dependent on the whim of his master, and/or filled with love for that master and the master's land. None of these figments of the writer's imagination (Lonnie Coleman) was given the opportunity to develop explanations for the historic origins of, or the motives for their questionable behavior.

There was little attempt by African American viewers to deny the existence of models for some of these roles. The argument from the black community stemmed from the fact that these distorted characters—the slave girl who slept with the "massa" (to save her husband, brother, or father), the freed slave who remained nearby (because part of his family was still enslaved), the black male lusting after white women—were presented on television as the rule rather than the exception, and they were presented with an almost absolute omission or distortion of motives. None of the characters was allowed to say or show why he was a participant in his own degradation. Moreover, throughout the series, viewers never encountered a slave who wanted to be anything other than a slave.[29]

Hollywood, in both film and television, had been tough on minority progress. Black actors and actresses, whose talents and energies were displayed so dramatically in the seventies, were bitterly disappointed by the inertia of the industry as it regressed to its pre-"Roots" mode of operation. The few African American writers, producers, directors, and other off-camera persons who had jobs in the industry felt intense dissatisfaction as they fought to move up to decision-making levels. The overwhelming majority of decision makers in the media were white males, who usually

Table 5.2   The Top-Rated Shows in History

Rank	Program	Telecast Date	Rating	Share
1	"M*A*S*H Special"	February 1983	60.2	77
2	"Dallas"	November 1980	53.3	76
3	*"Roots" (Part 8)	January 1977	51.1	71
4	"Super Bowl"	January 1982	49.1	73
7	"Gone with the Wind" (Part 1)	November 1976	47.7	65
8	"Gone with the Wind" (Part 2)	November 1976	47.4	64
11	"Bob Hope Christmas Show"	January 1970	46.6	64
15	"ABC Theatre, The Day After"	November 1983	46.0	62
16	*"Roots" (Part 6)	January 1977	45.9	66
17	"The Fugitive"	August 1967	45.9	72
19	*"Roots" (Part 5)	January 1977	45.7	71
20	"The Ed Sullivan Show" (Beatles appearance)	February 1964	45.3	60
21	"Bob Hope Christmas Show"	January 1971	45.0	61
22	*"Roots" (Part 3)	January 1977	44.8	68
26	*"Roots" (Part 2)	January 1977	44.1	62
27	"Beverly Hillbillies"	January 1964	44.0	65
28	*"Roots" (Part 4)	January 1977	43.8	66
29	"The Ed Sullivan Show"	February 1964	43.8	60
30	"Academy Awards"	April 1970	43.4	78

Source: A. C. Nielsen Company 1987.

Note: Rating is percentage of households viewing; share is percentage of households with television tuned to that program. Ranks 5, 6, 9, 10, 12, 13, 14, 18, 23, 24, and 25 are other Super Bowl games.

*African American-focused programs.

lacked sensitivity to minority concerns and interests, were entrenched in their positions, and were usually unwilling to encourage
minority aspirations.[30]

The Soaps

In the early days of television, when African Americans appeared
on daytime serials (soap operas), if they were seen at all, they had
small, insignificant *walk-ons* as elevator operators or passersby.
Occasionally, when some black faces were seen as extras, usually
they spoke fewer than five lines. This situation prevailed until the
mid-1960s. Then, gradually, African Americans began to play minor
roles in series such as "The Guiding Light" and "Another World."

In the early 1970s, soaps began to include black characters in
feature roles. For example, because of the creator and head writer
of "One Life to Live," Agnes Nixon, viewers were introduced to
Ellen Holly, a fair-skinned black woman passing for white. This
character was developed over a ten-year period and evoked much
controversy, as the story lines focused on touchy racial issues. In
the seventies and eighties, numerous black actors and actresses
appeared as guest stars in soap operas. "All My Children" and
"One Life to Live" pioneered in introducing black characters and
families and developing themes and stories about African Americans.
In the early eighties, other daytime serials followed suit, including
NBC's "Another World" and the CBS series "The Young and
Restless" and "As the World Turns."

In the late 1980s, African Americans had strong roles in some
daytime series. For example, there was Debbie Morgan in "All My
Children," Laura Carrington in "General Hospital," Marguerite Ray
in "The Young and the Restless," and Count Stovall and Tamara
Tunie in "As the World Turns." "Generations," commerical television's first daytime network serial focused on an African American
family, aired on NBC beginning in 1988.[31]

A frequent criticism of black characters seen on the soaps was
that they often lacked depth or dimension. The primarily white
writers for the soaps developed characters in the context of their
own world experiences. Often they were afraid of offending black
viewers and so made the characters perfect or wooden rather than
realistic. An answer to the "too perfect" criticism was provided in

the 1984–85 season's "Dynasty." The nighttime soap opera that year began featuring Diahann Carroll as the self-proclaimed "first black bitch" on nighttime television. Carroll's role as Dominque attracted African American viewers who had not been consistent viewers before. Still, the role was developed by whites and had little to do with African American culture. Dominique's values, views, and perspectives had a white, upper-middle-class focus.[32]

Supplier/Production Companies

The split in the black image in commercial television between what white decision makers elected to establish and what blacks attempted to disseminate about themselves has been described earlier. Implicit in this discussion is the point of view that African Americans can offer unique perspectives, if circumstances allow, about their views of America and about the black man in this society. Through the years there have been African American entrepreneurs who sought to enhance the economic and cultural empowerment of blacks in America by controlling portions of the businesses which projected American images. Supplier/production companies are among such enterprises. The group of African American–owned supplier/production companies includes Motown Productions, Parrott & People Productions, Bill Parker Productions, Flip Wilson Productions, Redd Foxx Productions, Bill Cosby Productions, Cosby's Jemmin and Jamel Productions, Topper Carew's Topo Alto Productions, Ossie Davis and Ruby Dee's Emmalyn II Productions, Oprah Winfrey's Harpo Productions, and Robert Townsend's Tinsel Townsend Productions. These program suppliers comprised a dismally insignificant proportion of the total suppliers to the networks as compared with the number of black viewers watching commercial television and appearing in programs on the networks.[33]

The supplier/production companies that achieved a measure of success in breaking down barriers established by the television industry have interesting stories. For example, in 1983 Motown Productions convinced NBC to air its "Motown 25" special in prime time. The show won an Emmy award and became a ratings blockbuster. Yet, by 1987, Motown Productions had not had another opportunity with any of the major networks. Then, in 1988, Berry

Gordy, Jr., founder and chief executive officer of Motown Industries, sold Motown Records and established The Gordy Company, a group of entertainment concerns. In early 1989, the centerpiece of the new company, Motown Productions, bargained to produce "Lonesome Dove," a highly acclaimed CBS television miniseries. Motown Productions made plans for the 1990s that included a search for new projects to position the company in all facets of electronic media: cable television, network television, home video, and the acquisition of a distributorship, particularly after "Lonesome Dove" garnered sixteen Emmy award nominations and three Emmys.[34]

Parrott & People Productions (P&P) produced award-winning television commercials, documentaries, and corporate industrial films and videos beginning in 1963. P&P awards included the coveted Clio award, and its client roster included many Fortune 500 corporations. In 1984, Columbia Pictures had P&P produce an on-location documentary, trailer, and television commercial on the making of the award-winning film "A Soldier's Story."

Bill Parker Productions was one of the few black production companies that was able to break into the new market for film and video artists, the rock-oriented Music TV (MTV). The Parker production of Shalamar's new-wave hit song "Dead Giveaway" on MTV in 1983 generated phenomenal business for the company beginning in 1984.

In 1989, Oprah Winfrey's Harpo Productions, Inc., which owned and produced "The Oprah Winfrey Show," the phenomenally successful talk show that originated in Chicago beginning in 1985, made a *Wall Street Journal* list as one of the twenty-eight rising stars in the *business* world. Called the richest woman on television in 1989, Winfrey had built and purchased a television and movie studio in Chicago from which she produced her talk show and many other television programs and films beginning in 1989. Winfrey, thus, became the third woman, and the first black woman in American history to own her own production company. (Mary Pickford and Lucille Ball preceded Winfrey on the list.) Harpo coproduced "The Women of Brewster Place," which aired in early 1989. Moreover, the company owned the rights to other production possibilities, such as Toni Morrison's Pulitzer Prize-winning novel *Beloved*, Mark Mathabane's *Kaffir Boy*, a book about his life in apartheid-ridden South Africa, and Zora Neale Hurston's *Their Eyes Were Watching God*.[35]

Like Winfrey, other major African American stars, such as Eddie Murphy, Bill Cosby, Richard Pryor, Robert Townsend, and Arsenio Hall, also established themselves as businessmen who owned the companies that used their creativity as a marketable commodity. Thus they prepared to obtain more control of the African American image as the turn of the century approached.

Conclusion

Commercial television had made some rather significant changes in the matter of race relations between 1950 and 1990, but much about the industry had stayed the same. Various ratings services and other research studies of America's viewing habits disclosed, through the years, that black viewers comprised a much larger share of the various audiences than did nonblacks. This information emerged when researchers began sampling African American viewers beginning in 1972 after pressure groups insisted that there might be a difference in the viewing habits of various audience segments, like the African American. Subsequently, researchers learned in the early 1980s that in Washington, D.C., while 7 percent of all households watched the daytime serial "All My Children," 17 percent of black households viewed it. In New York City, where 10 percent of the nonblack households viewed the serial "General Hospital," 18 percent of black households viewed it.[36] Moreover, in almost all areas of commercial television viewing African Americans ranked higher than did nonblack groups. With the advent of the alternative distribution systems (cable, multipoint distribution systems, and direct broadcast satellite systems), broadcasters probably reasoned that wealthier viewers would have more expendable incomes that would allow them to purchase the more expensive alternatives faster. Recall that when television replaced radio as the dominant form of mass entertainment, as mainstream listeners purchased television sets, many radio-station owners turned to black listeners as part of their targeted market. Similarly, broadcasters in the eighties began to turn their attention more and more to viewers whom they believed they still could depend upon to maintain their ratings. Black viewers were among that group. Thus, in the 1980s, with the advent of alternative distribution systems, commercials and programs alike began to include African

Americans as part of their targeted audience. Even with more involvement of blacks in the industry, much stereotyping remained endemic to commercial television, even in the late 1980s.

Elimination of stereotyping and other obviously hostile forms of programming from television would not totally solve the problem of the African American image, according to Michael Winston of Howard University. He contended that the most insidious distortions were found, not in *mis*portrayals of black culture, but in the exclusion of African Americans from programs depicting events in which they had played significant roles. Such exclusion reinforced the false but widely accepted notion that African Americans have contributed little to the United States and have significance in American society only as "a problem." As examples of this distortion, Winston cited television programs aired in the early 1980s about the Civil War, World Wars I and II, the Korean War, and the Vietnam War, which included few, if any, African Americans, although blacks were obviously full participants in the actual events. He further noted that a strange cultural situation had evolved in which television reflected a popular culture filled with the ideas, products, music, dance, and humor taken from black culture, although there were very few African Americans in evidence on the shows or as decision makers.[37]

What are the implications and the significance of Winston's insights? First, the pattern of use and denial of African American talent has repeated itself throughout the history of this industry. There were few African Americans among the program suppliers, producers, writers, and directors who brought viewers television programming from the 1940s through the 1980s. Therefore, the unique interpretations and perspectives that African American collective experience could contribute to productions were lost. However, despite such constraints many black people influenced television. They added credible lines or story ideas, used their talents whenever they could, refused to do things they found offensive, urged the network executives to look at other groups besides their own, and moved as much as possible among the powerbrokers, seeking answers, promises, and more work.

Second, implicit in Winston's assertions lies the issue of balanced television fare. Television of the 1990s, as a purveyor of shared cultural values, must deal with relevant issues and present contemporary concepts and stories characteristic of America's multicultural, multiethnic society, and do so with a balanced view rather than a one-sided and dominant-culture-controlled one. The African American experience in society can be used to create engrossing, entertaining, and informative television for all viewers—as "Roots," "The Cosby Show," and "In the Heat of the Night" so decisively proved. Certainly, the experience of African Americans reflects aspects of this culture, good and bad, which speak to a relevant shared heritage. It is my opinion that the infusion of authentic, African American–controlled images into mainstream popular culture, particularly television, could help all Americans better understand themselves.

The split image which Americans hold of their countrymen of African heritage, as could be seen in commercial television between 1949 and 1989, was the same as that described in the Introduction and demonstrated as existing in previous chapters. There we saw the dominant white-influenced and -controlled image and the concomitant African American thrust toward alternatives. Some of these alternatives emerged inside the mainstream framework as accommodations to the system ("Beulah" and "Gimme a Break"), while others resisted accommodation ("Good Times" and "Frank's Place"). As readers will see in subsequent chapters, the struggle over the image of the African American continued as the alternative media delivery systems developed.

1. See Eric Barnouw, *Tube of Plenty: The Evolution of American Television*, rev. ed. (New York: Oxford University Press, 1982).

2. Stanley G. Robertson, paper presented at "A National Conference on Black Families and the Medium of Television," University of Michigan, Ann Arbor, Spring, 1982.

3. "TV Reviews," *Variety*, 23 March 1988, 110.

4. Bishetta Merritt, "The African American Male as Undercover Agent on Primetime Television," a paper presented at the Speech Communication Association Convention, San Francisco, California, November 1989.

5. See: Paula Matabane (1987); "Subcultural Experience and Television Viewing," in *Television and Its Audience*, ed. P. Drummond and R. Paterson (London: BFI Publishing); Paula Matabane, "Television and the Black Audience: Cultivating Moderate Perspectives on Racial Integration," *Journal of Communication* no. 4 (1988): 38, 21–33; Robert Sklar, *Prime Time America* (New York: Oxford University Press, 1980); Melvin Moore, "Black Face in Prime Time," in *Small Voices and Great Trumpets*, ed. B. Rubin (New York: Praeger 1980); Nancy Signorelli, "Content Analysis: More Than Just Counting Minorities," in *In Search of Diversity*, ed.

Howard Myrick (Washington, D.C.: CPB (1981); J. Fred MacDonald, *Blacks and White TV: Afro-Americans in Television Since 1948* (Chicago: Nelson-Hall, 1983).

6. Sterling Brown divided the range of black character types in American literature into seven categories: the contented slave, the wretched freedman, the comic Negro, the brute Negro, the tragic mulatto, the local-color Negro, and the exotic primitive. Donald Bogle, *Toms, Coons, Mulattoes, Mammies and Bucks: An Interpretive History of Blacks in American Films* (New York: Viking Press, 1973); and "Marriages are Made in Heaven," from "The Beulah Show," Video Images, Video Yesteryear, Sandy Hook, Connecticut. "The Beulah Show" was withdrawn three years after it premiered, when black pressure groups like the NAACP voiced objections to its demeaning portrayals of African Americans.

7. Thomas Cripps, "Amos 'n' Andy and the Debate over American Racial Integration," in *American History/American Television: Interpreting the Video Past*, ed. John E. O'Connor (New York: Frederick Ungar Publishing Company, 1983), 33–54. See also "Sapphire's Sister," from "Amos 'n' Andy" in the Motion Picture, Broadcasting and Recorded Sound Division, Library of Congress; E. T. Clayton, "The Tragedy of Amos 'n' Andy," *Ebony* 16 (October 1961): 70; and Arnold Shankman, "Black Pride and Protest: The Amos 'n' Andy Crusade," *Journal of Popular Culture* (Fall 1978). In Thomas Cripps's *Black Film as Genre* (Bloomington, Ind.: Indiana University Press, 1978), he notes that, in the midst of serious debates about the demeaning portrayals of African Americans on "Beulah" and "Amos 'n' Andy," in 1953 New York's WOR-TV aired a series that at one point starred classical actor William Marshall in the title role of "Harlem Detective." Black pressure groups busy with concerns about denigrating images did little to help keep this positive image on the air, and the series was quickly canceled.

8. MacDonald, *Blacks and White TV*, 40, 48–50.

9. See Les Brown, *The Business Behind the Box* (New York: Harcourt Brace Jovanovich, 1971), 291–94.

10. Michael J. Arlen, *The View From Highway 1: Essays on Television* (New York: Farrar, Straus and Giroux, 1976), 53–66.

11. Neil Vidmar and Milton Rokeach, "Archie Bunker's Bigotry: A Study in Selective Perception and Exposure," *Journal of Communication* 24 (1974): 36–47.

12. Monica O'Donnell, ed., *Contemporary Theatre, Film and Television: A Continuation of Who's Who in the Theatre* (Detroit, Mich.: Gale Research Co., 1984), 1:173–95; Joseph McBride, *Filmmakers and Filmmaking: The American Film Institute Seminars on Motion Pictures and Television* (Los Angeles: J. P. Tarcher, 1983), 22; and Horace Newcomb and Robert Alley, *The Producer's Medium: Conversations with Creators of American Television* (New York: Oxford University Press, 1983).

13. Herbert J. Gans, "Black Poverty as Comedy," *Social Policy* (September/October 1974): 59–60.

14. Melvin Moore, Jr., "Black Face in Prime Time," in *Small Voices and Great Trumpets: Minorities and the Media*, ed. Bernard Rubin (New York: Praeger, 1980), 130–35; William Henry, "The Jeffersons: Black Like Nobody," *Channels* (March/April 1983), and Todd Gitlin, "Primetime Ideology: The Hegemonic Process in Television Entertainment," in Horace Newcomb, ed., *Television: The Critical View*, 3d ed. (New York: Oxford University Press, 1982), 426–77.

15. Eugenia Collier, "Black Shows for White Viewers," *Freedomways* 14, no. 3 (1974): 212–15.

16. Herman Gray, "Back in the Bighouse: Black Male Images in Prime Time Situation Comedies," a paper presented at the Popular Culture Association Annual Meeting, Toronto, Canada, 1984, 41–50.

17. Cf. H. Lewis, "Child Rearing Among Low Income Families," in *Poverty in America*, ed. L. A. Ferman et al. (Ann Arbor, Mich., 1965); Arnold Rose, *The Negro in America: The Condensed Version of Gunnar Myrdal's "An American Dilemma"* (New York: Harper & Row, 1964).

18. See Lerone Bennett, Jr., *Before the Mayflower: A History of Black America* (Chicago: Johnson Publishing Co., 1989), for more details about American slavery and the infamous middle passage, where so many Africans died before ever reaching the New World.

19. "The Talent That Refused to be Denied," *Ebony* (August 1982): 102–8. Perceptions about "Gimme a Break" were obtained from students in the author's classes at Howard University and at Coppin State College, 1981–87.

20. Telephone interview by author with Thad Mumford, executive producer of "A Different World," October 1989.

21. Lawrence Christon, "Dinner Gave Cosby Taste for Laughs," *Calendar*, Sunday, 9 May 1982, 80–81. Sally Bedell Smith, "Cosby Puts His Stamp on a TV Hit," *New York Times*, Sunday, 18 November 1984. According to network news, "The Cosby Show" was a favorite in countries such as England, Japan, and even South Africa; this was at a time when South Africa was struggling with severe racial turmoil because of its apartheid stance. Gary Dub, "Bill Cosby Ranks High on Personality List, " *The Tennesseean*, Friday, 1 March 1985. Jay Sandrich, personal conversation the author had with the director of many programs in the series. Richmond, Virginia, July 1986.

22. Georgia's governor, Herman Talmadge, assailed "The Ken Murray Show," "The Clifton Fadiman Show," and "The Arthur Godfrey Show" because they violated the southern tradition that called for separation of the races. Godfrey and CBS-TV defended their right to pick performers for their talent rather than for their race. Ken Murray and Clifton Fadiman continued to have black performers as guests. For further discussion, see "Georgia's Talmadge Assails Mixed TV Shows," *Jet*, 17 January 1952, 63, and "Television: Negro Performers Win Better Roles in TV Than in any Other Entertainment Medium," *Ebony* 5 (June 1950): 22.

23. Marilyn Fife, "Black Images in American TV: The First Two Decades," *The Black Scholar* 6, no. 3 (November 1974): 9; "TV Make Up Lady, " *Ebony*, February 1949, 27; and "TV Floor Man," *Ebony*, April 1954. White entertainer Martha Raye, in a January 1954 article in Ebony, wrote about what Harlem had taught her.

24. See Todd Gitlin, "Prime Time Ideology: The Hegemonic Process in Television Entertainment," in Newcomb, ed., *Television*, 426–77; MacDonald, *Blacks and White TV*, 40, 48–50, and Nat King Cole, "Why I Quit My TV Show," *Ebony*, February 1985, 30.

25. Gitlin, "Prime Time Ideology," 426–77; Cole, "Why I Quit," 30.

26. The Ebony Success Library, *1000 Successful Blacks*, vol. 1 (Nashville, Tenn., Southwestern Co., 1973); Eileen Southern, *The Biographical Dictionary of African American Musicians: The Encyclopedia of Black Music* (Westport, Conn.: Greenwood Press, 1982); Marjorie Dent Candee, *Current Biography—1956* (H. W. Wilson Co., 1956).

27. Robert Staples, "Roots: Melodrama of the Black Experience—Forum: A Symposium on Roots," *The Black Scholar* 8, no. 7 (May 1977): 37; and MacDonald, *Blacks and White TV*, 220. See also, Clyde Taylor, "Roots: A Modern Minstrel Show—Forum: A Symposium on Roots," *The Black Scholar* 8, no. 7 (May 1977): 37; Chinweizu, "Roots: Urban Renewal of the American Dream—Forum: A Symposium on Roots," *The Black Scholar* 8, no. 7 (May 1977): 38–39; and Melvin Moore, Jr., "Black Face in Prime Time," 134–35.

28. Robert Chrisman, "Roots: Rebirth of the Slave Mentality— Forum: A

Symposium on Roots," *The Black Scholar* 8 no. 7 (May 1977): 42; Melvin Moore, Jr., "Black Face in Prime Time," 135; William Henry, "The Jeffersons," 37.

29. Floyd Hayes, "A Position Paper Against the Airing of 'Beulah Land,' " a paper circulated to African Americans in colleges and universities and in the broadcast industry, March 1980, 2.

30. Bob Marich, "Hollywood Tough on Minority Progress," *Electronic Media* 11 (August 1983; David Robb, "Casting Report by SAG Shows Minorities Lose," *Variety* 6 (April 1983); U.S. Congress, House Committee on Energy and Commerce. Subcommittee on Telecommunication. *Hearings (Testimony of Peggy Charren).* (Washington, D.C.: Government Printing Office, 19 September 1983), 39.

31. "Who's New and Who's Back on TV," *Ebony*, October 1989, 96–101.

32. Valerie Turner, "Blacks in the Soaps: What's New and What's Next?" *Chocolate Singles* 3, no. 10 (September 1984): 10–13.

33. Both the Screen Actors' Guild (SAG) and the Directors' Guild of America, in a fifteen-month study of casting practices for the period July 1981 to September 1982, reported that: (1) although black people comprised 11.7 percent of the American population, they comprised only 7.4 percent of the SAG and were cast in fewer than 5 percent of all motion-picture and dramatic prime-time television roles; (2) black women (12 percent of the female population) were cast in 5.7 percent of roles available to women; (3) black men had 5.8 percent of the leading roles, compared to 89.8 percent for white males; (4) blacks were cast in less than 5 percent of all motion-picture and dramatic prime-time television roles; and (5) only ten black actors/actresses in the SAG earned more than $50,000 per year, while 312 whites earned more. In addition; a 1980 WGA report disclosed that, of the 1,540 members working on a weekly basis on television; only four were black persons.

34. Alfred Edmond, Jr., "Companies to Watch in the 1990s," *Black Enterprise*, June 1989, 300–301.

35. Andrew Feinberg, "The Richest Woman on TV? Oprah!" *TV Guide*, 26 August–1 September 1989, 2–7.

36. Turner "Blacks in the Soaps."

37. Michael R. Winston, "Racial Consciousness and the Evaluation of Mass Communications in the United States," *Daedalus* 3 (Fall 1982): 171–82.

6 PUBLIC TELEVISION

JANNETTE L. DATES

Public television, conceived as alternative programming to serve needs and interests not met by the commercial industry, has consistently failed to address the concerns of African American groups. For the most part, for nearly twenty-five years public television merely perpetuated the imagery of African Americans solidly established by the dominant culture. From the 1960s, when the system was vested with authority by federal government sponsorship and was funded through the public purse, public broadcasters were primarily concerned with audiences and ratings. Therefore they demonstrated little interest in working with minorities to assist them in diversifying the images of such groups. Though substantial rating figures were to elude "the fourth network" consistently, the negative effect of audiences who *failed* to watch it compelled public television to abandon the narrow markets it originally had been designed to serve. African Americans repeatedly appealed to the system for redress of grievances they harbored because of this neglect, but they were unable to penetrate the system in any viable way until well into the 1980s.

More than with other mass media systems, African Americans attempted to force the issue and insist that public television meet their media needs. During the 1980s some progress was made in this regard, as measured by programming and employee levels. The effects were still unclear, however. Scholars such as Gramsci, Hall, and Gandy have addressed some of the problems in their works. They have observed that the ruling class functions as thinkers and as producers of a society's ideas and that, as a result, the media increase the information and knowledge gaps between the less and better educated and thus between the races. Public television tended to attract the empowered and the well educated, reinforcing knowledge and information for this group, while the poorly educated watched fewer educational programs. Thus, public television would have had to exert a herculean effort to generate interest in its programming among minorities, who were most often found among the less educated group. For many years public broadcasters did not make this effort.

For years, therefore, public television fell in tandem with other established media; and, again, white cultural influence and control was pitted against African American culture. There was black resistance in this cultural war over African American images, just as there was black accommodation to white domination. Unlike the case with commercial television, however, by the late 1980s several viable programming alternatives had been developed and established in public television, by blacks, to counter the dominant culture's images of the group. In addition, there were significant opportunities for minority employment, even in mid-level decision making.

The Early Years

The passage of the Civil Rights Act of 1964 kindled hope among black Americans that they would at last be allowed to go as far as their talents and abilities would take them. "Civil Rights," "Black Power," "We Shall Overcome," and "Affirmative Action" were terms and slogans used by activists to right some of the wrongs African Americans had endured during the years of oppressive slavery and segregation. But during the sixties, at the height of the civil rights movement, when attention was focused almost daily on discrimination against African Americans in jobs, education, and housing, and when commercial television featured civil rights issues on news programs and documentaries, the educational broadcasting community, like the film, radio, recording, and commercial television industries that preceded it, consistently ignored minorities in both employment and programming. The report of the National Advisory Commission on Civil Disorders, often referred to as the Kerner Commission Report, focused on the causes of violence in America and singled out the media as one of the causes of discontent among the black populace. This report and the death of Dr. Martin Luther King, Jr., accelerated interest in meeting the need for television programs created by, for, or about African American citizens. Finally, in public television in 1968 two such shows aired.

To African American viewers, they both seemed to sparkle with talent and were relevant to African American interests and concerns. The first, "Soul!," was originally designed to give alienated black people a voice on television in New York City. Ellis Haizlip, the African American executive producer, focused on black artists: rhythm and blues groups such as "The Delfonics" and "The Sweet Inspirations," singers such as B. B. King and Joe Tex, and poets such as Nikki Giovanni and Amiri Baraka. The second show, "Black Journal," was an NET monthly, and then weekly, national program. It started as a four-week summer special in 1968. "Black Journal," the only national black public affairs series on either public or commercial television, for many years faced the almost yearly danger of cancellation. The show had premiered with a white executive producer, Al Perlmutter; under William (Bill) Greaves, the second executive producer, the show won the 1969 Emmy Award for excellence in public affairs television.

Bill Greaves, an African American producer-director who had received media training in Canada, returned to the United States in 1963. He produced television films for the United Nations and formed his own independent video-film company. In 1969, when the black staff rebelled against white control of "Black Journal," Greaves was appointed executive producer. Under his leadership, the program became an incubating center for a generation of young, independent black media producers and directors: St. Claire Bourne, Madeline Anderson, Stan Lathan, Kent Garrett, Tony Brown, Bob Wagoner, Lou Potter, and Horace Jenkins were among the group who hotly debated aesthetic and ideological issues of video programs they wanted to develop. Some of the flavor and excitement of that dialogue was caught by Greaves. For him the black producer in the mass media was an agent and catalyst for social reform and mass mental health improvement—a purifier of emotional and spiritual life. Greaves believed that television was just another word for "jazz" for the black producer. And jazz for the African American was a means of liberating the human spirit. For television to fulfill Bill Greaves's vision of presenting a visually and rhythm-ically stimulating montage to the eye, as jazz was to the ears of black people, programs like "Black Journal" would need regular airing and increased funding.[1] Instead, funding grew more scarce and, in the early 1970s, under the direction of Tony Brown, the series took on a different format and direction.

In June 1970, Tony Brown became executive producer of "Black Journal" and began immediately to cover special events such as the meeting of the Congress of African People, a documentary on Guyana (a newly independent black nation struggling to survive), and a ninety-minute special entitled "Justice," which asked and answered questions about the credibility of a just system for black people in a society where white supremacy was a fundamental belief. "Black Journal" also featured "Black Paper on White Racism," where six black scholars discussed their investigation of racism, a special on the killing of "Soledad Brother" George Jackson, and ninety-minute live specials in which a dozen or so African American speakers of varying views answered questions phoned in by national audiences.

African Americans responded enthusiastically to both "Soul!" and "Black Journal." "Friends of 'Black Journal' " clubs formed to sound the alarm if local stations dropped or capriciously changed the time of the programs. These clubs were instrumental more than once in saving the "Journal" from cancellation. For example, in early 1974, powerful forces in Washington, critical of the anti-Administration attitude of "Black Journal," set the stage for the board of the Corporation for Public Broadcasting to "dump" it. "Friends of 'Black Journal' " formed picket lines outside the Washington, D.C., headquarters, while such diverse groups as the Congressional Black Caucus, the National Newspaper Publishers Association, and the Urban League, along with scores of irate individuals, applied heavy pressure to keep "Black Journal" on the air. The Corporation for Public Broadcasting acquiesced and followed up by unveiling a project designed to move more African Americans quickly into upwardly mobile positions at local public television stations. Upward mobility failed to occur at this juncture despite the project, however, and African Americans inside public broadcasting continued to urge minorities to be vigilant about public television or it would remain almost all white.[2]

Peggy Pinn, program coordinator for "Black Journal" in the sixties, saw the need to establish a training program for African Americans who, she hoped, could later obtain employment within the television system, particularly public television. She realized that there were few technically trained black people available to be hired as opportunities arose. In 1968 she set up the Black Journal Workshop, later called the NET Television Training School. It offered instruction in cinematography, editing, and sound recording. Using borrowed equipment and laboratory facilities, Pinn and veteran filmmakers such as Ronald Mitchell, Madeleine Anderson, Bert Gerard, and Charles Stewart, with grants from the New York State Labor Department, offered year-round classes and graduated only a third of the students from the deluge of applications they received. The school grew and developed from 1968 through 1973.[3] It closed down after 1973, and Peggy Pinn began working at Howard University's fledgling School of Communications.

In 1969, the Johnson Foundation, the Kellogg Foundation, and the Corporation for Public Broadcasting funded a conference of the forty-five or so African Americans who were employed in various capacities in public broadcasting across the country. The group met in Racine, Wisconsin, to discuss ways to make the industry more responsive to black Americans. The organization that emerged from that meeting, the National Black Media Producers Association (NBMPA), elected Tony Brown, then a producer at a Detroit public television station, as its president. Established to oversee the improvement of the status of African Americans in the media, the group met sporadically during the next two years but eventually disbanded in 1971. A number of the issues raised by NBMPA and some of its members later emerged within other national media organizations: for example, Black Effort for Soul in Television and the National Black Media Coalition.

In 1965, in the article, "Is Educational Broadcasting Segregated?," David Berkman, a white educational broadcaster, noted that of the sixteen hundred persons attending the 1965 National Association of Educational Broadcasters (NAEB) convention, no more than five were blacks. Both in the article and at the conference, Berkman called upon fellow educational broadcasters to catch up with the racial realities of 1965 and try to recruit talented blacks into their industry. He believed that part of the reason for the reluctance of broadcasters to address and attempt to solve the problem of minority participation in educational broadcasting stemmed from the leadership role southerners played in the organization's growth. He cautioned NAEB members that they would be vulnerable to charges of de facto segregation unless they took immediate action. Berkman noted that discrimination is morally offensive and conflicts "with both the spirit and the letter of the Civil Rights Act's education title." The NAEB was unresponsive. In his 1969 article on the same topic, Berkman again took the NAEB to task, this time for entering "a formal comment before the FCC, lauding the successful efforts of educational broadcasting to insure equal employment and job advancement opportunities for minority group members. Yet during that very week, the NAEB was compiling data which conclusively showed that educational broadcasting was exercising the most racist, exclusionary personnel practices of any class of educational employer in America." Again the NAEB was unresponsive to Berkman's charges.[4]

That same year, two African American members of the NAEB (board member Laymond Robinson and regular member Lionel Monagas) presented a resolution from the floor during the membership meeting at the annual NAEB convention in Washington, D.C. It resolved that an office of minority affairs be established within the NAEB to encourage, support, and act as a clearinghouse and public broadcasting job placement center for African Americans and other minorities. The resolution was passed by the membership. Public broadcasting thereafter took a step toward more participation by African Americans in the industry in the 1970s.[5]

The 1970s

Public broadcasting in this country consisted of licensed local public radio and television stations. The industry also included the Corporation for Public Broadcasting (CPB)—the steward for most federally allocated money—the Public Broadcasting Service (PBS), the National Association of Public Television Stations (NAPTS), National Public Radio (NPR), American Public Radio (APR), and the National Federation of Community Broadcasters (NFCB). Together, they provided networking, distribution, production, or representation services to local stations. Funds for public broadcasting came from private sources (listeners, viewers, businesses, foundations, and so on); state and local governments; and the federal government, through CPB, the National Endowment for the Arts, the National Endowment for the Humanities, and the National

Science Foundation. The Public Broadcasting Act of 1967 authorized these various agencies to develop noncommercial radio and television programming for the American people.[6]

The Office of Minority Affairs (OMA) of the NAEB was opened in September 1970. It was directed by Lionel Monagas from 1970 through 1973 and by Arthur Cromwell from 1973 until its demise in 1976. It was the only nationally organized effort to recruit and place minorities in public broadcasting positions throughout the country. OMA's initial effort was to place African Americans on the board of directors of NAEB and the other national public media organizations based in Washington, D.C. The effort was successful. For example, attorneys Clifford Alexander and Frankie Freeman joined sole black board member Laymond Robinson on the NAEB board at the annual board meeting in 1970. OMA had complete control of its budget (funded by NAEB, the John and Mary Markle Foundation, and the CPB) and controlled its own operations, reporting its actions directly to the NAEB board of directors. Of particular importance to its autonomy, the OMA was accountable for its activities to African American and other minority members of the educational broadcasting community and was not questioned by other entities within the NAEB.[7]

Criticism of public broadcasting surfaced on several fronts in the early seventies. President Richard Nixon's White House expressed its displeasure through announcements from its Office of Telecommunications Policy. The president vetoed a two-year funding bill for public broadcasting and, as a result, public broadcasting had to seek yearly funding. Confusion and conflict over institutional roles arose from the process by which CPB and PBS were created; a majority of the conflicts were related to program control. In television, a system was designed to resolve the disputes over programming control. It allowed local stations to select and fund national programming and use lay representatives (local station board chairmen) in the support and governance of public television. This system was subsequently called the Station Program Cooperative (SPC) and is discussed later in this chapter.

As previously indicated, between 1952 and 1967 educational broadcasting ignored African Americans in employment practices and program offerings. A few critics occasionally addressed the issue of black participation, whereupon various educational broadcasting entities discussed the need to address the issue and then proceeded to *do* very little. During the seventies, however, public broadcasters consciously worked to become more diversified and reached out for commercially underserved audiences. In addition, minorities had begun to realize how much effect broadcasting could have on their lives. The possibilities of greater control of their own images and possible employment opportunities caused many African Americans to begin paying closer attention to noncommercial broadcasting. After a few minorities had entered this work force, they began to seek higher-level jobs. Very few rose to decision-making levels, however. This led a critic, Les Brown, to question the role of public broadcasting. He asked, "If the service was designed for an elite minority and did not care to reach numbers of people, in what sense was it a public network?" He also wondered whether "public service" was a euphemism for "government supported" programs? Brown believed that public television was interested in prestige and funding and cared little about underserved populations. He believed that the way the system functioned, running a public television station did not mean that one served the public in the fullest sense, but rather the local board of directors, by avoiding controversy and silencing critics of the establishment. He cited KQED in San Francisco and WGBH in Boston as exemplary independent and courageous public television stations. It is probably no coincidence that some of the finest programs offered on PBS by and about African Americans were developed and produced at these stations (Topper Carew's "Say Brother" and "Rebop" at WGBH, and Avon Kirkland's "Up and Coming," produced at KQED).[8]

In the spring of 1971, Lionel Monagas and Tony Brown met with the public television manager's council and representatives of several national public broadcasting agencies to discuss the issue of "institutional racism" as it existed in public broadcasting at that time. Monagas had worked in public broadcasting for more than twenty years, at the National Association of Educational Broadcasters, the FCC, and in commercial and noncommercial broadcast stations on the East Coast. As noted, Brown produced and hosted the television series "Black Journal." Also, he was the first dean of Howard University's School of Communications. Monagas was concerned because there was no "minority representation or black representation within the public television manager's council or among the representatives of NPB agencies or the constituency it represented." He observed that the only input this organization received from black people was when they were specifically invited. There were no African American public television managers. He told the council and representatives that there must be some consideration for the development of more minority programming for national distribution and for local consumption, and that the CPB must address these needs in terms of funding by giving priority to funding of local programs.

Brown observed that "if you are never in a situation where you have at least the counsel or participation of people other than yourselves then all of your decisions will simply perpetuate and maintain what is now." He hoped that the managers could understand why including people other than white people would enhance and benefit the public broadcasting television system. Brown charged that managers of public broadcasting television stations made subjective judgments about African American programs which they did not apply to other programs. For example, shows by and about teenagers or women usually did not reflect white adult male values, attitudes, or behavior patterns, yet such managers accepted programs that addressed these interests because they appealed to a market they felt needed to be served by public broadcasting. On the other hand, Brown believed that these same managers questioned what was said, how things were said, and by whom, when the speakers were black. In effect, they failed to accept African American programming as filling a specific need of a specific market that needed to be served. Brown was asked if white people should also watch black shows such as "Soul!" and "Black Journal." Brown explained that "Black Journal" was developed and produced by, about, and for African Americans, and that if persons from other racial or ethnic groups wished to watch that was all right. He noted, however that viewers should realize that the series was not designed to meet the needs or concerns of any group other than the African Americans.[9]

A 1974 article in *Black Enterprise* magazine noted that there seemed to be little doubt that "blacks . . . failed to get an adequate slice of the pie in commercial television." But the writer also noted that "the portion appears to be exceedingly generous when compared to the meagre crumbs offered by public television, a nonprofit operation receiving the greater part of its financing from the federal government."[10] Many critics of public broadcasting were concerned about the lack of participation of African American and other minority group members in programs offered by the public broadcasting system. The Ford Foundation's grant-making offices regularly reevaluated activities for which they had given support. The foundation's Office of Public Broadcasting, as part of this process, asked Robert C. Maynard, then associate editor and ombudsman of the *Washington Post*, to design a review and analysis of the portrayal of minorities on public television. A panel was appointed to view public television programs and appraise their treatment of minorities.

The panel concluded in its report that public television programs often ignored opportunities to use African American spokespersons, even when they were the most effective advocates of a particular position. The panel believed it was important that public television assist in destroying the stereotyped notion that blacks and other minorities know of nothing else but those things that uniquely concern them. Further, they believed that it was unrealistic to expect one or two shows, produced by and for African Americans, to do the entire job of presenting the African American perspective; in fact, the panel believed that to try to make two shows the sole voice of African American culture distorted the real world. They decided that public television should address itself to a fundamental issue of communications in America: to enrich the quality of the minority environment. The panel believed the issue deserved particularly high priority on the agenda of a publicly supported medium. They called upon public television to "provide information of basic interest to those outside the American mainstream, and make use of people belonging to those groups who needed service most: the non-white, women, adolescents, the elderly and the handicapped."[11]

Like other mass media industries before it, public television had failed to reflect the African American experience. It, too, steadfastly denied African Americans access to this system of communications, as it fell into place by helping the dominant, empowered group to retain its control and influence over the minds of viewers.

In the public television funding process during the 1970s, minorities had little success in obtaining grants to produce series for broadcasting. Carol Lawrence, an independent black producer, received CPB approval for her proposed series entitled "Were You There?," a series of five thirty-minute programs about important African American figures in American history. One delay after the other stalled the project until, finally, five years later, Lawrence received the money to produce the series. She only survived this period because she had another source of income to support her while she awaited the final outcome. Many other independent producers were not able to wait out the system and, discouraged, stopped trying to overcome the many obstacles to airing their creations on public television.

In the late seventies, Charles Hobson, former general manager at WETA-FM in Washington, D.C., became adept at obtaining funds for the production of African American minority programs for public television. In 1979, Hobson helped raise money from the Department of Education to produce "From Jump Street," a thirteen-part series that told the story of black music. It was the first nationally televised public television series that focused on African American contributions to American culture. The $1.7 million series, orginally aired in 1980–81, became one of the most popular series produced by the public broadcast system up to that time. It featured Oscar Brown, Jr., as host and highlighted the talents of Stevie Wonder, Dizzy Gillespie, and Quincy Jones, among others. It eventually spawned a radio series, books, teacher's guides, study guides, and teacher-training seminars. The series aired through the mid-1980s on commercial and public broadcast systems. Hobson subsequently raised money for productions that included "New Perceptions," a one-hour special about television in developing countries; "Spaces," an animated, humorous, music-focused science series designed to interest young African Americans, Hispanics, and Native Americans in the "hard" sciences; and he worked with producers at the British Broadcasting Corporation (BBC), in cooperation with PBS in America, to produce a $2.5 million series entitled "The Africans," hosted by a Black-African scholar.[12] ("The Africans" is discussed later in this chapter.)

Though commercial televison did not accept the numerous proposals introduced by program suppliers for soap operas with an African American storyline until the late 1980s, public television featured a few such series in the 1970s. For example, "Bird of the Iron Feather" appeared on National Educational Television in the early 1970s. It was written by Richard Durham, whose "Destination Freedom" (see chap. 3) had received critical acclaim and awards when it aired on Chicago's WMAQ radio station in the late 1940s. However, the television series was quickly canceled. Another example, "Our Street," was aired locally in Baltimore, Maryland, from 1966 to 1971. It concerned the vicissitudes of a lower-class black family and featured Howard Rollins as a troubled teenager. Rollins later received an Academy Award nomination for his role in the 1981 film "Ragtime," starred in numerous other films and, in the late 1980s, starred with Carroll O'Connor in the commerical television series, based on the 1967 film "In the Heat of the Night," discussed in detail in chapter 5 of this book.

In May 1974, the Station Program Cooperative (SPC) plan was ratified by public broadcasters. This plan involved having local stations bid for national programs and share the cost of producing them with CPB. The SPC was a blow to black programming on public television for a number of reasons. First, placing the decentralized buying power in the hands of local station managers (95 percent of whom were white males) left the African American community with more than 150 entities to convince of the merits of black programs, whereas before the SPC plan there had been only one such entity to convince, PBS. Second, it was difficult for any new series to obtain SPC funds because established series such as "Great Performances" and "Masterpiece Theatre," with their established audiences and known attractiveness to advantaged middle-class viewers, usually got the lion's share of the funds. Finally, votes for programs were on a one-per-station basis. This diluted African American viewer representation in three ways:

1. African Americans tended to live in larger communities. Therefore, since the votes from these communities represented greater numbers of viewers than did the votes from smaller ones, black input was diluted. The Chicago, Illinois, station received the same votes as the Bangor, Maine, station.
2. African Americans were unevenly represented geographically. Therefore, in many markets there was no incentive for a manager to vote for a black program. This would not have been the case if the same number of African Americans had been distributed evenly throughout the country.
3. African Americans were likely to watch black programs with high-viewer intensity per household. The SPC, by considering only the subjective preferences of white station managers, failed to take this factor into account, or to take into

account the absence of alternatives for African Americans on the commercial stations.[13]

For the 1974–75 broadcast season, the SPC offered "Black Journal" and "Black Perspectives on the News" to local affiliates. That year only 39 stations of the 152 broadcast licensees bid on "Black Journal," while 127 bid on "Black Perspectives," a severe drop in use for both series. "Soul!"—a regular on public television before the SPC was initiated—failed to attract a single underwriter. Hartford Gunn, director of PBS, responded to critics of the SPC by stating that the "programs are chosen from a list which the stations themselves have pre-selected, from a list of all programs that were submitted by the stations for possible production. We have a pure process of democratic selection, which is representative of the stations' wishes and desires."[14] He went on to note that the stations' choices were probably not far from what his staff and program committee would have chosen. Gunn failed to recognize that in the public broadcasting system at that time all of the management were white, the majority of the boards were white, and the majority of their subscribers were white. Thus, there was little opportunity for other perspectives to be accepted. Except for "Black Perspectives on the News," no minority-produced series obtained full series funding from the SPC from 1976 through 1978. It is likely that scholars would argue that the behavior of the decision makers in the industry reflected their beliefs, which they conveyed to viewers by their omissions, that African Americans were not important enough to be included in programming, or that dominant ideas should come only from the ruling class.

Until the 1970s, there was no minority representation on the Federal Communications Commission (FCC), the policy-making body for communications for the country. The first African American appointed as a commissioner on the FCC deserves special attention. African American special-interest activist groups, such as "Black Effort for Soul in Television" (BEST) fought tirelessly for years to convince the president and the Congress of the merits of such an appointment. They realized the important role that the FCC plays in establishing policies and regulations that set the course for public television. They had their own candidate in mind and were disappointed by the appointment of Dr. Benjamin Hooks.

Hooks was a minister in the African-Methodist-Episcopal-Baptist Church. He had been a civil rights activist and a respected leader, but he was not actively involved with the broadcast industry prior to this appointment. Disappointment with the Hooks appointment was quickly reassessed, however, as he became a strong advocate for civil rights in the communications industries and a leading supporter of black issues and women's rights concerns. He bullied and bargained with his colleagues on the commission, formed alliances at various points with fellow commissioners such as Nicholas Johnson, and helped make the FCC a powerful, though sometimes reluctant, ally of civil rights causes. Thanks to Commissioner Hooks and his allies, during the 1970s the FCC denied renewals of licenses to stations that were more blatantly discriminatory toward minorities, held minority ownership conferences, and made available tax certificates and distress sales to increase the involvement of African Americans and other minorities in decision-making positions and as owners of broadcasting facilities.

Public television was a particular concern to Hooks. He made his support of public broadcasting conditional upon the recognition by public broadcasters that they had underserved wide areas of the population. He accused public broadcasters of "arrogance" and of concentrating their efforts on the cultured, white cosmopolitans to the neglect of the less fortunate minorities. Styling itself as the electronic version of a Harvard liberal arts course, public broadcasting, Hooks believed, slighted those whose heritage derived from Africa, Latin America, or the Orient. In 1975, he urged that the congressional oversight committee establish a PBS accountability committee to submit semiannual reports on minority programming and employment. This suggestion went largely ignored.[15]

The Corporation for Public Broadcasting established a task force in the 1970s to address the concerns raised by African Americans about public broadcasting and their group, as targeted consumer and practitioner. CPB issued a report by the advisory panel entitled "Essentials for Effective Minority Programming." This report noted that the vast majority of all public broadcasting programs should be special interest programs, otherwise public broadcasting would lose its unique status as compared with commercial broadcasting. Audiences for special interest programming could include "women and men, and range from children to the elderly, from the atheist to the devout; from the mentally handicapped to the intellectual elite; and from the affluent to the disadvantaged minority." The report stated that those who presently received the least from public broadcasting were among the most disadvantaged in U.S. society: Native Americans, and Americans of African, Asian, and Hispanic racial or ethnic origins.   The report recommended that public broadcasting emphasize the positive elements of life and focus on authenticity and diversity within the minority communities; provide exposure to the diverse cultural lifestyles among minorities, and reflect, in a positive sense, the realism of life in local and regional minority communities; focus on the development of goal-oriented programs that motivate, as well as instruct, and lend themselves to the specific needs of minorities; and address and place in the proper perspective those issues that affect the lives and communities of minorities.[16]

In 1976, the House Communications Subcommittee of the Interstate Commerce Committee heard testimony from Black Caucus member Louis Stokes (D-Ohio) about the "grossly inadequate compliance with and enforcement of equal employment opportunity and related federal anti-discriminatory laws within the public broadcasting industry."[17]   CPB responded to Stokes's charges by organizing a task force to study the situation again.   "The Task Force on Minorities in Public Broadcasting" officially convened in February 1977 and issued its report in November 1978.[18]   The following are some of the observations contained in the report, "Formula For Change."

1. National minority programming (that is, programming by and about minorities) was seriously deficient.

2. PBS and NPR both had appalling records with respect to minority programming.

3. Since its inception in 1974, the Station Program Cooperative (SPC) had 811 program offerings submitted for funding by local public television stations.   Of this number, 87 (or 10 percent) were minority or multicultural programs.

4. Sixteen percent (26 of 160) of the public television licencees had no minority employees.   A review of the licensees' top three job categories (officials, managers, and professionals) showed that 59 percent (or 108) of the 184 public radio licensees and 33 percent (52) of the 160 public television licensees had no minority staff at these levels.

5. The scarcity of minority programs could be attributed directly to the insufficient number of minorities employed in public broadcasting, particularly in decision-making positions. For example, of the 26 major programming decision makers (officials and managers) at NPR, PBS, and in CPB's television and radio activities departments, only one (at NPR) was a member of a minority. In contrast, minorities were overrepresented in the office/clerical job categories in the programming departments of the three national organizations.

6. There were few minority-controlled public broadcast stations in the United States. Only 18 of the 471 stations (195 radio and 276 television) were minority-controlled public broadcast stations. Four radio and seven television stations were located outside the continental United States (for example, Alaska, Guam, Hawaii, Puerto Rico, and the Virgin Islands). This meant that only six of the ten minority-controlled public radio stations and only one of the eight minority-controlled public television stations were located within the continental United States. The television station was WETV-TV, licensed to the Atlanta, Georgia, school district, which had a black majority on its board of education.

Seventy "key recommendations" were included in the report, some of which were:

1. that continuance of long-range federal funding be contingent upon public broadcasting's "significant progress toward equitable minority hiring, placement, and programming practices";

2. that CPB, NPR, and PBS controlling boards reflect the diversity of minorities in the U.S.A.;

3. that CPB fund a minority-controlled and programmed transponder;

4. that funds be budgeted at the national and local levels specifically for minority programming;

5. that these three organizations insure that nationally distributed minority programming be equal to the percentages of U.S. minorities;

6. that no licensee (such as state ETV commissions) be allowed to control more than four transmitters;

7. that channels in markets with minority populations of more

than 20 percent be shared by their present licensee with minority-controlled licensees.[19]

The board of directors of CPB responded in November 1979 to this November 1978 report, at which time it failed to address more than one-third of the key recommendations or the decision-making policies that would have implemented the recommendations. The chairpersons of the subcommittee of the task force dissolved the task force in March 1980, reporting that "the continued unwillingness and apparent refusal of public broadcasting entities to effectively address corrective actions to historical discrimination and racism within the industry, constitutes a blatant disregard for the principles of justice and public broadcasting's legislative mandates."[20]

As can be seen, during the 1970s the various entities within the structure of public broadcasting repeatedly studied problems and issues related to minority participation in the system, and they issued numerous reports. However, they consistently failed to take meaningful action or to make substantive changes to encourage minority participation in their operation. In an article in *Black Enterprise*, Udayan Gupta, a freelance writer, asked the rhetorical question "how public is public television?" and answered that it was not, because he believed that an "old boy" network had screened out minorities in hiring, programming, and funding. He noted that PBS and CPB, at the national level, did not have a *single* black or minority person in a primary decision-making position. On the local level, Gupta noted, there was reason for a degree of optimism, since at least two stations—KCET-TV in Los Angeles and Howard University's WHMM-TV—each had a minority manager. Gupta also noted that the 1978 Public Telecommunications Financing Act made the Department of Health, Education, and Welfare responsible for equal employment opportunity in federally funded broadcasting. The agency stipulated that EEOC guidelines apply to all public broadcasting stations and implemented affirmative action programs. However, the conservative Reagan administration in the White House during the 1980s did not feel compelled to follow through on this act.[21] In the 1980s, partially as a result of the consistent, focused pressure by key individuals, writers, and the groups cited above, public television would become more responsive to minority interests in programming and employment. Inroads would, at last, be made for fuller African American participation in the industry during this era.

The 1980s

An overview of black programs, as reported by the Public Broadcast System (PBS) for the period 1981–88, reveals the following:

1981	1982	1983	1984	1985	1986	1987	1988	(Jan. to June)
56	85	106	131	109	120	86	51	

After the peak year of 1984, there was a declining trend in the number of black-oriented programs offered viewers, partly because public television was in trouble generally. Strong competition from cable systems and independent commercial television stations had begun an erosion of the already low numbers of viewers. In 1987, the last full year reported by PBS by this writing, a dismal eighty-six programs were black-oriented, a mere thirty more than when the decade began.

By the 1980s in general, PBS was increasing the number of its minority viewers. (See tables 6.1, 2, and 3.) For example, in a four-week period in March 1989, nearly three-quarters (72.4 percent) of all African American households watched some public television, although most of the programs watched were children's programs. By comparison, about 80 percent of non-African American households watched some public television during that period.[22] The 72.4 percent figure represented an increase in minority viewing, particularly because of the increased reception capability of PBS channels in the nation's urban areas where many African Americans were to be found.

Table 6.1   Top 32 PBS Programs among Nonwhite Households (Ranked by Total/cumulative Audience)*

Rank	Title	Rating (%)	Nonwhite households (in thousands)	Telecast date
1	Amer. Playhouse: "A Raisin in the Sun"	19.1	——	2/89
2	Great Performances: "Purlie"	16.2	1,980	1984
3	Amer. Playhouse: "Go Tell It on The Mtn."	15.0	——	1/85
4	Amer. Playhouse: "For Us, The Living"	14.4	1,740	3/83
5	Amer. Playhouse: "For Colored Girls . . ."	13.5	1,680	2/82
*6	"Lathe of Heaven"	13.4	1,240	1/80
7	"Eyes on the Prize" (pt. 1)	13.0	1,210	1/87
8	Amer. Playhouse: "Native Son"	12.2	1,170	6/88
9	"The Scarlet Letter"	12.0	1,040	4/79
10	"Death of a Princess"	10.8	1,000	2/82
11	"A House Divided: Denmark Vesey's Rebellion"	10.3	1,280	2/82
12	Amer. Masters: "Aretha Franklin"	10.1	990	8/88
13	National Geographic: "The Shark"	9.9	1,240	1/82
14	"Four Days of the Masai"	9.2	1,140	7/81
15	"Martin Luther King, Jr.'s Birthday"	9.1	1,140	1/82
16	Sound Stage: "The Temptations"	8.9	830	7/80
17	"Jazz at the Maintenance Shop"	7.9	730	7/80
18	Non-Fiction TV: "I Remember Harlem"	7.7	740	2/81
19	Great Performances: "Mrs. Reinhardt"	7.7	960	12/81

Table 6.1   (cont.)

Rank	Title	Rating (%)	Nonwhite households (in thousands)	Telecast date
20	Great Performances: "House of Mirth"	7.4	920	11/81
21	NOVA: "Anatomy of a Volcano"	7.3	700	2/81
22	National Georgraphic: "Etosha"	7.2	690	1/80
23	Life on Earth: "The Infinite Variety"	7.1	880	1/82
24	Hall of Fame: "Mr. Lincoln"	7.0	670	2/81
25	"Memories of Eubie"	6.9	640	1/80
26	National Geographic: "Great Whales"	6.6	560	2/78
27	National Geographic: "Dive to . . . Creation"	6.4	590	1/80
28	"Live from the Grand Ole Opry"	6.3	530	3/78
29	"Cosmos"	6.2	530	12/80
30	"Something Spectacular, with Steve Allen"	6.0	580	3/81
31	"Matinee at the Bijou" (3-survey average)	5.9	740	Fall 81
32	National Geographic: "Living Sands of Namib"	5.8	490	3/78

Source: Photocopy of collected data from PBS Research Department, Fall 1989.
* Listed in highest ratings for nonwhite and white households.

Table 6.2   Public Television—Highest Ratings

Rank	Program	Homes (%)	Date
General			
1	"The Sharks," National Geographic	17.4	1/82
2	"The Grizzlies," National Geographic	17.0	3/87
3	"Land of the Tiger," National Geographic	16.5	1/85
4	"Incredible Machine," National Geographic	16.0	10/75
5	"Great Moments with National Geographic"	15.7	3/85
6	"Best of Wild America: The Babies"	14.7	3/87
6	"The Music Man"	14.7	3/85
8	"Lìve from the Grand Ole Opry"	14.6	3/79
9	"Live from the Grand Ole Opry"	14.2	3/80
10	"Lions of Africa," National Geographic	13.8	1/87
Drama			
1	"Death of a Princess"	13.8	5/80
2	"The Sailor's Return"	9.8	1/84
3	"Smooth Talk," American Playhouse	9.3	2/87
4	"The Scarlet Letter" (part 1)	8.6	4/79
5	"Lathe of Heaven"	8.5	1/80
6	"Testament," American Playhouse	8.1	11/84
7	"Life on the Mississippi," Great Performances	7.7	11/80
8	"Flame Trees of Thika," Masterpiece Theater	7.5	1/82
9	"To serve Them All My Days," Masterpiece Theater	7.5	1/82
9	"Sweeney Todd," Mystery	7.3	10/82
9	"The Scarlet Letter" (part 4)	7.3	4/79
Classical Music/Dance			
1	"Classical Ballroom Dancing from Lincoln Center"	8.9	1/87
2		7.9	1/81
3	"Pavarotti/Mehta," Live from Lincoln Center		
4	"Pavarotti Plus!" Live from Lincoln Center	7.6	1/86
5	"The Nutcracker"	7.5	12/82
6	"Danny Kaye," Great Performances	7.3	9/81

Table 6.2   (cont.)

Rank	Program	Homes (%)	Date
7	"John Curry Skates Peter and the Wolf"	7.2	1/82
7	"Aida," Live from the Met	7.2	1/85
9	"Best of Broadway," Great Performances	7.0	5/85
9	Gala of Stars (part 2)	7.0	10/83
9	"Sutherland, Horne, Pavarotti," Live from Lincoln Center	7.0	3/81
Public Affairs			
1	"Shoah" (part 1)	9.8	4/87
2	"Unauthorized History of the NFL," Frontline	9.2	1/83
3	"Roots of War," Vietnam: A Television History	8.7	10/83
4	"Hiroshima Remembered"	8.3	8/85
5	"Death of a Porn Queen," Frontline	8.2	6/87
6	"Democratic Presidential Debate"	8.0	1/84
7	"Program for Parent-Child Sexual Abuse"	7.4	9/84
8	"Memory of Camps," Frontline	7.2	5/85
9	"The Real Stuff," Frontline	7.1	1/87
10	"Tet 1968," Vietnam: A Television History	7.0	11/83
11	"Visions of Star Wars," Nova/Frontline Special	6.8	4/86
11	"The First Vietnam War," Vietnam: A Television History	6.8	10/83
13	"88 Seconds in Greensboro," Frontline	6.7	1/83
14	"The Earthquake Is Coming," Frontline	6.6	2/87
15	"Shoah" (part 2)	6.5	4/87

Source: Phillip S. Cook, Douglas Gomery, and Lawrence Lichty *American Media* (Washington, D.C.: The Wilson Center Press, 1989), 235–36.

Note: About 57 percent of all households watched public television every week in 1988—up from 38 percent in the past decade. During the same period, the percentage of households watching public television every week in prime time increased from 20 to 34 percent. The programs above are ranked according to percentage of homes viewing.

Table 6.3   PBS Minority Programs by Cumulative Audience (in thousands)

Program/Episode	Date	Average (%)	Audience
*"Soul"	11/74	—	—
*"Harlem Voices/Faces"	10/75	0.8	560
"Indian Summer"	10/75	0.8	560
"Closing the Gap"	10/75	—	—
"Bill Russell Raps"	10/76	0.8	570
"Indian Summer"	10/76	—	—
"My Father Calls Me Son"	10/76	1.1	780
"Indian Summer"	09/77	—	—
*"Men of Bronze"	05/78	1.0	730
"A Day to Remember"	08/78	0.7	510
*"Black Caucus"	10/78	0.5	370
"American Indian Artists"	02/78	—	—
"I Sought My Brother"	06/79	0.5	370
"The Japanese Full Moon Lunch"	06/79	0.7	520
"Prime Time Elderly"	07/79	—	—
*"Memories of Eubie"	01/80	1.5	1,140
"Dateline Copenhagen (Woman)"	09/80	—	—
"Festival of Hands"	05/81	1.2	930
"Pueblo Presenre"	10/81	—	—
*"M. L. King, Jr., Birthday"	01/82	1.5	1,220
*"I Remember Harlem"	01/82	—	—
*"House Divided: Denmark Vesey"	02/82	2.2	1,740
*"American Play: "For Colored Girls"	—	2.6	2,120
"Elizabeth"	03/82	0.7	570
"Bad Moon Rising: Chinese American 2nd Century"	04/82	1.2	980
"Mitsuye and Nedlie"	04/82	—	—
	07/82	—	—
*"Frederick Douglass"	02/83	1.0	830
"Miles of Smiles"	02/83	0.5	420
*"Voices of Our People"	02/83	0.6	500
"Beyond Blindness"	03/83	—	—
"Carnival Miami"	04/83	—	—
"There But for Fortune"	06/83	—	—
"Voices of Native Americans"	04/83	0.6	500
"Closing Door"	06/83	0.8	670
"Latinos: Growing Force"	—	—	—
*"National Urban League Conference"	08/83	0.6	500

Table 6.3   (cont.)

Program/Episode	Date	Average (%)	Audience
*"Never Turn Back: Hamer"	10/83	—	—
"To Be Ourselves"	12/83	—	—
"I'll Fly Away"	12/83	1.3	1,090
"Nkuleleko Means Freedom"	02/84	—	—
*"Gotta Make This Journey: Sweet Honey in the Rock"	02/84	0.5	420
*"Bearden Plays Bearden"	02/84	—	—
"The Sailor's Return"	01/84	9.8	8,210
*"GP: Ellington: Music Lives"	02/84	3.1	2,600
*"GP: Purlie"	03/84	6.9	5,780
"Low 'n' Slow"	07/84	1.7	1,420
"Little People"	07/84	8.5	7,120
"Fritz Scholder"	08/84	—	—
"Great Spirit within the Hole"	08/84	—	—
"New Capitalists: Economics in Indian Country"	10/84	—	—
*"Fade Out: Erosion of Black Images"	01/85	—	—
"The Skin Horse"	10/85	2.4	—
*"Ossie and Ruby"	—	2.5	2,060
*"Martin Luther King: Dream and the Drum"	01/86	—	2,150
*"Bubblin' Brown Sugar"	02/86	2.3	1,980
"Trouble on Big Mountain"	03/86	1.3	1,120
"It's Up to Us"	08/86	—	—
"Diggers"	08/86	4.1	3,520
*"In Remembrance of Martin"	01/87	2.4	2,100
*"Eyes on the Prize: No Easy Walk" (pt. 4)	02/87	5.2	4,540
*"Eyes on the Prize: Awakenings" (pt. 1)	02/87	4.5	3,930
*"Eyes on the Prize: Fighting Back" (pt. 2)	02/87	4.1	3,580
"Eyes on the Prize: Ain't Scared of Your Jails" (pt. 3)	02/87	4.1	3,580

Table 6.3 (cont.)

Program/Episode	Date	Average (%)	Audience
"Eyes on the Prize: Is This America?" (pt. 5)	02/87	3.0	2,620
*"Eyes on the Prize: Bridge to Freedom" (pt. 6)	02/87	4.1	3,580
"A League of Their Own"	04/87	1.0	870
"World Without Walls: African Memoir"	04/87	1.8	1,570
"Blind Toms: Story of Thomas Bethune"	08/87	0.8	700
*"American Masters: Negro Ensemble Co."	09/87	1.4	1,240
*"Watch Me Move: (re. black dance)"	09/87	0.8	710
*"Black Champions: Athletes and the Sporting Life"	01/88	1.0	890
*"Chasing Rainbows: Josephine Baker"	02/89	3.6	3,250

* African American–focused program.

Source: PBS Research Department, Fall 1989.

A vast majority of the programs aired by PBS during the 1980s that focused on African Americans or their issues were those produced by Tony Brown Productions (see table 6.4). This production company emerged from "Black Journal," one of the first series in 1968 to air on the public broadcast system. As noted earlier in this chapter, "Black Journal" was continually under threat of cancellation. During the late 1970s and early 1980s, Brown obtained sponsorship for the "Journal" from Pepsi Cola and took it to commercial syndication. After a year or so, he negotiated with PBS and returned to the public broadcasting system, with underwriting by Pepsi Cola and with an established, loyal viewership. During this period, Brown renamed the program "Tony Brown's Journal," and expanded the reach of the company into production of a monthly magazine and other media products, such as films (*White Girl*).

The "Journal" usually examined serious issues regarded as important to black communities across America. Some of them included discussion of blacks killing each other; President Reagan's policies as they affected African Americans; minority students under stress at elite American universities; black cowboys of the Old West; South Africa and apartheid; whether blacks could make it in white corporate America; the need for black colleges in America; and the importance of creating economic growth in the black community.

In addition to Tony Brown, Topper Carew, an independent filmmaker and television producer, also found ways around the barriers usually placed before minority producers in public broadcasting. During the 1980s he was one of the few African American film and television producers who operated a viable program supplier business in Hollywood. In 1974, Carew produced "Say Brother" at WGBH-TV in Boston. He then produced "Rebop," a children's television series that received many national and international awards. In 1977, he received a $3 million grant from the U.S. Office of Education to produce ten one-hour children's movies, entitled "Rainbow Movies of the Week," about communicating effectively across racial and linguistic barriers. Before he left WGBH in 1978, Carew had been promoted to program manager of the station. In 1979, Carew's company, Rainbow Television Workshop (RTW) received $1.3 million from CPB to produce the ten half-hour shows that became "The Righteous Apples" series. The series focused upon a racially mixed singing group struggling toward success in the mainstream of the music industry. They faced problems felt by many adolescents, as well as the additional burdens of minorities.

"The Righteous Apples" was a landmark production. It was the first black, primetime, weekly situation-comedy on PBS and received the largest grant ever for a domestic comedy series. "In telling his tale of a teenage rock group in a newly integrated neighborhood, Carew used music to promote 'multiracial cooperation' that foreshadowed the commercial television version of "Fame."[23] Carew persuaded M&M Products (makers of Sta-Soft Fro, a hair-care product) to underwrite the show, at least in part. This was the first time an African American company had helped finance a PBS program. "The Righteous Apples" was funded by CPB for the 1979–80 and 1980–81 seasons but failed to obtain further support from the Station Program Cooperative after 1981. The cuts in PBS funding by the Reagan administration was blamed by some for the final demise of the series.

Carew's RTW produced the film "D.C. Cab" for Universal Pictures in the early 1980s, and his "Tales in a Golden Groove," an anthology of seven one-hour, family-oriented, dramatic musical specials were also seen on some public television channels. The latter series transformed traditional fairy and folk tales into reality-based musicals conceived in the vein of "Saturday Night Fever" and "Fame." In general, critics gave RTW productions high marks for technical skill, strong story lines, and social value.

Carew believed that black Americans had made a serious tactical error in stressing participation by African Americans in on-camera jobs. He believed there was a serious need for black entrepreneurs to become television suppliers (producers) and for black managers to employ people, thus becoming decision makers in the industry. Carew contended that black entrepreneurs needed aggressively to seek opportunities that would allow them to become television suppliers. He reasoned that if a new series were licensed by a network at a fee of one million dollars per hour for production, and if RTW obtained that contract for a twenty-six-week series, RTW would obtain twenty-six million dollars for operational purposes. This would immediately place RTW among the top five black businesses in *Black Enterprise*'s annual top one hundred listings. If African Americans became suppliers—that is, television film producers of shows—they would create broader opportunities for blacks in the television business. Carew believed that the impact of historical forces often kept the entrepreneurial mind-set from developing within the black community; that the service mentality dominated in many African American communities where few business initiatives were undertaken; and that this was true of black culture in general, and of the production industry specifically. He challenged young African Americans to acquire ownership of television supplier businesses so that they could become decision makers rather than "hired hands." Carew also noted that the African American employment issue was a peripheral concern that was dwarfed by the economics of television production. "Black people should understand," he contended, "that the person who hired Robert Guillaume, for example, to play the part of Benson could fire Guillaume whenever he chose to do so." However, if

Guillaume owned a part of the series or the company which produced it, he was in a stronger position financially.

In his discussion of the lack of African American participation in the television production industry, Carew saw the negligible number of African Americans in key positions at the networks (commercial and public) as a major problem. He argued that the scarcity of African Americans among network program development people, coupled with the general attitude that failed to support black entrepreneurship, made it extremely difficult for blacks to participate in the industry. He believed, however, that the networks were in critical need of African Americans among their development staff, to help blacks and other minority producers weave their way through a system that consistently viewed deviation from the white norm in a negative light. Carew saw pitfalls that producers needed to avoid: the separation from black culture and black audiences, concern about placating critics, and a tendency to allow creativity to falter because of the aforementioned. He believed that all producers should be challenged to balance entertainment and enlightenment creatively, to design ways of mainstreaming black material, to conquer fears because of being black, and to encourage the entrepreneurial spirit.

In addition to the nonprofit company Rainbow Television Workshop, Carew and his wife owned a profit production operation named "Topo Alto." Though Carew hoped to produce shows for commercial television and constantly submitted proposals, through the mid- 1980s he remained just outside the circle of producers who dominated the industry.[24] In the 1989–90 season, he acted as executive producer for a situation-comedy on commercial television.

Ossie Davis and Ruby Dee, one of the most celebrated husband-and-wife acting teams in America, could list credits for their creative works in theater, film, and the commercial electronic media. The duo also had impressive credits in public television. In 1980, Davis and Dee formed their own production company, Emmalyn II Productions. The company set out to develop television programs and films produced primarily for PBS. Davis wrote the powerful, highly acclaimed PBS docudrama "For Us the Living: The Medger Evers Story," about the slain civil rights activist.

"For Us the Living: The Medger Evers Story" was aired by the Public Broadcasting System in 1983. It starred Howard Rollins as

Evers and Irene Cara as his wife. As noted earlier, Rollins had been nominated for an Oscar (in 1981) for his portrayal of Coalhouse Walker in the film *Ragtime*. Even with an Oscar nomination to his credit, between 1981 and 1988 he rarely found good roles. Irene Cara had a large role in "Roots I," playing Alex Haley's mother, and she then starred in the film *Fame*. She, too, had trouble finding television and film roles. "For Us the Living: The Medger Evers Story" was turned down by all three commercial networks before PBS agreed to air it. It won high critical acclaim and good ratings. At this point, critics attacked the commercial television system for consistently failing to air programs with African American themes and applauded public television.

Davis and Dee's most celebrated production was "With Ossie and Ruby." Half-hour shows built around the hosts' fascination with storytelling, each had a different format and style. For example, one program told a ghost tale and featured Dee, Davis, and white actor E. G. Marshall, while another addressed the political commentary found in Gil Scott Heron's music. The series was widely acclaimed by critics and viewers. The *New York Times* named the series one of the ten best television programs of the 1981–82 season. The series was first coproduced with PBS station KERA in Dallas and then by PBS station WHMM-TV (Howard University's Channel 32) in Washington, D.C. "With Ossie and Ruby" received funding from the Alcoa Corporation and from the Corporation for Public Broadcasting. Davis and Dee believed their record spoke for itself and questioned why major film studios and networks were still reluctant to accept their proposals, even after such successes. They thought that whites who had fought against the same type of odds and won would have merited production rights to a two-hour TV movie, at the least. For the 1984 season, Emmalyn II was contacted by the Corporation for Education and Learning to produce two hour-long segments in the twenty-part series "A Walk Through the 20th Century," hosted by Bill Moyers. Davis and Dee were challenged to try something new with this project; they combined the art of storytelling with the science of documentary television. Their segments were well received.

According to PBS records, WNET/WETA was the second-ranked producer of black programming during the 1980s. The predominant number of shows contributing to this count were from the "McNeil/ Lehrer News Hour" when the programs included a subject or guest of special interest to African Americans. In my opinion, although the "McNeil/Lehrer News Hour" may have included segments of black-oriented materials in some of its programs, the series cannot, in good conscience, be considered black programming. The specific "McNeil/Lehrer News Hour" programs were, however, well researched and offered careful analyses of issues concerning African Americans—such as the Urban League's charge that the Reagan administration isolated itself from black Americans—and series features—such as profiles of black artists like Wynton Marsalis, a popular young black trumpeter who played both classical music and jazz.

Among independent producers who produced a large number of programs aired on PBS during this period was Carol Lawrence, mentioned earlier in this chapter. Lawrence finally saw her production "Were You There?" air on PBS, beginning in 1982. The segment "Oscar Micheaux: Film Pioneer" used interviews, film clips, and reenactments to profile Micheaux's works, which were described as films treating African Americans as mature adults in a period when such treatment was an exception among mainstream filmmakers. (See chapter 3 for more details about Micheaux's work.)

WNET, another station listed by PBS as a major producer of black programs, produced "The Dick Cavett Show." As it had the "McNeil/Lehrer News Hour," PBS listed the Cavett show within the black programming group when it devoted itself to black issues or personalities. One show featured an interview with Julian Bond, the Georgia state senator, in which he commented on his political career, the social upheavals of the 1960s, the Carter administration, and the Bakke reverse discrimination case. WNET also produced the highly acclaimed series "The Constitution: That Delicate Balance—Affirmative Action and Reverse Discrimination" in which panelists discussed the constitutional questions raised by a hypothetical case study involving affirmative action at a major university. They debated whether it was appropriate for an institution to use affirmative action to choose among job candidates of equal abilities. WNET, in conjunction with George Miles Productions, also produced a three-part documentary series, "The Different Drummer: Blacks in the Military," that combined archival footage, rare photos, and interviews to trace the history of black participation in the U.S. military from 1862 to the late 1900s.

Another major producer of black programming, WTVS, produced "PBS Latenight," a series that frequently featured guests who discussed black issues. Such guests included civil rights activist Kwame Toure (Stokely Carmichael); actor-director Ossie Davis and actress Ruby Dee; minister, civil rights activist, and politician the Reverend Jesse Jackson; NAACP president Benjamin Hooks; and former Miss America, Vanessa Williams.

WETA's black programs list included "Washington Week in Review," whenever panelists discussed major news events of the past week that related to African Americans. Such subjects included the debate over the proposed holiday to celebrate Martin Luther King, Jr.'s birthday, and the controversy over White House changes in the membership of the Civil Rights Commission. WETA also produced occasional specials such as "Gotta Make This Journey: Sweet Honey in the Rock," featuring a singing group formed in 1974 at a black workshop in Washington, D.C.

WNET and KQED joined forces to produce "A Walk in the 20th Century with Bill Moyers." In one segment, Moyers returned to his hometown to observe social changes in American culture. He interviewed James Farmer, founder of the Congress of Racial Equality (CORE), who had grown up on the black side of the same town. CORE was a civil rights organization of national stature, particularly during the 1960s and 1970s.

WGBH produced "Frontline," a series that documented issues and problems concerning Americans. One such documentary/ discussion focused on Birmingham, Alabama, where a power struggle emerged during the 1984 presidential election primaries as the Reverend Jesse Jackson sought the city's support for his candidacy as the Democratic nominee. WGBH also produced the highly acclaimed "Eyes on the Prize: America's Civil Rights Years," a six-part telecourse series detailing the stories, events, and spirit of the civil rights struggles in America between the years 1954 and 1965.

In 1986, "The Africans," which was developed by Charles Hobson for the Corporation for Public Broadcasting and Great Britain's British Broadcasting Corporation, was introduced as a major new prime-time series and as a telecourse for college credit, including print resources for instructional use. The host of "The Africans" was Dr. Ali A. Mazrui, a native Kenyan, professor of political science at the University of Michigan, and a research professor at the University of Jos, Nigeria. Mazrui guided viewers and students through the Africa of his experience, drawing on the works of scholars throughout the world. "The Africans" examined both cultural conflict and cultural synthesis as it explored the thesis that contemporary Africa is a product of three major influences: indigenous African heritage, the Western and Islamic cultures.[25] The series proved to be highly controversial, and at least one government funding agency withdrew its sponsorship, accusing the producers of an anti-Western bias. Moreover, a conservative national foundation placed advertisements in *Broadcasting* magazine in an attempt to discourage stations from airing the series. "The Africans" aired to a broad audience, probably in part because of the controversy preceding the airings. Matabane and Gandy noted, in their study of audiences for the series, that "The Africans" was not perceived as a program directed only to black viewers, but was expected to be widely viewed by various groups. They contend that the success of the series proves the need for informational diversity in public broadcasting.[26]

In the 1970s and 1980s, CPB established five consortia for funding, producing, identifying, and distributing minority programming for public broadcasting. The five included a consortium for Native Americans (established in 1977), Hispanics (1978), African Americans (1980), Asian Americans (1981), and Pacific Islanders (1981). During the 1980s the National Black Program Consortium (NBPC) was centralized in Columbus, Ohio, and then in Los Angeles under Mega Link, Inc., and Media Forum. It served as a collection, distribution, and archival center for programs produced by, for, and about African Americans. Primarily funded by CPB, the NBPC served as a supplemental programming service to PBS. The NBPC catalog contained new and original products, produced yearly by various entities, and classic programs from earlier years. It encouraged producers and distributors to submit programs and raised funds for producing, marketing, and promoting some of the black programs it obtained.

In 1981, CPB's Department of Human Resources Development (HRD), under the leadership of Mildred Morse, an African American woman with a strong civil rights background, responded to the minority task force report, discussed earlier in this chapter, in its publication, "Public Broadcasting Industry Responses to Minority Task Force Report: A Formula for Change." The response addressed each of the recommendations presented in "A Formula for Change."

Table 6.4   Producers of Public Broadcast Service Black-Focused Programming, 1981–1988

Producer	No. of programs	Producer	No. of programs
Tony Brown Productions	188	WETA/BBC	9
WNET/WETA	135	PTV Playhouse	6
Independents	74	KTVT	5
WETA	44	Documentary	
KQED	41	Consortium	3
WNET	38	KCET/WNET	3
WGBH	31	WHA	2
SECA	28	Georgia PTV	2
WTVS	26	WNET/KQED	2
KCET	12	WYES	2
WTTW	11	Iowa PTV	2
WHMM	9	WXXI	2
MCPB	9	KERA	2
Dallas County	9	WNET/WTTW	2

Stations producing one program each

Arkansas ETV	BBC/WNET	Living Design/WNET	KCTA
NBPC/WOSU	Idanha/WNET	WNET/WTTW/KERA	Nebraska ETV
WNYC/Roma	WOSA	KCET/SCETV/WNET	WHMM/B
KPBS	McNeil Lehrer/ WNET	Thames TV/WNET	

Generally, the plans, as presented in this report, showed a creative thrust in attempting to resolve the long-standing impasse between the public broadcasting industry and minority groups. The HRD department sought institutionalization of aspects of the system that could then offer long-term benefits to minorities. The staff at HRD theorized that the projects it developed, if made part of the system, would bring greater rewards to minorities in the long run than would one-shot programs, or even a few-program series. For example, HRD's Advanced Production Forum, later called the Program Enhancement Project, was designed to advise minority producers whose works had been rejected by helping them revise their work so they could obtain funding and air time for their productions. Moreover, their Public Participation Project tapped minority businesses around the country to work jointly with other organizations to build a minority public broadcasting constituency and increase the level of minority participation in public broadcasting. The Department of Human Resources Development encouraged stations to develop outreach programs to attract and invite ethnic groups as listeners and viewers. Evaluations of the effectiveness of these programs had not been completed by 1989 when the department was disbanded. At this point, however, the Department of HRD of the Corporation for Public Broadcasting could argue that it had been instrumental in increasing minority participation in public broadcasting. According to an August 1989 CPB report, between 1977 and 1988, of the 13,568 stations reporting (95 percent of the total number) there had been an 8 percent increase in minority employment, with a 12 percent increase in radio station employment and a 7 percent increase in television station employment. Further, CPB reported that between 1981 and 1989, as a direct result of its encouragement and assistance, minority employment rose to the point where approximately 11 percent of public television employees with authority to make major decisions about programming and production were minorities.[27]

Gramsci, Hall, and others have argued that the cultural and political power of the dominant group ensures that their ideas rule. In keeping with this theory, it should be noted that empowered Americans maintained firm control of public television, still denying African Americans a strong role in the industry as late as the 1980s, when there was a continued decrease in concern by empowered groups about the nation's minorities. By 1989, conservative Republicans had been in control of the executive branch of the American government for nearly a decade. They were able, therefore, to seize the opportunity to appoint Supreme Court justices whose conservative views would alter living conditions for all Americans. In fact, by 1990, the Supreme Court had issued rulings which appeared to reverse many of the civil rights gains of the preceding twenty-five years, some of which affected public broadcasting.

Three other important factors seemed to militate against continued advancement of black participation in public television: (1) Congress seemed poised to emphasize *programming* for minorities in public broadcasting, rather than a continuation of initiatives to increase employment and training; (2) minority groups often failed to voice their concerns to the industry's decision makers. This lack of action increased the perception that minorities were satisfied with the public broadcasting industry; and (3) the CPB determined, from the data it had collected, that minority ownership or control of public television stations might not be the most efficient way to provide service to minorities.   In its July 1989 report, the Corporation for Public Broadcasting noted that minority listeners and viewers responded to "general" programming more than they did to "targeted" programming.   Thus, PBS and CPB planned to involve minority groups, both on and off the air, in the production of general audience programming, while reducing their earlier thrusts toward productions of minority-targeted programs.[28]

As noted earlier in this chapter, in November 1980 Howard University became the first licensee of a public television station (WHMM-TV) on a black campus and the only black-owned public television station in the continental United States.   The station's signal was among the most powerful in the Washington, D.C., market (4.9 megawatts from a directional antenna).   In the 1980s, as a leader in public broadcasting, both as a member of the board of directors of PBS and as President of Howard University, James E. Cheek strongly argued that "the wave of the future for blacks was in the field of communications."   He envisioned the Howard University station as a fertile training ground for students in communications, engineering, fine arts, business, and other fields. He also envisioned WHMM (Howard University Mass Media) as "a communicative drum, not only for black people in the Washington and Baltimore areas, but for black and third world people around the globe."[29]   At the close of the decade the station focused on producing programs for the local market.

Conclusion

In its early years, public television had consistently denied black people opportunities to be involved in the system, just as commercial television had used black humor, music, and dance to enrich its offerings while it stubbornly denied opportunities to groups like African Americans to establish a diversity of views.   In later years, public broadcasting began to open some doors to other groups besides those from the empowered, dominant culture.   This policy allowed the system to begin to live up to its responsibility, as established by the Public Broadcasting Act of 1967: "to make noncommercial television service available to all citizens, in programs of high quality obtained from diverse sources."

By the late 1980s, the public broadcasting system at last included a variety of positive images of diverse groups who were treated as respected, valuable members of society, and it had moved closer to such public interests, particularly black interests, than had its commercial counterpart. Thus, public broadcasting could ask for strong support not only from government and private sources but from the many publics served, including the African American public. African American consumers and television practitioners alike, without dwelling on the negative elements that in the past had prevented their full participation, began to throw their support and interest into public television, hopeful that opportunities would increase to the degree they could eventually become full-fledged participants.

1. Interview with Bill Greaves by the author in February 1984.

2. David Berkman, "Minorities in Public Broadcasting," *Journal of Communications* 30, no. 3 (Summer 1980): 179–88. *Report of the National Advisory Commission on Civil Disorders* (Washington, D.C.: Government Printing Office, 1968), 383. Peter Bailey, "Black Excellence in the 'Wasteland,' " *Ebony* 28:45–53; Bill Greaves, telephone interview by author, June 1982; Sheila Smith Hobson, "The Rise and Fall of Blacks in Serious Television," *Freedomways*, 3d quarter (1974): 185–99; "Blacks and Public TV," *Black Enterprise*, January 1974, 31–33.

3. Peggy Pinn, retired Coordinator for Continuing Education, Howard University, personal interview by author, 1983.

4. Dave Berkman, "Is Educational Broadcasting Segregrated?" *The NAEB Journal* (January–February 1966): 67–70; Dave Berkman, "Inner City," *The NAEB Journal* (November 1969).

5. Lionel Monagas, Director, Franchise Development, Comcast Corporation, personal interview by author, 1983.

6. Donald E. Ledwig, *To Know Ourselves: A Report to the 101st Congress on Public Broadcasting and the Needs of Minorities and Other Groups*, (Washington, D.C.: Corporation for Public Broadcasting, July 1989), 2–3

7. Lionel Monagas, personal interview by author, 1983.

8. Robert Avery and Robert Pepper, "An Institutional History of Public Broadcasting," *Journal of Communication* 30, no. 3 (Summer 1980): 126–38. Gloria Anderson (Commission Chairman), "Essentials for Effective Minority Programming— Sponsored by the Corporation for Public Broadcasting" (May 1974). Les Brown, *The Business Behind the Box* (New York: Harcourt, & Brace, 1971).

9. Lionel Monagas, "Report of the NAEB Office of Minority Affairs on April 1971 Visit of Tony Brown and Lionel Monagas with the Public Broadcast Managers' Council," 1971; and interview with Monagas by author, June 1983.

10. Jacob Wortham, "In with the Big Boys," *Black Enterprise*, September 1974, 6–9.

11. "Replay: Minorities and Public TV—A Critical Appraisal," *Public Telecommunication Review* 2, no. 1 (February 1974).

12. Charles Hobson, Director of Special Projects, WETA-TV, personal interview by author, 1983; and "The Africans" public relations kit.

13. David Honig, Director of Research, National Black Media Coalition, and Assistant Professor, Howard University, personal interview by author, November 1983.

14. Vaughncille Molden, "Telecommunications and Black America: A Survey of Ownership, Participation and Control," (Ph.D. diss., Washington University, 1975); Wortham, see note 9 above; "Inside the Program Cooperative," *Public Telecommunication Review* 2, no. 4 (August 1974); Gloria Anderson, "A Formula for Change: The Report of the Task Force on Minorities in Public Broadcasting," *CPB* (November 1978).

15. Statement of Commissioner Benjamin L. Hooks, *Hearings* (Washington, D.C.: U.S. Government Printing Office, 10 April 1975).

16. Gloria L. Anderson (Commission Chairman), "Essentials for Effective Minority Programming in Public Broadcasting," Corporation for Public Broadcasting, May 1974, 35a–35e; U.S. Congress, House Committee on Interstate and Foreign Commerce, Subcommittee on Communications.

17. U.S. Congress, House Committee on Interstate and Foreign Commerce, *Hearings on the Enforcement of Equal Employment Opportunity and Antidiscrimination Laws in Public Broadcasting* (Washington, D.C.: U.S. Government Printing Office, August 1976), serial no. 94739; see Berkman (n. 1 above).

18. Berkman, "Minorities in Broadcasting." The task force was made up of twenty-eight members, of whom twelve were black, seven Latino, three Asian-American, three nonminority, two Native American, and one Hawaiian. They met eight times in seven cities and had a full time staff of three.

19. Gloria L. Anderson, "A Formula for Change: The Report of the Task Force on Minorities in Public Broadcasting," *Corporation for Public Broadcasting* (November 1978). After this report was published, other black-controlled public radio stations were established, and in 1980 Howard University's public television station (WHMM-TV, channel 32) went on the air. During the 1980s, it was the only television station on a black college campus and the first and only black-owned public broadcast television station in the continental United States.

20. See Berkman (n. 1 above).

21. Udayan Gupta, "How Public Is Public Television?" *Black Enterprise*, April 1980, 47–54.

22. Steve McGowan, *National Audience Handbook: 1987–88 Season in Review*, PBS Research Department, Alexandria, Va: 1988; PBS defines a program as "black" if it contains three of the following five elements while under production: a black producer, a black director, a black executive producer, black talent, or a black-targeted audience; See also Ledwig (n. 5 above), 13–14.

23. Topper Carew, "Rainbow TV Works," public relations brochure, fall 1983, and personal interview, Washington, D.C., July 1983.

24. Ibid.

25. John W. Fuller, "Black Programming on PBS—1981–April 1986," Program Data and Analysis Division of PBS (August 1986); S. Lee Hilliard and Nelson George, "Lights! Camera! Action!" *Black Enterprise*, December 1983, 48–56; "The Africans: An Annenberg/CPB Project," introductory brochure, 1986.

26. Paula W. Matabane and Oscar Gandy, Jr., "Through the Prism of Race and

Controversy: Did Viewers Learn Anything from 'The Africans'?" *Journal of Black Studies* 19, no. 1 (September 1988): 5–6, 14.

27. See Ledwig (n. 5 above), iv; Thomas Fuller, Assistant in the Department of Human Resources Development, CPB, personal interview, December 1983; and Mildred Morse, "Public Broadcasting Industry Responses to Minority Task Force Report: A Formula for Change," a report for the Corporation for Public Broadcasting, April 1981.

28. See Ledwig, (n. 5 above), 43–45.

29. Lon G. Walls, "WHMM-TV: Howard University's Black 'Super Station,' " *Dollars and Sense* 7, no. 4 (October/November 1981): 39–41.

Part Five

SMILIN' FACES TELL LIES:
THE NEWS INDUSTRY

7 PRINT NEWS

JANNETTE L. DATES

An incident that illustrates the difference between the operational modes of reporting on the black community used by the white print media and those of the black print media remains vivid even after a span of years. On a hot summer day in the early 1960s a group of black youngsters in Baltimore, led by a representative of the NAACP, integrated a public swimming pool in a park that blue-collar whites who lived around it regarded as their own special turf and thus off-limits to blacks.

The whites' view of who owned the rights to the park was well known, and rare was the black who attempted to set foot inside, despite the fact that the law said he or she had every right to do just that. Unwilling to accept the status quo, the NAACP announced it would integrate the pool and rounded up a group of black youngsters who lived fairly close to the public facility but who, dissuaded by fear, did their swimming in a pool several miles away, across town. On schedule, several carloads of black youngsters, with their adult leaders, drove up to the park. They had to walk some distance to reach the pool, and on the way they were subjected to curses and jeers from a white mob held at bay by a phalanx of policemen—all white.

Their time in the pool did not last long. With every passing

NOTE: E. Lee Lassiter, assistant professor at Coppin State College and former editor for the *Baltimore News American*, and James D. Williams of the National Association for the Advancement of Colored People contributed to this chapter. Wakeelah Mutazammil, Peter Nwosu, and Andrew Millington, Ph.D. candidates at Howard University, provided research assistance.

343

minute the mood of the mob grew uglier, until the police suggested that for their safety the children should call it quits. They were loaded into police vans and driven to their cars. On the short ride back to their neighborhood, they were followed by the police and several carloads of white teenagers. It was a pleasant day and a number of adults, including the worried parents of some of the children, were outside their homes, seated on the steps, awaiting the children's return. Once the children got out of the cars, the white teenagers followed suit and began a tirade of curses, racial taunts, and invectives. Instead of addressing their attention to the hostile whites, the police used dogs to force all the black people into their homes. This strange, and basically racist, way of restoring order went totally unreported in the white press. It was as though it never happened.

The only newspaper to report the use of dogs in this incident was the black-owned *Baltimore Afro-American*. It was the only voice to protest the action, and eventually the newspaper extracted an apology from the police and a promise that they would do better in the future. This situation was not atypical, for in truth the black press has always seen the black community in a vastly different perspective from that of the white press. And, at the heart of it, this explains the raison d'être for the very existence and continuation of the black press.[1]

The Black Press: The Early Years

The term *black press* is used in this chapter to include newspapers and magazines that are aimed at African American readers and speak to their issues. The term *general press* means publications directed to the general populace and usually erroneously perceived as presenting continuous objective coverage of issues and areas of interest. In reality not at all objective, the general press has been dominated by white Americans who disallow the use of publications under their control for the free expression of alternative views by African Americans. Thus, through the years, unless their views echoed those of the dominant culture, African Americans had no voice in the general press. As in other media, African American responses to this domination alternated between accommodation to white control and resistance to domination. While accommodationists, often unwittingly, marched to the tune played by the dominant culture, resistors among African Americans felt compelled to establish their own black press. Like the other media described in this study, in print journalism black responses to white influence and control this time meant that the black press needed to become— and, in fact, became—an established alternative for expressing African American views. Thus the war over who would provide images of the African American, so important in molding both self-esteem and opinion and setting the public agenda, became the catalyst for instituting a black press.

In the early 1800s newspapers were the primary vehicle of the black press, and their publication dominated the focus of the black press for more than a hundred years. In the middle 1900s, however, other types of periodicals gained popularity with black audiences. By the late 1900s, black magazines had taken over many of the functions that black newspapers had previously claimed for them-selves, particularly as the year 2000 approached. Part of the reason for the increased role of black magazines at this time lay in the declining quality of reporting and commentary in black newspapers. In fact, at this juncture, many black newspapers had become scandal sheets with sensational, screaming headlines and offensive pictures. Moreover, there was limited coverage of events, frequent misprints, outdated formats, smudgy ink, and a general perception that black newspapers were either too radical or too conservative and were thus failing to reflect true views of the black community. People were no longer proud to take black newspapers home to share articles with their families. Many hesitated to encourage their children even to see or read the papers. By the 1980s black newspapers across the country had lost much credibility in African American communities as providers of reliable and enlightened black perspectives and as protectors of black interests.[2]

As the black press lost ground with readers, it also suffered a general loss of economic viability. For, with integration, many black newspapers also lost their "natural" advertisers, black busi-nesses, to the general market press. In addition, many small black businesses had gone under, as black consumers, like their white counterparts, flocked to the major chain stores for their purchases. As their revenue decreased, black newspapers also lost much of their talent to the general market papers, which paid their staff higher salaries and offered them more career opportunities.

The black press, nevertheless, deserves special attention in this book because if it had not existed, there would have been no print medium of communications for African Americans that could instill a sense of community, a feeling of self-worth, or keep alive the often muted struggle to escape, first slavery, and then the clutches of segregation and discrimination. Therefore, this story cannot be told by looking at the black press as it had become in the 1980s— enfeebled to some degree by its own success in helping to create a more integrated society—but by looking first at its past.[3]

Nearly fifty years after America proclaimed herself a nation, the first faint rumblings of the abolition movement were heard in the land. Although a few white people courageously spoke out against slavery, many more were particularly strident in their firm opposition to any rights for the enslaved. Indeed, the animus toward blacks frequently spilled over into print.

Unwilling to allow African Americans opportunities to voice their views about slavery and oppression, the editor of a New York City newspaper launched vicious attacks against blacks, encouraged slavery, and denounced all thought of freedom. Other newspapers were equally racist and unwilling to give African Americans a hearing in their so-called free press. Samuel Cornish and John Russwurm, two brilliant, free black citizens, undertook the herculean task of issuing America's first black newspaper in response to these attacks by white publishers. With their publication, *Freedom's Journal*, Cornish, a young, militant, highly respected Presbyterian minister, and Russwurm, the nation's first black college graduate (Bowdoin College), launched an attack on slavery and its effects. The appropriately titled *Freedom's Journal* made its first appearance 16 March 1827. In the maiden editorial Russwurm set forth the principal reasons why the paper had come into being, reasons that are as pertinent today in explaining the need for the black press as they were in 1827.

> We wish to plead our own cause. Too long have others spoken for us. Too long has the public been deceived by misrepresentations in things which concern us dearly, though in the estimation of some mere trifles; for though there are many in society who exercise toward us benevolent feelings; still (with sorrow we confess it) there are others who make it their business to enlarge upon the least trifle, which tends to the discredit of any person of colour; and pronounce anathemas and denounce our whole body for the misconduct of the guilty one.[4]

Despite such stirring words, *Freedom's Journal* was not to have a long life. Very quickly a difference of opinion developed between Russwurm and Cornish, the former being in favor of the return of blacks to Africa and the latter opposed to colonization. Six months after its debut, Cornish left the paper. Russwurm continued to publish it for another year and then left America to settle in Liberia permanently. Cornish then returned to the paper and, in May 1829, changed its name to *The Rights of All*, which he continued to publish for a short time before that paper also disappeared, in October 1829.

In 1837, Cornish began editing another paper, *The Weekly Advocate*, which later changed its name to *The Colored American*, a publication that remained in business until 1842. A critic wrote of the paper that "its columns were filled with excellently selected and original matter. It ably advocated the emancipation of the enslaved and the elevation of the free colored people."[5]

Between the first appearance of *Freedom's Journal* and the advent of the Civil War, some forty black newspapers were published with antislavery titles such as *Alienated American*, *Mirror of Liberty*, *Freeman's Advocate*, and the like. Many of them had limited lives and would not be considered newspapers in the current sense of the word, but they served to create a print institution for the expression of views controlled by black people. All of these papers, because of their limited markets, were under extreme financial pressure. They most certainly could not be distributed to the blacks still in bondage, as their masters would never permit this. Thus readership was concentrated among free blacks and a few sympathetic whites. Most of the papers had to depend upon funds from the pockets of the publisher or contributors, both black and white.[6]

Two editorial themes predominated in these early papers: emancipation for those still in slavery and a fuller measure of basic rights for free blacks. The papers also reported on births, deaths, marriages, achievements, and social events in the black community, matters in which the white press took no interest.

The *New York Sun*, a general market publication, published frequent editorials, in the middle 1800s, proposing ideas that would negatively effect blacks, both free and enslaved. When the paper proposed curbing Negro voting rights in the state of New York, Willis Hodges, a militant, free black whitewasher, wrote a reply he wanted to have printed in the paper. The white editor told Hodges he would only print it as an advertisement for a fee of fifteen dollars. Furthermore, the editor changed the wording before printing it. When Hodges complained, he was told that the *Sun* "shone for white men only," and that he should publish his own paper if he had something he wanted to say. In response, Willis Hodges and a partner, Thomas Van Rensselaer, established the *Ram's Horn*, a notable black paper of the pre–Civil War era. Published in New York, the paper lasted only a year, but before its demise it carried the writings of both Frederick Douglass, the great black journalist and orator, and John Brown, the famous white abolitionist of the period.

Undoubtedly the most important paper of this period was the *North Star*, founded and edited by Frederick Douglass, a towering figure in black history. Irving Garland Penn called the paper "the beginning of a new era in the black man's literature." First published in Rochester, New York, on 1 November 1847, the *North Star* was named after the celestial reference point escaping slaves used to guide them on the trek to the North and freedom. Douglass set forth his credo in the first issue: "The object of the *North Star* will be to attack slavery in all its forms and aspects, advocate universal emancipation, exact the standard of the colored people; and to hasten the day of freedom to our three million enslaved country-men."[7]

Douglass's paper, which was later named *Frederick Douglass' Paper* to capitalize on his widespread fame, and the other black papers of the era were lonely voices crying in the wilderness. Even the most radical of the abolitionist papers—which were controlled by whites—were not prepared to go to the lengths the black press did of urging full citizenship for blacks. Freedom was one thing, but being equal was something entirely different. In many instances, blacks found that their agenda were not the agenda of their white friends. The insistent calls for emancipation and civil rights by the black press were regarded as militant and even ultra-radical. Its single-minded devotion to this cause, however, gave the black press its reason for existence.

Once the Civil War was over, there was a marked increase in the number of black papers. During the decade after 1865, publications were established in eight states which previously had had none, and in four others that already had papers. By 1890, 575 black papers were being published. Many were regular newspapers, while others were political organs, church papers, or publications designed to serve some specific interest group. Several papers born in the period were destined to exert national influence for years to come—the *Washington Bee*, the *Cleveland Gazette*, the *New York Age*, and the *Philadelphia Tribune*.

Along with the growth in the number of papers came a decline in their militancy. There were compelling reasons for this decline. It was not so much that the fires had gone out but that they had been banked. The social and economic milieu was such that black voices were muted. The national government, after the withdrawal of troops from the South, left the newly freed blacks to the mercy of former slaveowners. Black codes were rapidly instituted to create a society segregated by race from cradle to grave. Lynching was adopted as a way of keeping blacks in their place, and sharecropping replaced slavery as a method of keeping black people in bondage. If the South was hostile to blacks, however, the North was indifferent.

These were not the best of times for militancy. One black militant editor who tried and failed was Ida B. Wells, a teacher and publisher of the *Memphis Free Speech*. She had the courage to publish an article suggesting that white capitalists had instigated the murder of three black businessmen. Her printing plant was wrecked and she was forced to flee the city to save her life. Wells's fame as a journalist-crusader grew as a result of her interest in lynchings and other forms of oppression of and injustice toward African Americans. Wells's concern about the lynching of Henry Smith at Paris, Texas, began as a result of the handling of the event by the general press in the town, which had flagrantly publicized details about the lynching in their papers. Wells paid a Pinkerton detective to obtain for her a batch of the clippings. Subsequently, in lecture tours in Great Britain and in her pamphlet *The Red Record*, Wells told the world about the grisly death scene and the obvious disregard for due process by the town. As a result of her active crusade to end lynchings, the number of yearly lynchings decreased and were rarely rationalized or minimized by the "liberal" northern press as before.[8]

Also serving to dampen sparks of militancy were the program and goals of Booker T. Washington. Washington, an educator by profession, was a leading advocate of accommodation. He urged his fellow African Americans to work with white people on white people's terms, as blacks strove to establish enterprises and institutions for themselves with white support.   With his Atlanta Compromise Speech of 1858 at the Cotton States' Exposition in Atlanta, Georgia, Washington was catapulted by the general market press into the position of the nation's leading black spokesman. He advised black people to put aside their dreams of political and social equality and concentrate on earning the respect of whites by the sweat of their brow.   This accommodationist stance by a black man became a source of great controversy in the black community, particularly among those writing in black publications.   The split in the image of the African American, a basic theme of this book, was evident in this controversy.   On the one hand, white editors in the general press wanted Washington to be considered the leader in the black community because he expressed a view that echoed their beliefs about who and what the African American could and should be.   On the other hand, many African Americans disputed this view and sought to establish their own sense of what that image should be.   Firmly linked with the prominent weekly publication, the *New York Age*, which he eventually purchased, Washington exerted great influence on other newspapers as well as his own, as he used loans, advertisements, printing orders, and political subsidies to control published views on this issue.[9]

From the late 1800s until 1910, T. Thomas Fortune served as editor/publisher of the *New York Age*.   Fortune's rousing editorials attracted the attention of the general market press and even the president of the United States, then Theodore Roosevelt.   Moreover, the *New York Age* was the paper that Ida B. Wells joined when she was forced away from her home in Memphis, Tennessee, after one of her strongest anti-lynching editorials.   In addition, Fortune is credited with originating the term *Afro-American*.

Fortune published the *New York Age* in an era when few blacks could read and when most lived in the South, where strong black views were muted.   With little advertising income and a subscription rate of only one or two dollars per year, he managed to keep the *New York Age* thriving, largely with outside contributions from such luminaries as Booker T. Washington.   Toward the end of his career, because of his strong voice as a spokesman for the black press, Fortune was called the "Dean" of black journalism in America.[10]

The 1900s

A renewed tone of boldness, urgency, and demand was ushered in with the founding of the *Boston Guardian* by William Monroe Trotter in 1901. Trotter's paper, uncompromisingly militant, provided an outlet for anti-Washington views, which represented the first organized opposition to Booker T. Washington. Later, W. E. B. Du Bois would take up the mantle along with Trotter. The *Guardian* was designed to reach intellectuals and played an important role in the Niagara Movement, forerunner of the National Association for the Advancement of Colored People (NAACP). Robert S. Abbott's introduction of the *Chicago Defender* (discussed later in this chapter) also helped to renew the militant boldness of the race. This militancy was expanded as the *Defender* revolutionized the black press by establishing an unheard of *national* audience for the black publication. The trend toward militancy was further heightened by the one-year-old NAACP's publishing in 1910 of *The Crisis*, a widely read journal and the organization's house organ even today.[11]

The philosophies of the *Defender* and the *Guardian* set the stage for the establishment of militancy. Gunnar Myrdal, the noted Swedish scholar and author of *An American Dilemma* noted, however, that "it was the first World War that provided the tide of protest upon which the (black) press rose in importance and militancy."[12] The inconsistency of fighting a war abroad to safeguard democracy while democratic rights were being denied blacks wholesale back home was a topic of widespread interest to African Americans. Later, the pattern would repeat itself, when blacks watched as equal rights promises spawned by World War I were held in abeyance over the years while the nation prepared for and fought World War II. World War II inexorably linked the plight of blacks in the United States to the question of race relations around the world. Documenting and denouncing the mistreatment—domestic and global—propelled the black press to a level of prominence and influence that it was not to lose until the days of integration began to take their toll.[13]

Marcus Garvey deserves a special place in the story of the African American print medium. Though Garvey was not an African American, in his day he had a profound influence on African

Americans and on other black people round the world. Garvey, a descendant of Jamaican Maroons, ex-slaves who successfully defied the slave system, grew up in a home where his father, a skilled stonemason, possessed a library. Marcus developed an early taste for reading and at a young age became a printer's apprentice. As a young man, he traveled to many countries. In England, he worked for the *African Times and Orient Review*, the foremost Pan-African journal of the day, where articles regularly appeared about the worldwide sufferings of black people and articles by and about such leaders as America's Booker T. Washington, W. E. B. Du Bois, and John Edward Bruce. Upon returning to Jamaica, Garvey founded a racial movement entitled the Universal Negro Improvement and Conservation Association. Organized to foster a universal confraternity among the race and to establish a central nation for black people, the Universal Negro Improvement Association, as it was later called, reached its peak in the 1920s, claiming membership in excess of two million people in branches all over the world. The organization pledged to work for better conditions among Negroes everywhere. By the 1920s, Garvey had moved to America and published various newspapers, including the *Daily Negro Times* in Harlem, New York (1922–24), the weekly *Negro World*, also in Harlem (1918–33), the *Black Man* in Jamaica and England (1933 and 1933–39), and other papers in Costa Rica and Panama. Between 1910 and 1940, Garvey published nine newspapers, editing many of them himself, and he also established the first independent black publishing company, the Universal Publishing House. The program and goals of Marcus Garvey, so persuasively argued in his many publications, were to take root again during the 1960s civil rights era.[14]

Through the years, the unifying power of the protest theme was central to black press growth. The strong personalities of pioneer black editors and publishers, however, also share the credit for that growth. These black press leaders needed to be outspoken and articulate challengers of the status quo, defiers of convention, and risk-takers, gambling life, limb, and property. They also needed, and, in fact, exhibited an uncanny ability to carve out a clear direction for their publications that served well their times and their constituencies. Like Russwurm and Cornish, who in their maiden editorial articulated a black press purpose that has stood the test of time, the publications of those such as Frederick Douglass,

William Monroe Trotter, Robert Vann, and Robert Abbott reflected their individual frustrations and fighting styles, as well as the overall concerns of the race.

The influence of African American pioneers in journalism is particularly evident in the years 1910–54, sometimes called the "age of the black publisher." Such stalwarts as Robert Abbott, who remained at the helm of the *Chicago Defender* for decades, Robert L. Vann of the *Pittsburgh Courier*, P. B. Young of the *Norfolk Virginia Journal and Guide*, and John and Carl Murphy of the *Baltimore Afro-American* newspaper chain, exemplified the era. Abbott's *Defender*, with the help of J. Hockley Smiley, Ida B. Wells, and Roscoe Conkling Simmons, became a paper with strong mass appeal. Smiley, Abbott's general manager, was instrumental in molding the *Defender*'s front page, which he modeled on the style used by William Randolph Hearst, founder of the Hearst Corporation. Hearst began publishing the *San Francisco Examiner* in 1887, and his corporation grew to become the largest newspaper empire of its day. In the 1930s, the Hearst papers were the leaders in yellow journalism, where sensational headlines and strong editorial opinions captured America's readers in record numbers. For a long time the black press generally resisted using such yellow-journalistic tactics. They believed it was in the best interest of the race to show dignity and restraint in the print medium. However, when the *Defender* achieved wide success with tactics similar to those used by Hearst and others with sensationalized news, many in the black press followed suit. The *Defender* treated the news in a sensational manner, as it ran vociferous campaigns against such evils as prostitution or crime in the black community, and it published stories that emphasized the concerns, fears, and aspirations of the African American rank and file in rousing language. Smiley adapted for the *Defender* the slogan used by the Hearst Corporation for its *Chicago Tribune*. Whereas the *Tribune* called itself "the World's Greatest Newspaper," Smiley called the *Defender* "the World's Greatest Weekly." A crafty manager, he also adopted unique tactics to increase sales. For example, he used the services of porters and waiters, encouraging them to act as *Defender* salesmen while they carried out their regular duties. The system worked quite well. Ida B. Wells, at this point a vigorous and enthusiastic reporter for the *Defender*, investigated race riots, lynchings, and other such injustices, while Roscoe C. Simmons, a talented orator, toured the country promoting the paper.

The success of the "Abbott Age" of black newspapers was in part due to increasing literacy among African Americans. By 1910, seven out of ten African Americans over the age of ten could read. The newly literate race's hunger to see themselves reflected in publications and information about their communities as a part of current events reports also accounts, in part, for the *Defender*'s success. By 1920, it was at its peak, claiming a quarter of a million readers. (This estimate does not include the many unknown readers in the South who bought the paper and passed it from hand to hand.) The *Defender* not only reported on news events of the day, listing the lynchings, Jim Crow law problems, and inequities in the military but, in its editorial campaign, urged those African Americans who were sharecropping and living subsistence lives to "come North" in a search for better homes and jobs. The call was heard, and some three thousand African Americans fled the South during and after World War I for the industrial centers of Chicago, Pittsburgh, and Cleveland.[15]

Promoted as the national urban newspaper, Robert L. Vann's *Pittsburgh Courier* was directed toward the second generation of urban African Americans. The *Courier* took on many causes. For example, in 1931, Vann launched a campaign to have the radio program "Amos 'n' Andy" removed from the airwaves. Vann and the NAACP argued that this program degraded African Americans. (See chapter 4 for more details.) Before the campaign had ended, hundreds of black ministers, at Vann's request, had delivered self-respect sermons from their pulpits, and nearly 750,000 had signed their names to petitions demanding the cancellation of the program. Other black newspapers were divided on the issue: the *Chicago Defender* supported the airing of the series, while the *California Eagle*, like the *Courier*, opposed keeping it on the air. Though the *Courier* did not succeed in getting "Amos 'n' Andy" removed from the radio, it had used its influence to awaken African Americans to the image of them that was being instilled in the minds of America's listeners. The split in the image offered by the radio series and the one the *Courier* and its allies believed should be established by media was the focus of the debate. This image issue remains unresolved even today and again demonstrates others' views of how African Americans should be depicted versus the group's opinions of how they see themselves.

During World War II, the *Courier*, with its twenty weekly editions, became the number one African American newspaper in Washington, D.C., Birmingham, Alabama, Miami, Florida, and a dozen other cities with large and growing black populations. Vann died in 1940 (six months after Abbott), but under the leadership of Vann's widow, Jessie L. Vann, and P. L. Prattis, and Ira F. Lewis, two of the major black journalists of the day, the paper continued its role of spotlighting injustices, especially those occurring in the armed forces.

During World War II, the African American press uncovered abuses in army camps and army towns. As correspondents in war zones, this press polled and circulated the news of the black soldier abroad, through the National Negro Newspaper Publishers' Association and the Associated Negro Press (ANP).

The Associated Negro Press, the brainchild of Claude Barnett, began sending news releases in 1919 with the objective of gathering all news about the race for use, as a service, to black newspapers around the nation. For forty-five years the ANP received Barnett's attentive nurturance. When black newspaper publishers organized in early 1940, however, they met to establish a press service that would be under their own control. Thus, the publishers' own organization, the National Negro Newspaper Publishers Association (NNNPA) was founded in 1940. This confederation of newspaper publishers, which published daily and weekly, competed head-on with the Associated Negro Press, particularly during World War II. Gradually, the NNNPA became stronger, and Claude Barnett's Associated Negro Press finally suspended operations in the summer of 1964.

Through the years the NNNPA presented distinguished service awards annually to the black leader who had made the most significant contribution to advancement of the race during the previous year, maintained a hall of fame, sponsored annual workshops, and the like. In 1956 the organization changed its name to the National Newspaper Publishers' Association, dropping "Negro" as an outdated term. By 1989 the association boasted 148 member newspapers and a budget of $100,000. It offered members computerized services, mailing lists, and had organized committees of its membership for maintenance and control of its operations.[16]

During World War II, all African American newspapers realized an increase in circulation. Some newspapers capitalized on the war to make domestic demands. The *Courier* was in the forefront of this effort. "More importantly, the *Courier's* Double V campaign for victory abroad and victory at home provided the rallying cry for a phalanx of (other) black institutions."[17] At this point the African American press also rallied behind legal suits for equal teachers' salaries and school desegregation.

The Double *V* campaign of the *Courier* represented a moral and ethical dilemma faced by the black press. If wars can ever be said to be popular, then this was a popular war. The issue to the American people was clear: they and their allies were united against evil as reflected in the imperialist and racist campaigns of Germany, Italy, and Japan. For the Allies anything other than complete victory was unacceptable, and therefore the nation had to be totally in support of the war effort. However, black newspapers were faced with the reality that racism and discrimination were rampant on the home front at a time when blacks were being asked, again, to give their all in a war to save democracy. Could the black press ignore this paradox? They did not.

Black newspapers strongly supported the war effort. They also fought against segregation and discrimination, however, particularly in the armed forces and war-related industries. Thus, the black press provided positive coverage of black participation in the war effort, while also protesting segregation of blacks in the army and their virtual exclusion from the Navy, the Marine Corps, the Air Force, and from private industry.[18]

This effort at balanced coverage to a large degree went unappreciated in the white community. In a speech delivered before the first annual dinner of the Capital Press Club in Washington, D.C., in June 1944, Marshall Field, publisher of the *Chicago Sun* and founder of *P.M.*, a daily New York newspaper, observed that: "the American people's knowledge about our organization for war and the contributions all Americans are making toward it comes from news sources—the press, radio and newsreels; and from films, books and magazines. The Negro as a soldier and a war worker seldom appears in these channels. Many white Americans have no idea even of the number of Negros in the armed forces, let alone what their role has been."[19] The black press, with a few white allies like Field, continued to press the point. Publications such as the *Atlanta Daily World*, the *Norfolk Journal and Guide*, the *Baltimore Afro-*

American, the *California Eagle*, and the *Pittsburgh Courier*, though supportive of the war effort, were strongly militant about equitable treatment for black military men. They conscientiously dispatched correspondents to European and Pacific theaters, frequently printed big headlines on discrimination and segregation, and wrote articles and editorials denouncing anything less than respect for America's black fighting men. The armed forces' determined stand to maintain segregation forced many black papers repeatedly and vigorously to address this issue head-on. For example, the *Pittsburgh Courier* wrote vehement protests against racial discrimination and violence in a front-page editorial on 4 November 1944, headlined the "New Deal's Roll of Shame." In the editorial it mentioned "some of the Negro boys in uniform who have met death, not killed in action for their country, but murdered by their country" (Private Robert Specely killed by a white bus driver in Durham, North Carolina). For a time there was talk about censoring or suppressing some of the more militant papers. The Justice Department even considered issuing indictments against some militant black editors for sedition and interfering with the war effort. At one point many black papers suddenly found it difficult to obtain supplies to continue publication. After a time, cooler heads prevailed and there was a grudging acceptance of the importance of the black press. With the unofficial involvement of the NAACP, a compromise emerged and government intervention ceased.[20]

The Black Press After World War II

When the war ended, the black press was stronger than it had ever been. In September 1947, the four leading black newspapers were the *Pittsburgh Courier*, the *Afro-American*, the *Chicago Defender*, and the *Amsterdam News*. The combined circulation of more than a hundred black publications was in excess of two million copies a week. Based on the strength of their war coverage, the papers had established a loyal cadre of readers. The reporters and editors had brought to the black press a sense of professionalism that gave it a new degree of respect and importance that attracted talented people to its ranks. Moreover, it was an inescapable fact that if a black person wanted to be a journalist, the black press was then the only source of employment.

Indeed, the black press was "riding high" in the period immediately after World War II. At the beginning of 1948, there was a total of 169 newspapers, 56 college campus publications of all types, and more than 100 religious, fraternal, general, and other papers, bulletins, and magazines. Circulation figures for the 169 newspapers tell a lot about the health of the black press during this period: from a little more than one million in 1937, the figure stood at two million in 1947, very nearly a 100 percent increase. There was little mystery to the state of things. World War II had boosted interest in racial issues, and the black press had a virtual monopoly on readers in the black community. But in 1954 the first hint came that this situation would not last forever. The NAACP raised the issue of the legality of segregated schools in the case of *Brown v. the Board of Education* in Topeka, Kansas, and obtained a unanimous decision that such separation of the races was illegal.

The decade that followed saw the beginning of a permanent alteration in America's way of life. Discrimination and segregation lost legal status, and slowly there was a chipping away at the intricate Jim Crow structure that had been built up through law and custom over the years. With desegregation the question arose as to whether black institutions were needed any longer.

Black press leaders generally supported the move toward integration, notwithstanding its potential threat to black journalism. The reaction was not unanimous primarily because of press spokesmen representing such nationalistic groups as the Garveyites and others who were wedded to an ideal of racial separatism. But everyone seemed to sense that a new day was dawning—that with the bid for integration it was apparent black publishers and editors would need to adjust policies. Predictably, the signal produced two camps—optimists like John H. Johnson (discussed later in this chapter), who saw opportunity in the looming change, and others who forecast the inevitable demise of the black press.[21]

The overall question of relevance had bleak philosophical implications for the black press, but three practical factors brought changes in the black press that were as sweeping as the societal "alterations" taking place at the time. The first factor was competition from radio and television for readers and advertisers; the second, increasing costs of operations. These forces were compounded by a third, a new demand for black journalists by white publishers. The talent drain did not take its real toll until much later, when the firebombs of the fading 1960s left white reporters dumbfounded and storyless, for although the stories were unfolding in black communities daily, white reporters were understandably afraid to go into such areas. Suddenly general press publications began actively courting black reporters, whose skin color did not mark them as immediate outsiders; they could penetrate the black community and get the story out before their competitors.

At this point, black papers were running a distant second in each of the three professional considerations which counted most: salaries, prestige, and benefits. In the late 1960s and 1970s starting salaries at many black papers averaged $110 a week, while numerous metropolitan dailies paid salaries of $400 a week for reporters, some of whom had only a few months of experience. The combined effect of competition, rising operating costs, and talent drain was a drastic decline in circulation for black papers. This sent black publishers in search of solutions. In response, "many papers sought almost entirely to entertain readers, concentrating on local, social, and crime news and omitting news of developments and issues" of importance to the community. Often, too, they rewrote stories from general newspapers or culled information from radio and television.[22]

The changeover by the black press to entertainment and social and crime news was destined to fail. Not only did circulation dip, but critics cited the omission of serious issues as evidence of waning black press relevance. At the same time, complaints about the quality of reporting gained new credence because the loss of top talent was increasingly evident. The black press in the decade following World War II was a confused and groping institution. However, the need for change spawned some positive developments that brought the black press to the civil rights era weakened but not defunct.

Locked in the stranglehold of change, the press survived the period largely because of the personal determination and the business acumen of its handful of leaders: the Murphys of Baltimore, the Scotts of Atlanta, the Abbott/Sengstacke family of Chicago, to name a few. While building individual and, in some instances, family empires, these men and women simultaneously charted the course of the black press as an institution. They individually and collectively worked to create a different image of blacks *for* blacks to help instill a sense of pride and a feeling of self-worth within the race.

They had a tough fight, for the power and might of the dominant group consistently demonstrated the invisibility of the African American, projected the African American as a stereotype, or depicted the group as part of a social problem.

Black Press Leaders

Black press leaders charted a most important course when they recognized the need to go global in reporting racial wrongs. This was particularly significant because, before the changes brought about through the integration struggle, most black publications were more or less provincial or, at most, national in their focus. As the 1950s and 1960s unfolded, black publishers saw emerging African nations moving from colonialism to self-determination. They began to compare African Americans with people of African descent in all parts of the world in a way that had not been done since the glory days of Marcus Garvey's Universal Negro Improvement Association. Thus, an acknowledgment of kinship based on an expanding identification with what would later be referred to as the African diaspora increasingly became a focal point for many publishers. African American leaders included such legendary figures as John H. Sengstacke, Cecil E. Newman, Louis Martin, Carl Murphy, Adam Clayton Powell, Jr., John H. Johnson, C. B. Powell, Claude Barnett, and Carlton Goodlett.

For Sengstacke, journalism was a family tradition. He was the nephew of Robert Sengstacke Abbott, founder of the *Chicago Defender*, and, in the early stages of his career, worked at various jobs for a paper run by his father. The jobs covered everything—printing, advertising, and reporting. Sengstacke's practical experience was fortified by college study at Knox and Hampton Institutes. This was followed by graduate study at Ohio State University. His rise to leadership began in 1934 when he signed on to work for his uncle at the *Defender*. He never left the organization. As he had with his basic journalism, Sengstacke prepared for leadership by taking course after course in printing at Hampton Institute and studying business administration at Northwestern University. Eventually, he became a vice president, treasurer, and general manager of the *Defender*. By example, he showed the industry how to keep a business financially stable as he built the *Defender* into the largest chain of black newspapers in the United States. In the 1980s, with eleven newspapers, Stengstacke Enterprises became the largest chain of black newspapers in the nation. The chain included the *Chicago Daily Defender*, the *Memphis Tri-State Defender*, and eight papers in the *Pittsburgh Courier* group.[23]

Louis Martin, founder, publisher and editor in the 1930s of the *Michigan Chronicle*, was renowned, as well, for his work with the National Democratic Party from 1936 to 1976. In fact, Martin was vice-chairman of the Democratic National Committee and confidant to Presidents John F. Kennedy and Lyndon B. Johnson. Moreover, during the tenure of the Carter administration, he served as Special Assistant for Minority Affairs. However, politics did not prevent him from developing the *Chronicle* into a major weekly; nor did it prevent him from serving as editor of the *Chicago Daily Defender* from 1947 to 1959. In the 1970s, the *Chronicle* became part of the Sengstacke chain, and Martin was named editor and a vice president of the parent company. Martin's regular column during this period, "The Big Parade," written for his paper and others, included comments on current problems. He sometimes used an alter ego, Dr. O. S. Onabanjo, his Nigerian friend, to make a point. From 1981 to 1987, Martin worked as vice president for development and communications at Howard University.[24]

Carl Murphy, nephew of the founder, John Murphy, and second publisher of the *Afro-American*, developed a chain of newspapers from headquarters in Baltimore. Eventually, the *Afro* would be published in Washington, Philadelphia, Newark, and Richmond. "Mr. Carl" guided his editorials and news columns with a firm hand, advocating "America First" during the war years but fighting as well for the rights of black servicemen. He also fought for Paul Robeson, the great opera singer/football hero/actor, and for W. E .B. Du Bois, a founder of the NAACP and the publisher/editor of *The Crisis*, both of whom were accused of being Communists. These two black heroes lived some part of their lives in exile or under the dark cloud of government banishment or censorship. Murphy also stood up against U.S. Senator Joseph McCarthy's Communist scare tactics at a time when many influential general press publications were loath to take McCarthy on. Moreover, Murphy sent William Worthy as a correspondent for the *Afro-American* when the U.S. State Department denied him a visa to visit Red China to cover a breaking story. Second, third, and fourth generations of

Murphys continued to operate the newspaper after Carl's death in 1967. From 1961 to 1974, John Murphy III, great-nephew of John Murphy, Sr., served as president of the Afro-American Newspapers, and from 1974 through the 1980s was chairman of the board of directors. In the 1970s and early 1980s, Murphy served as publisher of the *Afro-American*. In the late 1980s, the newest publisher, Frances Draper, Carl's great granddaughter, set out with her cousins and other relatives to improve the paper's quality and sales. By September of 1989 it had become apparent that the *Afro* was in serious financial difficulty, however, and there was talk that one of the nation's oldest black newspapers would be forced to file for bankruptcy.[25]

C. B. Powell, the primary owner and operator of the *Amsterdam News*, was a Harlem physician who owned the publication from 1936 to 1971, when he sold it to a consortium of prominent African Americans. The *Amsterdam News* had been one of the four leading black newspapers during and just after World War II. Predominant in the campaign to have black soldiers treated equitably, at that time the paper boasted a circulation of over a hundred thousand. After 1971 the paper began a decline. It never regained its widespread popularity, and, as general market publications made more inroads into black readership, the publication declined even more.

Adam Clayton Powell, Jr.'s foray into journalism was like anything else he became involved in: controversial, colorful, and unique. His primary role in journalism was as editor of the *People's Voice*, a weekly New York tabloid. What set Powell's editorship apart was the paper's "tough, uncompromising militancy, brilliant editorial writing, and exciting layout."[26] Powell's weekly column, "Soapbox," was written to appeal to its readers' emotions. However, Powell aroused strong feeling without always paying close attention to the clear development of cause and effect. The paper's militancy was perhaps most readily demonstrated in its decision to be first to publish Richard Wright's *Native Son*. The effort had to be abandoned in midstream, however, because of complaints about the author's use of profanity in the work. In general, however, the paper's militant stance won plaudits and sold papers.[27]

Carlton Goodlett, a strong contributor to the black press, was a professor at West Virginia State College in the 1930s, earned his M.D., set up practice in California in the 1940s, and became copublisher of the *Sun-Reporter*. Goodlett was determined to have his paper serve as an advocate for improving social conditions for blacks, particularly in the San Francisco area where he practiced medicine. He served as president of the local branch of the NAACP and also for a time as president of the National Newspaper Publishers Association. Goodlett's theme, when he spoke about the role of the black press, focused on its role as the conscience of the nation. He believed that the general market press had lost its crusading zeal, whereas the black press, though smaller and poorer, served this function for the nation.[28]

In the ranks of the black press John H. Johnson (who will be discussed later in this chapter) is a giant among giants. While Sengstacke and others were developing historic, individual newspaper products and empires, Johnson, an optimist, ventured into black magazines. Like Sengstacke's *Defender*, the Johnson Publishing Company was based in Chicago.

It was with such leaders as these at the peak of their influence that the black press groped its way toward the civil rights era initiated by the 1954 school desegregation decision. While the activism of the 1960s provided new grist for the black media, the resulting civil rights breakthroughs renewed the nagging question of just how long the black press could remain a viable industry. It was apparent in the 1950s that, confused or not, the industry's demise was not imminent as long as its role was not preempted by the general press: as late as the mid-1950s, the majority press continued to take little or no interest in covering African American life in the United States. Then came the civil rights movement, with its demonstrations, marches, sit-ins, and violence. Here was a story that the white press could not ignore, though many newspapers and broadcast outlets, particularly in the South, chose to diminish the importance of the social revolution that was taking place under their noses and to blame most of what they reported on "outside agitators."

Thus, in the 1960s no longer was the black press the only medium telling the story of the black community. The general media—newspapers, radio, television, and magazines—joined in reporting on black affairs, and they specifically focused on the turmoil created when black interests collided with white resistance. There was a tendency by the general market press, even the liberal papers, to do little more than cover what was absolutely essential, exerting very little effort to probe deeper into causes of African American unrest and disenchantment with the dominant culture. Even at the height of the civil rights movement, for example, the general press found little room in its ranks for black journalists. Here and there a black face showed up representing the general media. In the main, however, the general press covered the movement through white eyes.

When meaningful change occurred, it came in the wake of the urban riots of the 1960s, when the general media discovered that they were ill-equipped to deal with the dynamics of covering stories centered in the black community. The National Advisory Commission on Racial Disorders (more familiarly known as the Kerner Commission) focused on these shortcomings in its report on the riots of 1967:

> They (general media) have not communicated to the majority of their audience—which is white—a sense of the degradation, misery, and hopelessness of living in the ghetto. They have not communicated to whites a feeling for the difficulties and frustrations of being a Negro in the United States. They have not shown understanding or appreciation of—and thus have not communicated—a sense of Negro culture, thought, or history.
>
> Equally important, most newspaper articles and most television programming ignored the fact that an appreciable part of their audience was black. The world that television and newspapers offered to their black audience was almost totally white, in both appearance and attitude. As we have said, our evidence shows that the so-called "white press" is at best mistrusted and at worst held in contempt by many Black Americans. Far too often, the press acts and talks about Negroes as if Negroes do not read the newspapers or watch television, give birth, marry, die and go to PTA meetings. Some newspapers and stations are beginning to make efforts to fill this void, but they still have a long way to go.[29]

Alternatives

This discussion of the African American has focused on the split between the image generated by the general market press versus the image of themselves which African Americans sought to establish. Within the African American group there have been at least two traditional approaches to how the African American should develop his own image. In general, this book has used the terms *accommodationists* and *resisters* to describe those two traditions. Among resisters to the dominant culture's control in the 1960s and 1970s in African American communities were the Nation of Islam and the Black Panthers, organizations that published, respectively, two popular publications, *Muhammed Speaks* and the *Black Panther*. *Muhammed Speaks*, the radical and therefore controversial publication of the Nation of Islam, started as *Mr. Muhammed Speaks to the Blackman* in Harlem, New York, in 1960. At first, the writings were published in a column written by Malcolm X for the *Amsterdam News*. Later, Malcolm X produced *Muhammed Speaks*, an entire paper devoted to Muslim views, which was published in New York and then in Chicago. In the later 1970s, in a modern, well-equipped plant, the paper employed more than thirty workers and offered training. The top-level editors were trained journalists like John Woodford, a Harvard graduate with previous newspaper experience. The paper, carrying a large amount of original news that often would not be given a single column in general market papers, had an orderly plan for content and made stimulating reading, particularly for followers of the movement. Moreover, it offered an alternative source of information and point of view to African Americans seeking a critical perspective about America. *Muhammed Speaks* led in circulation among black newspapers in the 1970s, with figures of six hundred thousand. In the 1980s, *Muhammed Speaks* was retitled *Final Call*. Although circulation figures were not as high in the 1980s, the publication still had a solid following in the black community.

The *Black Panther* was produced in California with an all-black staff working in Berkeley. The top editorial official of the paper, Eldridge Cleaver, focused on militant reactions to social conditions and on unremitting opposition to U.S. intervention in Indochina, condemnation of police behavior during the black community's opposition to Zionism and Israel, and support of the Arab and Cuban causes. By 1970, the paper had reached a circulation of one hundred thousand weekly.[30] These radical publications were two of the best known of the dissident black press, which enjoyed great success during the 1960s and 70s.

Ragin A. Henry, president of Broadcast Enterprises National, Inc., attempted to establish a viable national alternative to general market press reports about the black community, its leaders, aspirations, goals, and motivations. In 1982, Henry began publishing *The*

National Leader, with Claude Lewis as editor, a former associate editor of the *Philadelphia Bulletin*. Henry's company also owned radio stations in several states. Although it was well received as a solid publication, *The National Leader* suffered an early demise because of underfunding, and because it failed to attract sufficient advertisers and subscribers.[31]

The General Market Press

As noted, following the urban unrest of the 1960s, black reporters were hired by major newspapers for the first time. By the mid-1970s, black reporters and other contributors to general market publications numbered about a hundred. By the late 1980s, there were more than three thousand, with the *Washington Post* as possibly the largest employer of African Americans of any newspaper in the country.[32] The general market press thus included nationally known African American newspersons at this point, for example, syndicated columnist Carl T. Rowan, editor/publisher/president Robert Maynard, publisher Pam Johnson, and columnists such as William Raspberry, Dorothy Gilliam, C. Gerald Fraser, Luther Jackson, Monte Trammer, Mervin Aubespin, Earl Caldwell, Chuck Stone, Milton Coleman, and Juan Williams. (For a more complete listing see table 7.1.)

Rowan, for example, had been a reporter for the general market paper the *Minneapolis Tribune* from 1948 until 1961. From 1961 through 1963 he was deputy assistant secretary of state for public affairs. He was appointed ambassador to Finland in 1963, and from 1964–65 served as head of the United States Information Agency (USIA), becoming the first African American to sit in on meetings of the National Security Council. In 1965 Rowan became a syndicated columnist for the *Chicago Daily News*.[33]

In 1983, Robert Maynard became the owner and publisher of the *Oakland* (California) *Tribune*. Just four years earlier, he had been the first black to direct the editorial operations of a major American daily newspaper, also the *Tribune*. Prior to this, Maynard had worked at the York, Pennslyvania, *Gazette* as a police reporter, urban affairs writer, and night city editor, and he had served a year at Harvard as a Nieman Fellow. He then spent ten years at the *Washington Post* as its first black national correspondent, then as ombudsman and editorial writer. As owner/publisher of the *Oakland Tribune*, Maynard faced tremendous obstacles, but after six years of operation, by 1989 the paper was continuing to improve and earn respect.[34]

Pam Johnson, the first black woman to control a general market daily newspaper, became president and publisher of the *Ithaca Journal*, a small college town paper in Upstate New York, in 1982. After college Johnson began her career in journalism at the *Chicago Tribune*. Then she completed her Ph.D. degree in journalism and educational psychology and taught for a while at Norfolk State University. In late 1981, the Gannett Corporation, the largest and one of the most prestigious newspaper groups in the nation, which published *USA Today* and eigthty-seven other dailies, asked Johnson to become publisher of the *Journal*. Johnson thus joined Robert Maynard as a Gannett corporate executive, as she became the second black publisher of a daily.

In discussing the black press, which was established to allow African Americans an opportunity to have their views read, it seems pertinent to note that had the general market press allowed for diversity in its publications a black press probably would never have emerged to meet this need. After all these years in the 1980s, finally a general market press corporation began to seek diversity in its publication of news editorials, and in its corporate infrastructure. *USA Today* balances views of racially and ethnically diverse writers about diverse groups, and is aimed at diverse groups of readers. Under Chairman Allen Neuharth, the Gannett Corporation became the unchallenged leader in the newspaper industry in successfully implementing affirmative action goals. The corporation had four minority publishers (two of whom were Latino Americans) and fifteen women who controlled dailies by the late 1980s. While most general market publications rarely consulted African Americans or other minority groups for stories unrelated to racial issues, the Gannett company policy, initiated in 1988, "mainstreamed" news coverage through inclusion of members of various cultural groups as news sources in all stories. After more than a hundred and fifty years, the split in the image of the African American in the print medium has begun to be mended in at least one company's general market publications.[35]

Table 7.1   Black Reporters, Editors, and Columnists on Major Newspapers (19

Atlanta Constitution
Tony Cooper
Linda Horton
Burnis Morris
    (assistant city editor)
Ernest Reese (sports)

Atlanta Journal
Chet Fuller
John Head (assistant city editor)
Clem Richardson
Prentiss Rogers (sports)
Angela Terrell

Boston Globe
Ken Cooper
Jackie Green
Ron Hutson
Robert Jordan
Diane Lewis
Victor Lewis
Herman Lockman
Jim Lowery
Don McBride
Valerie Montague
Vola Osgood
Gayle Pollard
Mitcher Roberts
John Robinson
Miriam Tarver
Larry Whiteside

Charlotte News
Ramona Clark
Ted DeAdyle
Deborah Gates
Cassandra Lawton
David Porter
    (assistant city editor)
Oaker Spicer
Gail Westry (copy editor)

Chicago Tribune
Monroe Anderson
Joyce Brown
Vernon Jarrett
Janita McClain
John White

Detroit Free Press
Bruce Britt
Donna Britt-Gibson
Betty DeRamus
Andrea Ford
June Brown
Moses Harris
Kim Heron
Greg Huskisson
Luther Jackson III
Ben Johnson
Jackier Jones
Larry Olmstead
Ruth Seymour
Cassandra Spratling
Monte Trammer
Joyce Walker-Tyson
Susan Watson

Detroit News
June Brown
Denice Crittenden
Larry Davis
Brenda Gilschrist
David Grant
Jim McFarlan
Carl Payne
Arlena Sawyer
Michael Tucker
Monroe Walker

Louisville Courier-Journal
Mervin Aubespin
Marie Bradby
Leon Carter
Michael Days
Cheryl Devall
Angela Dotson
Keith Harriston
Donna Whitaker

Louisville Times
Bruce Branch
Michelle Chandler
Delma Francis
Clarence Matthews

Table 7.1 (cont.)

Newsday
Mike Alexander
Dennis Bell
Sid Cassesse
Merle English
Sheryl Fitzgerald
Betty Logan
Bill Mason
Les Payne (national editor)
Morris Thompson

New York Daily News
Earl Caldwell (columnist)
Ron Claiborne
Steve Duncan (copy editor)
David Hardy
James Harney
Bob Herbert
  (City Hall bureau chief)
Ron Howell
  (Harlem bureau chief)
Keith Moore
Cynthia Raymond
Rufus Rivers
  (copy editor)
Joan Shepard
Dave Sims
  (sports)
Causewell Vaughan
  (Bronx editor)
Joyce White
Hugh Wyatt
  (health affairs editor)

New York Times
Lee Daniels
Paul Delaney (national editor)
C. Gerald Frazier (arts and
  entertainment writer)
Dorothy Gaiter
George Goodman
Judith Gummings
Al Harvin (sports)
Ernest Holsendolph

Les Ledbetter
Sheila Rule
Nathaniel Sheppard
E. R. Skipp
Ron Smothers
Reginald Stuart

Oakland Tribune-East Bay Today
Marilyn Bailey
  (assistant city editor)
Sharon Bibb (copy editor)
Mary Ellen Butler
  (features editor)
Gerald Davis
Skye Dent (editorial writer)
Juadine Henderson (assistant city
  editor)
Denise Holt (education writer)
Lonnie Isabel
Annette John (sports writer)
Sidney Jones (columnist)
Will Jones (assistant city editor)
Brenda Lane-Worthington
  (columnist)
Robert Maynard (editor,
  publisher, president)
Tina Pania (copy editor)
Brenda Payton
Doris Worsham (columnist)

Philadelphia Daily News
Lorenzo Biggs
Joseph Blake
Prentice Cole
Wayne Faircloth
Juan Gonzalez
Frederick Lowe
Valerie Russ
Gene Seymour
Elmer Smith
Chuck Stone (columnist)
Leon Taylor
Linn Washington
Barnett Wright
Earni Young

Table 7.1   (cont.)

*Star-Ledger, Newark
New Jersey*
Edna M. Bailey
Kathy Barrett-Carter
Frederick V. Boyd
Bill Bright
Frederick W. Byrd
Kevin Dilworth
Larry Hall (editor, This Week
    Newark)
Jason Jett
Lisa Peterson
Ernest Roberson
Stanley E. Terrell
Joan Whitlow (medical editor)
Kenneth Woody

Washington Post
Vivian Aplin-Brownlee
    (assistant national editor)
Vanessa Barnes-Hillian
Alice C. Bonner
LaBarbara Bowman
Warren Brown
Dorothy Butler-Gilliam
    (metro-columnist)
Earl K. Chism (Treasurer—
    Washington Post Company)
Milton Coleman (city editor)
Leon D. Dash
Herbert H. Denton
David DuPree
Cheryl Eaves
    (assistant news editor)
Sandra R. Gregg

Carla Hall
Neil Henry
Michael Hill (assistant editor—
    style section
Donald Huff
Athelia Knight
Leah Y. Latimer
Wanda Lloyd (assistant-to-the-
    publisher)
Michel Marriott
Michel McQueen
Courtland Milloy, Jr.
Tom Morgan (editor, District
    Weekly)
Carol Porter (graphics)
Jacquelyn Powell (copy editor—
    style section)
Rudolf Pyatt
William Raspberry (columnist)
Vincent E. Reed (vice president—
    communications)
Keith B. Richburg
Joe Ritchie (foreign desk editor)
Eugene Robinson (assistant city
    editor)
Edward D. Sargent
Jane Seaberry
Jube Shiver, Jr.
Fred Sweets
Jacqueline Trescott
Joseph D. Whitaker
Ronald D. White
Michael Wilbon
Juan Williams
Leon Wynter

Source: "The Black Press and Broadcast Media," in *The Negro American Almanac*, ed. Harry A. Ploski and James Williams, 5th ed., (New York: Wiley & Sons, 1987), 1223.

Training Programs

Beginning in the late 1960s, various efforts were made to offer journalism training programs to minority groups. The intent went beyond skills training and included a systematic means of moving African Americans into the superstructure of media industries. Though such programs were successful at the time, they did not last long enough or broaden their funding sources enough to handle large numbers. Some programs continued through the 1980s, successfully placing most of the few African Americans they moved through the programs. One such effort, discussed in chapter 6, was the Black Journal Training Program (later called the NET Training Program). Another program, launched by the *Afro-American* newspaper and the Virginia Council on Human Relations in early 1969, was named the Frederick Douglass Fellowship Program. Financed by a $123,000 grant from the Ford Foundation, and designed by Raymond H. Boone, then editor of the Richmond edition of the *Afro-American*, and Frank T. Adams, former newspaperman and teacher, the program was open to fifteen aspiring African American journalists, who received stipends enabling them to spend a year learning about the newspaper business.

In 1968, Columbia University received a $250,000 grant from the Ford Foundation to offer an annual eight-week summer training program for minority students. Directed by Fred Friendly, a professor of journalism at Columbia, the program was quite successful. In 1969 there were twenty-two graduates, in 1970 there were thirty-seven, and each year the numbers grew. One of the program's most famous graduates was a young black woman named Michele Clark. Clark had risen through the reporters' ranks at CBS news to become co-anchor of its morning news program, when she was killed in an airplane crash. The training program was renamed the Michele Clark Summer Program for Minorities in her honor. By 1974, however, money for the project was unavailable. The program shut down for a time. Then, in 1975, with a grant from the Gannett Foundation, Earl Caldwell, a noted black journalist, helped raise the funds needed to restart the training program, now relocated at the University of California at Berkeley. Called the Institute for Journalism Education (IJE), the summer program prepared and found employment for young nonwhite newspaper reporters. Directors of the program in the 1980s included Robert Maynard and Dorothy Gilliam.[36]

Popular Magazines

In addition to daily and weekly newspapers, the black press includes popular consumer magazines, aimed primarily at the black middle class and designed to serve African American communications needs and interests that lie beyond what is offered in mainstream publications. Over the years, most black press magazines have addressed and presented African Americans as cultured, urbane, sensible, contributing middle-class citizens. By implication, these publications thus refute the notion, often implicit in general market press coverage of activities involving blacks, that somehow the group almost always represents a social problem. Black magazines feature entertainers, sports figures, and other African Americans who have "made the news" (such as America's first black astronaut), focusing attention on noteworthy activities, current issues and conditions, and the black cultural heritage. The first such magazines included *The Afro-American Magazine* (New York, 1859), and the *Douglass Monthly* (New York, 1859). *Alexander's Magazine* (Boston, Massachusetts, 1905–9), a national publication, provided a wide variety of news about the race. Designed to take note of significant actions and to act as an organ of pride for the race, the magazine commented on artistic and educational events, individuals of significance, and national politics. Subsequently, other publications followed this pattern, however, sometimes not so well as did *Alexander's*.

Johnson Publications: A Special Case

Between publication of the *Colored American* in 1900 and *Negro Digest* in 1942, approximately thirty-five magazines were published by and for African Americans across the country. The publication of *Negro Digest* in Chicago was John H. Johnson's response to a need for a periodical to summarize and condense articles and comments about blacks found in many daily, weekly, or monthly mainstream publications. Johnson had worked for an insurance agency, where he produced monthly articles summarizing news from numerous publications on a variety of topics. It was here that he conceived the idea for the *Negro Digest*, which he designed to include summarized news about the race, taken from publications such as *Newsweek* and *Saturday Evening Post*. The *Digest* was an immediate unqualified success, as circulation began a steady climb with its second issue.

The *Negro Digest* allowed blacks and whites a forum for their observations about public affairs issues, such as "The Negro Question." Since emancipation, America had been debating this issue. The impact of World War II had given the question a stronger emphasis, and many respected Americans, black and white, expressed their views on the subject—views that later found their way into the *Negro Digest*. From 1942 to 1970, the *Negro Digest* retained its wide popularity. Then it became *Black World*, in response to prevailing political and cultural forces that rejected the term *Negro* as an ethnic adjective.

The *Negro Digest/Black World* change typifies some of the confusion and lost direction that existed in the black press between the late 1940s and 1970. For more than twenty-five years *Negro Digest* was a major success for the Johnson Publishing Company. When it changed its name to *Black World*, thus reflecting a new militancy, its editor, Hoyt W. Fuller, and the Johnson Publishing Company sought to ride the wave of 1960s-style black nationalism then in vogue in the United States and abroad. The movement had run its course by 1970, however, and *Black World* proved to be out of step. It ceased publication in 1976.

In his autobiography, *Succeeding Against the Odds*, which covered the rise of the Johnson Publishing Company from the 1940s through the 1980s, Johnson candidly described his triumphs and failures as a black businessman whose vision, objectives, and social agenda centered on his attempts to provide a service to black people that he thought they needed and would want. In his book, Johnson gave his own prescription for success, while also describing how paying attention to black consumers might help to arrest the stagnation extant in the American enterprise system that was once the envy of the world.[37]

John H. Johnson's unprecedented success as a publisher with *Negro Digest* served as an incentive for him to publish the first issue of *Ebony* magazine in 1945. *Ebony* reported the successes black people were experiencing in various areas of American life. Imitating *Life* magazine in format and style, the politically active *Ebony* published editorials and encouraged black participation in the political process, while it promoted interracial understanding and emphasized the positive aspects of race relations. Between 1945 and the 1980s, the company also published, or bought out and published, *Jet, Tan, True Confessions, Hue, Ebony International, Ebony Jr.*, and *Copper Romance*.

Other Magazines

Other popular magazines of the forties included *The Negro* (St. Louis, Missouri, 1943); *Pulse* (Washington, D.C., 1943); *Headlines and Pictures* (Detroit, 1944); *Negro Story* (Chicago, 1944), *Southwestern Journal* (Oklahoma City, Oklahoma, 1944); and *The African* (New York, 1945). Between the 1945 publication of *Ebony* and the 1951 publication of *Jet* magazine, eight magazines began publications that targeted African American audiences. They included such titles as *Our World* (New York, 1946), *Sepia* (Fort Worth, Texas, 1947), and *Harlem Quarterly* (New York, 1949). *Jet* filled the need for a pocket-sized magazine that summarized the week's biggest "Negro" news in a well-organized, easy-to-read format. The magazine included a few in-depth news stories and items spreading across areas that focused on business, education, religion, health, medicine, journalism, politics, labor, poverty, and crime.

Between the 1951 publication of *Jet* magazine and the year 1970, eight popular magazines began publication, including *The Liberator* (New York, 1961), *Freedomways* (New York, 1961), *Harvard Journal of Afro-American Affairs* (1965–71); and *Black Theater* (1968–72). The latter two magazines started and then ceased publication in response to the sociocultural forces of the civil rights era. *Freedomways* thrived throughout the 1980s.

The year 1970 was a significant one in the history of the black press in the area of consumer magazine publication. In that year alone, thirteen consumer magazines were published. Some were short-lived; they included *Black Academy Review* (Buffalo, New York, 1970–74); *Black Business Digest* (Philadelphia, 1970–73); *Black Creation* (New York, 1970–75); and *Black World* (1970–76). Among those that continued to thrive through the 1980s were *Black*

Collegian (New Orleans), *Black Sports* (New York), and the two largest new publications, *Essence* (New York) and *Black Enterprise* (New York).[38]

Essence: The Magazine for Today's Black Woman, a privately owned periodical, enjoyed phenomenal success from the beginning. The publication was the brainchild of Jonathan Blount, an advertising salesman, and Clarence Smith, an insurance salesman, who had been inspired by a Wall Street brokerage firm's invitation to discuss ideas for black business ventures. Blount and Smith formed a partnership with a printing expert and a financial planner. The partners then sold their proposal for a black woman's magazine to financial backers on Wall Street, engaged an experienced and talented editorial and journalistic team, and began publication of a magazine that emphasized "more woman and less black." The publication relied more on prose than pictures and came close to being a black version of *Cosmopolitan*, a popular white general market publication.[39]

While *Essence* focused on black women's concerns, a new concept about African Americans and the corporate workplace in America's free enterprise system emerged at the same time. *Black Enterprise*, from its inception, focused on the economic viability of African Americans as an integral part of the nation's economic structure. The magazine emphasized businesses, job opportunities, and career options. It positioned itself as a source for practical answers and culled information on trends that affected opportunities for minorities, particularly African Americans. Though Earl Graves was the power behind the development and growth of the publication, the many participants in the concept-planning strategies for *Black Enterprise* included Whitney Young, Jr., then director of the National Urban League, and representatives from the National Association of Marketing Developers, the National Business League, the Congress of Racial Equality, and others. Though *Black Enterprise* had a business orientation, it also highlighted for African Americans those political and social forces which had effects on or were impacted by economic factors. As a leading proponent of black entrepreneurship and political and social awareness in the black community, Earl Graves developed *Black Enterprise* and his other businesses as the authorities on the progress made by African Americans, and other culturally diverse groups, in business endeavors. By the 1980s, Earl Graves Associates also owned radio stations in several cities, and Graves served across the country as a consultant on urban affairs and black economic development.[40]

Photojournalists

Like African American news reporters, photographers who wished to see their works in news publications found it extremely difficult to break into the mainstream. Until the 1970s, except for a select few individuals, if they were to work at all it had to be in the small market of black publications. Early photojournalists included Cornelius Marion Battey of Tuskegee Institute (*The Crisis and Opportunity*), Arthur Bedou (*Louisiana Weekly*), Clifton George Cabell (*Norfolk Journal and Guide*, the *Pittsburgh Courier*, and the *Washington Afro-American*), Harvey James Lewis (*Pittsburgh Courier*), Carroll T. Maynard (*Ebony* and the *Chicago Defender*). Later photojournalists comprise a long list of names (see Appendix 3).

Gordon Parks is one of the most famous photojournalists of the period from 1940 to the present. As a young man, Parks decided to become a photographer after he saw the photographic works of the Farm Security Administration during the 1930s. He began working for FSA and the Office of War Information during World War II. Because of traumatic events (lynchings, death of his mother) that had occurred in his childhood in Kansas City, and because of the racism he had to face during his army years, Parks decided that his choice of weapons in the fight against racism and bigotry would be the camera. After some years of struggle, Parks's works began appearing in numerous publications in both the black and the general market press. Eventually, highly respected and world-renowned as a photojournalist, Parks has also directed major feature films (*Sounder, Cotton Comes to Harlem*) and written books (*A Choice of Weapons, Born Black,* and *The Learning Tree*).

Among other African Americans who have fought their way to the top in the field of photojournalism are Moneta J. Sleet, Jr., staff photographer for Johnson Publishing Company, whose striking picture of Coretta Scott King at her husband's funeral won him a Pulitzer Prize in 1969, and Matthew Lewis, Jr., the *Afro-American's* freelance photographer, who later worked for the *Washington Post* and won a Pulitzer Prize.

As a child, Louise Martin yearned to become a photographer.

Despite obstacles, she realized her dream. Although she could not attend a school in the South to pursue a photography career because of racial discrimination, she attended Chicago's Art Institute and the American School of Photography. Her photographs of the funeral of Martin Luther King, Jr., appeared in *The Forward Times* and *The Informer*, two Houston black newspapers. Michelle Agins, an orphan living with her grandparents, was befriended by white *Chicago Daily News* photographer, John Tweedle, when, like Louise Martin, she showed interest in photography as a child. Agins later became the official photographer for Mayor Harold Washington of Chicago. Her photographs have appeared in *Ebony*, *Jet*, the *Chicago Tribune*, the *Chicago Sun Times*, the *New York Times*, the Associated Press, United Press International, and Wire Service Publications.[41]

The Relevance of the Black Press

The efforts, in the 1970s and 1980s, of the general print media to respond to the black community, for whatever reason and however minimally, fanned anew the old controversy of the relevance of the black press. Was the risk of blacks being misrepresented by the majority press a real concern given the gains of the 1950s and 1960s? Increasingly, the call for a so-called color-blind society, heard with mounting frequency in both black and white circles, brought up the question of the continued need for a black press, which was challenged as a form of self-segregation. "Buppies"—Black Up-wardly Mobile Youths—a term coined by *Black Enterprise* magazine, were particularly prone to accuse the black press, as well as most other all-black institutions, of being "contradictory" to the espoused goals of the civil rights campaign of the 1950s and 1960s. On closer scrutiny, however, those who made such assertions were found to have ignored two facets of the "color-blind society" drive. First, in reality, the concept received little more than lip service, being voiced particularly where no firm actions or hard choices were required. Second, the heartiest advocates of the color-blind society were some white Americans who were pleased by the phenomenon of a new quiet on the African American front. To them, color-blind meant no calls for guaranteed participation of minorities in lucrative muncipal state or federal contracts. Color-blind meant no push by minorities to attain parity in management-level positions. Considering these attitudes, the dawning of a color-blind society seemed a weak reed on which to justify the abandonment of such stalwart institutions as the black press.

Within the print media, there was a more concrete reason for concern. More than a hundred and fifty years after Russwurm and Cornish had started the black press, the issue of fair representation of minorities in the majority press was far from settled. Three questions remained salient: (1) Did the majority press devote an equitable share of positive coverage to the minority community? (2) Did the majority press employ a representative number of minority journalists? (3) Did the majority press provide adequate minority participation at most decision-making or management levels? Despite the gains cited earlier, none of these questions could be answered in the affirmative in the late 1980s.

To raise such concerns before 1950 had been out of the question. But then came the rebellions and Martin Luther King, Jr., Malcolm X, Rap Brown, Stokely Carmichael, and others whom the media could not ignore. Suddenly, against their will, the media were permitting blacks to be heard—sometimes patronizingly, but heard nonetheless. This development precipitated a second, the hiring of blacks by newspapers.

The trend to hire African Americans made a fresh surge forward when President Lyndon Johnson's riot commission (1968) leveled harsh criticism at the media for their lopsided racial coverage and discriminatory hiring policies,[42] and when the American Society of Newspaper Editors (ASNE) launched a campaign in the 1970s to lure more minorities into the media. The National Urban League, using ASNE figures to describe the work-force picture for the print media for 1985, stated:

> In the workforce of daily newspapers, 2,862 minority persons, including blacks, Hispanics, Native Americans and Asian Americans, are employed as newsroom professionals. ... Blacks represent approximately two-thirds of the total—roughly 1,900. This means that of the 49,000 employees in newsrooms of the nation's 1,710 dailies, about 3.8 percent are black and around .8 percent are of Hispanics, Native American and Asian American ancestry.

The ASNE statistics released another fact worth noting: "Almost 95% of the journalists of daily newspapers are white. Four minority groups share 5.8 percent of the newsroom jobs. In the ranks of senior editors, minorities almost drew blanks. Ninety-two percent of the nation's newspapers have not one minority person in a news executive position." The report's overall conclusion speaks for itself and addresses all three of the major concerns raised about minorities in the media. Further, the *National Urban League's 1986 State of Black America* summary, sometimes quoting the ASNE report, read: "The newspaper industry remains largely segregated, especially in positions where decisions are made on what news to cover and on what play and space to give the news. For example, 97 percent of all news executives are white. Ninety-five percent of all copy editors are white, as are 98 percent of all reporters, photographers and artists."[43]

The immediate issue of equal opportunity for employment in the general print media was an important one, particularly since the discouraging picture did not improve a great deal after the late 1980s. But numbers and even minority access to the field were not the primary concerns. These conditions were only pieces of the larger problem—how was the image of the African American affected by the low number of minorities in the media? Did the danger of "misrepresentation" automatically arise in a situation where minorities were underrepresented in the print arena?

In the waning years of the 1980s there remained a serious discrepancy in the positions and places whites ascribed to blacks and the images that African Americans held of themselves. Differences in the response of blacks and whites to the age-old query "What do blacks want?" furnished further proof that a tremendous gulf existed between black and white Americans. For example, set-asides in federal projects, whereby a specific percentage of a project was earmarked for minority contractors and vendors to supply or provide, were seen by most blacks as minimal steps to correct many past years of deliberate denial of opportunity to minorities. The effort was viewed by many whites, however, as "handouts" and "reverse discrimination," and in 1989 the Supreme Court, with a dissenting opinion by the lone African American on the nation's highest judicial bench, declared such set-asides unconstitutional.

Many other clear-cut examples existed which suggested that the perceptions of blacks and whites remained at loggerheads even as the nation approached the threshold of the last decade of the century. The success of political and social conservatives of the 1980s in rolling back civil rights gains of previous eras was additional strong proof of the schism in race relations.

This chapter began with an incident that occurred in Baltimore in the 1960s in which the white and black print media handled a newsworthy story in totally different ways. Almost thirty years later, America was to see another newsworthy story handled totally differently by the white and black print media. The black press again interpreted the dynamics of African American involvement in society from a different perspective from that of the general press.

On 13 June 1988, syndicated columnist and television-radio commentator Carl T. Rowan was awakened as he and his wife slept, at about 2 A.M., by persons in his yard and near his house. Rowan, a staunch advocate of gun control laws, called the police and, thinking they had arrived, opened a sliding door, only to see one of the intruders. The accounts of what transpired after that differ, but the intruder was shot in the wrist. Rowan was held up to ridicule by the National Rifle Association and others, many of whom were opposed to gun-control legislation.

The white press carried headlines such as "Columnist Shoots Teen Skinny Dipper" and "Rowan's Explanation of the Shooting was Off Target." Further, the white press focused on the fifteen or so columns that Rowan had written throughout the years in strong favor of the banning of handguns. Many majority newspapers focused on what they preceived as Rowan's "elitist attitude," which they noted favored gun control "for others." A black journalist on the staff of the *Baltimore Evening Sun* ridiculed the Rowan incident by describing how others would want to use guns as he had—frivolously.

The issue here is not whether Carl Rowan should or should not have shot the intruder or should or should not have had an unregistered gun in his home. The issue here is that the black and white press, by definition, still look at the same event/action from different perspectives, thus testifying to the continuing need for a black press.

Through the years, those who were reading black press articles about various incidents received a very different message from those who only read the writings of general market press writers. Views expressed in the black press allowed black readers to see another side of issues, thereby increasing their understanding of where they fit in society and what an agenda could or should be for African Americans on given issues.

A survey of twenty-three articles published about the Rowan shooting incident in the *Los Angeles Times, Washington Afro-American, Chicago Defender, Kansas City Star, Washington Post, Washington Times,* and *Baltimore Sun* between 15 June and 25 June reveals that eleven were negative toward Rowan, exhibiting themes such as:

1. Local gun-control lobby group believes Rowan is singing their tune.
2. Rowan is the new Charles Bronson. (Bronson starred in films about vigilante-type heroes who shot and killed hoodlums after they had experienced horrendous traumas at their hands. "Death Wish" was the first of the series.)
3. Welcome to the nasty world of self-defense Carl.
4. Own up to true beliefs if they are different now than when you wrote them.
5. Rowan is a hypocrite, calling for strict gun control while he owned one for himself.
6. Rowan is now facing criminal charges.
7. Rowan's acts were inconsistent with his espoused principles.
8. The parents of one intruder say Rowan used appalling judgment.
9. Rowan's reputation as a liberal was irreparably damaged when he "grabbed an unregistered handgun and shot a teenaged intruder."
10. Expressed shock that Rowan would own, much less use, a gun.

Of the twenty-three articles, seven were neutral, coming from general press and black publications; of the five positive articles, three were from the *Washington Afro-American,* and two were from the *Washington Post,* one of which was written by Rowan himself.

The *Washington Afro-American* looked at the shooting incident in a different perspective from most articles in general press publications, noting or raising issues that were not covered or were given much less space in articles in other publications. As noted, numerous articles were negative toward Rowan, whereas the *Afro-American* devoted more space to positive aspects of the incident, as viewed by Rowan supporters. For example, it noted that the

National Newspaper Publishers Association—the national minority press organization discussed earlier in this chapter—passed a resolution in support of Rowan. Radio talk shows were flooded with complaints about the handling of the case in favor of Rowan. Some callers believed the case would have been handled quite differently had the intruders been black, as whites always carried the presumption of innocence, while blacks carried the presumption of guilt. The *Afro* stated that their readers were shocked at how little blame law enforcement officials and media placed on the teenagers who had intruded.[44]

Thus, in the late 1980s the words of Russwurm and Cornish resounded again: "though there are many in society who exercise toward us benevolent feelings; still (with sorrow we confess it) there are others who make it their business to enlarge upon the least trifle, which tends to the discredit of any person of colour."[45]

Russwurm and Cornish probably did not have minorities in the white media in mind, but their further admonition was still applicable in the statement, "We wish to plead our own cause." The cause at the dawn of the 1990s was for full and fair participation in the decision-making process. The National Urban League's 1985 report put the problem in clear perspective:

> The most significant problems of blacks in mass communications may be subsumed under two categories—content and control. The categories are not mutually exclusive. They are interdependent. By virtue of sharing media control, blacks become a part of media content, even when the measurable evidence is limited to their bylines. That, in part, explains why news content that is fair and beneficial to blacks won't come until blacks achieve parity in media employment, which would assure them of control functions that are associated with news selection, news filtering and management, the decision-making functions that are the main determiners of news content.[46]

The report left little doubt that at the heart of the problem was the underlying war of images that is being discussed throughout this book:

> When excluded from the gathering and processing of news, blacks are subjected to being defined by whites who view minorities through prisms distorted by personal and institutional racism. A news item rounding up Christmas Eve prayer services, for example, is likely unwittingly to omit black churches because the reporter lacked interest or contacts in the black community.[47]

Samuel Adams, professor of journalism at the University of Kansas, referred to the task of bringing adequate numbers of blacks into the print media as the "process of blackening in" the media. A staunch advocate of the process, he warned, however, of one major limitation. The process of blackening in the media would not provide an "automatic, total solution to the problem . . . because black journalists who are whitenized in their training and experience also are likely to define as 'non-news' that which does not titillate whites."[48]

Adams's note of caution had major implications for schools of journalism. Obviously, they faced a new challenge of significant dimensions. But just as important was Adams's implied warning to would-be journalists from African American communities. While a key mandate was to master the trade, black journalism students also carried the burden of somehow managing not to become "whitenized." The challenge was not one to be taken lightly. The point raised an issue to which every minority journalist needs to give some thought. Does one indeed have a special obligation to self and to the black community that transcends the job as a journalist?

In a paper presented at the "One-Third of a Nation Conference" at Howard University in November 1989, Clint W. Wilson II, a former journalist, recalled the admonition given to the National Association of Black Journalists at their 1986 convention by then U.S. District Judge Alcee Hastings. Hastings warned of the "illusion of inclusion" by which African American journalists could find themselves deluded into believing that their presence in the newsroom of a major mainstream news organization ensured their inclusion in and acceptance by its Eurocentric social system. Wilson noted that, on the contrary, their ethnicity could be used as a measure against which they would need to prove to what degree they had abandoned their own cultural perspective in favor of the Eurocentric value system. Wilson subsequently called upon higher educational institutions to structure course content to include multicultural perspectives. He believed that educators need to develop texts with a culturally pluralistic view and noted that "good" reporting should be defined and taught as inclusive of multicultural news sources.[49]

Lionel Barrow, Jr., writer and former dean of the School of Communications at Howard University, provides an instructive assessment of the black press:

The conservative press is still apt to depict lazy black men as the major recipients of welfare and to condemn black crime without any consideration of its cause—white racism. . . . And even today, less than two percent of the editorial employees on the nation's newspapers are black. . . . Thus, the need for the Black Press continues. We need a vigilant, fighting press, sure in its blackness, concerned and knowledgeable about the facts and images needed by its community.[50]

Black newspapers, particularly those located in urban centers across the country, in the waning years of the 1980s began to upgrade their publications through diversification and innovative uses of available technology (such as desktop publishing). For example, Ernie Pitts, publisher of the *Winston Salem Chronicle*, launched the paper in 1974 to "provide a fuller picture of African Americans and to chronicle their accomplishments and aspirations."[51] Later, Pitts printed and distributed an insert for his and many other black newspapers, entitled "Sports Review," a monthly review of black college sports accomplishments. Like William H. Lee, publisher of the *Sacramento Observer*, Pitts believed that the role black papers played was vital.

Although the perennial problem of a solid base of advertisements to maintain the vitality of operations continued to plague black newspapers, the National Newspaper Publishers Association in 1989 manifested a new initiative when it obtained advertising commitments for its membership worth more than two million dollars from major corporations (K-Mart, Chrysler). Lawrence Kaggwa, chairman of the Department of Journalism at Howard University's School of Communications, believes that many capable black journalists could be attracted to black newspapers in the future as they become group-owned rather than predominantly family-owned operations. Kaggwa suggested that with group ownership the perception among up-and-coming young journalists would be that the papers offer a better chance for upward mobility. Further, Kaggwa believes that black newspapers need to see their role as one of a responsible, critical watchdog for the black community. The *City Sun* of Brooklyn, New York, took such a role very seriously: in the 1980s it consistently discussed public leaders and the black establishment despite pressures from others to distance itself from such issues. Andrew Cooper, publisher of the *City Sun*, believed, as Pitt did, that the way to have influence and increase readership in the black community was to cover the community—warts and all. Cooper noted, in an article in *Presstime*, that the black press had a unique role and responsibility and therefore needed to endure for future generations: "We have a rich history and culture that belongs to us. We ought to read about it, teach our children about it, and take pride in it."[52]

1. James D. Williams, personal recollections with author, Fall 1987.

2. Phyl Garland, "The Black Press: Down But Not Out," *Columbia Journalism Review* (September–October 1982): 43–50; Vishnu V. Oak, *The Negro Newspaper* (Yellow Springs, Ohio: Antioch Press, 1948), 43–50.

3. The black press had tirelessly hammered away at expressing the need for integration in the armed forces, public education, housing, and the workplace. For more information on this, see, for example, Garland, "The Black Press," 43–50; Roland E. Wolseley, *The Black Press, U.S.A.* (Ames: Iowa State University Press, 1971); Penelope L. Bullock, *The Afro-American Periodical Press: 1838–1909* (Baton Rouge: Louisiana State University Press, 1981); Walter White, "It's Our Country, Too: The Negro Demands the Right to Be Allowed to Fight for It," *The Saturday Evening Post*, 14 December 1940.

4. John Russwurm and Samuel Cornish, *Freedom's Journal* (New York), 26 March 1827 (copyrighted 1891 by Willey & Company, Springfield, Mass.); Lerone Bennett, "Founders of the Negro Press," *Ebony*, July 1964, 96–102. George M. Fredrickson, *The Black Image in the White Mind: The Debate on African-American Character and Destiny, 1817–1914* (New York: Harper & Row, 1971), 110–59.

5. Martin E. Dann, *The Black Press, 1827–1890: Quest for National Identity* (New York: G. P. Putnam Sons, 1971), 16–17; Luther P. Jackson, "The Beginning: The Spirit of the Early Black Press," *Encore American and Worldwide News*, 20 June 1977, 16–17; Armistead Scott Pride, "Negro Newspapers: Yesterday, Today and Tomorrow," *Journalism Quarterly* 28, no. 2 (Spring 1985): 179–82; Frederick G. Detweiler, *The Negro Press in the United States* (Chicago: University of Chicago Press [through McGrath Publishing Co., College Park, Md.], 1968): 1–31.

6. Irving Garland Penn, cited in Detweiler, 32–52; Bennett, "Founders of the Negro Press," 102–3.

7. Jackson, "The Beginning," 16–20; Wolseley, *The Black Press, U.S.A.*, 17–24.

8. For more information on Ida B. Wells, see Jackson, "The Beginning," 22–23.

9. Wolseley, *The Black Press, U.S.A.*, 31–33.

10. Wolseley, *The Black Press, U.S.A.*, 7, 29, 33; Jackson, The Beginning, 22–23; and "The Black Press and Broadcast Media," in *The Negro American Almanac: A Reference Work on the Afro-American*, 5th ed., ed. Harry A. Ploski and James Williams (John Wiley & Sons, New York 1987), 1212.

11. Detweiler, *The Negro Press*, 55–78; William Loren Katz, *Eyewitness: The Negro in American History* (New York: Pitman, 1968), 337–50.

12. Wolseley, *The Black Press, U.S.A.*, 52–57; and Gunnar Myrdal, *An American Dilemma* (New York: Harper and Brothers, 1944), 908–24.

13. Wolseley, *The Black Press, U.S.A.*

14. For further information on the life and works of Marcus Garvey, see Tony Martin, *The New Marcus Garvey Library*, 9 vols. (Dover, Mass.: The Majority Press, 1986). The volume used most in this chapter is 8: *Race First: The Ideological and*

Organizational Struggles of Marcus Garvey and the Universal Negro Improvement Association.

15. Pride, "Negro Newspapers," 179–81. Wolseley, *The Black Press, U.S.A.*, 30–54. Detweiler, *The Negro Press*, 53–78. Mabel Smythe, *The Black American Reference Book* (New York: Prentice Hall, 1976), cited in Luther P. Jackson, Jr., "The Age of the Publisher, 1910–1954," *Encore American and Worldwide News*, 5 July 1977, 16–20; and James Kelly, "Press: Spurning a Father's Advice," *Time*, 1 June 1987, 62–63.

16. *Encyclopedia of Associations*, 23d ed. (Detroit, Mich.: Gale Research, Inc., 1989), 2947: 58; and Lawrence D. Hogan, *A Black National News Service: The Associated Negro Press and Claude Barnett, 1919–1945* (N. J.: Associated University Presses, 1984).

17. Jackson, "Age of the Publisher," 19.

18. Roi Ottley, *Black Odyssey: The Story of the Negro in America* (New York: Charles Scribner & Sons, 1948), 262–314. Smythe, *Black American Reference Book*, 16–20.

19. Marshall Field III, "The Negro Press and the Issues of Democracy (1944): An Essay," *Encore American and Worldwide News*, 5 July 1977, 21–24.

20. "The Black Press and Broadcast Media," in *The Negro American Almanac: A Reference Work on the Afro-American*, 5th ed., ed. Harry A. Ploski and James Williams (New York: John Wiley & Sons, 1987), 1213; Wolseley, *The Black Press, U.S.A.*, 55–60; Henry G. La Brie III, ed., *Perspectives of the Black Press: 1974* (Biddleford, Maine: Mercer House Press, 1974), 28–29; Oak (see n. 1), 57–60; and Lerone Bennett, Jr., *Before the Mayflower: A History of Black America*, 5th ed. (Chicago: Johnson Publishing Co., 1982), 305–7.

21. "The Black Press and Broadcast Media," 1213; Henry G. La Brie III, "The Black Press 150 Years Old," *Negro History Bulletin* 40 (May–June, 1977): 705–10; Wolseley, *The Black Press, U.S.A.*, 61–64. Sherman Briscoe, "150 Years of Fighting for Self-Respect and First-Class Citizenship in America," *Black Press Handbook—1977* (Washington, D.C.: Howard University Press, 1977), 62–63; and Oak, *The Negro Newspaper*, 70–71.

22. Luther P. Jackson, Jr., "The Age of The Publisher 1910–1954," *Encore*, 5 July 1977, 17; Briscoe, "150 Years of Fighting," 64–65; "The Black Press and Broadcast Media," 1211.

23. Wolseley, *The Black Press, U.S.A.*; "The Black Press and Broadcast Media," 214–20.

24. "Louis Martin," *Washington Post*, 10 October 1978, B3,1; Wolseley, 60–61.

25. Wolseley, 57–65; "The Black Press and Broadcast Media, 1214 and 1220.

26. Jackson, "Age of the Publisher," 19–20; and Wolseley, 57–65.

27. Jackson, 19–20; Wolseley, 57–65.

28. Jacqueline Trescott, "Black Papers as 'Conscience,' " *Washington Star News*, 13 March 1974; "Publishers' President Triple Career Threat," *Michigan Chronicle* (April 1979).

29. Otto Kerner, Commission Chairman, Report of the National Advisory Commission on Civil Disorders, 1968. The report criticized the press for failing to report adequately on black America and for excluding black professionals from the news-gathering and editing process.

30. Wolseley, 80–87; and Lauren Kessler, *The Dissident Press: Alternative Journalism in American History*, The Sage CommText Series (Beverly Hills, Calif.: Sage Publications, 1984), 13:43–47.

31. "The Black Press and Broadcast Media," 1215–19.

32. Ibid.

33. W. Augustus Low and Virgil Clift, eds., *Encyclopedia of Black America* (New York: McGraw Hill, 1981), 736.

34. Hollie I. West, "Oakland's Black Voice," *Washington Post*, 9 September 1979), D7–D8; and Alex S. Jones, "Oakland Publisher in Uphill Struggle," *New York Times*, 5 June 1985, A16.

35. S. Lee Hilliard, "Pressing for Power," *Black Enterprise*, April 1985, 42–50; see n. 32 Clint W. Wilson II, "Pressures Against Change: Black Journalists in White Newsrooms," paper presented to the National Conference on One-Third of a Nation: African American Perspectives, Howard University, Washington, D.C., November 1989.

36. Wolseley, *The Black Press, U.S.A.*, 213–16. See also West, D7-D8, and Jones, A16 (n. 33).

37. John H. Johnson, with Lerone Bennett, Jr., *Succeeding Against the Odds* (New York: Warner Books, Inc., 1989).

38. Walter C. Daniel, *Black Journals of the United States* (Westport, Conn.: Greenwood Press, 1982), 21–175; Wolseley, 62–63; Oak, *The Negro Newspaper*, 129–32; Bullock, *The Afro-American Periodical Press*, 75–149.

39. M. J. Sobran, Jr., "Having It Both Ways," *National Review*, 8 November 1984.

40. Daniel, *Black Journals*, 53–68; "The Black Press and Broadcast Media," 1218–19.

41. Valencia Hollins Coar, *A Century of Black Photographers: 1849–1960*, 19 (Providence: Rhode Island School of Design, 1983), 181–85; Deborah Willis-Thomas, *Black Photographers, 1840-1940: An Illustrated Bio-Bibliography* (New York: Garland Publishing Company, 1985), 13–22; Deborah Willis-Thomas, *Black Photographers 1940–1988: An Illustrated Bio-Bibliography* (New York: Garland Publishing Company, 1989); Jeanne Moutoussamy-Ashe, *Viewfinders: Black Women Photographers* (New York: Dodd, Mead & Company, 1986); and Gordon Parks, *A Choice of Weapons* (St. Paul: Minnesota Historical Society Press, 1986).

42. Kerner, National Commission (n. 28).

43. Samuel L. Adams, "Blackening in the Media: The State of Blacks in The Media," in *The State of Black America: 1985* (New York: The National Urban League, 1985).

44. See the *Washington Post*, the *Washington Afro-American*, the *Chicago Defender*, and the *Kansas City Star*, between July 14 and July 25, 1988, on coverage of Carl Rowan's shooting of a teenage intruder.

45. Russwurm and Cornish, *Freedom's Journal* (see n. 3).

46. Adams, "Blackening In the Media," 65–71.

47. Ibid.

48. Ibid.

49. Wilson, "Pressures against Change," (n. 34 above), 16.

50. Lionel C. Barrow, Jr., "Role of the Black Press in the Liberation Struggle," *The Black Press Handbook—1977*(Washington, D.C.: NNPA Publishers Inc., 1977).

51. Christine Reid Veronis, "Black Press Comeback," *Presstime* July 1989, 20–22.

52. Ibid.

8 BROADCAST NEWS

LEE THORNTON

The relatively brief history of blacks in mainstream broadcast journalism might be illustrated by an event that occurred in the autumn of 1989 when Norfolk State University, at its annual communications conference, presented media "pioneer" awards to several people, me included, who entered the field in the early 1970s. In broadcast news, suffice it to say, blacks were not there at the creation. Indeed, it would be decades after Edward R. Murrow, H. V. Kaltenborn, William Shirer, Robert Trout, and other pioneers in radio and television laid the groundwork that blacks would be heard or seen at all.

The first black network correspondent was Mal Goode, hired by ABC in 1962. A decade later Goode had been joined by only a few others at the network level, but at the local level blacks were being seen in increasing numbers. However, it was not until twenty years later that African Americans were in highly visible roles at all of the commercial networks and in the local markets—large, medium, and small—in every part of the country. Today, blacks are in anchor positions in every market and, at the networks, have regularly covered such top beats as the White House and Congress. The late Max Robinson became the first black man to anchor a primetime network news program. Ed Bradley of CBS anchored a weekend newscast and joined the ranks of the top professionals·of the highly rated "60 Minutes." Bryant Gumbel became the first African American to act as host of NBC's "Today" show. At CNN, Bernard Shaw was the first black anchor. On camera, by any measure, the gain has been significant. But to this day, there are still very few African Americans in managerial, decision-making positions of authority. There is perhaps more than a little irony that, in this respect, broadcast journalism resembles professional sports. In the broadcast news industry, as in other industries discussed earlier, blacks suffer from a split image—in this case being considered good enough to be seen up front and on camera but not to be trusted to "do the thinking" and hold the reins of power.

Blacks and the Evolution of the Evening News

Ironically, it was a "black" news event that helped to foster the ritual of the American family gathered round the television set for the evening news. The story was the real and recurring drama of the struggle for desegregation that began with an act of defiance by a black seamstress—an act that inspired the young preacher Martin Luther King, Jr., to lead a year-long bus boycott in Montgomery, Alabama.

The images of the events of those years were burned into the collective American consciousness by television: hundreds of paratroopers escorting nine black youths back and forth to Central High School in Little Rock, Arkansas; attack dogs and fire hoses; club-wielding law enforcement officials attacking demonstrators who sat in at Woolworth's lunch counter in Greensboro, North Carolina, and then at other lunch counters, bus depots, movie houses, and elsewhere; bus burnings; angry mobs defending "white only" public facilities—the images of racial strife seemed endless. Outrage followed shock at the brutal racial encounters in Anniston, Birmingham, Montgomery, and Jackson, and at the assassination of NAACP leader Medgar Evers, shot down at his home in Mississippi. On the evening news violence proved to be, as Student Nonviolent Coordinating Committee leader H. Rap Brown put it, "as American as apple pie."

One of television's finest hours was its coverage of the massive and moving civil rights march on Washington, D.C., in August 1963. It was then that broadcast journalism captured the essence of the civil rights movement and made Martin Luther King's "I Have a Dream" speech a cry of hope heard round the world.

It was five years of racial trial by fire played out on television that foretold the tremendous drawing power of the medium as a disseminator of news. So powerful was the effect of the network coverage that local stations and newspapers had little choice but to give detailed and serious attention to the story, although some were not able to do it accurately. WLBT-TV in Jackson, Mississippi, slanted the story so obviously that in 1965 its management was rebuked by the Federal Communications Commission (FCC). In 1969, WLBT's license was revoked when the station lost a suit brought by the United Church of Christ acting on behalf of Jackson's black community.

In my own experience, the civil rights struggle and the story of African Americans in broadcast news crystallized one cold Christmas morning over breakfast at a highway pancake diner in Albany, Georgia. Seventeen years earlier, Albany had been the scene of a violent and unsuccessful effort to desegregate public places. I, who had been a college student in 1962, was now a White House correspondent for CBS News, covering President Jimmy Carter, who was at home in nearby Plains, Georgia. As a friendly waitress set a steaming cup of coffee on the table, it was clear that Albany had come a long way since the time when an African American would have been barred from entering that diner for a simple bacon-and-egg breakfast.

CBS News had come a long way, too. Just a decade earlier the network had hired George Foster, its first black correspondent. Now CBS was the first of the three major commercial news networks to assign a black woman to a regular beat covering the White House.

The Urban Riots and the News Media

Several years after the March on Washington, newspapers, radio, and television were strongly urged to hire African American journalists. The request came from a federal investigative panel, the National Advisory Commission on Civil Disorders, after prolonged urban unrest. The first major outbreak occurred in the summer of 1965, in Watts, a black community in Los Angeles. When it was over, nearly three dozen people were dead and hundreds of others had been injured. Property damage ran into the tens of millions. In *Responsibility in Mass Communication*, William Rivers observed that never had a riot been publicized "so starkly and in such extravagant detail." Wrote Rivers, "So intense was the reportage that millions of television viewers could have identified in a police lineup two looters who were followed by the camera as they trudged out of a burning store and down the street carrying a huge couch, as they stopped occasionally to sprawl on it and rest."[1]

Neither the riots nor the intensity of the coverage was to end with Watts. In the summer of 1967 and again in the spring of 1968, violent disorders brought some degree of destruction to predominately black sections of dozens of American cities. As noted in earlier chapters, President Lyndon Johnson appointed the National Commission on Civil Disorders, which came to be known as the Kerner Commission after its chairman, Otto Kerner. The panel studied twenty-three of the riot-torn cities and concluded that the chaos—the violence, looting and arson—grew out of grievances about police practices, unemployment, underemployment, and inadequate housing, among many other things. An entire chapter of the commission's report was devoted to the news media and the disorders. The media were criticized for failing to analyze and report adequately the racial problems in the United States and for failing to meet what the report called blacks' legitimate expectations in journalism, of failing to bring more African Americans into the profession.

In essence, the Kerner Commission indicted the media for treating African Americans as invisible people and the profession of journalism for being "shockingly backward" in not seeking out, hiring, training, and promoting black Americans.[2] The commission noted that in 1967 fewer than 5 percent of all editors and supervisors were black and most were at black-owned newspapers and radio stations. The panel noted the existence of only one black newsman, Carl Rowan, with a nationally syndicated column.

Stating that tokenism was not enough, the panel issued a clear call for change. It said African American editors and commentators were essential to the policy-making process and urged the news media "to do everything possible to train and promote their Negro reporters to positions where those who are qualified can contribute to and have an effect on policy decisions."[3] In the collective mind of the commission there was no split: blacks would do both. In no uncertain terms, the commission called on the nation's newspapers and broadcasters to make a commitment:

> Journalism is not very popular as a career for aspiring young Negroes. The starting pay is comparatively low and it is a business which has, until recently, discouraged and rejected them. The recruitment of Negro

reporters must extend beyond established journalists, or those who have already formed ambitions along these lines. It must become a commitment to seek out young Negro men and women, inspire them to become—and train them as—journalists. We believe that the news media themselves, their audiences and the country will profit from these undertakings. For if the media are to comprehend and then to project the Negro community, they must have the help of Negroes. If the media are to report with understanding, wisdom, sympathy on the problems of the black man—for the two are increasingly intertwined—they must employ, promote and listen to Negro journalists.[4]

As a first step, the commission called for the creation of an Institute of Urban Communications, private and nonprofit, to be run by journalists and distinguished public figures.

In broadcasting, the first notable step in that direction was the Program in Journalism for Members of Minority Groups. As noted in chapter 7, it was established at Columbia University in 1968 with funding from the Ford Foundation and leadership from Fred Friendly, Columbia Graduate School professor and former president of CBS News. For the next two years of its existence, the program concentrated on training minorities for broadcast journalism only. In 1971, it expanded to include print. An estimated 150 minority-group Americans completed the program, most of them sponsored by cooperating stations, and most of whom later went to those stations to work. Many of today's leading black broadcast journalists are graduates of the Columbia program. Other minority journalists who finished the program got jobs but did not manage to keep them. One fault of the program, as some saw it, was that it accepted a number of applicants who did not have high school diplomas, applicants who were not educationally equipped to keep up with the demands of the training or the profession.

For broadcast journalists, the Columbia program came to a close in June of 1974. *Washington Post* writer Joel Dreyfuss reported that Fred Friendly admitted to doubts about finding positions for future graduates. "I think the desire of the broadcasters is a little less than it used to be," Friendly is reported to have said. "The pressure is off. Maybe they feel they've done as much as they can."[5]

Two years later, CBS News began a limited minority training program of its own. Some individual stations as well as station groups also inaugurated their own programs. While the Institute for Journalism Education at Berkeley continued to train print journalists, there has been no other program like the Columbia model for preparing minority broadcast journalists.

"Never mind how good they are, how black are they?"

In 1967, researcher Royal Colle related the astonishment of British journalist Beverly Nichols on seeing for the first time a black newscaster on American television. "The unfamiliar is always frightening," said Nichols. "And here he was, in my room, in a million rooms, speaking to me." For Nichols, the sight of that African American newscaster seemed to be part of some grand solution to racial inequality. "It's simple ideas like these," Colle noted, "ideas that spring from the people with a heart, that change the lives of nations."[6]

The degree to which the life of this nation was changed by the sudden appearance of black faces on television newscasts may never be known, but as the sixties moved into the seventies, more African Americans entered the profession, although perhaps not as many as there *appeared* to be.

Researcher Waltraud Kassarjian observed that, even without conducting an analysis, "the layman lately can observe a much greater utilization of the Negro in all the media."[7] But Kassarjian raised questions about the impact, asking whether the inroads were being overestimated simply because any change was highly noticeable and apparently more than a little surprising. If there was a dominant image of blacks in television and radio up to that time, it had more to do with Rochester on Jack Benny's program and Beulah on radio than a reporter delivering the news.

Like women, African Americans in television news had a high visibility factor. Most of those black faces were there in large part because the urban riots had forced the hiring of many black reporters and camera operators who were needed to go into the riot corridors. Although some white reporters toughed it out, they were the exception and not the norm. Rivers noted the bravado of some white journalists covering the violence in Watts, observing that some of the riot leaders considered those reporters and photographers so laughably audacious that they were simply allowed to roam at will. But as Dorothy Gilliam, then a freelance writer, described it, "Here was a new phenomenon: white reporters were chased away when they showed up. Black copyboys and messengers, even, became instant reporters during that period. And most metropolitan newspapers, wire services, and TV stations started taking the hiring of black professionals seriously—more or less."[8]

Joel Dreyfuss wrote of this period, "Black reporters, sometimes freshly promoted from secretarial and menial jobs, gave on-the-scene reports from locations that resembled postwar Germany."[9] Robert Northshield, then an NBC executive producer, said: "There is a tendency to say, 'Never mind how good they are, how black are they?'" Fred Friendly of CBS "half expected finder's fees for identifying African Americans with journalistic potential."[10] The sudden demand for black journalists at the time extended all the way to the proverbial top. CBS News hired its first African American correspondent, George Foster, during this period. Actually, as Foster tells it, he had been on the premises working with the production unit for a religious program for a year. As the riots erupted he suddenly found his opinions sought after by "Black Rock," the famed Manhattan headquarters of CBS—and soon he was reporting the riot story. For the first time, television news needed the image of a black news reporter, and there was no mistaking the exploitation of that black image doing standups against a backdrop of chaos in the streets.

Enter the FCC

In June of 1969 the FCC adopted rules prohibiting discrimination in employment in the broadcast industry. Under the regulations, broadcast licensees with five or more full-time employees were required to file annual reports showing the number of minority workers in nine job categories. The FCC released its first study of industry employment practices in 1973, finding that the previous year about one in ten of all workers surveyed was a member of one of four key minority groups: African American, Oriental, American Indian, and Spanish-surnamed Americans. African Americans accounted for 6.6 percent of all workers in the field, the largest minority representation. Spanish-surnamed workers were second, with 3 percent. Orientals accounted for .5 percent. And native Americans accounted for only .4 percent. All categories combined did not come close to the 23 percent representation of women in the industry that year, this latter group comprised white females overwhelmingly.

But compared with the Kerner Commission's findings, the FCC numbers seemed encouraging. However, late in 1972, the United Church of Christ released a survey showing that one in five of all commercial stations had no minority employees. One in three stations had no minority group members in the upper four job classifications: officials and managers, professionals (newswriters, reporters, announcers), technicians, and sales account executives. According to the UCC, African Americans and other minorities held only 8 percent of the higher salaried jobs in an industry where two-thirds of all full-time workers were in the upper salary categories. Nearly eight of ten stations had no minority employees in management positions. The stations' discrimination against blacks and other minorities was obvious.

"They *use* you, man!"

Little exists in the literature on the subject of how much black and other minority broadcast journalists were utilized during this period. What is available tends to indicate that after the period of the urban riots, their participation was not a matter of priority for management. In a study covering two time periods in 1972 and 1973, Churchill Roberts counted fourteen African Americans in ninety television newscasts—eleven during the 1972 period, and three during the viewing period in the following year. In the period studied in 1973, no black reporters at all were seen on CBS News, and only one appeared on ABC News. Journalist Jules Witcover, surveying the Washington journalism scene, wrote that the three major networks had only two full-time black correspondents. Observed Witcover, "TV directors particularly say they are looking for qualified blacks, but, as Frank Jordan of NBC says, 'All the networks in Washington are way past the point where we just hire readers. We need a man who is qualified as a good correspondent with solid reporting credentials, who also can go on the air—with voice, appearance and delivery.' "[11] Witcover added that the combination was rare among African Americans "for the same reason there are not more experienced black newspaper reporters—the early days of closed doors."

The relationship between those black pioneers of 1973 and white managers appears to have been an uneasy one at best. Dorothy Gilliam, who went on to become a *Washington Post* columnist, reported an outburst by a "top black reporter" speaking to a group of journalism students. "They *use* you, man! And when you get out there—way out there—they often don't back you up!"[12] It was a complaint that with some variations would be heard repeatedly over the next decade and longer, even as the numbers of African Americans in the field continued to increase.

By 1975 black representation in the industry had grown from the 6.6 percent of 1972 to a total of 8 percent.

Illusion or Reality?

In August of 1977 the United States Commission on Civil Rights issued a report entitled *Window Dressing on the Set: Women and Minorities in Television*. In essence, the report said the broadcasting industry had employed members of minority groups and women but had not made significant progress in promoting them. The Civil Rights Commission took the FCC to task for the inadequacy of its reporting instrument, Form 395, used to survey those stations with more than five full-time workers. The commission attacked the form for being too broadly defined and for including such a wide range of job classifications as to obscure the degree of decision-making responsibility. The study singled-out forty television stations for further study but agreed with the FCC that minority and female employment did indeed increase between 1971 and 1975. Moreover, the commission said the numbers rose in each of the upper four job categories. But the conclusion was that things were not all that they appeared to be. "Contrary to the impression one may form from these data," the commission said, "minorities and women have not necessarily made significant employment gains at these stations."[13] The commission said its own detailed analysis of job titles and job categories showed that women and minorities were neither being fully utilized at all levels of station management nor in all levels of station operations. In the judgment of the commission, it was white males who held the vast majority of the decision-making positions in every job category and within every department of the stations studied. Sounding much the same as the Kerner Commission nine years before, the Civil Rights Commission said its finding was particularly important with regard to programming because of the potential impact of television programs on American society.

Window Dressing on the Set also raised questions about the presence of women and minorities on network news programs. The study examined a composite week of ABC, CBS, and NBC broadcasts randomly selected from March 1974 to February 1975. It found that white males outnumbered minority and female correspondents by almost nine to one and noted that minority and female correspondents rarely covered crucial national stories but tended to cover issues related to minorities' and women's interests.

In 1982, Michael Massing, executive editor of the *Columbia Journalism Review*, conducted a management head count at the three commercial networks and found that the highest-ranking African American at NBC was chief of a midwestern bureau. At ABC, the top off-screen job was held by an assignment editor on the nightly news show. At CBS, like NBC, the top position was held by a bureau chief. Massing observed that there was not much hope for an increase in the numbers of African Americans and other minorities in top management because very few of the people in the "pipeline" jobs to such positions were minority group members. As Massing stated, "These are the producers and associate producers who do much of the day-to-day work behind the camera. Of the approximately two hundred such producers at NBC, only eleven were black. At CBS, which has two hundred and sixty-five such producers, only twelve were black. ABC, with a similar total, has about fifteen blacks in production (about half of them in lower-level slots)."[14] But for the industry overall, the FCC continued to report increasing minority representation. Of all workers in the upper four job categories in 1981, the FCC reported that 12.7 percent were minority group members. The figure was the same for 1982.

What seems most obvious about the struggles of black broadcast journalists is that many, if not most, fought their way to the local or national level only to become disillusioned with the role they were to play. They had sought to be journalists, reporters, and producers who would not only do the job well but affect the status quo. Relatively few were able to claim that accomplishment. Many pointed with frustration to a system of unconscious racism that relegated them to roles of inferiors.

But no serious examination of the concerns of African Americans in broadcast journalism should neglect one salient point: broadcast news is a tough, highly competitive, and complex business. The reality of it is very different from the uninformed public perception of the work as "glamorous." It was David Brinkley who described the essential nature of the business as one of monotony, of working holidays, and, when there is little news, of working relentlessly difficult hours and of fighting off a certain psychological corrosiveness. It is a business that is extremely demanding of everyone connected with it. The show must go on. But if there was psychological corrosiveness, African Americans wanted an equal opportunity to share in it. What they experienced was another, more serious, form: a psychological corrosion having to do with the feeling of not being heard and of having no control—what Joel Dreyfuss called "presence without power," because, again, there was a certain problem with their image.

Black professionals who might otherwise have been primarily concerned only with editorial issues, with balance, and with the problems inherent in presenting ethical and accurate ninety-second stories (including fifteen-second sound bite and on-camera close) instead found themselves fighting to maintain their personal and professional dignity. Of his pioneering days as the first black correspondent at a network, Mal Goode said flatly, "There was never a day that something didn't come up to remind me I was black."[15] In 1974 others were also speaking bluntly about their frustrations. CBS News associate producer Marquita Poole, then with public broadcasting, said: "We helped put ourselves in a box. It is an understandable process we went through, but that has left us as unnecessary to the operation. We were always minorities, extras."[16] Max Robinson, then a WTOP-TV anchorman, said: "On one level, I've become more successful. I make twice the money I used to make three years ago, but I have half the influence."[17] Robert Reid, then with NBC News, said: "There is still a tendency to hire the average white guy and to look for the superblack. If an employer can't make a case for one guy being better than another, and if there are no pressures from the FCC or otherwise, which one do you think is going to be hired?"[18]

A broadcaster who declined to have his name used out of apparent fear of reprisal said, "News is a quasi-cultural effort—it's a view of the world. The whites who control it are not willing to deal with those who see the world differently. That's the big psychic factor."[19]

Bill Matney, then with ABC News, told the writer during a press stakeout of presidential daughter Amy Carter that he could rarely get anything at all on the air. Matney's observation came not at the beginning of a career but after long years as a network correspondent. He was one of the first African Americans in broadcast journalism, hired away from the *Detroit News* in 1963 by NBC. He covered the urban disorders and from 1970 to 1972 was a White House correspondent for NBC. His network tour of duty also took him to ABC. Matney once joked about running into CBS's Hal Walker on an assignment at dawn and Walker asking about the lone black at NBC. Said Matney, "Hal facetiously asked, 'Where's Gordon Graham? Doesn't he know we're having a meeting here?' "[20]

Although humor might have been good for the soul, those African Americans who spoke out most often and most forcefully found the going rough, and certainly no joking matter. It was unavoidable that the split in the image of African Americans in broadcast news, their view of themselves versus the views of those in power, would eventually collide.

"Their time had come and gone . . ."

At the outset of the 1980s, white journalists looked in on what they called the "plight of black reporters" and found much the same kind of frustration that had been voiced nearly a decade before. There was, as *TV Guide* put it, "a pervasive feeling among blacks in network news that their time had come and gone."[21] Former CBS newsman Randy Daniels revealed why he had chosen to leave the network and work as an adviser to the Nigerian Television Authority: "I met with every level of management of CBS News, both past and present, over issues that specifically relate to blacks and minorities. When it became clear to me that such meetings accomplished nothing, I chose to leave and work where my ideas were wanted and needed. I have found my race an impediment to being assigned major stories across the entire spectrum of news."[22]

ABC News correspondent Carol Simpson, who left NBC at the same time as several other black reporters, noted: "Not only isn't there any pressure to promote blacks—I see an erosion of progress. They just don't care any more. We're not voguish any more."[23] CBS News correspondent Lem Tucker, speaking to the Radio and

Television News Directors Association in 1981, said: "We took the jobs for the wrong reasons. We saw fame. We saw glory. We saw a chance to change the world. We wanted to be up front. The long, hot summers of the late sixties created a need for me, for many of my brothers and sisters on television—'up close and personal,' I believe the expression goes. The cry went out, 'Let's find us some blacks. Not too threatening, if you please. Hopefully with a well-trimmed afro. Let's hope they're reasonably intelligent. And let's get them on the tube.' You did not pay as much attention to their careers as you did to those of white staffers. So in came young, sometimes extremely bright minorities. They may have needed help in writing, or in how to conduct a better interview. . . . But too often you did not give them that kind of support. Well, of course, many of them didn't make the cut."[24]

Those who did make the cut wrestled not only with those concerns but with the basic need of the reporter, which, as Roger Mudd has said, is to report. African Americans were brought into the industry to report stories about blacks, and they recognized that if they did not do that reporting there was the risk of losing some of the sensitivity, if not the objectivity, that black journalists can bring to the business. At the same time, there was a type of split in the internal image: the need among some to be *journalists* first. Bernard Shaw often said he thought of himself as a journalist who is black rather than as a black journalist. Ed Bradley repeated that sentiment: "I'm a reporter who happens to be black. It's too easy to paint yourself into a corner. On '60 Minutes' I want to break down doors and interview Bette Davis, the same as Mike Wallace. Or do a piece on the Muppets, like Morley Safer. Did Morley do that because he was a Muppet?"[25] Bob Teague, who had a long career with NBC, chafed at being interviewed for a magazine story on the problems of the black reporter: "I am one of dozens of TV news reporters and I resent the fact that I'm only interviewed for a story like this one, on black correspondents. I'm a professional journalist, not a professional black."[26]

How pervasive that feeling was is impossible to say. But for every Shaw and Bradley there were probably hundreds of others who felt that if black reporters did not cover stories revolving around African American concerns, did not push for those stories, who would?

If the concerns of black broadcast journalists were heard (and they were all but inescapable) by those in power in the industry, rarely, if ever, was there a satisfactory response. More typical was the response of an NBC executive who said the character of the journalist is what counts—that the "less negative" the reporter, the higher the climb. As was so often the case, whether an African American *thought* of himself as a black reporter or not, there was an absence of a reasonable response.

A System of Unconscious Racism?

It would be simple, as some have done, to attribute the grievances of African Americans in broadcast journalism to pure and simple racism, although it is undeniable that journalism has historically and systematically excluded members of minority groups.

Bob Maynard, as noted in chapter 7, became the first African American to edit, publish, and then own a major metropolitan daily newspaper. But long before that, he met with the kind of rejection that would have killed many a career. In 1956, Maynard was granted a job interview with an editor in White Plains, New York. "The interview was late at night. There was no one around, and only one light on in his office in a darkened building." The editor told Maynard, "He 'wouldn't have a problem,' but he 'didn't think his employees would accept it.' "[27]

Over a ten-year period, Maynard wrote letters of application to more than three hundred newspapers and was turned down by virtually all of them because of his race. He said he was sure of that because a number of times he removed his black story clips and deleted the names of black newspapers from his résumé. The result was that he got the interviews, but not the jobs. Maynard confessed that there were times when he thought about becoming a "bomb thrower," but instead of getting angrier he decided to "get even."

The treatment Maynard received was racist in its nature and its intent. But racism can come in many forms. What of the broadcast organizations who hired blacks to be be on-air reporters and were unable to trust them to do the job? What of the broadcast managers who created the so-called weekend ghettos comprised of minority production and on-camera personnel? Why, in my experience, have a considerable number of young black reporters, complete strangers, called or written to ask advice about how to handle what they labeled blatantly unfair treatment by news directors and producers?

Richard Levine, writing in *TV Guide* about the problem, said: "It was a tricky business, this disillusionment on the part of blacks in network news departments, caused less by conscious racism than by the insensitivity of white management. The trouble was that black reporters could never be certain if they were getting routine assignments, or none at all, because of the inevitable but evenhanded workings of an increasingly competitive system, or because they were the fall guys for the system."[28] In the past quarter of a century the system has grown increasingly large and complex. The advances in technology, the huge budgets for news divisions, the vast numbers of personnel, and the public demand for broadcast news in the mid-1980s bore little resemblance to the state of the industry even a decade earlier.

What did not change was the amount of air time available for news on a daily basis. That fact affects not only the kinds of stories that make air but also is a determining factor in who will report those stories. Few would deny that there is a hierarchy of reporters who are given most of the air time at virtually every broadcast outlet. This is the so-called star system, based sometimes on excellence, sometimes on other factors, including physical appearance. Industry veteran Gil Noble wrote about the phenomenon in his book *Black Is the Color of My TV Tube*:

"Reporters are called into the news director's office with increasing frequency and are criticized on such vital points as their wardrobe, their makeup, and the need to smile at the camera more often. News teams are currently popular, since the consulting firms found teams to be more effective with audience ratings. The motivation behind these concerns is not to provide more and better news service, but to impress the viewing public. It is not uncommon to hear of reporters who have been hired because they possess a certain 'kinky' quality."[29]

Noble went on to describe how this process actually alters the content of news stories: "Newsroom executives have told me that reporters must become more involved in the stories they cover. We are to be visually prominent in film and taped reports, even if it takes more time to set up the camera crew to record the reporter striding into and out of a news clip."[30]

In one form or other, the system is alive at both the local and network levels.   Shortly after he inherited the anchor desk from Walter Cronkite at CBS News, Dan Rather issued a call for the Washington reporters he wanted to see on the "CBS Evening News" on a regular basis.   At the time there were three black correspondents at the network's Washington bureau, Jacqueline Adams, Lem Tucker, and me.   None of us was on the list.   Racism on the part of Rather? Certainly not.   But Rather's action was fairly typical of a business that is, as even Murrow acknowledged, a mixture of journalism, advertising, and entertainment, a business where standards are ever-changing, a business where only a very small number of African Americans are in positions to affect those standards, and a business of *image*.

Management: "Why are there so few?"

Massing reported an outburst by Hispanic reporter J. J. Gonzalez at an October 1981 forum on issues involved in press coverage of New York City.   It was a large gathering with WNBC-TV newsman Felipe Luciano among the panelists.   At one point Luciano spoke of "racism, sheer racism that happens all the time in our newsroom. It infuriates me, it sickens me."[31]   As Massing related it, WNBC newsman Gabe Pressman then "countered by asserting the importance of traditional standards of quality and objectivity."   It was then that Gonzalez exploded, "Who passes the goddam judgment on competency?   Come on, now!   Don't tell me 'competency.' [Even] when you get the competent person in, he is not allowed [to do the job].   So stop your bull!"[32]   Massing reported that this naked display of hostility left the audience stunned.

If there has been wordplay and a lack of evenhandedness about the competency of minority broadcasters, there seems to have been even more of both about the ability of minorities to be part of the management of news operations.   Renee Pouissant, then a CBS News correspondent, made an appointment with a CBS management recruiter who told her that she "didn't have a chance, that there really is an old boys network."[33]   Former CBS News president Richard Salant is among those who have denied the existence of such a system, although Salant admitted that there is what he called a "friendship" network from which management tends to be selected.   Salant also said there are "very few slots that open up.   If someone, black or white, had decided he wanted to be head of CBS News back in 1961, he'd have had to wait 18 years for me to get the hell out of there."[34]

But Salant was acutely aware of the lack of black producers at CBS News. He called the situation a real problem, one he would bring up at every staff meeting but get nowhere with because the pool of qualified people was so small.

As late as 1981, *TV Guide* reported that there was not a single black executive producer or vice president in news at any of the networks. That there were not more middle and top black managers in the industry cannot be blamed entirely on the system. In fact, far fewer African Americans sought to enter this arena. Michael Douglass, vice president and general manager of WTOP-AM, an all-news radio station in Washington, D.C., said: "I think too many people in the minority community are star struck. They want to be on the screen or behind the microphone. They do not appreciate the importance of sales or what you can do with a sales background in the broadcasting business."[35] And it seems clear that the majority of those African Americans most interested in entering the field held an image of themselves as on-air talent. Still, many of those who wanted the management track met with discouragement.

In 1982, the chairman of the National Black Media Coalition, Pluria Marshall, noted that in Washington, D.C., with a very large proportion of black on-air reporters and anchors, there was not a single black news director in TV, not one executive producer of the news, or a general sales manager. There was one station manager. Again, sounding much like the report of the Kerner Commission, Dwight Ellis of the National Association of Broadcasters said in 1983 that the shortage of black managers results in a loss to the industry of "the opportunity to give an accurate, positive image of black Americans."[36]

Those few African Americans who have successfully entered the management mainstream attribute their rise to training and internship programs, and to strong affirmative action programs, which are, like the Columbia program, all but defunct. Ron Townsend, now a top-level executive with Gannett, was one of fewer than a half-dozen black general managers of major television stations in the entire nation. Tony Rose of the Washington Area Media Organization asked plaintively, "Why are there so few? That's the question we're addressing. Why are there so few?"[37]

One Reporter's Story

There are as many stories of success and hardship in the business of broadcast news as there are broadcast journalists. What follows is just one such story, that of Phyllis Crockett of National Public Radio, told in her words. Crockett's story is one with themes common to many blacks in the industry, a story of struggle and concern for being given an even break as well as concern for how issues of importance to African Americans are covered—or not covered. It is the story of a black reporter struggling with her own split image, wanting to be a part of mainstream media but remain true to her African American cultural ideals, the story of a black reporter who followed all the rules and yet came up against a brick wall of resistance to her black image. It is a very personal story by a reporter who fought the odds, overcame the split image, and won.

> My situation is not typical. If anything I am one of the lucky ones, a person who through sheer perseverance and the grace of God at long last won the opportunity most African Americans in broadcasting never get. Sure this smacks of racism that the gatekeepers in the industry will deny. But I believe there is no other explanation.
>
> In August of 1985, after nearly ten years in the business as a reporter, producer, writer, editor, commentator, talk show host as well as guest, lecturer, teacher and consultant, I was offered a reporter trainee position at National Public Radio. In 1978 I received a master's degree from Northwestern University's Medill School of Journalism. I had worked for three national news organizations, including NPR, where I was an assistant producer for "All Things Considered" for more than two years. On a freelance basis for NPR, I had worked as an on-air reporter, covering more than seventy stories in a three-year period, including twelve documentaries.
>
> Each time I applied for a full-time reporting position at NPR I was turned down. Each time a white male was hired instead. In two instances their experience was less substantial than mine. Not being one to take injustice without a fight, I found the best lawyer in town for equal opportunity cases and contacted the National Black Media Coalition. The Coalition functions in an advocacy role on behalf of blacks in the industry as well as those who want to be in the industry. The NBMC agreed that African Americans at NPR were not getting equal treatment and decided to take my case. I never filed suit, instead my lawyer and the Coalition wrote letters to NPR pointing out the problems and suggesting that we work out a solution. Of course there was an implied threat of a suit if things did not work out.
>
> During this time, NPR sent a crew of about ten people to the United Nations Decade for Women conference in Nairobi, Kenya. I applied to

go but was turned down. Instead, NPR sent an all-white editorial team to Africa where the problems of black and other third world women were high on the agenda. When asked why I was denied the opportunity to go, my superiors told me that the white folks who were chosen had "third world experience." I had a third world experience by having been married to an African for seven years. I had covered third world issues in the past. I had personally known poverty and the problems of single female-headed households. All of this I felt would make me a valuable addition to the African assignment, but my superiors felt this experience was unimportant.

To me this was another example of my being denied not only the reporter's job that I wanted, but the assignments I wanted. In addition to these outside pressures, there was at least one highly placed person on the inside who went to bat for me. Since I had done numerous pieces and work with various producers and editors on NPR programs, I was not an unknown quantity. My work was known to be good and I had never missed a deadline. I also got along with my coworkers.

I believe it was because of these external and internal pressures that I was offered the reporter trainee position. Since the position meant doing work I wanted to do and since it paid nearly $10,000 more than my salary as an assistant producer, I felt I had no alternative but to take the job. However, in a memo to the news director I did ask why I was being relegated to reporter trainee. He replied that my experience was indeed comparable to other reporters. He failed to explain why I was to be a trainee while they were not.

One might conclude that I was being treated differently. What was different about me? Unlike most of my colleagues, I am not white, Jewish, male, well-off, or from the northeast. I am black. My parents are from a working-class background. I was raised in the inner city of Chicago's South Side. None of my relatives own a media outlet or worked in the media. I am a single parent with an African ex-husband who does not pay child support. My view of the world is a legitimate one, although different from the whites I work with. They do not know or understand what I think. I once told a white editor that if she were the only white female from the rural south at an all-black urban paper in the north, she would definitely be inclined to see stories from a different point of view.

Despite my background, I was determined to get the education and experience I needed to be successful in broadcasting. I believed in my ability to do it and diligently prepared myself. I did everything they said you were supposed to do: I went to a smaller market to get experience; I joined professional associations; I networked, and got a mentor. And I had gone to one of the "right" schools. I paid my dues, yet, despite my best efforts, I remained in low-ranking, low-paying positions.

There is a great irony in all this. Among the people I interviewed with after completing graduate school was the manager of the reporters' bureau at NPR. I asked him what was necessary to become a reporter there. He told me I needed at least five years of experience and suggested I get it in a smaller market where the opportunities were greater. Since I had received this same advice from professors and other professionals in the field, I set off on that course. Yet this same man, who later became NPR's news director, told me when a reporter's position opened that I did not have enough experience and needed more. When I reminded him that I had already done everything he had advised me to do some years ago, he was unable to justify what he had said previously. At one time I believed it was basically ability and nerve that determined who got ahead. I learned along the way that it wasn't necessarily so.

One of my first steps on the career ladder took place at a Radio and Television News Directors' Association convention meeting in Atlanta. I met the news director of an all-news station in Charlotte, North Carolina. He had an opening for a reporter at his station. A month later I was flown in for an interview and hired. I did not want to leave my family, give up my social life and cultural activities for a job in a city and state where I knew no one. I did it because I was convinced it was the only way to get ahead. To complicate matters, I was a single parent with a house full of furniture that the new job in Charlotte would not pay to move. My meager funds were exhausted by graduate school. Because the course work was so demanding, I could not work for the nearly two years I was there.

After my first paycheck ($200 for a six-day work week), I was able to find an apartment. My daughter was then seven. She and I slept on the floor until I saved enough money to bring my furniture down from Chicago.

I got excellent experience at the job in Charlotte. I reported breaking news daily. I also developed the black community beat because a lot was going on there that was newsworthy but was not being covered. I covered the school board, the housing authority, and the banking industry, as well as entertainment. I had an opportunity to produce the early news, which meant arriving at work at three in the morning. The program featured a live interview as well as regular traffic reports. I also began anchoring the five-hour news show on Saturday morning, engineering my own board. When an opportunity came a year later to produce and anchor daily, I left. The new job paid nearly $5,000 more and called for working only one Saturday a month. In Fayetteville, North Carolina, I was a big fish in a small pond. I was able to interview every important person who traveled to town. Because the town is the home of Fort Bragg, a huge military base, there were many people passing through. I interviewed the governor, the congressmen, and a great many celebrities.

In each of these, my first two full-time jobs in broadcasting, I became aware of differing perceptions of what is news, especially as it relates to so-called black issues. At the white organizations where I worked, the editors were at a distinct disadvantage when it came to stories in the black community. Without exception, these editors knew virtually nothing about these stories. Many times their inclination was to push off a piece simply because they did not know anything about it. I found my credibility with them slowly growing as stories I suggested regularly turned up later in other media—the local newspaper, the *New York Times* or the national news magazines. Still, their primary interest was in stories they knew and felt comfortable with. So I spent a fair amount of time on regular beats like police, education, and city hall. This was fine, yet I have an intense personal interest in covering stories in the black community. I did not consider this a controversial stand until some black reporters began to make it an issue by saying they were reporters first who just happened to be black. After lots of thought I found I had problems with that concept. First of all, I was born black and I will die black. I was not born a reporter and I may not be a reporter when I die. White reporters don't find it necessary to say, "I'm a reporter first and white second." The fact that they are white and happen to be a reporter is simply taken for granted. If they show interest in covering a particular beat—politics, education, economics, the environment, it's not a big deal. Yet African Americans in journalism are often pushed into being defensive and fall for the ruse that stories in the black community are insignificant, therefore they often do not want to cover these stories because they are afraid of being stereotyped. I don't believe every black reporter should be assigned black stories exclusively, nor do I believe that if a reporter wants to cover the black community beat, the choice should not be treated with as much respect as if he wanted to cover defense or any other beat. And just because a reporter is black does not mean he or she will be good at covering the black community. It takes someone who has an interest in doing it, who has knowledge of the black community from having been around, and who studies the issues involved.

When I left the job in Fayetteville, I went to work for a black-owned national radio network, Sheridan Broadcasting. At that time, Sheridan's editorial staff was based in the Washington, D.C. area. As executive editor, I supervised the work of the reporters, assigned stories, and managed logistics. I also hosted a monthly news interview program and did occasional special assignment reporting. Among the reasons I enjoyed my time at Sheridan was that race was never an issue. We felt we were performing a valuable service by providing news to black listeners. Many of the stories we covered were ignored by the major media. The main frustration with working for a black-owned media company was lack of sufficient resources. On the one hand, our mandate was to cover news around the world for regular broadcasts, yet there was never enough money to do things the way they should have been done. Sadly, this is the case for virtually all black-owned media, with only a few notable exceptions.

I left Sheridan, as the company began to undergo a financial crunch. I landed a job in television as a writer for WTTG-TV for their evening news broadcast. I worked there only a few months, long enough to learn that I preferred working in radio. While at WTTG, I worked as a full-time freelancer at NPR, a 40-hour week. I was paid for the pieces I completed, not the number of hours I put in. As a freelancer I received no benefits, but I was on the air regularly and worked on interesting assignments. After about a year I was hired on staff at the relatively low level of assistant producer. This happened during a period of rapid expansion at NPR. I took the position because I needed a full-time job, although I was disappointed at not getting one of the higher, better-paying positions. Three months after I began, NPR was hit with a major financial crisis that threatened its very existence. The unit I worked for was eliminated. Nearly a third of the entire NPR staff was let go over a six-month period. To this day I maintain it was only through the grace of God that I was kept on and eventually placed on the "All Things Considered" staff. The feeling among some was that I was so vocal that they were afraid to get rid of me.

There had been several instances in my early days on staff in which I felt compelled to speak out. For example, I missed a promotion simply because I didn't know about it. This is not unusual. There is an "ole white boys" network that excludes us. A coworker, who happened to be a white male, was also an assistant producer. He was promoted to a level that paid about $5,000 more. I pointed out to my boss that this wasn't fair. I was ignored. At the numerous staff meetings held during the period of the cutbacks, I often raised questions about why African Americans, who were already few in number, were being let go at a highly disproportionate rate. I was told it just happened to be that way.

At one point I tried to organize the remaining African Americans at NPR to press for a better deal. I was devastated to learn that while the great majority, if not all, felt we were being mistreated as a group, virtually none was willing to fight for his rights. Most seemed to feel they would jeopardize their jobs and be branded as troublemakers. They were willing to quietly agitate for change but when we discussed filing a class action suit, putting up money for a lawyer, and having several others stand with me as plaintiffs in the suit, I found myself standing alone. At that point I decided to go forward alone and got my own lawyer.

Above my typewriter at work I have this quotation from Frederick Douglass, the great orator and abolitionist: "If there is no struggle, there is no progress. Those who profess to favor freedom and yet deprecate agitation are people who want crops without plowing up the ground. They want the rain without the thunder and lightning. They want the ocean without the awful roar of its many waters. This struggle may be both moral and physical. But it must be a struggle. Power concedes nothing without a demand. It never did and it never will." I read this often as I pondered my situation at NPR. It is a good place to work in many ways and I realized that the higher-ups were never going to give me the reporter's position I knew I deserved without a fight. Because of my cultural background, I am perceived as too different from them and they find this threatening. But I deeply believe in the concept that the media should reflect the different voices that the exist in society. They may not want to hear these voices, but the voices cannot be silenced.

Looking forward, I don't believe there will be much change for African Americans in journalism. If you are a carbon copy of a white person with the only difference being black skin, your chances are probably no better than those of a black who celebrates the black experience. Those raised in a black cultural environment know the difference. Few whites know these cultural differences. They may like you personally but being different is not something they handle well. Journalism is an exclusive field which by definition means excluding certain people. The gatekeepers don't necessarily want to share.

Of course, there are notable exceptions, and, in the face of great disenchantment, there will sometimes be one or two individual whites who are in a position to make a difference and who are willing to do so. The business needs more like them who are aware of how African Americans in journalism, with rare exceptions, continue to be treated differently from our white colleagues. But those of us who, despite it all, want to pursue journalism careers need to be aware of what we're up against and we must press on. If we don't, there'll be no hope of change.

Some will read my story and question whether it is really racism that works against me. I gave a draft of this manuscript to a white colleague for her reaction. She read it and said, "This would never have happened to me if I'd had your experience and education." I played by the rules of the game. Why else, if not for my race, did it take me as long as it did to achieve the reporter's position I wanted? Also, why is it that at NPR out of hundreds of full-time staffers there are only a handful of blacks? Is it just a coincidence?

White friends have told me they could not imagine being given a reporter-trainee position after having worked as a reporter, producer, writer, editor, commentator, talk show host and guest, teacher, and consultant for a total of ten years. I am not the first black to raise questions of racism at NPR. In two other instances, suits were brought by African Americans, resulting in an out-of-court settlement and a promotion. Apparently, there is some merit to charges of racism at NPR and, indeed, throughout the industry.

What I find now is that the stories I do involving black people are not highly valued. There are exceptions, such as major productions, which I suspect are appreciated more for their production value than for the subject matter. But run-of-the-mill stories consistently get the go-ahead. Perhaps this is to state the obvious, but I know this would be different if there were more African Americans here, particularly editors and producers.

For those who read my story and see racism on my part, here is my response: To grow up black in America is to grow up with problems white people do not have. This is a result of racism. What I am coming to understand is that most white journalists go about their business and rarely even think about African Americans or whether we are treated differently. As I said, one solution at National Public Radio would be to hire more African Americans. But then that's the story of this industry, isn't it?

Maybe it was the power of prayer and determination, I don't know, but every editor who stood in my way, including the then news director, was either fired or transferred to a position where they no longer had control over my professional life.

By 1989, I was earning $50,000 and would earn $60,000 in 1990, including overtime and freelance work. I was way past the rank of "trainee." An important part of this was a reorganization of the blacks at NPR. We documented our lack of opportunity here. We had support on the board and eventually enlisted the support of NPR president, Doug Bennet. Another news director was hired, Adam Clayton Powell III, son of the late congressman. I didn't make any assumptions about him because his daddy was a famous race man. His style is totally different but, by and large, Adam has done right by me.*

I got an editor, a white woman, who genuinely cared about my development and made sure I got assignments that would enable me to grow. I had an opportunity to cover the presidential campaigns of Jesse Jackson, Michael Dukakis, and George Bush. I delivered. I was assigned to the White House.

But the story has not ended. There's a new managing editor, a white man, who questions whether I am enough of a heavyweight to cover the White House. I presented my case and he agreed to let me stay there for a few months to see what I can do. I refuse to look at this development as another probation. Instead, every day I try to do my best work. I am still growing. That's one of the joys of journalism. I'm constantly learning. And I know I have paid my dues. I have a right to be here. When I leave it will be because I am ready to go.

Twists and New Turns

In September of 1985, black anchorman Harry Porterfield was demoted at CBS-owned WBBM in Chicago to make room for Bill

---

* AUTHOR'S NOTE: From the beginning of his two and one-half year tenure at NPR, Adam Powell III was a controversial figure. He resigned abruptly in February, 1990. Inside the organization the resignation was perceived as unwilling, but Powell said he had accomplished what he set out to do in public radio. Some blacks at NPR said Powell was a victim of a certain high-handedness and lack of confidence on the part of a few powerful white reporters at the network.

Kurtis, who was returning to local broadcasting after a stint as anchor of the "CBS Morning News." In response, Jesse Jackson accused CBS of what he called "de facto apartheid" and launched a boycott of the CBS network and CBS-owned stations, demanding the hiring of more black executives and black news anchors. From its Chicago base, Operation PUSH (People United to Save Humanity) initially targeted only WBBM, but later expanded its boycott to a national campaign.

Like most such efforts, that boycott accomplished relatively little. In response to Jackson's charge, then CBS chairman and president Thomas Wyman said the network had "broken some ice"[38] and cited a few appointments of minority group members to executive jobs, including the post of general manager of WBBM.

By 1986, another issue that had long simmered among African Americans in the industry broke into the open. This one had to do with self-image, the feeling of many black men that the industry favors and promotes black women. Dwight Ellis of the National Association of Broadcasters was firm in his belief that black men, along with Asian Americans, and Native Americans were "becoming endangered groups in the industry."[39] Others, including Percy Sutton, agreed that the ranks of white women and Hispanics were growing at the expense of black men. The chief negotiator for PUSH in the WBBM boycott, the Reverend Henry Hardy, felt that "historically, white America has always sought to undermine black men and sometimes use black women as a double minority."[40] In fact, in the WBBM dispute, PUSH originally specified that black male anchors be hired rather than qualified African Americans regardless of gender. It was a demand that the organization later abandoned, but within the ranks of black broadcast journalists the damage was done.

ABC correspondent Carole Simpson said she "went berserk" when she learned of the original PUSH demand for hiring black males. Said Simpson, "What is so amazing to me is that a civil rights organization that is against discrimination would put itself in the position of discriminating against black women."[41] Simpson went on to point out the obvious, saying, "Name a black woman who has ever been in such a highly visible role as Bryant Gumbel or Ed Bradley or Max Robinson."

But by 1989, Simpson herself had made broadcast history, gaining the distinction of becoming the first African American woman to anchor a network evening newscast. In the summer of that year, Simpson sat in on two consecutive nights for anchorman Peter Jennings. At the time, Simpson was also regular anchor of ABC's Saturday evening newscast, another first. The image of the gender and color of the person behind the anchor desk had changed and, given the history of blacks in television and radio journalism in the United States, its significance deserves note.

"Better late than . . ."

At the network level, television journalism has been most thorough in its coverage of blacks and their concerns through the use of the "special," and not ongoing day-to-day reportage. J. Fred MacDonald, author of *Blacks and White TV* has noted the absence of much research in this area, but there is general agreement that local television and radio newscasters can be credited with more and better coverage of minority group issues on a continuing basis. However the networks, commercial and public, have done admirable in-depth coverage.

Not so admirable has been the relative infrequency of such reports. Perhaps the richest and best period was 1963, when National Educational Television produced the series "Desegregation," "Heritage," "Perspectives," "Decision," and "Anatomy of a Revolution," focusing on the black plight and black concerns. That was also the year ABC produced "Crucial Summer," a five-part series that showed, among other things, blacks attempting to overcome racial stereotypes. On Labor Day of 1963, NBC took to the air with the widely praised "The American Revolution of '63," a massive special report that sampled opinions on race in seventy-five areas of the country. As noted earlier in this chapter, all of the commercial networks were thorough in their coverage of the 28 August 1963, "March on Washington for Jobs and Freedom," and the "I Have a Dream" speech by Dr. Martin Luther King, Jr.

While those and other sporadic attempts over the years deserve note, what has been less noteworthy is black participation in the networks' efforts. It was not until the summer of 1989 that ABC News president Roone Arledge gave Ray Nunn, an African American and a senior producer at ABC News, the go-ahead to pull together a special called "Black in White America." What made the broadcast a first was ABC's decision to use only black reporters and a black production staff. The special was also designed to take a deliberately nonobjective look at African Americans. For the first time in prime-time on a commercial network, it would be an image of black Americans by black Americans for all Americans.

At a colloquy at Norfolk State University, a student noted that such a report had been "better late than never" but asked Nunn why ABC had waited so long to take such a step. Nunn responded by praising Arledge, saying the head of ABC News had given him carte blanche in terms of program content and budget. The simple answer to the question would have been to note that the special was part of an evolutionary process, and a slow one at that.

"Black in White America," like all creative endeavors, had its supporters and its detractors. In its prime-time slot, the special drew good, but not top, ratings. For the better part of forty-eight minutes it ran the gamut from showing black children who were asked to decide which of two drawings was ugly—identical drawings except for skin color—and pointing to the sketch of the black child; to a profile of the black chief executive officer of one of the largest black-owned firms in the United States; to a segment on the Tuskeegee airmen and their heroic role in World War II. "Black in White America" might aptly be compared to the dancing bear. It was remarkable not because it did everything *well*, but because it did what it did at *all*.

In his review of the program, *Washington Post* columnist William Raspberry said the show "seemed to be aimed at white viewers, calculated to elicit white guilt over the terrible plight of black Americans." Raspberry accused the broadcast of never arranging the pieces in a "coherent pattern, and—the bigger sin—they never suggested how blacks themselves might undertake to minimize the crippling effects of racism. They never even described the routes that led to their own considerable success in network television."[42]

What Raspberry overlooked is that the latter is a story still very much in progress and not one that broadcasters or the African Americans who work for them are ready to use the power of the medium to tell. If the history of blacks in broadcast news is any indication, that is one television news special that will be a long time coming.

"Smilin' faces . . ."

In 1981 the FCC reported that minorities held 9.2 percent of the jobs in broadcast news. By 1988 the number had nearly doubled. That year, minorities occupied six thousand positions in the broadcast news industry. According to these numbers, black Americans would appear to have surmounted the problems revolving around the split image, and to have overcome a system that had previously embraced them only on an as-needed basis. But the reality at the end of the decade was that, at the three major commercial networks and at stations across the nation, black employees had banded together in associations to ensure equal treatment. The reality was that at a time when black reporters should perhaps have been as concerned with the ethical questions inherent in such then current practices as news "re-creations," too often they were concerned with equitable treatment for African American employees and with getting more of them hired and into positions of authority. The reality was that, while their numbers had increased, the image problem had not been solved, for too often blacks were still chosen only to replace a black who had been lost. The reality was that, by the late 1980s, African Americans were creating their own forms to fill the gap in the coverage of issues relating directly to their lives. By then, Black Entertainment Television was airing its "BET News" with stories by, about, and decidedly *for* black consumption nationwide.

Just as television and radio journalism had a long way to go to come into greater congruence with the rapidly changing institutional, cultural, and intellectual diversity of American society, news media have a long way to go to heal the split image, one that it can be fairly said they created themselves.

1. William L. Rivers, "The Negro and the News: A Case Study," in *Responsibility in Mass Communication*, ed. William L. Rivers and Wilbur Schramm, rev. ed., (New York: Harper & Row, 1969).

2. *Report of the National Advisory Commission on Civil Disorders*, "The News Media and the Disorders," Chap. 15 (Washington, D.C., 1968), 362–86.

3. Rivers, "The Negro and the News."

4. Ibid.

5. Joel Dreyfuss, "Presence without Power," *Washington Post,* 3 September 1974, B1.

6. Royal D. Colle, "Negro Image in the Mass Media: A Case Study in Social Change," *Journalism Quarterly* 45(1) (1968): 55.

7. Waltraud M. Kassarjian, "Blacks as Communicators and Interpreters of Mass Communication," *Journalism Quarterly* 50 (1973).

8. Dorothy Gilliam, "What Do Black Journalists Want?" *Columbia Journalism Review* (May/June, 1972): 47

9. Joel Dreyfuss, "Television Controversy: Covering the Black Experience," *Washington Post,* 1 September 1974, K1.

10. Ibid.

11. Jules Witcover, "Washington's White Press Corps," *Columbia Journalism Review* (Fall 1968): 42.

12. Gilliam, "What Do Black Journalists Want?"

13. U.S. Commission on Civil Rights, *Window Dressing on the Set: Women and Minorities in Television* (Washington, D.C.: Government Printing Office, August 1977.) See also *Window Dressing on the Set: An Update* (1979).

14. Michael Massing, "Blackout in Television," *Columbia Journalism Review* (November/December 1982): 38.

15. Anne P. Jones, "Inside the FCC," *Television/Radio Age,* 15 November 1982, 93.

16. Dreyfuss, "Presence without Power."

17. Ibid.

18. Ibid.

19. Ibid.

20. Richard M. Levine, "We're On the Team, But We're Not Playing," *TV Guide,* 18 July 1981, 8.

21. Ibid.

22. Ibid.

23. Massing, "Blackout in Television."

24. Ibid.

25. Richard M. Levine, "Why 'Unconscious' Racism Persists," *TV Guide,* 25 July 1981, 26.

26. Ibid.

27. Jane Freundel Levey, "Profile: Robert Maynard," *Washington Journalism Review* (April 1981): 44.

28. Levine, "We're on the Team."

29. Gil Noble, *Black is the Color of My TV Tube* (Secaucus, N.J.: Lyle Stuart, 1981).

30. Noble, *Black Is the Color of My TV Tube.*

31. Massing, "Blackout in Television."

32. Ibid.

33. Levine, "Why 'Unconscious' Racism Persists."

34. Ibid.

35. Alice Bonner, "Minorities in Broadcasting," *District Weekly, Washington Post,* 24 March 1982, 1.

36. Dwight M. Ellis, "Minority Progress in Majority-Owned Media since the Kerner Commission," text of address to the CBS Black Employees Association, 19 September 1983.

37. Bonner, "Minorities in Broadcasting."

38. John Carmody, "The TV Column," *Washington Post*, 18 April 1986, D 10.

39. Dorothy Gilliam, "A Troublesome Remedy," *Washington Post*, 10 April 1986, D3.

40. Ibid.

41. Ibid.

42. William Raspberry, "The Deadly Theme of 'Black in White America,'" *Washington Post*, 3 September 1989, C7.

Part Six

**HALF A LOAF:
THE ADVERTISING INDUSTRY**

9 ADVERTISING

JANNETTE L. DATES

We have seen them hundreds of times: short dramatic sequences with images to shape our perception of what we must purchase and why:

> "The subject is chicken. . . . Cause I can't stand your eating even a leg in any other place. That's why I made July chicken month at Roy's. . . . For just $2.99 you can have . . . Now, if that's not the best deal in town, you're in the wrong zip code honey. . . . Cause I want to see your face in my place."

The above monologue is a 1989 Roy Rogers chicken commercial featuring a sassy, African American woman speaking directly to the camera while people cook and order food around her in a fast-food restaurant. Until the 1980s, such a commercial would not have been recurrent on network television. Extremely cautious in developing ties with the African American community, the American advertising industry only began to focus on the black consumer market after the civil rights era had come and gone. Thus, it was well into the 1980s when the industry began actively to court African Americans as consumers of their products. There are many explanations for this caution, but whatever the complex reasons, the effect was that advertising treated African American citizens as though they were invisible for many years, and then included them, grudgingly, for a long time almost exclusively, in massive advertising of unhealthy products such as fast foods, tobacco, and alcoholic beverages. By the late 1980s, however, the $203-billion-dollar buying power of black Americans and the growth of minority spending power (see table 9.1) reflected the growing affluence of African Americans. The advertising industry took note. This,

421

Table 9.1   Growth of Minority Spending Power (in constant 1986 dollars)

	Number of households (in thousands)		Mean income		Total after-tax income (in billions)		After-tax income change
	1981	1987	1980	1986	1980	1986	
All households	82,368	89,479	$21,652	$23,683	$1,783	$2,119	19%
Nonminority	71,872	77,284	$22,424	$24,570	$1,612	$1,899	18%
Minority*							
Black	8,847	9,922	$15,236	$16,398	$ 135	$ 163	21%
Hispanic	3,906	5,418	$18,030	$18,817	$ 70	$ 102	45%
Asian/Other	1,649	2,273	$21,831	$25,077	$ 36	$ 57	58%

Source: Census Bureau, American Demographics. From "Minorities in the Newspaper Business," ANPA 5 (Summer 1989).

*The sum of minority and nonminority does not equal all households because Hispanics may fit either category.

coupled with the increasing influence of black Americans in network television programming, precipitated the use of this newly perceived constituency as targeted consumer and marketing talent in a variety of ways.[1]

The advertising industries changed their policy of totally ignoring African Americans, as the music, film, radio, and television industries had done, only when decision makers had overwhelming evidence that it would bring them huge profits to do so. Thus, it is apparent that the engine that drove the media to include minorities as employees and to recognize the interests of minority markets was fueled by money. Although this explanation has some validity, the issue is more complex. The following discussion will demonstrate that even when there were clear indications that targeting the black consumer would profit the industry, its policy remained largely unchanged for years. Obviously, other factors besides profit were at play in the decision-making process within the advertising industry.

Hall argues that there is no social practice (human interaction) outside of ideology, and that ideology is conveyed through images tied to mythologies and rituals that help to legitimate society. In addition to profitability, then, what was the ideological basis that caused decision makers in the advertising industry to ignore and then engage itself with African American consumers? We can decipher the set patterns of the controlling ideology by deconstructing the language and behavior of those who made decisions about policies and procedures within the advertising industry. The emerging pattern will reveal the decision makers' framework for thinking and calculating about the world, and the inherent ideas they had concerning how things were or ought to be.

In deciphering such an inherent ideology we shall first describe the treatment of the African American consumer by the advertising industry, then describe the African American images created by white decision makers inside the industry, and go on to focus on the images that African American practitioners sought to establish as they and black activists outside of the industry fought to develop their own views of how the black oriented market should be targeted and reflected by the industry. We will also look at the special case of African American radio station owners and the advertising industry. Finally, we shall take a brief look toward the future and at the possible relationship of the advertising industry and African Americans.

African American Consumers

Ever since the beginning of advertising, three rules have prevailed: "to advertise to people ready, willing and able to buy; to use the media which reach them, [and] to make advertisements which [would] win their business."[2] In practice, advertisers rarely worked at reaching African American consumers.[3] In contrast, there were two important reasons why black American consumers wished to be targeted by advertisers: (1) they wanted to be courted for their money as others were, and (2) they responded to the respect implicit in the courting process, when the advertisement was neither patronizing nor condescending. As Julian Bond, a state senator in the 1970s and 1980s in Georgia, noted in an article in *Black Enterprise* magazine, American blacks wanted to be sought but not bought, and reached but not grabbed. He observed that black Americans "want to believe that we are buying the best of the line—the top ticket item . . . that the company that sells to us also hires us and has us on its board . . . that our pictures will be in some of the ads without the use of patronizing, specious street jargon."[4]

Gradually, corporate America attempted to address the issue of how to tap this market, which had grown from $77 billion in earnings in the mid-1970s to more than $140 billion in the mid-1980s, and to over $200 billion as the 1990s approached. The advertising industry began relatively heavy marketing of the African American at this juncture. To understand how the African American consumer and advertising practitioner became a prime target for Madison Avenue's overtures, we can briefly look back to the beginning of the relationship between the American advertising system and these descendants of slaves.

As noted in chapter 7, the first paper published by African Americans, *Freedom's Journal*, carried advertisements. The first issue, published on 16 March 1827, had an advertisement for B. F. Hughes' School for Colored Children of Both Sexes. Black American consumers were seen as a specific advertising market by cultural outsiders as early as 1916, when a gas company in Rock Hill, South Carolina, working with a church group and the local government, conducted a cooking school for "Negro" servants. Advertisements of their efforts led to the sale of twelve gas ranges by the gas company. The Fuller Brush Company, in 1922, hired four teachers as salespersons for the "Negro" population in Tulsa, Oklahoma, while a 1928 article in *Advertising and Selling* reported on "the attractive sales possibilities" in Harlem, New York. The National Negro Business League conducted a study of income and living habits of the Negro in the 1930s. This was the first national approach to a study of black consumers. The study was subsidized by Montgomery Ward, Lever Brothers, and Anheuser-Busch. The report placed the overall spending power of this consumer group at $1.65 billion.[5]

Paul K. Edwards, professor of economics at Fisk University, wrote a definitive article "The Negro Commodity Market," in 1932, which paid systematic attention to black consumers for the first time. Edwards reported that black and white southerners had different spending habits and that black people were particularly concerned about quality products, brand names, and their personal appearance. In the 1940s, Negro marketing consultants were used when a few black advisers and salesmen were added to staffs; thus began a systematic means of advising manufacturers and advertisers about ways to advertise to the "Negro" market. Researchers Friend and Kravis, in a study based on Bureau of Labor Statistics data for 1950, compared black and white spending habits and firmly established similarities and differences between the races. The studies by

Edwards and Friend and Kravis were used as points of reference for a number of subsequent studies.[6]

After World War II, numerous market surveys were commissioned by African Americans to assess the black market: a 1946 study in Milwaukee and Omaha; a 1947 study in Washington, D.C., Baltimore, and Philadelphia made for the *African American News*; a 1950 survey by Starch for *Ebony*; and, in the mid-1950s, Professor Henry Bullock's study of the black American market for a chain of radio stations. The Bullock study revealed that the African Americans surveyed resented appeals aimed at them that were differentiated from others—they were offended by jive-talking radio disc jockeys. During the late 1950s and early 1960s, African Americans were described as consumers who frequently purchased leading brands in their search for status and prestige. Numerous articles in trade publications stressed the brand loyalty and brand consciousness of the black consumer. *Printer's Ink* (1958) reported to marketers the first report of social class distinctions among African American consumers; they noted that the upper class valued security and status; while the lower class valued conspicuous consumption and splurging. However, a mid-1960s study revealed that African Americans saved more than whites of comparable income and that they spent "less on automobiles than whites of comparable income."[7] These findings were the opposite of widely held stereotyped ideas about black consumers.

Until the 1960s, the advertising industry's amoral attitude to social concerns usually went unquestioned. Before then the industry was observed as having "no motivation to seek the improvement of the individual or to impart qualities of social usefulness. . . . Though it [wielded] an immense social influence . . . it [had] no social goals and no social responsibility."[8] A *New York Times* article of the period noted that "though advertisers have traditionally assumed that they could divorce themselves from the nation's social issues, the 'Negro' revolution proved otherwise."[9] During this time, both the Congress of Racial Equality, the NAACP, and other civil rights groups held meetings with advertising organizations such as the American Association of Advertising Agencies (AAAA) to argue for fundamental alterations of sponsor and advertising agency attitudes about black consumers and toward minority marketing strategies. During the latter part of the decade, national and regional conferences of advertiser industry and trade associations included panels that, for the first time, focused on racial integration in advertising and on the black minority consumer. At this juncture, advertisers actively questioned themselves and others about the Negro consumer, what he was like and how to reach and satisfy this market. Subsequently, however, although the advertising researchers of the 1960s studied African Americans as consumers and practitioners little changed in the industry regarding African American consumers and minority markets, except for a few integrated advertisements.[10]

Throughout the decades, advertising placed by blacks for blacks and by whites for blacks dealt in the hierarchy of skin color, a concept that was a central theme of "School Daze," a 1980s film by Spike Lee, a young filmmaker discussed in chapter 3. In the film, as in America of the eras preceding the civil rights/black awareness period of the 1960s, darker-skinned blacks were ignored or placed in an inferior position, while the fairer-skinned of the group were allowed more recognition and freedom by both black and white cultural factions. Aware of this sociological phenomenon, the advertising industry used models in their advertisements with Caucasian features, fair complexions, and straight or straightened hair. For example, not until the 1960s did *Ebony* magazine, a black publication discussed in chapter 7, begin to carry advertisements where Caucasian features gave way to Negroid ones, and straightened hair to the natural "Afro" hairstyle. Black people in the 1970s were aggressively concerned about being black enough to be acceptable to other blacks. Moreover, in a 1979 research study, Kerin found that black women attributed higher quality ratings to products when a comparison model exhibited a black image, and that black and white women significantly differed in their responses to the physical characteristics of models in judging the quality and suitablity of an advertised product.[11] However, by the 1980s the pendulum had again swung in the other direction. Lee made the point in his film that skin color was a significant factor in social circles and psychologically in the black community.

In the late 1960s and early 1970s, advertisers learned that African Americans constituted twenty-three million Americans, were 11 percent of the population, and spent about $30 billion a year for consumer goods and services. Black entrepreneur/writer D. Parke Gibson's widely discussed *The 30 Billion Dollar Negro* suggested that purely from an economic perspective, advertisers with an eye toward their business would realize that this market should be a prime target for cultivation. However, fearful that the white market might become alienated by "integrated" advertising campaigns, advertisers resisted the idea of appealing to the two distinct markets in one advertisement, while they also resisted targeting black consumers alone.[12] Various studies were conducted to examine the credibility and viability of this perceived fear of "white backlash." The studies revealed that whites were indifferent to well-conceived integrated advertisements; that there were no negative effects from the use of blacks as models, either by themselves or integrated with whites; that the presence of African Americans in main roles in advertisements produced only a moderate but significantly lower than expected reaction from highly prejudiced students; and that commercials that used black models had more meaning for African American viewers than did all white commercials. Thus, while these ads were clearly favored by African American viewers, they also made little difference to white viewers. Still, the policy persisted, and well into the 1980s black advertising practitioners and other businessmen consistently complained about the small number of advertising dollars being used to target black consumer groups

A 1973 article by Barrow noted that "minority media (were) a good advertising medium for any company,"[13] since advertisers could no longer have a single mass market in mind for all their products. Marketers, advertisers, manufacturers, and consumers all increased their awareness at this juncture that segments of the mass market had to be identified, defined, understood, and then marketed. The potential for this segmented approach was desirable if the segments "were easily recognized, reasonably large, and if the consumption patterns differed substantially."[14] Black consumer groups met all the criteria outlined in the segmented approach. In the seventies major advertisers were told that if they sought to attract or hold a minority market, advertising in minority media was vital, because such advertisements offered the advertiser the unique opportunity to sell to the black consumer "directly by speaking to his needs and desires, in his language, in his medium, without running the risk of confusing or . . . alienating other projects."[15] The majority of the advertisers were unresponsive to this advice.

An early-seventies article by Sexton described black consumer

buying behavior. The writer noted that African American consumers spent more on socially visible items than on nonsocially
visible items than did whites in the same income bracket (black
consumers spent proportionally more than whites for clothing,
personal care, home furnishings, alcohol, and tobacco and less for
medical care, food, transportation, education, and utilities). The
writer believed that marketers subscribed to one of two broad views
about black consumers: (1) black people are too poor to purchase
national brands, or (2) black people desire the brands and labels they
imagine the *best* white consumers purchase. He argued that income
level was the major determinant of two major segments of the black
consumer's market. Consumers who could live a middle-class life
comprised one segment and those who lived at a subsistence income
level made up the other. This writer optimistically believed that
as African American income levels gradually increased, many
apparent differences between black and white markets would diminish. Further, he believed that higher income African Americans
could become innovative consumers in numerous and diverse
products in the future.[16]

A 1977 study by Surlin noted that research had documented the
following explicit parallel between authoritarianism, racism, and
advertising: highly authoritarian individuals were attracted to the
advertising field; highly authoritarian types exhibited more favorable
attitudes toward advertising; and advertisers probably tended to be
authoritarian types who used their profession to support their
interpretations of society's values. The writer concluded that
"advertisers tend to be highly authoritarian and racially prejudiced
in their beliefs. This would lead them to resist using black models
in advertisements in order to keep their interpretation of society's
value system congruent with (their) expectations."[17] He noted that
numerous studies reveal that whites react the same way to advertisements with black models as white models, while African Americans feel more favorably disposed toward advertisements with
black models. Yet, advertisers consistently resisted the use of black
models, claiming fear of white backlash. The findings of this study
supported the idea that highly authoritarian advertising executives
had predispositions against the use of black models, probably because
of their internalized belief about society's values which they perceived as negative toward African Americans. In any case, by the
close of the 1970s African Americans still were not viable practi-

tioners in the advertising industry. Moreover, many advertisers believed that black people had been incorporated into mainstream target advertising. They failed to recognize the opportunity they had to address black consumers directly to attract more business from this group. Given the consistency of these research findings, underrepresentation of black people in advertising was probably more an indication of prejudice on the part of the Madison Avenue-dominated advertising community than of the often claimed prejudice of white consumers.[18]

Responding to the powerful effects of the civil rights movement, in the 1970s some large corporations did target the black consumer for marketing campaigns. One of the most successful of these included the corporate-style ads designed by American Telephone and Telegraph (AT&T). These advertisements focused on AT&T's record in equal opportunity employment that used two or three generations of black AT&T employees as central, featured characters. Print ads were placed in African American print media, while radio spots run on the National Black Network and the Sheridan Network employed actor Ossie Davis to interview the workers. AT&T also used numerous black entertainers in their "Reach Out and Touch" campaign. Some believed that competition from independent telephone networks had encouraged AT&T to seek a solid foundation of loyalty in the black community by conducting advertising campaigns like these.

The black consumer market underwent important changes in the 1970s, as revealed in the U.S. Census Bureau's 1980 Population Profile. The most significant developments included the steady increase in the migration of African Amerians to the suburbs and the rise in college enrollments among the black population. A majority of African Americans continued to live in urban areas, but 21 percent of the total black population, by the beginning of the 1980s, lived in the suburbs. Advertising and marketing experts suggested that these shifts might lead to an eventual fragmentation of the black consumer market. Marketers noted that the African American market was no longer one, homogeneous group in a geographically bound setting. Some experts further predicted that a definitive middle-class (upscale) African American market, often referred to as *Buppies*, a term coined by *Black Enterprise* magazine, could become a distinct entity, to be heavily targeted by marketers.[19]

In the 1980s, upscale black consumers presented a distinct

challenge to the marketers who had targeted the group for marketing. Many of these African Americans were first-generation middle-class consumers, who still maintained tastes for food, atmosphere, and life-style from their early years. The common traits and common vocabulary that marketers used when advertising to middle-class whites often did not apply to middle-class blacks, for the African American community had a unique culture and a distinct personality. Very often the high-salaried, highly successful black who worked on Madison Avenue still enjoyed, and often preferred, many of the same foods, recreation, and other products and services that poorer blacks enjoyed.[20]

The Wellington Group, the nation's largest black-owned market research firm in the 1980s, warned marketers that brand loyalty among black consumers could easily erode if marketers failed to work at maintaining loyalty. Wellington believed that the fastest way to destroy brand preference and loyalty was to ignore the revealed differences between the black and white markets and to use mainstream marketing strategies and tactics to promote products in African American communities. Wellington illustrated differences between the black and the general population by noting that the number one toothpaste among whites was Crest, while the number one toothpaste among African Americans was Colgate, with Crest running second. Wellington found that 80 percent of the blacks surveyed bought mouthwash, compared with 62 percent of the whites. African American consumers preferred brand-name paper napkins and towels, whereas the general populace used generics as their first choice. African Americans also used more sugar-filled products. According to Wellington, the black woman was a prime consumer, as she made most of the purchasing decisions in a family where, more often than her white counterpart, she was head of the household. She often purchased not only food, but a car, lawn mower, and other household items.

While African Americans made up less than 12 percent of the general populace, they consumed higher percentages of products such as instant mashed potatoes (14 percent), floor wax (17 percent), chewing gum (23 percent), malt liquor (32 percent), and hair conditioning products (36 percent). Black consumers purchased almost double the amount of cornmeal as the general population. Aunt Jemima led in commerical consumption, with 55 percent of this brand being purchased by black consumers. The parent company for Aunt Jemima products normally spent only a small portion of its advertising budget in black markets, however. Wellington challenged the marketers of Aunt Jemima: If Aunt Jemima led in sales in black communities when few advertising dollars were spent to market the product there, if the company were to spend 55 percent of its advertising budget on advertisements targeted to the black market, what then would be their share of the black consumer market for cornmeal purchases?

Wellington pointed out that the term *disposable income,* used to define the money that families used for purchases after essential purchases had been made, was not so applicable to all black consumers. Often, in some parts of the black communities of the past, instant gratification had taken precedence over long-term goals, and this life-style pattern was often passed on from generation to generation. Thus, disposable income needed to be defined in a different way for the black consumer group. This phenomenon usually escaped the notice of white marketers.[21]

All types of persons in the African American population tended to consume "all black" media in the 1980s. That is, black people of all income levels purchased black magazines, listened to black radio stations, and watched blacks when they appeared on television. Moreover, during this era, all segments of the African American community were heavy viewers of off-network reruns of former prime-time network programs such as "The Jeffersons" and "Sanford & Son," two shows with predominantly African American casts.

By the mid-1980s, however, African American consumer groups generally were not prime targets for marketers. George Edwards, president of the National Black Network in the 1980s, then the largest African American radio network in the country (with more than a 110 affiliated stations), believed that advertisers assumed that since African Americans spoke English, they should treat them in the same as they did any other English-speaking citizens. Thus, advertisers would develop commercials especially for Hispanics but not for African American consumers. The Mattel Toy Company, which developed special commercials for reaching the Hispanic market, explained that since black people spoke English and there was no black television network (as there was with the Hispanic/Latino community's Spanish International Network), they found no need to create special advertisements for reaching black consumers.[22]

Network television broadcast programming oriented to African

American viewers on the Public Broadcasting System and cable's Black Entertainment Network service (BET) allowed for more direct network video access to black consumers in the 1980s. In 1989, when BET moved into its new studios in Washington, D.C., after ten years of operation, it declared itself "the information voice of black America," as it continued to grow at a rate of two million subscribers per year. BET president Bob Johnson noted the viability of black spending power and encouraged cable system operators to take note of the obvious economic opportunities to be found in black cable-viewing audiences.

In the 1980s, Gulf Oil switched from print ads in *Ebony* and *Jet* magazines and cosponsored "America's Black Forum," a syndicated talk show that aired on many cable systems. At the same time Goodyear Tire and Rubber Company developed national spot and cable television commercials targeted to black automobile owners.[23]

The advertising industry's consumer marketing strategy in the late 1980s, called *target marketing* increased in importance at the same time African American social and economic viability also increased. Because of foreign competition and the softening American economy, many in the industry needed new opportunities and new markets. So, they often looked toward markets they had once bypassed. Many looked to the black and Hispanic/Latino communities, particularly since industry experts realized that between them the African American and Hispanic/Latino markets controlled almost $300 billion annually, representing the ninth most profitable market in the world. They realized by the year 2000, the African American/Latino communities would be one-third of the nation.

Even at this point, however, some marketers questioned the use of black advertising agencies to reach the black consumer market. For example, a beer vice president noted that it was possible to communicate with an audience to whom one does not demographically belong. He stated that the target market for beer was the 21–34 year old, but that the company never demanded that the account be handled by members of that age bracket. What he failed to realize, of course, was that all account executives would be, had been, or were 21–34 years old, and knew something about that age group from experience, whereas they had never been, were not, and would never become members of an ethnic minority group if they were members of the usual white, male decision-making group that controlled American industries.[24]

Even if reluctantly, most marketers increasingly turned to black advertising agencies during the late 1980s to help them gain better access to the rapidly growing and increasingly powerful black market. At this point, the African American community were 12 percent or 30 million of the American population, had an annual income of $203 billion, and was growing faster than the general population. (See Table 9.1) Moreover, 46 percent of the black population lived in twenty-five cities, where, in many instances, they had reached majority status. These factors made them easily reachable for marketing overtures.[25]

Black Images in Advertising

As the industry developed advertisements that reflected society's myths and rituals, which were usually absorbed and accepted as real, decision makers in advertising were concerned with profit, and not with the side-effects their decisions might produce. They believed that advertising paid the way for Americans to maintain the high standard of living that made them the envy of the rest of the world, and, as solid members of the nation's free enterprise system, the industry fought fiercely to return profits to stockholders.

Advertisers' decisions reflect a bias that is revealed by African American memorabilia. According to Margaret Ross Barnett, a political science scholar at Columbia University in the 1980s, the memorabilia of black American citizens are "Nostalgia as Nightmare," as most of the items featuring black people developed during the years of slavery and segregation revealed negative, racist images. Advertised products had names such as the "Alabama Coon Jigger," while salt and pepper shakers of black men and women with bulging eyes, thick red lips, and expressions of stupidity were popular as well. More gruesome items included black people being chased or eaten by animals or portrayed as dismembered utilitarian objects, such as a black man's head used as an egg cup and a black woman's mouth used as a bottle opener. Like scholars Hall and Jefferson (See Introduction), Barnett believes that popular culture, in this case including advertisements, was an important vehicle for the transmission of ideologies related to black inferiority and white supremacy.

Rastus, the advertising world's version of the obsequious faithful black servant, appeared in advertisements for the cereal "Cream of

examples

examples

Wheat," where he usually was shown serving whites in a happy, contented fashion. Aunt Jemima personified the mammy stereotype. One Aunt Jemima advertisement stated, "Oh the meals that Colonel Higbee's Jemima used to cook." A 1919 Johnson Smith & Company catalog, advertising the "Alabama Coon Jigger" toy, described the ways in which the toy could be made to dance fast or slow, and stressed how it was *in the firm control* of the owner. Barnett notes that "careful analysis of black memorabilia materials (such as these advertisements) and their sociopolitical and economic contexts underscores the fact that racism was not an isolated mistake or [an] aberration of the distant past, but an intrinsic feature of past and recent American cultural reality and political structure."[26]

A study in *Life* magazine that examined the use of African Americans in advertisements revealed that of the 413 editions published in the years 1937–67, the total pages of advertisements with African Americans featured in them were: two in 1937, two in 1942, nine in 1952, two in 1957, one in 1962, four in 1967, and twenty-two in 1972. These numbers probably reflect the degree to which black people as consumers were the concern of the advertising industry in these typical years. An article in *The Crisis* revealed that in 1962 the NAACP in New York City launched a project to desegregate advertising. The organizers examined various print and broadcast media and concluded that, from the advertisements, visitors "would conclude that there are no Negroes in the USA. Or that if there were Negroes in America, they didn't wear clothes, own automobiles . . . or that advertisers were indifferent to their existence."[27] The organizers noted that "if visual advertisements of merchandise included the highly visible Negro, along with white people, the American public would get a new and more accurate image of the Negro."[28] They believed that Negroes would then be appreciated for their real worth.

In the early 1970s, the NAACP Legal Defense and Educational Fund appealed to the FCC to use its power against discriminatory advertising. The NAACP studies revealed that although a number of commercials used African Americans, very few of them had more than bit-player roles even in sports advertisements. This study followed an NAACP report on the employment of African Americans in commercial sports telecasts. The percentage of black persons used in advertisements had increased from 5 percent in 1968 to 14 percent in 1970, but only 2 percent of those ads featured blacks in major roles. The study found that in most of the monitored cities, African Americans in commercials were seen only for momentary flashes. The NAACP made several recommendations for specific FCC action: "(1) require the stations, whose licenses must be renewed every three years, to review commercials for racial content just as they did for good taste and suggestiveness; (2) issue guidelines to the industry concerning its responsibility to obey federal laws against color discrimination in employment; and (3) set up a monitoring apparatus to determine the racial composition of programs and commercials or ask stations to provide such data."[29] The NAACP believed that television was too important an influence for the FCC to ignore the fact that television commercials affected viewers in ways not necessarily intended by their producers and sponsors. They noted that one of the side effects of commercial advertisement on television was viewer perception that these advertisements reflected images based on truth, reality, and shared values.[30]

At about the time of the NAACP's appeal to the FCC, African American actors and actresses began to appear with more and more frequency in integrated advertisements in the print and electronic media. In the 1970s, the advertising industry began to use African Americans as star presenters on television and in print ads. During this period, African American entertainer Lola Folana advertised "Tigris" perfume, while Bill Cosby began to pitch for the Del Monte Corporation. Cosby did an unidentified voice-over, using his gentle, whimsical humor to make the product name heard and remembered and, through humor, to make the commercial palatable. The General Foods Corporation began using Cosby as a spokesman for Jell-O pudding in 1973, and in 1976 he began appearing as star presenter for the Ford Motor Company. Bill Cosby thus traveled between a position as a mass volume salesman (Del Monte and Jell-O pudding) and a big ticket item presenter (Ford). Cosby was chosen by these companies (and subsequently by Ideal Toys, Texas Instruments, Coca Cola, and Kodak) because research had proven that he exuded an unusual amount of believability and warmth. Thus, he could help each company in its campaign to build a youthful, warm, and modern image, as it positioned itself in the market. Critics and media observers believed Cosby's sweet, cozy commercials helped make him one of the best known and most liked personalities on television. His smash hit television series "The Cosby Show," which began airing in the 1984–85 season, increased interest in him as a star presenter. However, after years of doing commercials for these various products, Cosby generally limited himself in the 1980s to Jell-O, Coke, and Kodak commercials.[31]

Philip H. Dougherty of the *New York Times* noted in the 1980s that "if TV commercials using black actors and actresses have a positive effect on black consumers, while not having a negative effect on white consumers, it would be natural for big national advertisers to use such advertising in heavily black markets. But even if the results in other markets were less positive, wouldn't it be nice if the advertiser would go ahead and use the spot anyhow, just for the sociological impact?"[32] Dougherty argued that big national advertisers would need to use network television in addition to spot advertising to achieve this end. He noted that Proctor & Gamble, the nation's biggest commercial user of television and the sole sponsor of the 1982 made-for-television miniseries "Marco Polo," aired 103 commercials for thirty brands during seventy minutes of commercial time for that series, but they used very few African American actors or actresses in these commercials. When Dougherty questioned the company about the scarcity of black talent in their commercials, the company professed an "interest only in a commercial's ability to communicate a message, not about the talent in it."[33] The William Morris talent agency, in response to Dougherty's query, noted that their company was "color blind," but they also revealed that "nobody ever calls and says they want black actors unless they're going after the black market."[34] This was said as if the issue were settled as a result of the statement.

Until the mid-1980s, African American people consistently employed as talent in advertisements were fairly scarce to find except in a few companies such as fast food chains, soft drink, alcoholic beverage, and cigarette companies. The psychological implications of the types of advertisements that were considered acceptable for targeting to African Americans deserve future study to address the question: why were products that were known for their unhealthy qualities (cigarettes, liquor, sodas, fast foods) the ones first introduced and the ones most heavily advertised in the black community? Obviously, the uneducated, frequently unemployed, and often unskilled are among the most vulnerable and least knowledgeable about health care. Implicit in the decision to target poorer, urban areas for massive advertising of unhealthy products is the belief that it might be all right to urge this group toward self-destruction via consumption of such products. This issue deserves research, discussion, and full analysis.

After the phenomenal success of network television's "The Cosby Show," in 1986, E. F. Hutton, a securities firm, commissioned Cosby to help rehabilitate its severely tarnished public image. Its highly successful commercials, which employed the theme "when E. F. Hutton talks, people listen," were retired from use after Hutton pleaded guilty to mail and wire fraud and paid a two-million dollar fine for illegalities committed by company administrators. Cosby's task in 1986–87 was to make people believe in E. F. Hutton again. The Hutton/Cosby commercials featured very simple statements by Cosby. In one, he told viewers that when he was a child he had not needed a company to handle his money because he had none. Now, however, he said "I trust E. F. Hutton with *my* money."[35]

Creative marketers, realizing that music is a universal language, began to use the language of the young and youthful to sell products to that target group. The music and jargon of young whites has African American roots. In fact, black culture can be seen in music to a larger degree than in the language. Thus, after years of using "whitened" imitations of black music (See chaps. 1 and 2 for more details), advertisers finally sought the authentic sounds of African Americans: Ray Charles, Diana Ross, B. B. King, the Pretenders, the Imperials, and more. Black music, featuring black and white artists, was used as background for numerous advertisements during this era. Moreover, since each generation has its nostalgia music— the music which they courted by—people who were in their forties in the 1980s had been in their twenties during the 1960s and much of their courting music from the 1960s, as noted in chapter 1, had included black music's rhythm and blues songs. A catalyst for such use of black music can be found in the success of the 1982 film "The Big Chill," which effectively used 1960s songs as part of the development of "moods" for the movie. Subsequently songs from *Billboard's* Rhythm and Blues Charts of the sixties began to find their way into advertisements to sell a wide variety of products.[36]

The 1980s advertisements also saw a proliferation of African American talent in the forefront as star presenters. In addition to Bill Cosby, the recording industry's Michael Jackson and Lionel Ritchie appeared for Pepsi Cola, and Whitney Houston for Diet Coke. There was former defensive lineman for the Baltimore Colts,

Oakland Raiders, and Houston Oilers, Bubba Smith for Miller Lite Beer; and Will "The Refrigerator" Perry, tackle for the Chicago Bears, for McDonald's hamburgers; as well as Herschel Walker selling Big Mac's and Adidas sneakers; Julius Erving (Dr. J.) pitching Crest toothpaste and Converse basketball shoes; and Reggie Jackson selling Pentax cameras, Panasonic video equipment, and Nabisco cereals.[37]

It appears, however, aside from using the obvious celebrity, advertisers chose to use black music but few black faces. As black singers sang the jingles, white models flashed across most television screens. For example, Chevrolet used Motown 1960s hits sung by Martha and the Vandellas and the Four Tops, while whites drove the cars. Bill Withers sang "Lean on Me" as white models leaned on trucks. The Pointer Sisters sang "Jump" while whites jumped for Bounce commercials. "Only You" was sung by the Platters for Amorall Wax, and "You Are So Beautiful" by Brook Benton for Mercury automobiles, again as white models polished, leaned on, or sat in the cars.[38]

This is not to say that there were no commercials featuring black noncelebrities. In fact, in the 1980s some television advertisements began targeting black consumers with sensitivity, by blending attractive African American actors and actresses, "catchy music, eye-appealing action and honest representation of black life-style"[39] in a way that was brand-new for television. Minority advertising agencies, the primary force behind the new trend, authenticated these ads by featuring situations that reflected the different tastes, rules for living, codes of conduct, life-styles, and other motivational factors that differentiated black consumer groups from the general market. At the same time, however, the purveyors of entertainment programs supported by these new types of advertisements continued to restrict black talent as they had always done.[40] Media scholars might argue that industry decision makers thus maintained their beliefs: whites would not accept African Americans in programming, or they wanted to maintain the old programming focus because they believed that was the way it should be, or they merely allowed their own racism to control their decisions.

African American Advertising Professionals

As we have seen, most often the portrayal of blacks in advertising showed an insensitivity to the African American consumer, and a lack of understanding of the market. Moreover, white advertising agencies and their clients allocated few dollars to influence the purchases of black consumers, whom they usually claimed to believe were undifferentiated from the general market. As noted earlier, in the late 1970s major advertisers began to realize that future growth lay in reaching untapped market segments, particularly after an economic downturn threatened profits. It was then that industry decision makers turned to the handful of African Americans working in mainstream advertising for their assistance in reaching the black consumer. Knowledgeable African Americans sensed an opportunity, and black advertising agencies suddenly appeared. The African American entrepreneurs who set up their own enterprises were often talented but frustrated professionals who had left creative and managerial positions because of the limited opportunities available to this group within the advertising industry.[41]

During this period, *Black Enterprise* magazine listed thirteen advertising agencies as specialists in the black consumer market. One of them, the Burrell McBain Advertising Agency in Chicago, opened in early 1971 and waited for six months before landing the company's first client. However, by 1972 they had convinced McDonald's that their company could help increase its share of the black consumer market. They accomplished this goal, and between 1972 and 1984, Burrell Advertising developed more than a hundred commercials and advertisements for McDonald's, including their 1979 television commercial "A Family Is," which won a CLIO award for excellence in advertising. Burrell Advertising, as it became known after McBain pulled out in 1976, gradually became a specialist in ethnic-market advertising and built up a roster of satisfied clients, including Coca Cola, Canadian Mist, Jack Daniels, Johnson Products, and the L'eggs subsidiary of Consolidated Foods Corporation. The Burrell firm obtained an assignment from the Johnson Products Company (JPC), in 1980, when JPC sought ways to fight off giant general market competitors for black hair care and facial cosmetics. The Burrell Advertising Company helped JPC products to establish a corporate advertising campaign to strengthen its image. JPC had the largest research and development department in the industry for black hair care and facial cosmetics, and Burrell helped JPC successfully convey this message to consumers.

In November 1983, Proctor and Gamble hired Burrell Advertising to develop a black-oriented marketing effort for its Crest brand toothpaste. As readers will recall, the Wellington Group had brought it to the attention of the manufacturers of Crest that though they were number one in the general populace, they were number two among African American consumers. For the first time Proctor and Gamble went outside of its regular list of general agencies for specialty help with increasing their market share for Crest toothpaste. African American advertising agencies hoped this was the first step in a wide swing in their direction. An important aspect of this marketing assignment was that many marketing companies would follow the lead established by Proctor and Gamble, the country's largest national advertiser. (See Table 9.2) Until Proctor and Gamble named Burrell for black-oriented marketing, few companies other than the marketers of soft drinks, alcoholic beverages, and fast foods, had signed up with black-owned agencies for help in their particular area of expertise, the black consumer market. It is highly probable that the Proctor and Gamble influence helped, because by the late 1980s Burrell was billing over $50 million in accounts annually and had become the nation's largest black-owned advertising agency.

In 1977, Frank Mingo, a senior vice president at McCann Erickson Advertising, formed a partnership with Carolyn Jones, vice president

Table 9.2   Largest Advertisers on TV (in millions of dollars)

Corporations	Expenditure
Procter & Gamble	779
Philip Morris	478
McDonald's	303
Pepsi Cola	266
R. J. Reynolds	263
General Motors	259
General Mills	239
Pillsbury	232
Ford	229
Anheuser-Busch	227

Source: Television Bureau of Advertising, *Broadcasting Yearbook*, 1989, xv.

and creative supervisor for BBDO Advertising. The two resigned their respective senior-level positions in mainstream advertising agencies and established the New York-based Mingo-Jones Advertising Agency, specified as a general market advertising agency. By 1984, the firm had acquired 30 percent general billings, 10 percent Hispanic, and 60 percent African American oriented. The company included among its clients Heublein's, Kentucky Fried Chicken, Seagrams, Miller Brewing Company, Philip Morris, Goodyear Tire and Rubber, Liggett & Myers Tobacco, and Westinghouse Electric. One of their general accounts included the New York region advertising accounts for Kentucky Fried Chicken, with billings of about three million dollars. For the assignment Mingo-Jones came up with the tagline "We do chicken right." that was later used by the national agency. Mingo-Jones was determined to continue to apply for general market accounts as well as minority targeted accounts. Thus, they were pleased in 1984 when Mingo-Jones began its first corporate campaign for Walt Disney Productions. The contract was for the general market, but it was also designed to increase the number of African American visitors to Disneyland and Disney World. The 1986–87 campaign for Disney World included thirty-second network spot commercials featuring Felicia Rashad, Keshia Knight Pulliam, and Ahmad Jamal Warner of "The Cosby Show" having fun at Disney World.[42] In 1987, after Caroline Jones left the company to form her own advertising agency, the company changed its name to the Mingo Group.

In President Ronald Reagan's 1984 State of the Union address, he discussed Barbara Proctor. According to Reagan, Proctor was an example of America's best spirit of free enterprise. She had risen from a ghetto to build a multi million-dollar advertising agency. The firm, Proctor and Gardner, was the nation's second largest black-owned advertising agency in the mid-1980s, employing twenty-five persons and billing $12.5 million in accounts in 1983. Most of the company's accounts were from national companies aiming at black consumers. Proctor noted two years later, however, that in 1985 she believed the federal government and the American corporate leadership no longer set affirmative-action goals as a priority. Thus, in the late 1980s black advertising agencies, like hers, had difficulty in sustaining their earlier momentum.[43]

The top six African American-owned advertising agencies, Burrell

Advertising, Mingo-Jones, Uniworld, Lockhart and Pettus, J. P. Martin and Associates, and Proctor and Gardner, collectively reported billings of $155 million in 1985, a 70 percent increase over 1984 billings. These advertising agencies argued, however, that although they billed some of the largest names in corporate America as clients, their billings were dismally small when compared with those of mainstream agencies, and in comparison to African American consumption of advertised products.[44]

The Wellington Group, founded in 1978 by Alphonzia Wellington and his wife Karen Montague, became a marketing research organization that specialized in black and Hispanic consumer markets. Wellington created a new research methodology which established the firm as a major force in its field. This methodology, *Access Brand Preference Audits*, used a full-color 35 millimeter slide presentation to guide respondents through a simulated shopping excursion, allowing marketers to see what products consumers purchased in a market. The Wellington Group became one of the nation's foremost sources of information on black and Hispanic consumer preferences, where as before most marketers had relied solely on general market shares and gross revenues to figure out consumer preferences. Prior to the Wellington Group's research, demographic and psychographic information about consumers was rarely broken down to examine the black and Hispanic markets. By the mid-1980s, the Wellington Group had a dozen full-time employees, annual sales of more than $2 million dollars, and more than forty clients, including such national firms as Campbell Soup, Anheuser-Busch, and Burger King.[45]

Other entrepreneurs also set up services to assist advertisers in reaching black consumers. For example Tri-Ad Consultants, Ltd., a syndicated consulting firm, offered marketing, advertising, and research for the black consumer markets, as well as sales promotion, planning, and implementation of campaigns targeted to the African American. It also offered a specialty service, "Black Trak," which tracked the product purchasing and usage habits of African Americans. The service gathered information four times yearly, based on personal interviews, for publication in a quarterly report that focused on the top twenty-five markets.[46]

In the late 1980s a fierce struggle erupted between black advertising agencies and mainstream agencies. Earlier, in the 1970s and early 1980s, it had been routine for the same product to be shared by a black agency and a mainstream agency for serving a client's needs, since each agency supposedly tapped a different market. The cause of the battle was the success of black advertising agencies, for in some instances these small black agencies' campaigns had reached not just the black consumer but the general market consumer as well. For example, the previously cited Mingo-Jones campaign slogan "We do chicken right" for Kentucky Fried Chicken became the tagline for the general campaign as well as the African American segment. Similarly, Burrell Advertising's campaign, targeted for the black consumer, which simply said, "I assume you drink Martell," obtained a tremendous general market response. Subsequently, Burrell obtained the entire mainstream account for Martell, as well as the black segmented market.[47]

Although the billings did not represent huge sums of money in terms of percentages, the general market competitors did not take such intrusions lightly. Some general market firms began to test the feasibility of offering their own black consumer marketing services, in house. For example, in 1986 BBDO, one of the largest general market advertising agencies in the country, formed a separate in-house unit called "Special Markets" to handle everything that was not considered mainstream marketing. They named Doug Alligood, an African American with years of experience in black marketing campaigns and a seasoned BBDO employee, as manager of the division. As readers might guess, the general market agencies had an advantage over minority-owned agencies because of the nearly unlimited resources general market agencies had at their command.

Black advertising agencies responded to the attack by general market agencies in two ways: (1) They noted the strong reinforcement such actions gave to the legitimacy of the segmented black market. Mainstream advertisers had said for years that the African American market was undifferentiated from general market consumers, and (2) They went after *more* of the general market accounts for themselves.[48]

At the beginning of this chapter, a question was raised concerning the ideological beliefs that drove mainstream advertisers in their decision making as it affected African Americans. It has been demonstrated in answer to that query that white decision makers acknowledged reasons in the 1980s—after years of denial—to develop more positive black images for targeting larger groups of black consumers.   They used varying methods to achieve this end, including in-house services, and the specialized assistance of the black advertising agencies.

A Special Case:
Black Radio Stations and Advertising

Beginning in the 1970s, minority entrepreneurs began obtaining ownership of radio broadcast properties in America (see chap. 4); However, their share of the advertising dollar was not what they had dreamed it would be.   The reason: many advertisers claimed that they could as readily reach black consumers through general market broadcast advertising, and they claimed that the African American consumer was not upscale enough to have much discretionary income.   As a result, advertisers argued that it was not profitable for agencies to target African American markets through black formatted and black-owned radio properties.   Many black radio entrepreneurs were nearly ruined by this new economic constraint.   Originally, they had believed that ownership would allow them an opportunity to "get a piece of the pie," as white entrepreneurs had done.   The new rules dictated that though they had, individually or in small groups, struggled to leverage money to purchase stations, unlike white investors, the return on their investments would be in slow dribbles.   Black owners responded to this new threat to their economic survival in a number of ways. First, they banded together and formed an organization called the National Association of Black Owners of Broadcasting (NABOB). NABOB believed that there was strength in collective bargaining and that common experiences with peripheral industries and organizations (NAB, advertising agencies, and the like) could be better addressed in a public forum, organized to work within the system. At the organization's scheduled meetings they shared information and heard from spokespersons representing the FCC, NAB, advertising agencies, research organizations, and others.   Second, they urged their sales staffs to think of innovative strategies for getting around the ratings books that advertising agencies used in determining "media buys" for their clients (the product manufacturers), such as Proctor and Gamble or Ford Motor Company.

    In fact, ratings books presented a unique problem for black

broadcast owners. Most research organizations, which published ratings books like Nielsen, Arbitron, and Simmons, had data collection systems that until the early 1970s bypassed or gave short shrift to black listeners. These major research organizations did not begin to collect data from persons residing in black neighborhoods until 1972. Even after 1972, black entrepreneurs cited numerous instances where the system worked against their economic viability. For example, a black radio station owner relates that the City of Buffalo, New York, which had a fairly large black population in the late 1970s, had, according to the data collected by the ratings research organizations, only a negligible number of listeners for Buffalo's only black-formatted radio station. In fact, the figure was so negligible that it was not even counted and therefore did not appear in the ratings books. As a result, advertising agencies, their clients, and advertisers paid a disproportionately lower rate for commercials broadcast on this black radio station than they paid for advertisements on general market stations in the same city. The black-formatted station had strong evidence that the large black population in fact listened faithfully to their station. In appealing to advertisers to purchase airtime on their stations, they cited such evidence as self-administered surveys and community awareness activities. It should be noted, however, that general market radio stations also charged varying rates for commercials that were dependent upon periodic ratings in the research books.[49]

In the early 1980s many stations that were calling themselves "soul stations" switched their names to "urban contemporary," seeking to appeal to general market listeners as well as the black community (see chap. 4 for further discussion). One of the most successful of these stations, WBLS/WLIB in New York City, was purchased in 1972 by former Manhattan borough president Percy Sutton and about fifty original shareholders, including Jesse and Jackie Jackson. Called Inner City Broadcasting, the company devised sales strategies that allowed them to capitalize on black, Hispanic, and white targeted listeners, and boost their ratings. Often listed as the number one AM/FM station in the country, WBLS/WLIB soon demanded and received top rates for commercials aired on their stations. Most black-owned properties, however, even when they switched to the new "urban contemporary" format, were unable to obtain top rates for advertising. Often, too, they faced the gradual erosion of their black listening audiences as the black stations played the music of more and more white artists, while the general market stations continued to play black artists' music very infrequently. Because of these developments, African Americans (both entrepreneurs and artists) usually lost ground and revenues.

Civil Rights Activists

In 1961, the Reverend Leon Sullivan, a Philadelphia minister, had organized four hundred black ministers in Philadelphia to use their pulpits to convince people to withdraw patronage from businesses heavily dependent on black dollars unless those businesses responded to black community concerns about employment and ownership opportunities. These boycotts were not a direct result of what was happening to black-owned radio properties but ultimately helped these entrepreneurs. Other activist organizations also began to devise ways to make businesses such as the advertising industry and industries with close ties to broadcasting more sensitive to minorities.

For example, in the late 1960s, Reverend Jesse Jackson, as director of Operation Bread Basket, an ancillary organization to Martin Luther King, Jr.'s Southern Christian Leadership Conference, took note of the series of successes that Leon Sullivan's civil rights group in Philadelphia had achieved. Sullivan's theme was "Don't shop where you can't work." As a result of pressure brought to bear by the ministers in Philadelphia, major advertisers began to use African American-owned and targeted radio stations to advertise their products more often. When the Reverend Jackson founded and became president of Operation PUSH in 1971, economic development became a primary concern of his organzation. In the 1980s, Jackson contended that President Reagan's cutbacks in social programs affected black people disproportionately. He believed President Reagan's emphasis on deregulation sought to assure the Congress and the private sector that affirmative action was no longer in vogue. Further, the Reagan guest-worker programs and other devices to increase opportunities for foreigners further undercut opportunities for black citizens, according to Jackson. So, Jackson concluded that black people had to become their own equal employment opportunity agents. He believed that the enforcement lever for this was the billions of dollars that black consumers spent yearly on goods and services.

Jackson's concept was based on a development formula. He noted that when Coca Cola went to Europe or Nigeria, it could not just offer jobs. It also had to make supply-side offers in terms of business opportunities, financing, and ownership. He believed it was unconscionable for them to go into America's black communities offering merely jobs. Furthermore, Jackson also reported that none of Coca Cola's 550 bottlers or its thousands of fountain wholesalers were African Americans and that the company had just $254,000 on deposit in ten black banks. This, at a point in history when black consumers purchased more Cokes than any other soft drink and in vast disproportion to their percentage in society, impelled Jackson to encourage the use of consumer power in African American communities. He also urged large corporations to include economic development in African American communities, not just offer jobs. Further, Jackson requested shelf space for black products in supermarkets, the use of black-owned banks for financial arrangements, the use of black certified public accountants and advertising agencies, and the purchase of airtime for advertisements on black-owned broadcast facilities. Jackson argued that if a given company used thousands of goods and services in operating its business, some given proportion of those goods and service supplier opportunities should go to black businesses, especially when blacks consumed the product of the company in percentages as high as 40 to 50 percent. Jackson obtained moral agreements (covenants) with various major corporations, such as Anheuser Busch, after complicated and sometimes heated negotiations. Prior to these settlements, Operation PUSH had taken direct action in encouraging African American consumers *not* to purchase Anheuser Busch products (manufacturers of Busch beer, and other products) for over a year. A 1984 article in *Advertising Age* noted how short-sighted beer companies were in not capitalizing on their loyal black consumers by directing ads to reach them. The article noted that although Anheuser Busch and Miller Brewing Company each had increased their involvement in targeting marketing campaigns toward the African American community, there was no balance between what these consumers actually spent and the amount of marketing dollars that were used to keep them.[50]

The Coca Cola company, after nine months of secret negotiations, agreed to establish a venture capital fund for loans to African Americans in businesses associated with the soft drink industry, appoint wholesalers and distributors from the African American community, to double advertising in black-owned newspapers and magazines, and substantially to increase advertising on black-owned broadcast properties. As a result of the efforts of Operation PUSH, advertising agencies such as Proctor and Gardner began to obtain more clients from among the larger corporations, and black-owned radio stations began to receive more of the media buys purchased through advertising agencies from some of the nation's largest corporations.[51]

Major advertisers increased their radio advertising or the amount spent on advertising on African American owned and targeted enterprises during the 1980s for a number of other reasons. First, in the middle of the decade, of the 250 African American programmed radio stations, 127 were owned by blacks. Many of these stations upgraded community services, news, and job listings in their attempt to develop an image as a "voice of the community." The stations also pushed voter registration to help give the black community more clout in the sociopolitical sphere. Thus, black-owned stations increased their credibility and respect among African American listeners which increased the size of their audience. African American entrepreneurs used audience-increase figures as leverage for higher rate cards for selling air time to advertisers on their stations. They were able to improve profit margins, as a result. Second, inspirational music, a program format that became popular on black stations during this period, mixed traditional gospel and contemporary songs with "positive" lyrics designed to promote love of family and God combined with messages such as "Keep trying," "Hang on and do your best," and "Things will work out in the end." Musical recordings included such songs as Diana Ross's "Reach Out and Touch Somebody's Hand" and George Benson's "The Greatest Love of All." Inspirational programming was featured on stations such as WWRL in New York and WEBB in Baltimore. Many advertisers purchased air time on these stations during inspirational programming periods because of their high ratings. Third, "urban contemporary music" was a format that blended soul music and soft rock. Although some believed that the term *urban contemporary* was a laundered name for black radio,

WKTU and WBLS (both New York City urban contemporary stations) cut across all ethnic boundaries, attracting white youngsters as well as black and Hispanic listeners. Further, the owner of WBLS, Percy Sutton, believed many middle-class black listeners had disliked black radio in the fifties and sixties because of the context in which the music was played (screaming and jive-talking dejays). Sutton believed he was giving sophisticated New Yorkers music that sold itself because of its inherent beauty and that it did not need a hard pitched deejay *salesman*. WBLS played all types of music and considered itself mainstream radio. (See chap. 4 for further details) As noted earlier, as one of the top radio stations in the country, WBLS obtained top rates for advertisements aired on its station, while other urban contemporary stations using this model met with varying degrees of success.

African Americans and Alternative Media Distribution Systems of the 1980s

The advertising industry, unreceptive to African Americans as both consumers and practitioners for many years, had a new opportunity to include minorities with the emergence of the electronic advertising environment created by the various alternative distribution systems such as cable, direct broadcast satellite systems, and satellite master antenna systems. Activist groups, like The National Black Media Coalition, serving as advocates and tireless fighters, attempted to assure African Americans opportunities in these emerging systems. They had minimal success, however, because local cable system operators derived their advertising revenues primarily from the sale of time on local origination channels and from "spot" time on satellite services to local businesses. Few of the cable system operators were African Americans. Advertising revenue was usually measured as a dollar amount per subscriber, per year spent by local businesses. However, the bulk of advertising revenue generated in the cable industry was the advertising time sold, not by local system operators, but by the owners of the national satellite services such as the USA network, and the Cable News Network. Since African Americans did not own satellite services they were again shut out from many slots in the practitioner's side of this communications industry. However, there were still opportunities for the creation and development of advertising packages for cable systems. As noted, Bob Johnson of Black Entertainment Television was a prime example of a program supplier for cable television.

Johnson's BET sells airtime directly through three core advertising offices. These offices, located in New York, Chicago, and Los Angeles, have six, two, and one account executive, respectively. As is usually the case, the account executives solicit advertisements through agencies that represent clients. BET's account executives market their service by presenting the value of BET as a program supplier that reaches large numbers of African American and other ethnic consumers. According to BET, this targeted market has high viewing habits and makes more consumer-oriented purchases than other similar groups.

For years in its programming, BET used a large number of infomercials, which are program-length commercials that give viewers general related information as they generate interest in products. For the 1990s, BET planned to move away from heavy reliance on infomercials to specialized programming, produced in-house, for which they would obtain commercial advertisements and sponsored support. Moreover, in 1990 the BET news department planned to videotape "The Black Agenda-2000" from Chicago in October, and from Los Angeles in January, with sponsored support and commercials to underwrite costs.[52] Many believed that with the growing number of minority entrepreneurs and politically and economically strong activists and businessmen emerging in urban centers across the nation more African American media supplier entrepreneurs, like Bob Johnson at BET, would emerge.

Conclusion

In the past, African American entrepreneurs were the main advertisers that sought black consumers in black print publications and on black-formatted radio stations. General market advertisers, reluctant to target black consumers, spent very little money in the African American community. When they used African American figures, it was as comic or as stereotypic characters in their advertisements that were targeted to white consumers. Black resisters to these images argued against their use and for more positive images targeted to the African American *and* general markets.   The split in the image of the African American as a targeted consumer group, as talent, and as a professional in advertising is apparent.

From this review of the advertising industry, it is also apparent that the decision makers' frame of reference was based on maintaining the status quo.   Empowered white male decision makers believed that the social order should remain as they found it, and, despite information that could have influenced them to the contrary, they chose to remain disengaged from the African American consumer and practitioner for many years.   Finally, when economic and sociopolitical forces precluded any further delays, the industry acquiesced.   In the meantime, well-prepared African American entrepreneurs, poised to push their way into the system with innovative marketing strategies to establish an authentic black presence in advertising, capitalized when the opportunities arose. Their authentic, yet personable images of the African American make it possible to believe that the split in the image of African Americans as developed by those within the advertising industry might dissolve in the twenty-first century.

1. "Urban Contempo Radio Listeners 40% Non-Black," *Variety*, 10 August 1983, 1; Morry Roth, "Black Inroads in Broadcasting: Dramatic Change in U.S. TV Audience and Viewing," *Variety*, January 1985, 1; and Marianne Paskowski, "Cover Story: Shades of Grey," *Marketing and Media Decisions* 21 (March 1986): 30–40.

2. William Boyenton, "The Negro Turns to Advertising," *Journalism Quarterly* 42 (Spring 1965): 227.

3. Ibid., 234.

4. "Urban Contempo Radio—Reaching the Black Consumer," *Black Enterprise*, June 1974, 125–34.

5. Raymond A. Bauer and Scott M. Cunningham, "The Negro Market," *Journal of Advertising Research* 10 (April 1970): 3–13.

6. Irwin Friend and J. B. Kravis, "New Light on the Consumer Market," *Harvard Business Review* (January–February 1957): 112–15; Bauer and Cunningham, The Negro Market, 7.

7. Bauer and Cunningham, 8–9.

8. David Potter, *People of Plenty* (Chicago: University of Chicago Press, 1954), 177–83, as cited in Boyenton, "The Negro Turns to Advertising," 227–28.

9. Peter Bart, *New York Times*, 6 January 1964, 88.

10. Sylvia Appelbaum, "On Desegregating Advertising," *The Crisis* (June–July, 1962): 313–17.

11. Roger A. Kerin, "Black Model Appearance and Product Evaluation," *Journal of Communication* 29 (Winter 1979): 23–128; Michael Chapko, "Black Ads are Getting Blacker," *Journal of Communication* 26 (Autumn 1976): 175–78; and George

Gitter, Stephen O'Connell, and David Mostofsky, "Trends in Appearance of Models in Ebony Ads Over 17 Years," *Journalism Quarterly* 49 (Autumn 1972): 547–50.

12. James E. Stafford, Al E. Birdwell, & Charles E. Van Tassel, "Integrated Advertising-White Backlash?" *Journal of Advertising Research* 10 (April 1970): 15, 20; Lester Guest, "How Negro Models Affect Company Image," *Journal of Advertising Research* 10 (April 1970): 29–33; Mary Jane Schlinger and Joseph T. Plummer, "Advertising in Black & White," *Journal of Marketing Research* 9 (May 1972): 149–53.

13. Lionel C. Barrow, Jr., "Minority Media Means Money," *Contact* (Winter 1973): 46–47, 64.

14. Ibid.

15. Ibid.

16. Donald E. Sexton, Jr., "Black Buyer Behavior," *Journal of Marketing* 36 (October 1972): 36–39.

17. Stuart H. Surlin, "Authoritarian Advertising Executives and the Use of Black Models in Advertising: Implications for Racial Relations," *Journal of Black Studies* 8 (September 1977): 105–16.

18. Surlin, "Authoritarian Advertising . . ." 105–16; and Lawrence Soley, "The Effect of Black Models on Magazine Ad Readership," *Journalism Quarterly* 60 (Winter 1983): 690; Stafford, Birdwell, & Van Tassel, "Integrated Advertising . . .": 15, 20; Guest, "How Negro Models Affect . . .": 29–33; Schlinger and Plummer, "Advertising in Black & White": 149–53.

19. Theodore Gage, Jr., "Marketing to Blacks RSVP: An Invitation to Buy," *Advertising Age*, 16 May 1981, sec. 2, 5–7, 58; and Franklin Joseph, "Blacks' Ambition Enters the Picture," *Advertising Age*, 14 March 1985; 26–27.

20. Djata, "Madison Avenue Blindly Ignores the Black Consumer," *Business and Society Review* 60 (Winter 1987): 9–13.

21. "Black Broadcast: The Market," *TV-Radio Age*, February 1983; A-3; and Herbert Allen, "Product Appeal: No Class Barrier," *Advertising Age*, 1 May 1981; Alphonzia Wellington, The Wellington Group Marketing Packet, 1982.

22. Gail Bronson, "No Hurry to Reach the Black Consumer," *U.S. News & World Report*, 8 August 1983, 43.

23. Kasey Jones, "Washington-based Cable Network Expands in Size, Strength and Scope," *The Sun*, 16 April 1989, and Bronson, "No Hurry . . ."43.

24. Paskowski, Cover Story: 30–40; and Rich Blake, "Minorities: Reaching the World's Ninth Largest Market," *Public Relations Journal* 41 (January 1985): 30–31.

25. Paskowski, Cover Story: 30–40.

26. Margaret Ross Barnett, "Nostalgia as Nightmare: Blacks and American Popular Culture," *The Crisis*, February 1980, 42–45

27. Mary Alice Sentman, "Life in Black and White: Coverage of Black America by 'Life' Magazine, 1937–1942" (paper presented at the Annual Meeting of the Association for Education in Journalism, East Lansing, Michigan, August 8–11, 1981), 19, and Appelbaum, "On Desegregating Advertising," 313–17.

28. Appelbaum, 313–17.

29. Maurine Christopher, "NAACP Asks FCC to Eliminate Racism in Ads," *Advertising Age*, 5 October 1970, 29; Phillip Dougherty, "Advertising: Frequency of Black in TV Ads," *New York Times*, 27 May 1982, D19.

30. Ibid.

31. John W. Gould, Norman Sigband, and Cyril Zoerner, Jr., "Black Consumers' Reactions to 'Integrated' Advertising: An Exploratory Study," *Journal of Marketing* 34 (July 1970): 26; John Revett, "Cosby Top Star Presenter of 1978," *Advertising*

Age, 17 July 1978: 1; Gary Dub, "The Ever-popular Cosby," *Dallas Morning News,* 16 March 1985.

32. Dougherty, "Advertising": D19.

33. Ibid.

34. Ibid.

35. "Robert Fomon," *Business Week,* 18 April 1986, 229–30; "Why E. F. Hutton Scandal May Be Far From Over," *Business Week,* 24 February 1986, 98–101.

36. Bill Backer, Creative Director/Owner — Backer and Spielvogle Advertising Agency, telephone interview with the writer, July 1986.

37. Bryan Burwell, "Super Deals for Superstars: Top Jocks Put On the Hardsell for Big Bucks," *Black Enterprise,* July 1984, 37–57.

38. Djata, "Madison Avenue" . . . :9–13.

39. J. Fred MacDonald, "Stereotypes Fall in TV Ad Portrayals," *Advertising Age,* 19 November 1984, 44.

40. Ibid.

41. Ken Smikle, "The Image Makers," *Black Enterprise,* December 1985, 44–52.

42. Smikle, "The Image Makers . . .":44–55; Joseph Winski and Kathy Lampher, "He said 'No Thanks! to Handouts," *Advertising Age,* 1 March 1982, M2–3; "P & G. Seeks to Build Market Among Blacks," *New York Times,* 12 November 1983, 8; Phillip Doughtery, "Advertising: Minority Marketing," *New York Times,* 28 June 1982, D6; and Phillip Doughtery, "Advertising: Eagle/One Telephone Starts Out," *New York Times,* 7 March 1984, D23.

43. See Kevin Klose, "In the Spirit of Enterprise," *Washington Post,* 27 January 1984: D1; Ricki L. Francki, "Success Story Good News: Proctor Takes A Gamble and Hits the Jackpot," *Working Woman,* August 1979, 19; and Smikle, "The Image Makers," 44–55.

44. Paskowski, "Cover Story," 30–40.

45. John Briggs, "Reshaping Product Ad Campaign," The *Courier-Post,* 15 January 1984, 1–2.

46. "Black Trak, Advertisement," *Advertising Age,* 29 November 1982, M14 and 25 August 1986, S6.

47. Smikle, "The Image Makers", 44–52.

48. Ibid; Paskowski, "Cover Story", 30–40.

49. Les Brown, *Television: The Business Behind the Box* (New York: Harcourt Brace Jovanovich, 1971); Donald Brooks, Station Manager, personal interview by the writer, WEBB-AM, Baltimore, Maryland, Summer 1982.

50. Udayan Gupta, "Is Minority Advertising Falling Flat?" *Advertising Age,* 16 January 1984, M24.

51. Frank Watkins, Director of Communications, Operation Push, Chicago, Illinois, telephone interview by the writer, October 1984.

52. Cheryl Holmes, Director of Advertising, Black Entertainment Television, telephone interview by the writer, December 1989.

CONCLUSION: SPLIT IMAGES AND DOUBLE BINDS

JANNETTE L. DATES AND WILLIAM BARLOW

White domination of the mass media, with its pervasive control over the portrayal and participation of African Americans in those media, has disclosed major cultural contradictions. In all the media industries surveyed in this study, white owners and producers have appropriated aspects of African American culture to enrich the mass-media mainstream and enrich themselves. The black images mass-produced by them, however, have been filtered through the racial misconceptions and fantasies of the dominant white culture, which has tended to deny the existence of a rich and resilient black culture of equal worth. Throughout most of the twentieth century, whenever white image makers have developed media products (records, films, radio and television programs, news stories, and advertising campaigns) featuring African Americans, they invariably did so in terms of codes and criteria based on their own racial and class background. Historically, there has been very little African American involvement at decision-making levels in these industries.

Given this situation, it has been only natural that African Americans should devise their own ways of resisting white domination, just as they had in the past, and that one of their first priorities would be to reconstruct more accurate images of themselves. Both the social reconstruction and the control of black images in the mass media came to be additional points of contention along Du Bois's prophetic "color line."

In the preceding chapters, we have focused on this schizoid racial representation in the American mass media, noting how, more often than not, the images of African Americans favored by the mainstream media were based on long-standing black stereotypes. These one-dimensional caricatures not only gave white Americans a false impression of black life, art, and culture but they also helped to mold white public opinion patterns, and set the agenda for public discourse on the race issue, thus broadening the cultural gap between black and white Americans. On the other side of the racial divide, the stereotyped imagery provoked a defiant response from many black image makers, who consciously sought to undermine the prevailing black representations by parodying or negating those stereotypes.

This war between white and black image makers and media practitioners over the African American image is a classic example of group/class power relations, where social class divisions have been complicated by the added dimension of race. Incorporating insights and concepts gleaned from thinkers like Du Bois, Gramsci, Lippmann, Brown, Hall, Gandy, Bakhtin, and Gates, we have endeavored to show how the dominant cultural group has worked to define, control, and maintain its influence over the subordinate one, while the latter has struggled to recreate an authentic self-image, and hence to reclaim its historical identity.

In the mainstream media industries, the overwhelming constraints placed on African Americans have forced them to adopt (sometimes consciously and sometimes unconsciously) a dual strategy in the ongoing chess match to control the destiny of the black image. Within the corporate mass media there are African American "insiders," media professionals who are working to broaden and upgrade black images and input as best they can, even as they establish their own credentials at the various levels of those industries. A second strategy has involved cultural entrepreneurs and activists who have developed alternative media products, outlets, and services that target the interests and needs of African American audiences and consumers. Some of these black media practitioners outside the mainstream have increasingly gained a modicum of both control over their products and success in marketing them, but a far greater number have paid the price for going against the corporate current and are no longer in business. Another factor in the cultural resistance equation has been the organized political action of African Americans, most often led by progressive media professionals or civil rights groups. They have worked diligently to expose and discredit the lingering black stereotypes, as well as to agitate for greater black participation and ownership in the media industries. Yet while considerable progress has been made in all of these areas, especially during the past twenty years, new factors are emerging that can only complicate the racial situation in the mass media in the very near future.

As the twenty-first century looms on the horizon, African Americans have made some significant inroads as entrepreneurs and decision makers within the white-dominated media industries, which suggests that a promising trend may be in the making. Oprah Winfrey's Harpo Production Company marks only the third time in American history that a woman has owned her own production facility and produced her own media products. Obviously, it is the first instance for an African American woman. Spike Lee, the African American independent filmmaker, director, and actor, with his three films "She's Gotta Have It," "School Daze," and "Do the Right Thing," seems to promise a new wave of cinema that speaks with a black voice rather than the white one hitherto dominant in films about African Americans. However, there is also a growing disparity between the demographic projections of the general population, on the one hand, and both current ownership and employment patterns in the media industries, on the other. The white population in the United States is projected to lose its numerical majority to nonwhite populations in the country sometime toward the end of the next century.[1] In contrast, even the projected gains in ownership of media outlets by American minorities, including African Americans, lag far behind their current percentage in the total population.[2] Moreover, the gap is growing wider, not vice versa.

Another contradictory tendency, or double bind, that has emerged recently concerns the new revisionist black representations in the mass media, best exemplified by the popular acclaim and success of "The Cosby Show" on network television. Henry Louis Gates, Jr. has characterized Cosby's character of Cliff Huxtable as a new "Noble Negro" stereotype living in an upper-middle-class utopia. Furthermore, Gates attributes the popularity of the programs to the "black characters in them," who have "finally become, in most respects, just like white people":

> As long as all blacks were represented in demeaning or peripheral roles, it was possible to believe that American racism was, as it were, indiscriminate. The social vision of Cosby, however, reflecting the minuscule integration of blacks into the upper middle class (having

"white money," my mother used to say, rather than "colored money"), reassuringly throws the blame for black poverty back onto the impoverished.[3]

The selective bifurcation of the black television image along class lines has been the focus of sociologist Herman Gray's recent research. Gray has found that, while idealized black middle-class families living the American Dream have come to the forefront of mainstream fictional television fare, in particular entertainment television, the black underclass, in contrast, has been a major focus of television newscasts and documentaries. These two seemingly disparate black representations are linked, because they tell opposite sides of the same mythical story of African American success and failure. As Gray points out:

> The assumptions that organize our understanding of black middle-class success and underclass failure are expressed and reinforced in the formal organization of television programming. . . . Where representations of the underclass are presented in the routine structure of network news programming, it is usually in relationship to such extraordinary offenses as drugs, homicide and crime. In contrast, middle-class blacks are very much integrated into the programming mainstream. . . . The failure of blacks in the urban underclass . . . is their own, since they live in an isolated world where contemporary racism is no longer a significant factor in their lives. The success of blacks in the television middle class suggests as much. In the television world of the urban underclass, unemployment, industrial relocation, ineffective social policies, power inequalities and racism do not explain failure, just as affirmative action policies, political organization, collective social and cultural challenges to specific forms of racial domination, and the civil rights movement do not explain the growth of the black middle class.[4]

Similar reservations have been expressed by media critic Nelson George concerning crossover acts in black music and crossover formats in black commercial radio. George equates the crossover phenomenon with black yuppie assimilation into the dominant corporate structure of the media industries. He warns that such an exodus from the black community by the black bourgeoisie is tantamount to "cultural suicide" because it undermines the ability of the community to develop indigenous cultural institutions, while exacerbating the class divisions among African Americans.[5] Success and failure, middle class and underclass, the noble Negro and the brute Negro, crossover and stand pat, divide and conquer—these are just some of the double binds confronting African Americans in the mass media as they look toward the future.

This study has raised issues and offered explanations concerning the role of African Americans in the mass media. In the future, the authors believe that the task of making media systems more congruent with the increasing cultural diversity of American society does not rest solely on the shoulders of African Americans and other minority groups. Only a concerted, systematic effort within the media mainstream, academia, and industry can ensure that the future will be different from the past for African American and other minorities with respect to the development and control of their media images. Respect for the multicultural society that will characterize America in the twenty-first century must be engendered by all image makers who shape the worldviews of the American public, regardless of their race. America's future can be one of either relatively smooth transition or great upheaval. The task is great and the hour is late. We encourage all those of goodwill and stout heart to begin the transformation now.

1. Clint C. Wilson II and Felix Gutierrez, *Minorities and Media: Diversity and the End of Mass Communication* (Beverly Hills, Calif.: Sage Publications, 1985), 19–20.

2. John Downing, "Minority Radio in the United States," *Howard Journal of Communications* (Spring 1990): 31.

3. Louis Henry Gates, Jr., "TV's Black World Turns—But Stays Unreal," *New York Times*, 12 November 1989, sec. 2, 40.

4. Herman Gray, "Television, Black Americans, and the American Dream," *Critical Studies in Mass Communication* 6 (December 1989): 384.

5. Nelson George, *The Death of Rhythm and Blues* (New York: Pantheon, 1988), 200.

GALLERY OF PHOTOGRAPHS

Duke Ellington was one of the first African American dance band leaders to be recorded by a major record label, RCA Victor, in the 1920s. (Courtesy of the Frank Driggs Collection)

Billie Holiday, recorded by Columbia Records, was the most acclaimed female jazz vocalist of the postwar era. (Courtesy of Paul Hoeffler)

461

Ray Charles, a pioneer of the postwar rhythm and blues sound, was the first black recording artist to make country and western crossover albums in the early 1960s. (Courtesy of *RCM International*)

Left: Terry Lewis and Jimmy Jam Harris from Minneapolis have produced a number of hit albums for pop artists, such as the 1986 Janet Jackson album, "Control." (Courtesy of *Stafford Mpls.*) Run-DMC *(above)* was typical of the black rap groups heard in the 1980s. (Courtesy of the Afro-American Newspapers)

Oscar Micheaux, a producer of "race movies," combined tenacity and self-promotion in a filmmaking career that spanned more than a quarter of a century from 1919–48.

This frame enlargement from the film *Body and Soul* (1924) shows Paul Robeson in his first movie role.

World War II provided the political crisis that led African Americans to renegotiate their status in American society. John Huston's *In This Our Life* (1941) featured Ernest Anderson in a role that so challenged the status quo that black soldiers demanded this scene be run over and over, and Bette Davis (here on the right) remembered it the rest of her days and included it in her memoirs.

With the opening up of the screen to African Americans during and after World War II, Hollywood began to win the black audience away from black-oriented movies. Even French-produced *Native Son* (1951), here with Richard Wright playing Bigger Thomas, was not so well attended.

Nurtured by the Black Filmmakers Foundation, contemporary African American filmmaking has achieved higher quality. Its most famous alumnus is Spike Lee, director of *She's Gotta Have It*, *School Daze*, and the widely discussed *Do the Right Thing*. (Courtesy of the Afro-American Newspapers)

Warrington Hudlin, until recently, president of the Black Filmmakers Foundation and a producer of much admired independent films like *Black at Yale* and *Street Corner Stories*, is shown here with his brother Reggie. He recently released the feature film, *House Party* (1990). (Courtesy of New Line Cinema)

Paul Robeson, an early African American presence on network radio in the 1930s, embodied black resistance to white domination. He provided the narration for the famous "Ballad for Americans," broadcast on CBS in the 1930s. (Courtesy of Paul Robeson, Jr.)

Percy Sutton is president and founder of Inner City Broadcasting Corporation in New York City. (Courtesy of the Afro-American Newspapers)

Debbie Allen, hired by Bill Cosby as producer-director of "A Different World," is one of the first African American women to reach a decision-making level in network television with a primetime top-ten series. (Courtesy of Arnold Turner for the Afro-American Newspapers)

Howard Rollins starred in the television series "In the Heat of the Night," one of four dramatic, weekly network series featuring African Americans that premiered during the 1988–89 season. (Courtesy of the Johnson Publishing Company, Inc./Ebony-Jet Showcase)

Oprah Winfrey's successful talk show has made her influential in television. (Courtesy of Joffre Clarke for the Afro-American Newspapers)

Bill Cosby's comedy, in various media since the 1960s, has appealed to various cultural groups. (Courtesy of the Afro-American Newspapers)

Blues artist Willie Dixon *(left)* and the "Black Valentino," Lorenzo Tucker *(right)*, two pioneers of American show business, were among the many personalities featured on "Were You There?" the public television series on African American heritage produced by Carol Lawrence with Nguzo Saba Films. (Dixon Photo by Michael Weinstein/Photo Reserve)

Public television's "American Playhouse" production of Lorraine Hansberry's classic drama, "A Raisin in the Sun," starred Esther Rolle as Mama, Kim Yancy as Beneatha, Danny Glover as Walter Lee, and Starletta Du Pois as Ruth. (Photo by Mitzi Trumbo, Courtesy of American Playhouse)

News veteran Tony Brown *(left)* addresses issues confronting black Americans on the highly regarded "Tony Brown's Journal," the nation' longest running African American public affairs series. (Courtesy of Tony Brown Productions)

Below: "Eyes on the Prize: America' Civil Rights Years, 1954–1965" is a chronicle of the people and events o: this watershed period in American's social history. (Courtesy of James H. Karales)

Ida Wells-Barnett, publisher of the *Memphis Free Speech* newspaper, published numerous articles and waged a campaign against lynching at the turn of the century. (Courtesy of the Afro-American Newspapers)

Marcus Garvey, founder of the Universal Negro Improvement Association, established a series of newspapers in furtherance of his racial and political goals. (Courtesy of Moorland-Spingarn Research Center, Howard University)

David Cannady, AT&T Communications market manager, Suzanne de Passe, president of Motown Productions, John H. Johnson, founder and publisher of Johnson Publishing, and Jewell Jackson McCabe, president of the National Coalition of 100 Black Women. John H. Johnson is publisher of: *Ebony, Jet, Negro Digest/Black World, Tan, True Confessions, Hue, Ebony International, Ebony, Jr.* and *Copper Romance.* (Courtesy of the Afro-American Newspapers)

The "Grand Daddy" of them all, Mal
Goode was the first black ever hired at
the network news level. He was still
working well into his 70s. Goode was
also much in demand on the national
lecture circuit—where he spoke openly
about racism in television news. (Courtesy of the Goode family)

Lee Thornton was the first black woman assigned the White House television
news beat. She covered the administration of President Jimmy Carter for CBS.
(Courtesy of CBS TV News)

Max Robinson was the first black to anchor a primetime network news program. (Courtesy of the Afro-American Newspapers)

A veteran of both ABC and NBC News, Carole Simpson became the first black woman to anchor a network news program regularly. She was part of the history-making broadcast, "Black in White America" on ABC. (Courtesy of Capital Cities/ABC, Inc.)

A BIBLIOGRAPHICAL ESSAY

The war of images continued even in the descriptions and analyses used throughout the country to document information about the mass media. Very few scholarly books, for example, focused substantively on the participation and the portrayal of African Americans in media industries. Thus, the African American is perceived by scholars, historians, and the general populace, alike, as not having viable participatory roles in the creation and evolution of the various mass media. Almost no books written before the 1970s include African American participation. A look at selected books published since 1970 reveals the following materials on African American participation in the music industry: Robert Dixon and John Godrich, *Recording the Blues* (1970); Arnold Shaw, *Honkers and Shouters* (1975); David Ewen, *All the Years of Popular Music* (1977); Charlie Gillett, *Making Tracks: The History of Atlantic Records* (1975); and Steve Chapple and Reebee Garofalo, "Black Roots, White Fruits" in *Rock 'n Roll is Here to Pay: The History and Politics of the Music Industry* (1975). Most recently, William Barlow published a book on black music, *Lookin' Up at Down: The Blues Culture* (1989).

Books dealing with African Americans in the film industry are more plentiful. The works of historians Thomas Cripps and Donald Bogle dominate the list, including *Slow Fade to Black: The Negro in American Film 1900–1942* (1976) and *Black Film as Genre* (1978) by Cripps; and *Toms, Coons, Mulattoes, Mammies and Bucks* (1973), *Brown Sugar: 80 Years of America's Black Female Superstars* (1988), and *Blacks in American Films and Television: An Enclyclopedia*, by Bogle. Other works include Daniel Leab, *From Sambo to Superspade: The Black Experience in Motion Pictures* (1975), and James R. Nesteby, *Black Images in American Films 1896–1954: The Interplay Between Civil Rights and Film Culture* (1978). Cripps's numerous articles and chapters in other books have been used to supplement book lists in many instances.

There is very little published on African Americans in the radio industry. Erick Barnouw, *A Tower in Babel: A History of Broadcasting in the United States*, vol. I (1966), and *The Golden Web: A History of Broadcasting in the United States*, vol. II (1968) include some information on the subject, as does a chapter in the book by J. Fred MacDonald, *Don't Touch That Dial* (1979).

Few books focusing on television have featured the African American. J. Fred MacDonald, *Blacks and White TV: Afro-Americans in Television Since 1948* (1983) is an exception. This book is the definitive work on the subject. Other works that augment MacDonald's include *Black Faces in Primetime* by Melvin Moore; *Blacks on Television: A Selectively Annotated Bibliography* (1983) by George H. Hill and Sylvia Saverson Hill; *History of Blacks on Television* (1985) by Cynthia E. Griffen and George H. Hill; and *Role Portrayal and Stereotyping on Television* (1985) by Nancy Signorielli.

There are no books that address the black experience in public broadcasting, and few about African Americans and the broadcast news industries. In the print industry there are: *The Black Press, 1827–1890: The Quest for National Identity* by Martin E. Dann (1971); *The Black Press U.S.A.* (1971) by Roland Wolseley; and *The Negro Press in the United States* (1926) by Frederick G. Detweiler. In broadcasting there are *Black is the Color of My TV Tube* (1981) by Gil Noble; and *Live and Off-Color—News Biz* (1982) by Bob Teague. The advertising industry has one major book that focuses on African American experience, D. Parke Gibson, *The $30 Billion Negro* (1969). A few textbooks in marketing classes have devoted a few pages to discussions about black culture or about African Americans as consumers with unique marketing needs.

INDEX

Abbott, Robert Sengstacke, 351, 353–54, 360–61
Abby, film, 163
Accommodationists, 364–65
Adam Ant, 109
Adams, Frank T., 371
Adams, Samuel, 383
Adorno, T.W., 126, 127
Advertising, 421–51; advertising packages for cable systems, 449–50; African American actors and actresses, appearance in integrated advertisements, 435–37; African American advertising practitioners, 439–44; African American celebrities in, 437–38; African American consumers, relationship to, 423–33; African Americans as used in advertisements, 434; alternative media distribution systems, 449–50; amoral attitude to social concerns, 425–26; black consumer buying behavior, 427–28; black consumer market, changes in 1970s, 429; black images in, 433–38; black music and, 437–38; black radio stations and, 444–46; civil rights movement and, 429, 446–49; direct network video access to black consumers in 1980s, 432; discriminatory, 434–35; focus on black consumer market, 421–22; growth of minority spending power (table), 422; hierarchy of skin color, fac-tor in, 426; "integrated" advertising campaigns, 427; largest advertisers on television, 440; marketing campaigns, black consumer as target for, 429; market surveys commissioned by African Americans, 425; minority media as advertising medium, 427; ratings books, significance in radio, 444–45; struggle between black and mainstream agencies, 442–43; "target marketing," 432

AFM (American Federation of Musicians), 61

African American actors and actresses, appearance in integrated advertisements, 435–37

African American advertising agencies, 432–33; struggle between black and mainstream agencies, 442–43

African American advertising practitioners, 439–44

African American businesses, as advertisers in black press, 345

African American capitalism in music, 98–101

African American celebrities in advertising, 437–38

African American college radio stations, 237–40

African American consumer market, changes in 1970s, 429

African American consumers: buying behavior, 427–28; direct net-

475